POR

KNOW THYSELF

G. C. Ter Morshuizen

PUBLISHING

© G. C. Ter Morshuizen

Second Edition 1999

ISBN: 81-86822-05-4

All rights reserved. No part of this publication may be reproduced, stored in a retrieval system, or transmitted, in any form or by any means, electronic, mechanical, photocopying, recording, taping, or otherwise, without the prior written permission of G. C. Ter Morshuizen. Reviewers may quote brief passages.

Published & Distributed by:
Sai Towers Publishing
Sai Towers Brindavan
23/1142 Vijayalakshmi Colony
Kadugudi, Bangalore 560 067
Tel : (080) 8451648
Fax : (080) 8451649
Email : saitower@vsnl.com
Web : saitowers.com

Printed at
D.K. Fine Art Press Pvt. Ltd.
Delhi - 110 052 INDIA

KNOW THYSELF

the Gateway to physical, mental and spiritual Health

Sathya Sai Baba's Messages in His own Words

by

Gerard T. Satvic

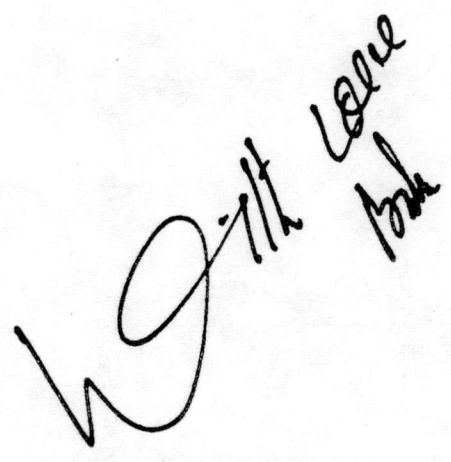

This book and the work it involves are dedicated to my most beloved Bhagavan Sri Sathya Sai Baba in love and gratitude and service to His creatures.

CONTENTS

PREFACE ... I

PART I: SELF-KNOWLEDGE ... 3
1. The Message I Bring ... 4
2. The Moving Temple ... 9
3. The Gross, the Subtle and the Causal Worlds ... 22
4. The Four Bodies and the Four States of Consciousness ... 29
5. The Five Sheaths and the Chakras ... 34
6. Purusha and Prakriti, Male and Female ... 44
7. Maya or Illusion ... 50
8. Dharma for Men and Women ... 55
9. The Five Elements and the Five Pranas ... 61
10. Mastery of the Senses ... 65
11. Conquest of the Mind ... 72
12. The Manas, the Chitta, the Buddhi and the Ahamkara – I ... 79
13. The Manas, the Chitta, the Buddhi and the Ahamkara – II ... 93
14. Know Thyself ... 97

PART II: HEALTH, FOOD AND SPIRITUALITY ... 106
15. The Three Gunas ... 107
16. The Heart of the Bhagavad-Gita ... 121
17. Food and Character ... 128
18. Food, Health and Goodness ... 140
19. A Comprehensive Satvic Diet ... 145
20. A Seaworthy Boat ... 152
21. Limits (*Miti*) and Progress (*Gati*) ... 156
22. Food, Health and Sadhana ... 160
23. Satvic Food, Rajasic Food and Tamasic Food ... 171
24. Purification of our Food ... 186
25. Health and Illness ... 192

26. Karma, Suffering and Grace	203
27. The Doctor's Profession	209

PART III : YOGA — 213
28. Bhakti Yoga, Karma Yoga and Jnana Yoga	214
29. Dhyana Yoga	226
30. Seva Sadhana: Spiritual Endeavor through Service	240
31. Education for Transformation	243

APPENDIX — 256

A. AYURVEDA — 259
1. History	259
2. The Rishis	260
3. Ayurveda, the Science of Life	261
4. The Triumvirate of Vata, Pitta and Kapha	263

B. THE WESTERN NATUROPATHY — 267
1. The Bio-electronigram of Professor L. C. Vincent	267
2. Uncooked Food	271
3. Uncooked Food and Vital Strength	275
4. Uncooked Food and Healing Power	276
5. The Digestive System	281
6. The Digestion	288
7. The Natural Physical Cycles	292
8. The Correct Fruit Consumption	293
9. The Switch–Over to Raw Food	296
10. The Second Step Towards Raw Food	299
11. The Principle of Correct Food Combinations	302
12. The Fourth Step to Living Food	312
13. Classification of Food According to Jan Dries	314
14. Proteins: the Most Important Nutritious Substances	315
15. Milk and Milk Products	319
16. Nuts and Seeds	322
17. Germinating Cereals, Pulses and Seeds	324
18. Grasses, Grass Juices and Fermented Seeds	328

19. The Carbohydrates	330
20. Oils and Fats	334
21. Vitamins	336
22. Life–Extension Science and Premature Ageing	342
23. Minerals and Trace Elements	343
24. Rough Fibrins	348
25. Fruit and Nuts - a Nourishment of Full Value	349
26. One, Two or Three Meals a Day	350
27. Fasting	351
28. A Few Instructions and Recipes	353
29. Living Food and Motherhood	364
30. Bodily Exercise Fresh Air, Bathing and Sunlight	366
C. AYURVEDA AND THE WESTERN NATUROPATHY	367
1. A Comparison	367
2. The Living Foods Lifestyle of Dr. Ann Wigmore	369
3. Ayurvedic Spices and Herbs	373
4. Some Special Satvic Spices and Herbs	377
5. Purification and Cure	380
6. Correct Breathing, a Straight Back and Correct Singing	385
7. My Personal Experiences and Vision	389
8. Satvic Food and Family Life	392
9. Epilogue	397
References	397

PREFACE

Simple living is the best prescription for health. The name of God is the most reliable and efficient drug. Faith in God and in one's own atmic reality can guarantee continued health, both physical and mental, more than all the drugs in the world. Develop health, both in body and mind. I am urging you to do this, for you have still to witness and delight over many more leelas (divine plays) and mahimas (miracles) of Swami, leelas and mahimas far surpassing those you have witnessed so far.

Sri Sathya Sai Baba,
Sanathana Sarathi, November 1978, pp. 218-219

Modern man has no notion of the importance of the control of the senses: for his health, for the development of his spiritual faculties, and for gaining the ultimate goal, the so-called the unification with God. Even spiritual people mostly neglect this essential discipline. "Modern man lives like a libertine - and such a life can only result in destruction and ruination," says Sathya Sai Baba. Both the *Vedas* and the doctrine of the Essenes, declare that control of the tongue, of taste as well as speech, creates the gateway to Divinity. In addition to God's Grace, the control of the senses and spiritual discipline must go together in order to attain God.

Hippocrates, the father of medical science in the West, declared that health is the same as purity. Sathya Sai Baba says that purity is almost the same as Divinity. It follows then, that health is almost the same as Divinity. So we can say that health is synonymous with divinity. Health is the constitution or state of body and mind in which all parts function and co-operate in the right way. It is the state of optimum well-being from a physical, mental and spiritual point of view. Especially for those on the spiritual path health is of vital importance.

Health should be a priority, but the contrary is often the case. It is deplorable and tragic that most people only become interested in health when it is impaired. Our body has a great natural ability to keep itself in a healthy condition and cure itself. This, however, only occurs when man co-operates closely with nature and respects the laws of God. In olden times, an illness was cured with rest, diet, simple remedies from nature, common physical exercises, sun, air, water, mud and ash baths, and spiritual exercises. It is widely known, both from allopathic doctors and natural physicians, that the common state of health, especially of young people, gives rise to great anxiety.

The so-called urban and pollution diseases, such as heart and vascular diseases, and cancer, occur more and more. The number of sick people who can be helped with present medical science is restricted, in spite of all the technological and scientific progress.

Only naturopathy, such as *ayurvedic* or the western natural art of healing (if necessary in co-operation with allopathy), and due observance of the laws of nature, of God (*dharma*), can ensure good health. *Ayurveda* and the western natural healing art do not only teach how illnesses can be cured, but more importantly, how illnesses can be prevented and how good health can be maintained till old age, or death. Unfortunately, most people are unacquainted with these forms of medical science. Sathya Sai Baba has made me aware of this situation and I think it is my duty to provide accurate information on the subject.

"What about a Sai Health Centre?" I asked Baba in the summer of 1991. After an explanation about centres, He said, "I bless." Later, He softly said, full of love, like a mother's, "Only write, I shall help you." I was totally surprised and many questions remained. So, for the time being, I had to concentrate on writing. I had already written a few books about *satvic* food and spirituality, but from His attitude and words I understood that He meant a fuller work.

For me, and for many millions of people in the world, Sathya Sai Baba is the Divine *Avatar* of this era, an incarnation of God in human form. Baba's life is His message. He is the embodiment of love *(prema)* and love is His instrument. He often says, "Start the day with love, fill the day with love, end the day with love, that is the way to God. There is only one religion, the religion of love, there is but one language, the language of the heart and there is but one God and He is omnipresent. God is everywhere. We are all one, man is Divine."

On the twenty-third of November, 1926, Sathya Sai Baba was born as the fourth child of the married couple, Srimati Easwaramma and Sri Pedda Venkappa Raju, in the small village of Puttaparthi in South India. It was at sunrise that the Lord was born. His birth announced itself as imminent by the awakening of the household in the night by the *tambura* twanging automatically and the *maddela* beating rhythmically as if an expert hand was playing it. After His birth, a cobra was found below the bed of the charming baby.

As a little boy He kept away from places where cattle or fowl were killed or tortured or where fish were trapped or caught. When a bird was selected for dinner he would run towards it and clasp it to His bosom, trying to persuade the elders to spare the bird. Even as a child, He spoke of the degraded ideals of the cinema, and how it made a muddle of music. Even to this day, Sathya Sai Baba is a relentless critic of the arts, especially literature and films that wilfully drag ideals down into the dust in order to make money.

On the twenty-third of May, 1940, He declared, "I am Sai Baba, I am Sai Baba of Shirdi." Shirdi Sai Baba is a well-known saint in India, who predicted before His death in 1918 that He would be born again in South India eight years after His death. Sathya Sai Baba has said that He will be born again after His death as Prema Sai Baba in the Mysore region of South India. Sathya Sai Baba is the *Sanathana Sarathi* (the timeless charioteer), and the supreme supporter of *Sanathana Dharma* (eternal religion), and He is the Divine Mother of all humanity. He is both the Divine Mother *(Sai)* and the Divine Father *(Baba)*.

I had already been at work on translating His texts, now I decided not only to gather His teachings about health, food and spirituality, but also His teachings about mind and different forms of spiritual disciplines *(yoga)*. That's why this book consists of three parts:

* Chapters 1 to 14, with the subtitle 'Self-knowledge'
* Chapters 15 to 27, with the subtitle 'Health, Food and Spirituality
* Chapters 28 to 31, with the subtitle *'Yoga'*

The whole book consists of texts and discourses of Sathya Sai Baba Himself; nowhere have I inserted words of my own. Besides, I have always exactly mentioned the sources. Only the preface and the appendix are mine. In order to clarify in what way all this inspired me I would like to say a few things about myself which may help the reader to form an idea about my intentions.

After I had worked for a number of years as a chemical engineer at a university and in a chemical industry, I heard about 'silent meditation'. This method of meditation fascinated me so much that I immediately started practising it very intensely. I was not content with life, and frankly speaking, I thought life had no meaning at all. I thought silent meditation would lead me to a real expansion of consciousness. At that time, however, I did not realise that it was going to be a long and difficult way ahead. At a given moment I started dreaming. That was quite an eye-opener for me, for I had not been conscious of a dream till then. Here is one of my first dreams (about thirty years ago). It holds great significance for me:

I fell into a dream and I saw two rooms separated by a doorway. One room was to the right and the other to the left. From the left room appeared two identical little boys carrying a big stretcher full of beautifully coloured balls of wool. They both wore little round yellow caps. I liked the balls of wool very much. They put the stretcher into the right room, which appeared to be a storehouse with wooden shelving. The little boys put the balls of wool on the shelves. The little boys disappeared and, instead of beautifully coloured balls of wool, I saw bricks lying on the shelves. The balls had changed into bricks. Then, to the right of the doorway, I saw a very thick column on a broad pedestal, it's top disappearing into the clouds. On closer investigation, I found that it was built with the same bricks that I had seen on the boards. I shrugged my shoulders and turned around. I looked into a terrible depth and saw a tempestuous sea covered with a solid and transparent film. This film was lifted up in such a way that two concentric circles could be seen and, in the centre of each of these circles, I could see a beam of the light from heaven. In the path of the light I distinguished Mary, Joseph and the Christ-Child. Then a voice was heard, "You do not want to recognize any of them, do you?"

This dream proved to be the turning point of my life. As so many other intellectual people, I had thus far given significance to the beautiful appearance of illusory thought-forms, the beautifully coloured balls of wool which eventually became the bricks with which I built up my towering ego (the column), and its dualistic way of thinking (the two little boys wearing the yellow caps). I had to turn around in order to discover my reality, my soul (or the *atma*, the Infant Jesus). Then came a period of introspection.

For more than twenty years, thousands of dreams gave me a deeper understanding. For ten years I walked about in monasteries, churches and cathedrals in my dreams. I became aware of many negative emotions and I was forced to go deeply into Christianity and its history, western philosophy and the works of C. G. Jung, Rudolf Steiner, Teilhard de Chardin, Sri Ramakrishna, Sri Aurobindo and others.

I had my eyes opened to the fact that at the university and in trade and industry most people only strive for money and power. They are hardly, if at all, interested in their own inner life, in each other, in friendship, honesty, morality or love. Because I hoped I might find this in the teaching profession, after having worked as a management-consultant in industry for another couple of years, I became a teacher in a Roman Catholic secondary school. There too, I found little interest for character formation, self-knowledge and religion.

Even after years of meditation I couldn't get rid of continuous headache which would come all of a sudden and was dismissed on medical grounds and granted a pension. In search of recovery, I vainly tried various alternative ways of healing. I became interested in the religions of India. It dawned on me that the real cause of my headache had to do with my past *karma*. I went to India and went to see Sri Hairakhan Baba (Babaji) in North India. His message was the path of truth, simplicity and love. Above all, He taught the repetition of the *mantra*, 'Aum Namah Shivaya', *karma yoga* and selfless love for one's fellow-man and God. Though I can hardly put it into words, I am convinced that Babaji worked a great change in me.

One and a half years after Babaji's death, I went to Sri Sathya Sai Baba in Puttaparthi, South India, for the very first time. That was in August 1985. Fortunately, our group got an interview fairly soon. Deeply moved, I entered the room which is known to so many devotees. When I put a question to Baba about my *karma yoga* and health, He put me at ease. He answered, "Don't worry, I heal you." This promise was a great help to me, especially during the hard times that followed. In a subsequent interview, Sathya Sai Baba said to two Indian students who lived in the U.S.A., "My teachings, that's Baba! Don't bow to this body but do what I say. Practise my teachings!" That's why, in this book I have gathered those sayings of Sathya Sai Baba which refer to practice.

Shortly after coming home from my second visit, I had an almost fatal car-smash. For nine days I was balanced on the very edge of the grave. A few months in hospital, and a deep depression which was mainly caused by administering excessive medicines radically changed my vision of life. The days became gloomy and almost unbearable. I was perplexed by the fragmentary public health service and the piling up of blunder after blunder. The food was very bad. Afterwards, I realized that is the case in most hospitals, mental homes, children's homes, homes for elderly people and barracks all over the world.

In the book, *'Harper's Review of Biochemistry'*, written by David W. Martin, Jr., MD and others (1985) it is said, "Typical protein-energy malnutrition also occurs in developed countries among adults as a consequence of malabsorption, gastrointestinal surgery, or severe illness. Surveys of medical and surgical wards in major urban hospitals suggest that as many as 30% - 50% of patients hospitalized for more than two weeks meet World Health Organization standards for protein-energy malnutrition. Many of these patients require nutritional support to aid their recovery." (pp. 673) In most cases that does not happen. In any case, not in the right way! In addition to this, any knowledge of the natural healing arts and of religious inspiration were completely absent in that hospital. In the midst of all this, my inner self remained true to Sathya Sai Baba. In so far as I could, I repeated the *mantra* 'Om Sai Ram'. I knew the whole experience meant great grace and my eyes were opened to the grief, both physical and spiritual, and the ignorance in this world.

Fortunately, after some time, I was well enough again to go to Sathya Sai Baba. For five months I spent an unforgettable time in Kodaikanal, Ooty, Whitefield and Puttaparthi. He freed me from my depression and since this release, I have known an almost continuous happiness, something I had not experienced before. During an interview, He assured me that my health was entirely in His hands and that I should no longer pay attention to my headache. Henceforward, one-pointed attention to God should be my attitude in life. Though I preferred to stay with Him, He finally sent me home saying, "Go back to Holland and do some work." All these experiences form the basis of this book.

I started by asking myself what Sathya Sai Baba had said about health and medical science and discovered the report, "How to maintain health till we breathe our last. A humble presentation from Haryana and Chandigarh Sri Sathya Sai Organisation on the auspicious occasion of the Commemoration of the 60th Birthday Anniversary of Bhagavan Sri Sathya Sai Baba." At first I could hardly believe the contents of this report. Feeling that the report was not complete I started to read as many books and discourses of Sathya Sai Baba as possible. It was only a short time ago that I finally finished reading all the issues through all the years of publication of the magazine *'Sanathana Sarathi'*, which they keep in the library of the University at Puttaparthi. At the same time, I began to dive deep into western naturopathy, at first especially in the Natural Hygiene Movement in the U.S.A. I gathered the sayings of Sathya Sai Baba on health, food and spirituality and wrote my first book (108 pages) entitled, *'Live Healthily by Good Activities and the Right Food. Sayings of Bhagavan Sri Sathya Sai Baba and from the Natural Hygiene Movement.'* Baba was very pleased with the book. Turning over the pages He said, "Very happy, very happy."

The Natural Hygiene Movement takes up a clear position in the field of health. The doctors of Natural Hygiene declare that it is not the bacteria, viruses, etc. (against which modern medical science has put up such a vigorous fight) that are the cause of disease, but that man falls ill by a wrong way of life, by faulty food or too much activity, over-excitement and through all kinds of dissipation. They take drugs, alcohol, tobacco, coffee, tea, narcotics and all physiological and psychological practices which injure life and disturb health. Besides, they suffer from the use of chemical medicines, vaccinations and X-rays. Scientists of the University of Munich say that in Germany every year about 20,000 people die as a result of diseases caused by too many X-rays.

In the meantime, my investigations proceeded. I found out that at different places in the world there were and still are naturopaths and institutes which prove that most of the diseases are caused by faulty food and, what is more, that these diseases can be cured with only the right food as remedy. Also several prominent naturopaths and biochemists say that no single treatment, not even a treatment by a natural healing practitioner, a homeopath or an acupuncturist, is significant so long as a good diet is not followed.

All these natural doctors and biochemists tell us that we poison our body with faulty food and, by doing so, we undermine our immune system and, finally, fall ill. Mostly the poisoning is not noticed; a disease often develops very slowly and may remain unnoticed for many years at a stretch. As early as 1884, S. Graham (Natural Hygiene Movement) said, "For a very long period of time I have taught in public that man is inclined to bring about his own diseases and sufferings; it is more or less his own fault that he is ill and suffers. Just like drunkenness, he is in case of diseases obliged to offer his apologies to society."

In Sathya Sai Baba's *Geetha Vahini* (see Chapter 26) Krishna says : "Moral conduct, good habits, spiritual effort all depend upon the quality of food: disease, mental weakness, spiritual slackness – all are produced by faulty food."

Meanwhile, a Dutch devotee found a cassette containing a complete lecture of Sathya Sai Baba in the Telugu language (with hardly an understandable translation of it in English) about the connection between food and character (see Chapter 16). Of course, it was not by chance that at the same time I met two Indian people who knew the Telugu language and who were willing to translate Baba's discourse for me. This discourse of Baba's was the reason that every doubt in me disappeared like snow under a hot sun.

In the chapter, 'Sai Baba and the Animal Kingdom' in the book *'The Embodiment of Love'*, written by Peggy Mason and Ron Laing, Sathya Sai Baba says: "Birds and beasts need no Divine incarnation to guide them, for they have no inclination to stray away from their *dharma* (right living). Man alone forgets or ignores the goal of life. Animals did not come for the purpose of supplying food for human beings. They came to work out their own lives in the world. Man is incurring very bad *karma* for his immoral, unethical and unspiritual treatment of animals. See God in every creature."

Man needs to look upon nature as a university for *satyam*, *sivam* and *sundaram* (truth, goodness and beauty). Sathya Sai Baba encourages everyone to appreciate the beauties of nature; He directs attention to the charm of a flower, the colourful magnificence of a sunrise or sunset, the grim grandeur of an overcast sky, the timorous twinkling of the stars in the midnight sky or jasmine-garland cranes in flight.

And what does the human being do? Hundreds of millions of animals are misused for all sorts of experiments in the laboratories of industry, the universities and hospitals. Countless is the number of animals that are raised in an agonizing way and slaughtered for consumption. Without this madness there would be sufficient vegetable food for all people and there would also be fewer diseases.

The human being needs no meat and fish. The natural doctors have arrived at the conclusion that meat and fish are actually injurious to health. Cancer, heart and vascular diseases and many others are related to the consumption of meat and fish.

Sathya Sai Baba stresses the importance of *satvic* food, i.e., living, raw, unheated and biologically grown food, especially fruit, nuts, vegetables and just germinating pulses. Small quantities of milk and certain milk-products are *satvic* as well. Man is awfully ungrateful and cruel to the cow. Instead of being able to finish her life in a natural way, she is prematurely slaughtered for economic reasons in most cases. On Sathya Sai Baba's farm, all cows die a natural death. This is an example for the world. A summary of His division of *satvic* food, *rajasic* food and *tamasic* food is given in Chapter 22, and the tables belonging to it. *Satvic* food is full of vitality. Recently, in a dream, Sri Sathya Sai Baba instructed me to eat exclusively *satvic* food.

I have studied various important schools of western naturopathy and compared them with Sathya Sai Baba's teachings. Some prominent schools or associations have developed a more or less similar science of nutrition and hygiene. I can mention here the Natural Hygiene Movement in the U.S.A., the European University for Natural Healing in Belgium, the Ann Wigmore Foundation in Boston and Puerto Rico, the International Biogenic Society in North America and the Gesellschaft Gesundheitsberatung in Germany. In an appendix I have tried to give a short summary of the dietetics of these groups, using the words of Sathya Sai Baba as a touchstone.

The most important purpose of this appendix is to help the reader to change over to *satvic* food and *satvic* habits of eating. By this switch-over the body is rid of poison. However, in doing so, many poisonous materials may be freed to enter into the blood giving rise to all kinds of complications and problems. Besides, most people's digestive system has degenerated by the years of faulty food and has become unable to digest raw food. So, it is best to change step by step. Some people manage to switch over fast; others take months or even years. I advise especially the sick to have themselves treated by an expert (doctor) on naturopathy.

By eating *satvic* food both the body and mind are gradually purified. This purification takes many years. You need much discipline and perseverance. The current habits of eating make man ill and weak, shorten his life, and form an impediment to his spiritual aims. According to the *Vedas*, in a life span of one hundred sixteen years, man has to attain liberation (*moksha*) from slavery to the body. The period as a youth lasts twenty four years, the period as a grown-up lasts forty four years and the waning of life lasts forty eight years.

During an interview with Sathya Sai Baba in the summer of 1991, He promised to help me. While writing this book I experienced His help and guidance several times. For some time, I had wondered whether Sathya Sai Baba's message about health, food and spirituality was something that could be found in Christianity. One day I received a letter from Italy. The sender was a devotee from Australia who wanted to have an interview with me about *satvic* food. Very soon, indeed, it appeared that he had not only come to ask something, but had also come to give something. He told me about the books of Dr. E. B. Szekely who had concerned himself deeply with the history and the teachings of the Essenes. Their teachings are already very old and date from thousands of years.

The Essenes formed a brotherhood. They lived during the last two or three centuries B.C., and the first century of the Christian era, around the Dead Sea in Palestine and at Lake Mareotis in Egypt. In Egypt they were known as the Therapeutae. We know two identical versions of *'The Essene Gospel of Peace'*: one written in Aramaic and the other in Old-Slavonic. Fleeing from the marching troops of Genghis Khan, the Nestorian priests brought this gospel along with them to the West.

In this 'Gospel of Peace' Jesus says: "For I tell you truly, he who kills, kills himself, and who so eats the flesh of slain beasts, eats of the body of death. In his blood every drop of their blood will turn to poison. Kill neither man, nor beasts, nor yet the food which goes into your mouth. For if you eat living food, the same will quicken you, but if you kill your food, the dead food will kill you also. And everything that kills your body kills your soul as well. With the fire of death you cook your food. It is the same fire which destroys your food and your body, even as the fire of hatred which ravages your thoughts, ravages your spirit. Therefore don't eat anything which a stronger fire than the fire of life has killed. Eat all fruits of trees, the grain and grasses of the field, the milk of beasts and honey of bees. For everything beyond these is of the Evil One, and leads by the way of sins and diseases unto death. But the food which you eat from the abundant table of God, gives strength and youth to your body, and you will never see disease. For the table of God fed Methuselah of old, and I truly tell you, if you live even as he lived, then the God of the living will also grant you a long life on earth.

"When you eat at the table of the Earthly Mother, eat all things even as they are found on her table. Cook not, neither mix all things one with another, lest your bowels become as steaming bogs. For I truly tell you, this is abominable in the eyes of the Lord. And desire not to devour all things you see round about you. Be content with two or three sorts of food, and when you eat, never eat unto fullness.

"And your fasting is always pleasing in the eyes of the angels of God. Trouble not the work of the angel in your body by eating often. For I tell you truly, he who eats more than twice in the day does in him the work of the Evil One. And if you wish that the angels of God enjoy themselves in your body and that the Evil One ignores you, then eat only once a day from the table of God." Here they speak about the air angel, the water angel, the angel of the earth, etc., the five elements of which Sathya Sai Baba speaks.

In the *'The Essene Gospel of Peace'* Jesus proceeds: "Breathe long and deeply at all your meals, so that the angel of air may bless all your repasts. And chew well your food with your teeth, so that the angel of water may turn it into blood in your body. And eat slowly, as if it were a prayer you say to the Lord. For, I tell you truly, the power of God will enter into you if you eat at His table in this manner. For the table of the Lord is as an altar, and he who eats at the table of God is in a temple. The body of man is turned into a temple and his bowels into an altar if he keeps God's commandments. Wherefore put naught upon the altar of the Lord when your spirit is vexed, neither think upon anyone with anger in the temple of God, for all that you eat in sorrow, or in anger, or without desire, becomes a poison in your body.

"And forget not that every seventh day is holy and consecrated to God. On the seventh day eat not any earthly food, but live only upon the words of God. And let not food trouble the work of the angels in your body throughout the seventh day. Let the angels of God build the kingdom of heaven in your body. On six days feed your body with the gifts of your Earthly Mother, but on the seventh day sanctify your body for your Heavenly Father."+

Whoever has the disposal of the financial means in order to switch over to *satvic* food is a privileged man. *Ayurveda* and the doctrine of the Essenes are not only individually aimed, but also socially and universally. Just like Sathya Sai Baba, they teach that if man wishes to lead a healthy, happy and long life, he should be full of compassion towards his fellow man in distress, and should actually help him. There are many sick people, but also many people who are starving. Between five hundred million and a billion people in this world live on the verge of starvation. Every minute about twenty-eight people die because of lack of food. Together with the victims of diseases caused by malnutrition about one hundred thousand people daily die owing to lack of food.

Hunger is a solvable problem. The world food problem would already have been solved if people would not eat meat. Besides, the well-to-do people in general eat far too much. In order to digest food properly, we need pure drinking-water and proper sanitary provisions. It is exactly the poorest who are in need of this. The whole world should exert itself to its utmost in order to solve the hunger problem.

A wonderful example is the work of the Indian missionary, Sai Shankar, (1935-1986), who, inspired by Sathya Sai Baba, has established in his country the Sai Shankar Trust head-quartered in the village of Ponnamapet in Karnataka, and its sister organization, the People's Trust of India in Sriramanahalli near Bangalore. Sai Shankar spent all his energy and abilities for the very poor and his work is continued by both trusts. He inspired many educated people belonging to various religious traditions.

+ Dr. E. B. Szekely, The Essence Way, biogenic living, pp. 75 - 79.

Sai Shankar said: "The rich need peace of mind and the poor need clothes, a home, and so on, and especially selfless love. Real devotion is serving the poor, instructing them how to provide for their own livelihood, rendering them self-reliant and teaching them spirituality."

The Sai Shankar Trust and the People's Trust of India help the poorest of the poor in India. They provide for food, clothes, new houses, medical assistance (hospitals), material help and instruction in the field of agriculture, cattle-breeding (purchase of cows), irrigation and drinking-water and sanitary supplies. And, last but not least, education (schools). They help the people to help themselves, so that in the end they become independent. The Sai Shankar Trust has adopted fourteen villages and the People's Trust of India eighteen (10,000 people). Their work is sustained by the People's Trust of Holland, by the People's Trust of Belgium and the People's Trust of the United Kingdom. Recently, the People's Trust of Nepal was established.

One of the latest things I received from Sathya Sai Baba, through two of His Indian devotees, is the original *ayurvedic* text, the *Charaka Samhita*, consisting of six volumes. I got these volumes from the Shree Gulabkunverba Ayurvedic Society at Jamnagar in India. In the appendix I have tried to illustrate the essential items of *ayurveda*. Delving deeply into the *ayurveda* and the western natural healing arts, I discovered a lot of similarities and unifying factors between them. For both natural healing arts, and correct food form the basis. Closing the circle of my research, I rediscovered modern biochemistry. The *yogis* already knew the secret of so-called 'eternal youth'. With the aid of the electron microscope and the most advanced biochemical methods, scientists have observed and understood the natural basis of this secret (see appendix). Eating pure *satvic* food is a precondition.

Sathya Sai Baba's teachings are universal. Difficult essential conceptions such as the ego and evil are made understandable and clear. He says: "The correct meaning of ego is the mistaken identification of oneself with the body (Chapter 12). Just like plants, animals and human beings, the demonic and the Divine forces can be described as waves (Chapter 3). Evil is one of the temporary manifestations of the Divine, (this is not a concept of Christian belief) and it is our task always to choose the good. We have to be obedient to the Divine laws - that is our *dharma*." Sathya Sai Baba has come to restore *dharma* in the world. He says: "Disaster now dances madly on the world stage, because right is neglected and there is disbelief in the essentials of *dharmic* life. The *Bhagavad-Gita* declares that without control of the tongue it is impossible to follow the path of devotion and enter the mansion of *yoga* which leads to God. The most important basis of all kinds of yoga is the right food. The food man eats nowadays is mainly *rajasic* food and *tamasic* food. That's why cruelty and restlessness are prevalent in the minds of people. Their physical health is bad as well. *Tamasic* food kills the intellect, (*buddhi*), and forms the basis of the ego. Most illnesses can be cured by simple living, simple exercises and by intelligent control of the tongue. Allow nature to fight and to cure disease. Follow more and more the principles of naturopathy. Live long so that you can witness the career of the Divine *Avatar* for years and years."

The best way to maintain and regain your physical, mental and spiritual health is to direct your attention to God, and use the four 'medicines' of Sri Sathya Sai Baba:

* Sai-lence or Divine silence, both outward and inward (sense-control and mind-control); talk only when there is need.
* *Satvic* nourishment by way of all the senses, especially the tongue; and the associated good habits of eating, such as eating with *satvic* feelings and thoughts, chewing well, eating slowly, moderately, in silence, with devoted people, in a clean room, and once or twice a day, and fasting one day a week; and *satvic* habits of life, such as regulated sleeping habits, disciplined spending of spare time, good music, sufficient exercise and sunlight, fresh air, pure water and a good living environment;

* *Sadhana* (spiritual discipline) consists of devotion (*bhakti yoga*), selfless service or work (*seva, karma yoga*), acquisition of wisdom and spiritual knowledge by self-inquiry and reading holy scriptures (*gnana yoga*), and meditation (*dhyana yoga*). Living according to the five fundamental human values: truth (*satya*), righteousness or right conduct (*dharma*), love (*prema*), equanimity (*shanti*), and non-violence (*ahimsa*) eliminating negative emotions such as anger, fear, and worry, and striving for bliss (*ananda*). *Dharma* comes from the food sheath (*annamaya kosha*), *prema* comes from the vital sheath (*pranamaya kosha*), the mental sheath (*manomaya kosha*) and the intuition-centred sheath (*anandamaya kosha*), *shanti* comes from the mental sheath, *satya* comes from the intellectual sheath (*vignanamaya kosha*), and *ahimsa* comes from the intuition-centred sheath. Purity, patience and perseverance are very important.

* *Bhajan* singing (singing hymns in the glory of God), and the repeating of the name of the Lord (*namasmarana*), and talking about the glories of God with form. Recite prayers and chant mantras in the correct way. The *Gayatri Mantra* is the most important *mantra*; it should never be given up. Listen only to good and heavenly music.

  The medicines of Silence, *Satvic food*, *Sadhana* and *Bhajans* can easily be remembered because the letters SSSB are the initials of Sri Sathya Sai Baba. His fifth medicine is:

* *Vibhuti*, the holy ash which Sathya Sai Baba materializes. One of the meanings is: "The protection of humanity by the Lord." For many people *vibhuti* is a tangible proof of Sathya Sai Baba's love and protection. Man's efforts and God's grace have to come together; without God's grace and protection nothing can be attained and reached.

Sathya Sai Baba has said that methods such as *hatha yoga* and *kriya yoga* cannot make us realise God; these *yogas* may only improve health and prolong life. He advises against most schools of western psychology and transcendental meditation (TM), and generally speaking against *pranayama* and spiritualism. Without a good *guru*, *pranayama* may be dangerous. Having a straight spine in all postures, good breathing and chanting *mantras* in the best possible way are extremely important. (At the end of the appendix some attention will be paid to these three subjects).

Sathya Sai Baba often asks: "What is the way to God?" In psychological language: how can we expand our consciousness and merge back into cosmic consciousness? According to Sathya Sai Baba the answer should be: be good, do good, see good, think good, talk good, do no evil, see no evil, hear no evil, think no evil, talk no evil. We should emphasize the good qualities in our fellowmen and also in ourselves. During the process of self-inquiry we should discover our good qualities, and burn up our bad qualities, after facing and witnessing them, in the Divine light by meditation and other spiritual disciplines. With the four medicines of Sathya Sai Baba we should purify our mind and body with patience and perseverance. That is real spiritual therapy.

To be able to discriminate between right and wrong we have to read the holy scriptures and to develop and purify our conscience (*buddhi*). In August 1993, Sathya Sai Baba said during a discourse, "Do not criticize other people. Forget the past and the future. All problems in the world come from brooding over the past. Know what you should do in the present. Be perfect in the present. Think continuously of God and His commands."

When I was about thirty-five years old I came heavily under the influence of the ideas of modern western psychology, of psycho-analytical thoughts (Freud, Fromm, Jung, Adler) in particular. After imbibing these ideas I made several big mistakes in my life. I needed a serious car-accident followed by a deep depression (more than one year) to get rid of the negative impact of these ideas and other negative *karma*. It is only due to the immense mercy of Sathya Sai Baba that I have survived and can finally transcend modern psychology.

In psycho-analysis, dream-analysis is considered to be very important. I analysed thousands of dreams on my own and with the help of a psychiatrist, but now I know that in spiritual therapy hardly any attention is paid to dreams. The only exception relates to the dreams given by God or a God-realised *guru* to provide solace and support to the individual. Generally speaking, interpreting dreams means brooding over the past, binding the individual with new ideas and strengthening of all kinds of lower desires and instincts, especially of the sexual instinct. I realised that psycho-analytical practice and theory are false in the ultimate analysis and had lowered the level of my consciousness.

Interpreting dreams and other psychological practices, also in groups, without spiritual knowledge and discipline (prayer, meditation, etc.), is dangerous. The ideas incorporated in psycho-analysis and other psycho-therapies tend to take us to the lowest levels of consciousness whereas genuine spiritual therapy takes us to the highest levels of consciousness. The basis of all therapies, should be spiritual, not mental and material. Psycho-therapists, no, all therapists should treat their patients in such a way that their patients tend to develop firm faith in the Lord and try to connect themselves with Him. A good example of a spiritually inspired psychotherapy is the method of Phyllis Krystal; Sathya Sai Baba has blessed her work. Phyllis Krystal describes her method in her book *'Cutting the Ties that Bind.'*

Many psychiatrists, and psychological counsellors of all hues, have no idea of the importance of morality (*dharma*) or of human values, and of the influence of *tamasic*, *rajasic* and *satvic* food on body and mind; and they do not understand the genesis of the ego and its working. They also have no idea of the spiritual journey to God or of the fundamental reality of the soul and God. When I was deeply depressed I talked to the chief psychiatrist of a Roman Catholic hospital in Amsterdam. I asked him cautiously if he believed in God. He answered, "No, we do not need a God anymore."

Modern psychology says that lust, hatred, jealousy, egoism, pride, attachment, etc. are natural, and hence cannot be eradicated; it states that we should recognize our desires and accept them emotionally. In the spiritual path on the contrary, one has to become a witness to ones desires, instincts and qualities, avoiding all repression. The desires should not be fulfilled but only looked at, starved honestly and, finally, totally uprooted; thereby the whole structure of the mind can be pulled down, thus granting spiritual liberation and bliss (*ananda*). Sex is a very powerful instinct; it can bring down the level of consciousness to the most gross level. That is probably the most important reason why all religions teach one to restrain the sex urge. During an interview Sathya Sai Baba in Kodaikanal said, "Sex in the West is very bad. Sex is only allowed between husband and wife, only in marriage. Before marriage everyone should live as brother and sister."

By identification with the body, the mind builds a cage around the real 'I' (*soul, atma*), and replaces it by the false 'I'(ego), and the possessive sense of 'mine'. The ego is externally oriented. The mind expresses itself through attraction and repulsion, affection and hatred towards the external world. In this context the following words of Sathya Sai Baba are important, "Both *ahamkara* (ego) and *mamakara* (senses of 'mine') are results of consuming improper food. You must realise that food is mainly responsible for your feelings of attachment and hatred as well as for *ahamkara* and *mamakara*," (Chapter 12). The walls of the cage are built of innumerable sense-impressions, desires, emotions, feelings and thoughts related to human beings and material objects. Modern psychology states in great ignorance that this cage is the reality and that by nature the ego is the centre of consciousness. Psychotherapy tries to reconstruct and modify the cage by making minor repairs; the human body and its needs remain the central truth. Psychotherapy only gives some superficial and illusory relief, but after the treatment the suffering goes on. Spiritual therapy (the four 'medicines' of Sathya Sai Baba) dismantles the cage step by step and finally destroys it completely. The warder of the cage, the ego, is killed and dies, and the individual is liberated. All suffering disappears and one acquires real freedom and bliss. The process of the extrication of the individual from the cage is very painful, although after extrication, it is all joy. Only the mercy of God can shatter the deep-rooted illusory identification of one's self with the body, and grant liberation.

Dr. B. S. Goel, a very ardent devotee of Sathya Sai Baba, has given a very lucid, authentic account of his journey to God in his book *'Third Eye and Kundalini, an Experiential Account of the Journey from Dust to Divinity,'* (Third Eye Foundation of India, 1992). When he was young, Dr. Goel came heavily under the influence of Marxist thought. After going into a state of severe depression, he underwent classical psycho-analysis for four and a half years. When he was about thirty-five years of age, Sathya Sai Baba appeared in his dream and told him that everything was happening according to His will for the particular purpose of exposing the limitations of both Marxism and psycho-analysis, which are false in the ultimate analysis, and cannot provide happiness to the individual. He indicated to him that the Godward inner path is the only path to achieve bliss and peace.

Sathya Sai Baba activated his *kundalini* and opened his third eye. He had to pass through intense painful sufferings, and he experienced the destruction of his cage and reached the seventh *chakra*. As a result of these experiences, Dr. Goel can give a fascinating commentary on psycho-analysis and a unique account of the *kundalini* process with all its problems, sufferings and states of bliss. To my mind, the most precious book about the human evolution process is the *Ramakatha Rasavahini, (Ramayana)*, written by Sathya Sai Baba Himself. Sathya Sai Baba has said, "The *Ramayana* happens in everyone's heart. It does take place systematically and in the same sequence" (chapter 8). I read this book several times and I feel that it conscientiously describes the different stages of the process of God-realization.

If any human being does not undergo spiritual crisis or change, his physical disease is at least a spiritual opportunity. Disease is often a lack of love, including a lack of caring for oneself and one's physical body. Self-examination is the first step - the fundamental basis of understanding and resolving any disease. The sick person should start realising that the purpose and meaning of his life is the expansion of his consciousness, and the spiritual evolution of humanity as a whole.

According to *ayurveda*, both mental and physical diseases have three causes. First, *karmic* causes: the effects of wrong thoughts, feelings and actions in this life and in previous lives. Second, they can be caused by the disequilibrium of the three *gunas*: *satva*, *rajas* and *tamas*. Third, diseases can arise from physical causes: the imbalance of the three biological humours, *vata*, *pitta* and *kapha* (see appendix), and the accumulation of toxins.

Western naturopathy says that most diseases are caused by the accumulation of toxins (toxemia) and the deficiency of nutritional requirements such as enzymes, vitamins and minerals. Allopathy believes that most diseases are caused by bacteria and viruses. *Ayurveda* is not as concerned with nutritious substances, bacteria and viruses, but is concerned primarily with the subtle energies in food and man.

Spiritual therapy includes all three viewpoints. Most disease conditions involve spiritual, mental and physical factors, and require treatment on all three levels. Spiritual therapy (the four 'medicines' of Sathya Sai Baba) includes the use of *satvic* food and also of *satvic ayurvedic* and other spices and herbs (see further part C of the appendix). A *satvic* diet is a generally healthful and balancing diet, safe for all three humours. *Rajasic* foods aggravate *vata* and *pitta*, *tamasic* foods increase *kapha* and *ama* (*toxins*). Eating *satvic* food is tantamount to purification of the mind and healing of the body by balancing the humours, removing the toxins, supplying all nutritional requirements, and strengthening the immune system.

Spices, herbs and foods follow the same energetics and can be looked at according to the same principles. Herbal therapy requires the support of proper food to be effective. Diet can enhance, neutralize or counter the effect of spices and herbs. For medicinal purposes, when it is absolutely necessary, we may also make use of non-*satvic* spices and herbs, *rajasic* methods such as surgery and allopathic medicines, which are mostly *tamasic* in the long run. For instance, antibiotics can save lives but, mostly, they are misused.

We must realize that by these curative methods, the mind becomes *rajasic* and *tamasic*. After the required changes have been brought about, we have to purify the mind by eating *satvic* food and by other spiritual methods. Several people get depressed and even commit suicide after surgery or long treatments with strong medicines; that could be prevented if they got good food at the same time.

Although Sathya Sai Baba prefers naturopathy, *ayurveda* in particular, He has built an allopathic Super-Speciality Hospital near His *ashram* in Puttaparthi. On His sixty-fifth birthday in 1990, Sathya Sai Baba said: "In the name of the Lord free education and medical relief should be provided. What is the plight of the poor? Who looks after them? That is why we have launched this big hospital project. Whether it is a heart bypass operation, or a kidney transplant, or a lung operation or brain surgery, everything will be done free. This hospital will be opened on the twenty-second of November, 1991." And so it happened. Sathya Sai Baba inaugurated the Super-Speciality Hospital on the twenty-second of November, 1991.

In *ayurveda*, *yoga* therapy is a special branch of treatment; it makes use of specific *yogic* postures (*hatha yoga*), breathing exercises and *mantras*. Without a good *guru* these *yoga* practises can do more harm than good. Sathya Sai Baba said in one of His discourses ('*Summer Showers in Brindavan*', 1993, pp. 91-93): "There is a proliferation of pseudo *yogic* systems all over the world. Many physical exercises are paraded as *yoga* today. True *yoga* is based on Patanjali's *yoga sutras*. It is a serious mistake to take *yoga* as a physical exercise. *Yogic* practices should be accompanied by *yogic* discipline as well. Sage Patanjali devoted his whole life to the study of *yoga*; he defined a *yoga* as the observance of discipline for the physical, mental and spiritual well-being. *Yoga* lays down certain disciplines like eating moderate, balanced and pure food, sense restraint, control of thoughts, one-pointed concentration and meditation. But modern man flouts *yogic* discipline by helping himself with spicy and sumptuous food to cater to his greedy tongue. He ignores the ancient doctrine that food should be taken like medicine, for the disease of hunger. We should take medicine whether it is tasty or not to cure our illness.

"Modern man continually flouts this discipline and feeds voraciously on spiced food. Indians make use of a lot of *tamarind* to flavour their dishes, though *tamarind* is detrimental to health. Man in his frantic scramble to amass wealth has lost his proper sleeping habits. Man forces himself to take sleeping pills to induce sleep into his worried mind. Pills and drugs take a heavy toll of his health and make him a target for blood pressure and heart ailments. The hurry and insatiable greed of man have brought in their wake a host of mental maladies. The chaos and the confusion, the agitation and upheaval that you see in the world today arise from ill-health.".

On the ninth of July, 1993, during the interview, Sathya Sai Baba blessed this book and signed it 'With love Baba' on the title-page. In the manuscript I had put a photograph of Sathya Sai Baba with a baby opposite the title-page. To my amazement He also wrote 'With love Baba' on the baby in the photograph. I understood that He wanted to emphasize the importance of these teachings for children and this inspired me to write a smaller book for parents, children and teachers about the same subject during my stay in Puttaparthi, Whitefield and Kodaikanal during 1993-1994. When He signed the book, Sathya Sai Baba said: "It has to be put into practice, otherwise it is of no use. Love all, serve all." No doubt it is good service to teach children, in addition to human values, the value of *satvic* food. The proper care of children is the foundation of culture, and the prevention of disease is better than its cure. Above all this book aims to be a practical book. Sathya Sai Baba says, "A thick wall of books disconnects man from God." I do hope that this book will not serve as a 'brick'. Three-fourths of spiritual discipline should be introspection. That is why the first part is concerned with Self-knowledge. Health and food form the basis of Spirituality (second part). *Yoga*, the third part, leads to unification with God.

I should like to express my acknowledgement and gratitude to all those who have made possible the realization of this book, in particular Martina de Pater who has made the beautiful illustrations and the recipes and typed the whole manuscript with patience and great interest.

May you all walk in the Light of God and may the Lord bless you all with good health, a long life, peace and spiritual enlightenment.

Loka samastha sukhino bhavantu	*Aum Namah shivaya*
May the inhabitants of all the worlds have peace and happiness	*Aum,* bow to God

Gerard T. Satvic
(Ter Morshuizen)
Eindhoven
The Netherlands
1994

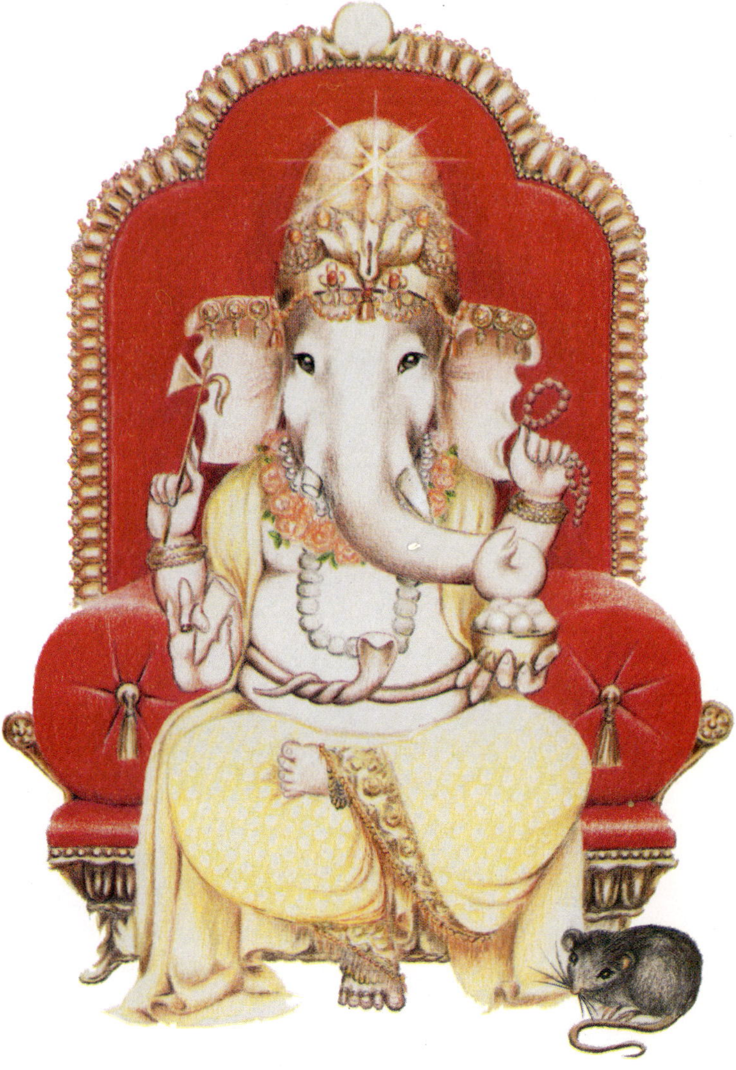

PART I

SELF KNOWLEDGE

1. THE MESSAGE I BRING

"Your reality is the *Atma* (soul), a wave of the *Param-atma* (God). The one object of this human existence is to visualise that reality, that *Atma*, that relationship between the wave and the sea. All other activities are trivial; you share them with birds and beasts; but this is the unique privilege of man. He has clambered through all the levels of animality, all the steps on the ladder of evolution, in order to inherit this high destiny. If all the years between birth and death are frittered away in seeking food and shelter, comfort and pleasure, as do animals, man is condemning himself to a further life sentence.

"Man is endowed with two special gifts: *viveka* (the faculty of reasoning) and *vignana* (the faculty of analysis and synthesis). Use these gifts to discover the truth of yourself, which is the truth of everyone else, of everything else. All countries are borne and sustained by this earth; all are warmed by the same sun; all 'bodies' are inspired by the same Divine Principle; all are urged by the same inner motivator. The *Vedas* are the earliest testaments to the victory of man over himself, his discovery of the underlying unity in all creation and his pulsating contact with the truth that unifies. They declare, God is *Sarva bhuta antar atma* (God is the inner self of all beings), *Isa vasyam idam sarvam* (all this is enveloped by God), *Vasudevah sarvam idam* (all this is God, Vasudeva). The Divine Principle that is in everyone is like the electric current that illuminates the bulbs before Me here, of different colours and of different candle powers. The same God shines in and through everyone, whatever be his creed, colour, tribe or territory. The current animates and activates all bulbs; the Divine animates and activates all. Those who see differences are deluded; they are befogged by prejudice, egoism, hatred or malice. Love sees all as one Divine family.

"How does this *Atma*-principle express itself in man? As *prema*, love! Love is the basic nature that sustains him and strengthens his resolve to march ahead. Without love man is blind; the world, for him, will be a dark and fearsome jungle. Love is the light that guides the feet of man in the wilderness. The *Vedas* laid down four goals before man, two pairs of goals, rather, *dharma-artha* (morality-wealth: the earning of the wherewithal for living through moral means) and *kama-moksha* (desire-liberation: the attainment of liberation from the twin experiences of pain and pleasure and the desire for that liberation and for nothing less than that supreme treasure). All these goals are attainable through the practice of Love. Love is regulated by *sathya* (truth), *dharma* (righteousness) and *shanti* (equanimity). The *Vedas* teach that man must earn wealth through the path of *dharma*. That is not taken to heart; wealth is accumulated anyhow! The *Vedas* teach that man should have only one *kama* (desire), namely, for *moksha*, or liberation; this is not respected; man is drowning himself in a maelstrom of desire. The fulfilment of that desire can never quench his deeper thirsts. How can a prisoner have any desire but liberation? Widespread anxieties, fears and unrest, evident all over the world, are consequences of this mistaken course.

"The human body, so filled with skills, so capable of great adventures, is a gift from God to each of you. It has to be used as a raft, on which to cross this never-calm sea of *samsara* (relativity) that lies between birth and death, bondage and liberation. Awaken to this primal duty even while your physical and mental faculties are keen; awake even while your power of discrimination is sharp. Do not postpone the launching of the raft, for it may become unserviceable soon. It may be burdened with illness, so that all your attention will have to be spent on its upkeep. Think of the incomparable joy that will surge within you, when you approach the shores of liberation! Ride safe on the raging waters of *samsara* (relativity); be a witness, do not crave for the fruits of action, leave the consequences of all acts to God's will. He is the Doer, you are but the instrument. Pursue nobler ends; have grander ideals; sensory pleasures are trinkets, trivialities. The sages have discovered the disciplines that will keep you unaffected by defeat or victory, loss or gain. Learn them, practice them; establish yourself in unruffled peace.

"In homes and schools, training of the minds of the young on these lines has to be taken up earnestly by teachers and parents. Of course, they must equip themselves for this work by steady practice in meditation and *namasmarana* (recital of the name of God). In every home, a certain length of time must be fixed everyday, in the morning as well as the evening, for readings from spiritual books and *namasmarana*. Parents and children must join in singing the glory of God. In fact, one's time must be dedicated to God: as a first step, a few minutes may be devoted to the adoration of His glory or the gauging of the depth of that glory. Gradually, when the sweetness of the habit heartens you, you will devote more and more time and feel more and more content. The purpose of 'living' is to achieve 'living in God'. Everyone is entitled to that consecration and consummation. You are the truth - do not lose faith. Do not belittle yourselves, you are Divine, however often you slide from humanity to animality or even lower.

"Cultivate love; share that love with all. How can you give one person less and another more, when they are both the same as you? If you forget the basic Divinity, hatred sprouts; envy raises it's hood. See the *atma* in all. Love sprouts, peace descends like dew. You are *prema-svarupas*, embodiments of love. You have been sitting here for hours, in the open, putting up with great discomfort, awaiting Me, eager to hear Me and see Me. I am speaking to you from this dais, only to satisfy that ardour. When I sense your *prema*, I feel I must share it and allow you to share My *prema*. That is the best of all communications and communions. The mediation of words is then unnecessary.

"I have come to light the lamp of love in your hearts, to see that it shines day by day with added lustre. I have not come to speak on behalf of any particular *dharma* (religion), of the Hindu *dharma*. I have not come on any mission of publicity for any sect or creed or cause; nor have I come to collect followers for any doctrine. I have no plan to attract disciples or devotees into My fold or any fold. I have come to tell you of this universal unitary faith, this *atmic* principle, this path of love, this *dharma* of *prema* (religion of love), this duty of love, this obligation to love.

"All religions teach one basic discipline: the removal from the mind of the blemish of egoism, of running after little joys. Every religion teaches man to fill his being with the glory of God, and evict the pettiness of conceit. It trains him in methods of detachment and discrimination, so that he may aim high and attain liberation. Believe that all hearts are motivated by the one and only God; that all faiths glorify the one and only God; that all names, in all languages and all forms man can conceive, denote the one and only God. His adoration is best done by means of love. Cultivate that *eka-bhava* (attitude of oneness) between men of all creeds, all countries and all continents. That is the message of love I bring. That is the message I wish you to take to heart.

"Foster love, live in love, spread love - that is the spiritual exercise which will yield the maximum benefit. When you recite the names of God, remembering all the while His majesty, His compassion, His glory, His splendour, His presence - love will grow within you, its roots will go deeper and deeper, its branches will spread wider and wider, giving cool shelter to friend and foe, to fellow national and foreigner. God has a million names. Sages and saints have seen Him in a million forms; they have seen Him with eyes closed and eyes open. They have extolled Him in all the languages and dialects of man; but yet, His glory is not exhausted. Select any name of His, any name that appeals to you, select any form of His; everyday when you awaken to the call of the brightening East, recite the name, meditate on the form; have the name and the form as your companion, guide and guardian throughout the toils of the waking hours. When you retire for the night, offer grateful homage to God in that form with that name, for being with you, by you, beside you, before you, behind you, all day long. If you stick to this discipline you cannot falter or fail.

"I must give you one more advice. Endeavour always to promote the joy and happiness of your fellow countrymen in this continent; be sharers in their joy and happiness. Bharat is so called because the people of that country have *rathi* (great attachment) to *Bha* (Bhagawan, that is God). They are devoted to God and so to all the children of God. They are afraid of sin; they are eager to acquire *gna͡ a*.

"Resolve to carry on the quest for your own reality. Resolve to live in the inspiration of the constant remembrance of God. Cultivate love and share love.

"I bless you that you may achieve success in this endeavour and derive great joy therefrom."

References:
1. Sathya Sai Baba, *Sathya Sai Speaks*. Vol. VI, pp. 242-247
2. Nairobi (Kenya, East Africa); 4 - 7 - 1968

2. THE MOVING TEMPLE

This body is a valueless iron safe.
Like the precious jewels kept in an iron safe,
There is the Divine inside the body.
This Sai's word is the path of truth.

What you call God is not in a distant place,
That God is in your very body.
What you call sin is not in a faraway country,
It is there in the very acts that you perform .

Embodiments of the Divine *Atma*!

"Although the human body is worthless in itself and is impermanent, it has to be carefully looked after, because it enshrines the Divine *Atma*. This is man's primary duty. Without a healthy and strong body, man will fall an easy victim to numerous ailments. The body is verily the foundation for human life. That is why the ancient Romans, who were aware of this truth and who were the pioneers of modern civilisation in the West, used to carefully undertake various measures for the proper upkeep and development of the body.

"The body is a world in itself. It is not merely the outer form. It is the collective assemblage of many organs and limbs. Each organ has its own beauty, which has to be fostered. A weak and unhealthy body is incapable of any resolute action. Pure, noble and sublime ideas can emanate only from a strong and healthy body. All religions are agreed on this point. Although the body is impermanent, special care should be taken to maintain it properly because it provides residence for the eternal *Atma*. The Divine spirit illumines the body although the latter is composed of flesh, blood, faeces, urine and other foul smelling and impure things. *Atma* does not grow with the body, nor does it decay along with the body. The *Atma* Principle is not subject to growth or decay. It is ever pure, precious and immutable.

"A big and brilliant diamond if found on a garbage heap, does not lose its lustre or value. Just because a good variety of pumpkin is grown in a thorny hedge, it does not lose its taste or nourishing quality. Even though a peahen's egg is hatched under the warmth of an ordinary hen, the young peacock that emerges will not lose its beautiful plumage. So also, the splendour and effulgence of the selfless, stainless, eternal *Atmic* Principle will in no way be diminished, although it is associated with the human body which is full of impurities.

"What is the reason for people professing different faiths to agree on the need to nourish the health and happiness of the body? It is because all of them regard the body as the temple of the Lord within. Therefore, it is man's primary duty not to neglect this holy temple called the body, but to take utmost care for its proper maintenance and for using it for the discharge of one's duties and obligations in life. Persons who do not recognise this truth, subject the body to various ordeals in the name of worship, religious vows, fasting and penance. Thereby they are missing the goal, the recognition of the eternal *Atmic* Principle. By hitting an ant-hill, can you kill the snake inside? By subjecting the body to torture, can you realise the *Atma*? By giving up good food and water, can you attain liberation? Self-realisation is possible only through knowledge of your own real nature.

"Therefore, the first step in the quest for Self-knowledge is to understand the nature of man. Whatever the number of lives one might have had, the body one has now assumed is new. This shows that Divinity is inherent in man. The discovery of this Divinity, or real Self of man, calls for appropriate enquiry leading to the perception of the Real. When one perceives one's real Self through prolonged contemplation on the Self, one becomes a *drashta* (seer). The ultimate aim of *bhakti* (devotion) is to become such a *drashta*, and to experience the world with this spiritual perspective or background. Without this attainment, man remains a human being in form only, with no realisation of his true Self. The Sanskrit word *manava* designating man, means 'not new', because his reality is the *Atma*, which is ancient and eternal. Another meaning of the word *manava* is: *ma(agnana)*-ignorance; *na*-without; *va*-conducting oneself.

"In other words, he alone deserves the name of *manava* (man) who conducts himself without ignorance. Can all green birds talk like a parrot? Can every insect found on a flower be called a bee? Can a donkey become a tiger by merely putting on the latter's skin? Just because a pig has grown as huge as an elephant, should it be called an elephant? Likewise, can everyone that has human form be considered a true man? He alone can be rightly called a man who has harmonised his thoughts, words and deeds.

"The body is like a water bubble which emerges from water, stays on water for a while, and merges back into water. So also the bubble called *nara* (man) has emerged from the water called *Narayana* (God), and merges back into Him. Only when we recognise this Divine origin of human beings, will we take care to maintain and use our human body in an appropriate manner. Although the body is a mere instrument, its use has to be regulated according to prescribed standards and limits. Every object in the world is governed by certain regulations. It has rightly been said that we cannot achieve any success or progress without observing such discipline. The body, too, is governed by certain regulations. We should develop purity in our thoughts, feelings, looks, and actions. If, on the other hand, one uses one's senses and limbs in impure ways, one's nature will degenerate from human to demonic. Our life can be compared to a business enterprise. The body's normal temperature is 98.6°F; if the temperature goes up to even 99° F, it is a symptom of disease.

"Our normal blood pressure, is 120/80 mm, but if it becomes more or less, it is considered a disease. Even our eyeball can see light only within a particular range. Similarly, our ears can hear sound within a given range. Thus, our body may be called a limited company. Hence we should observe these limits while making use of the body. Whether in the food we eat, the water we drink, or the words we speak and hear, in fact in all our living habits, moderation should be the keynote. Exceeding the limits will entail danger. Excessive eating or talking results in mental aberrations, while moderate eating or talking is conducive to pleasantness in life. Therefore the body should always be used only in such a manner which confers happiness in man's life.

"Man's knowledge can be classified into five categories. The type of knowledge which is most widely prevalent nowadays is book knowledge. We are wasting our entire lives to acquire book knowledge, which is merely superficial. On account of this, general knowledge and common sense have become conspicuous only by their absence. These two, general knowledge and common sense, cannot be gained from books, but only from various experiences in actual day-to-day living, especially through service to society. The fourth one is discriminative knowledge. This type of knowledge is nowadays being used perversely to selfish ends. This is not the right use of discrimination. What is wanted is the kind of discrimination which keeps in view not the selfish individual good, but the collective good of society at large.

"Young people should particularly avoid justifying the wrong use of their discrimination, that is, only for self-interest. They should develop what may be called 'fundamental discrimination,' that which is equally applicable to all people, irrespective of the country to which they belong. Unlike the logic of ordinary arithmetic, $3-1=1$ in spiritual arithmetic. You may argue that this equation is incorrect, but I firmly assert that it is correct. Why? Because it is based not on selfish worldly calculation, but on selfless *Atmic* calculation, which aims at universal welfare. Of the three entities: God, *maya* and the universe, God is the object, *maya* is the mirror and the universe is God's reflection. If the mirror is removed, there can be no *maya* or universe. Then only God remains. Therefore,

3−1=1. People are not in a position to understand such things, because they lack the fifth type of knowledge, practical knowledge.

"This practical knowledge is highly essential for man, but it is woefully lacking today, because every individual thinks that it is enough to take care only of himself. He should realise that he is part of society and that he should be equally concerned about the welfare of society as a whole. There is no difference at all between the sun and its rays, or between the sea and its waves. Likewise, there is no difference whatsoever between God and love, because God is the source of love. Similar is the relationship between the body and the *Atma*, which are interdependent and intimately associated with each other.

"Although the body is transient, it should be properly cared for, till *Atma* is realised. Not recognising this truth, many persons neglect the body and expose themselves to the onslaught of many diseases. Even to achieve the four *purusharthas* (goals of human life), viz., *dharma*, *artha*, *kama*, and *moksha*, bodily health is highly essential. Man today is subject to maladies caused by more mental worries than by consuming bad food. What is the shape of worry? It is only a mentally created fear. There should be a limit to speculation, anxiety and worries. Otherwise they will lead to mental troubles and derangement. A study showed that eighty to ninety percent of the students in several universities were suffering from some kind of mental disorder. Students should see to it that in this most precious stage of their lives, they do not become a prey to physical or mental ill-health. They should keep their minds away from unnecessary thoughts and worries, and also avoid excessive reading, playing, singing and sleeping, etc., because excessive indulgence in any such activity has an adverse effect on the body.

"Moreover, you have been told, off and on, about the programme of 'Ceiling on Desires' which has four important components. The first one is: 'Don't waste food'. Why? Because food is God. Food is indispensable for human life, since the body cannot survive without food. The second one is: 'Don't waste money'. The misuse of money is an evil. Today's youth especially are wasting money in a number of ways. This will lead to bad habits, loss of peace of mind and to the ruin of your life itself. Our country is today facing grave economic problems and, therefore, indiscriminate spending of money for selfish purposes should strictly be eschewed in the interest of society at large. The spirit of co-operation has to be promoted. National unity and integrity should be safeguarded.

"A balance has to be maintained between individual interests and national interests. Everything in life depends on maintaining the proper balance: whether it is walking, sitting, cycling or driving a car. Today this balance has been lost because of excessive knowledge and its misuse. If knowledge is to be put to right use, it should be transformed into skill. However, instead of skill, young people in particular are killing knowledge. You are wasting knowledge and energy in seeing, hearing, talking, thinking, etc., in wrong manners, and in excessive measures. Therefore, the third item in the 'Ceiling on Desires' says, 'Don't waste energy'. A small illustration in this connection: you have tuned the radio to a particular station. Whether the volume is kept high or low, whether you listen or not, so many units of electrical energy will be wasted. Likewise, your body is a radio. You are constantly engaged in thinking as well as talking in a loud or low tone, talking to others or to yourself, talking while awake and even while asleep. Due to such continuous talking day and night, how much energy is being wasted, thereby causing lethargy in your lives. Every act involves the use of energy. If the energy in the body is properly used, then balance can be maintained and the body will be in good shape.

"The fourth dictum of the 'Ceiling on Desires' is 'Don't waste time'. Students, only when the body is strong, healthy and happy can you enjoy the proper state of balance in life. Man's life is wasted in brooding over the past and worrying about the future. What is the root cause of man's sorrow and sickness? Not being content with what he has, and hankering after what he does not have, man forfeits peace of mind. There is no need to think about what is past or about what is in store in the future. Of what avail is it to think of the past which is irrevocable or to worry about the future which is uncertain? It is a sheer waste of time. Past is past, future is future. You can do nothing about either.

"What is most important is the present. This is not the ordinary present. It is the omnipresent. The result of the past and the result of the future are both present in the present. You are reaping in the present what you had sown in the past. And what you are sowing in the present, you will reap in the future. Thus, both the past and future are contained in this very present moment. So make the best use of the present. Give up all sorts of worry and lead ideal lives leading to immortality and fulfilment of the purpose of human life.

"Students, don't underestimate the value of the body. Everything in this world is impermanent; on that account, are we neglecting such things? So, even though the body is transient, you should take good care of it so long as it lasts, because it is a moving temple of God. Develop self-confidence instead of confidence in the world. Self-confidence may be compared to the foundation for the edifice of life, self-satisfaction is like the walls, self-sacrifice is the roof and Self-realisation is the happiness of living in the mansion of the human body. Therefore, with self-confidence, you can accomplish anything and secure joy. You will be able to face and surmount any difficulty in life.

"What do you mean by Self? Self is of two kinds. One is the single lettered 'I' The other is the three-lettered 'eye', which stands for the body. The single-lettered 'I' refers to the *Atma*, which is present in all. There may be some people who may not have the three-lettered 'eye', or even if it is there, it may be covered by a cataract or suffer from other defects or diseases. But the single lettered 'I' exists equally in all persons irrespective of whether one is a *bhogi* (hedonist or pleasure-seeker), *rogi* (diseased person), *yogi* (realised person), *viragi* (renunciate or monk) or *byragi* (mendicant).

"Whenever a number of people are called severally by their names, each of them will respond saying 'I'. Although their names and forms are different, the 'I' in all of them is one and the same. That is why the *Vedas* have declared, *Ekam sat vipra bahudha vadanti*, which means truth (or existence) is one, the sages call it by many names. You should, therefore, try to experience the unity underlying the diversity in the universe. It is because you see the diversity ignoring the unity, that there is so much restlessness and lack of peace in the world. For instance, nations are many but the earth is one; stars are many but the sky is one, beings are many, but breath is one. Therefore, if man remembers this unity in diversity, there will be no room for differences, quarrels or wars in the world.

"Students, you are now in the most precious period of your life. You should never give room to differences and discrimination in your thoughts, words or deeds. Such unhealthy ideas arise from an unhealthy body. Each of you can judge for yourself whether you are strong and healthy or weak and unhealthy, based on the nature of ideas that arise in you. That is why it is said, *Yat bhavam tat bhavati*, i.e., as you think, so you become. Just as you take care of the iron safe for the sake of the valuable jewels inside, so too, you should take care of your body for the sake of the precious *Atma* in it. You should eat to live, but not live to eat. If you have self-confidence, the required food will come walking to you, as it were. You need not go in search of food. That is why it is said in the *Bhagavata Purana*, that one who seeks the *Atma* is a *gopi* (devotee), while one who seeks food is a *papi* (sinner). It is a pity that having earned the invaluable human birth, people are running after *anna* (food) instead of seeking the *Atma*. *Vedanta* has been exhorting man to seek who he really is. Instead of using the mirror of your intellect for looking at your Self, you are placing the mirror in front of others to see them. That is why you are not able to see yourself.

"Develop self-confidence which will lead you to bliss. Never give room to worry and anxiety. Gain sufficient strength of body and mind to face boldly the difficulties, losses and sorrows that may confront you in life. This will be facilitated if you practise the four F's taught in our educational system viz., 'Follow the Master (your conscience),' 'Face the Devil,' 'Fight till the end' and 'Finish the game.' What is the inner meaning of the first three letters in the alphabet A, B, C of the English language? It means Always Be Careful. The same dictum is given in the *Upanishads* by exhorting a man to 'Arise, awake and stop not till the goal is reached'."

"However long you may live, whatever scientific knowledge you may acquire, whatever position you may occupy, some time or the other you have to know the truth about yourself. Start knowing it from now. You should be on the alert all the time because you can never know when the Lord's grace, His love and benediction will be showered on you, at what time and at what place and in what circumstances. Unlike worldly matters, you cannot understand what is happening in the spiritual domain or what the Divine plans are. Therefore, if you go on discharging your duties and obligations in the proper manner with enthusiasm and joy, that in itself will confer bliss on you. Don't worry about the future. Don't brood over the past. All are just passing clouds. In this world, there is nothing permanent, whether people, objects or other things. The very name *jagat* (universe) means 'coming and going'. Knowing this truth, why should you worry at all? So give no scope whatsoever to any kind of worry. Only then can man be entitled to become Divine.

"It is only man that is endowed with the capacity to discover his Divinity. In this context, food habits play an important role. Out of 8,400,000 species of living beings on earth, 8,399,999 species of creatures like insects, birds, animals, beasts, etc., live on what is provided by God in nature, and hence they do not generally suffer from diseases. Man is the sole exception in this regard. By becoming a slave to his palate, he relishes only cooked and spicy foods of various kinds, without realising to what extent such foods are curtailing his own longevity.

"Besides this, it is significant to note that those who live on vegetarian food are less prone to disease, whereas non-vegetarians are subject to more diseases. Why? Because animal food is incompatible with the needs of the human body. Doctors speak of proteins being present in non-vegetarian food, but the fact is that there are better quality proteins in food articles like vegetables, pulses, milk, curds, etc. Non-vegetarian food not only affects man's body but also has deleterious effects on his mind.

"Food, Head, God - these three are inter-related. By consuming animal food, animal tendencies are aroused. As is your food, so are your thoughts. Men today are behaving worse than wild animals in the forest. They have become cruel, pitiless and hard-hearted. There is no sympathy or understanding even between man and man. The main reason for this condition lies in the kind of food that is consumed. Students, be careful about the food you eat. See that it is conducive to your health and happiness. Our ancestors used to take food twice a day and our ancient sages used to eat only once a day. They declared that the man who eats only once is a *yogi*, the one who eats twice a day is a *bhogi* (enjoyer) and he who eats thrice a day is a *rogi* (sick). Today people go on consuming food at all times, not to speak of drinks and snacks in between. How then can they escape from indigestion and other diseases? Man needs food which supplies him with energy equivalent to about one calorie per minute. Young people should be satisfied with 2000 calories of food per day. For a healthy life, man needs only 1500 calories per day. But nowadays, the food intake has increased upto 5000 calories. As a result, people suffer from indigestion and sleeplessness. Loss of sleep gives rise to many ailments. Don't worry about sleep. If you go to bed without any worry, you will have a sound sleep automatically.

"Observe moderation in your intake of food, as well as in other living habits, to keep your body in good shape and to perform your duties properly. However, do not develop undue attachment to the body. The two feelings of 'I' and 'mine' are solely responsible for the problems and evils prevailing in society. You should try to minimise, if not eliminate altogether, the feelings of 'doership' and 'enjoyership'. Then only will you be able to lead ideal lives.

"We suffer from ill-health due to psychological reasons, too. If you examine your pulse, blood pressure, temperature etc., with a feeling or fear that you are unwell,' you will get abnormal readings. If you have the apprehension that you will not sleep well, it will happen accordingly. So always try to have a positive outlook and be self-confident that your health is all right. Our ancients wished to live long for the sake of a godly life and, therefore, they tried to preserve the health of their bodies as well as their minds accordingly. Today, one is called an old man if one attains the age of sixty or seventy. But, in olden days, people were considered young even at the age of eighty, ninety or hundred. Students, you might have read in the *Mahabharata* that at the time of the Kurukshetra War, Krishna and Arjuna were eighty six years and eighty four years old, respectively. But they were in youthful condition and participated in the war with vigour, vitality and valour.

"Who was the Commander-in-Chief of the Kaurava Army? It was the one hundred sixteen years old Bhishma. If it were to be today, a one hundred sixteen -years-old man would be confined to his bed, with his body shaking all over and needing others' help even for getting out of bed. But Bhishma fought fiercely for nine days. How do you account for this? It was because of their mental strength, physical strength supported by nourishing food and, above all, Self-confidence (confidence in the real Self, or *Atma*). Today, such spiritual strength is totally lacking in people. Self-confidence is constantly going up and down. Their minds are unsteady and subject to jumps and bumps from moment to moment. If their wishes are fulfilled, they will install ten pictures of God instead of one in their shrine room. In case their desires are not complied with, they will remove even the one picture which they used to worship previously. This is an indication of the waywardness of their mind. This is not the right attitude.

"You may worship a picture as God but not God as a picture. If your mind wavers from moment to moment, how can there be steadiness or stability in life? Everyone must endeavour to develop the courage to face the vicissitudes of life, joys or sorrows, gains or losses, with equanimity.

"Today there are many who profess themselves as believers in God. But because these so-called believers do not conduct themselves properly, many are becoming atheists. Talking about *bhakti* (devotion), they resort to *bhukti* (hedonism). This is no genuine devotion. A devotee should be willing to gladly accept anything as God's gift. Can you get sugar by merely requesting the sugar cane, instead of crushing it to extract the juice from it? Even if it be the best kind of diamond, will it shine in all its effulgence unless it is subjected to cutting and polishing? Similarly, it is only when man undergoes trials and tribulations, hardships, losses and sorrows that his real worth will shine forth. *Bhakti* (devotion) is the nectar obtained as a result of churning the essences of many *Upanishads* and scriptures. Real devotion is that which is buttressed by firm faith, and is steadfast and unchanging under all circumstances. Only then does one deserve to get the fruits of real *bhakti*.

"Embodiments of Divine Love! Although you may have body-consciousness, your lives should be guided by the *Atmic* awareness. The body, the senses, the mind, the intellect and the *Atma* are to be considered as your five breaths *(pancha pranas)*. Once you have understood the mysteries or subtleties of each of them, you need no other spiritual discipline. Truth is everything. Without realising this, what is the use of troubling yourselves with all sorts of *sadhanas*? I am explaining to you, during this summer course, the subtle truths relating to the five vital constituents of your personality in compliance with the request of your Vice-Chancellor. You speak about meditation. What do you do in meditation? You are merely sitting in a comfortable posture, with your eyes closed. But your mind is wandering in the barber's shop, or the laundry or in the bazaar. Instead of engaging yourself in such futile exercises, you had better enter into society and undertake selfless service. Without understanding what real meditation is, your attempts at meditation will result only in sound sleep. First of all, try to understand the nature of the mind. Then only will you be able to control it. Once an old woman came to me and complained that her mind was giving her endless trouble by its restless wanderings. Then I asked her, 'Where is that mind which is troubling you? Show it to me and I shall destroy it.' She replied 'Swami, I don't know where it is.' I told her, 'If you do not know where the mind is, how do you say it is troubling you? Is it the mind that is troubling you or are you troubling yourself?' So, without understanding anything about the mind, to blame it is meaningless, and to sit in meditation is sheer idleness. You must, therefore, have a thorough understanding of the nature of the mind as well as the senses.

"Everything in the world has a useful secret to reveal. God does not create anything without a purpose. All things are purposeful, meaningful, blissful and valuable. But we are not making any effort to understand their mysteries. So, I hope and bless you that during this fortnight you will understand thoroughly the nature and the role of the body, the senses, the mind, the intellect and the *Atma*, so that you may blossom forth as ideal students endowed with purity and equanimity."

Sathya Sai Baba, *Summer Showers in Brindavan* 1990, pp.24-38

3. THE GROSS, THE SUBTLE AND THE CAUSAL WORLDS

"Wherever you look in this world you will find only the five elements and nothing else; there is no sixth element to be found anywhere.

"There are three types of *akashas* (spheres of consciousness or spaces), which can also be considered universes or worlds. These are the *Bhutakasha* (the gross physical universe), the *Chittakasha* (the subtle universe of the mind), and the *Chidaakasha* (the subtlest and most extensive of all three, referred to as the causal universe). Beyond these, and serving as the basis for all three of them, is the Divine Principle, what has been called *Brahman* or God, and what has also been called *Atma*, the immortal Self. A devotee who is anxious to know the Divine Principle and merge in it, should have understanding of these three types of *akashas* or universes.

"The *Bhutakasha* is made up of the five great elements, that is, ether, air, fire, water, and earth. Ether, which is also called space, is the first of the five elements; it is very subtle. Ether does not have any specific attributes except sound. After that comes air. Air has two attributes, sound and touch. Next is fire. Fire can be seen; it has three attributes, namely, sound, touch and form. Following the fire there is water. Water, like fire, can also be seen by the naked eye; water has four attributes, namely, sound, touch, form and taste. Earth, the last element, has all five attributes namely, sound, touch, form, taste and smell. You see that only the last three elements, namely, fire, water and earth have form; the first two, ether and air, have other qualities but no form.

"All things found in the *Bhutakasha*, the physical world, are impermanent and subject to constant change. In time, all objects undergo complete modification from one name and form to another, and then to still another, and so on. In the *Bhutakasha*, everything is in perpetual motion. The various atoms which exist in a given place will make up a particular form at any given time. As the atoms move and change their position, the form they make up will also change. The atoms which form the human body, like atoms in any other object, change every moment, causing the body to undergo modification. These changes are something like an endless wave. Once every seven years all the atoms which constitute the human body undergo a total change.

"Humanity can be described as a wave, and the other living beings, such as animals and birds, can be described as another wave, plants make up another wave, and so do insects and crawling things. The demonic forces can also be described as a wave, and the Divine forces are still another wave. In nature it is impossible to say what aspect of any wave will merge with any other wave. Therefore, just as drops of one wave in the ocean mingle with and merge into another wave, so also you may find that a wave containing human characteristics may merge into another wave containing characteristics of other living things. It is one continuous process of change and modification. In this way, life can be described as a series of waves. Human nature is associated with the process of thinking which results in a continuous sequence of thoughts. These thought processes are all impermanent. They constantly undergo change. In the same way, the body undergoes change. Unless you are able to recognize the six types of changes which occur in human life, namely, birth, growth, maturation, decline, decay and death, you will be deluded into thinking that human life is permanent. The root cause of such a lack of understanding is ignorance.

"The physical universe, *Bhutakasha*, contains billions of suns, each with its own world; there are countless planets, big and small, and innumerable beings; and in this entire vast universe, the earth is smaller than even a tiny drop; on this earth, India is just a little country.

"And in a little house there sits a very small body. Isn't it ludicrous to think that such a small body could ever feel egoistic and blown-up with self-importance, considering its minute size in this huge universe?

"The whole vast physical world, the *Bhutakasha*, is something like an atom in the *Chittakasha*, the mental world, just as your body is like an atom in the *Bhutakasha*. And this incredibly huge *Chittakasha* is only the size of an atom in the *Chidaakasha*, the causal world. The *Bhutakasha* being made up of the five gross elements, can be apprehended by the five senses of perception. But since everything in the *Bhutakasha* is made up of the five elements and only the five elements, the *Bhutakasha* is inert and insentient.

"Yet, the Divine Principle is inherent in it. Similarly, this Divine Principle is also to be found in the *Chittakasha*, although, since the *Chittakasha* is made of the same five elements (in their subtle aspects), it is also inert and insentient. But, just as the Divine Principle as indweller is inherent in the inert body, vitalizing and activating it, so also it is inherent in these inert physical and mental worlds, the *Bhutakasha* and the *Chittakasha*, energizing and vitalizing them. This Divine Principle shines forth from the *Chidaakasha*, the subtlest of these infinite universes. All the apparent lustre of objects in the world arises from the *Chidaakasha*, the causal world, and is then reflected by the *Chittakasha* and *Bhutakasha*, which act as mirrors. Just as the effulgence of the sun is reflected by the moon, the effulgence present in the causal state of the *Chidaakasha* is reflected in the subtle mental state of the *Chittakasha*, and then the gross physical state of the *Bhutakasha*.

"Untruth in untruth is what you find in the *Bhutakasha*, in the gross world of the senses; here everything is transient and impermanent; here not only the reflection is untrue and illusory, but the object that is being reflected, which arises from the mental state, is also untrue and illusory. Untruth in truth is the situation you find in the *Chittakasha*, where the projections are temporary and untrue, but they reflect that which is permanent and true. Truth in truth is to be found in the *Chidaakasha*; it is free of all illusory projections and reflections; it is the very essence of truth because within it shines the unchanging light of *Atma*.

"The *Bhutakasha* is the gross. You experience it during the waking state. The same thing in a subtle form is associated with the *Chittakasha*, which you experience in the dream state. In the waking state, you are able to see objects because of the light emanating from the sun and the moon; but the sun and the moon of your waking state are not present in the dream state. It is only the light which emanates from the *Chittakasha* which helps you to see the objects of that world. The moment you push aside the gross, the subtle light becomes evident inside.

"There is something that transcends both the gross and the subtle. That is the *Chidaakasha*. The *Chidaakasha* does not have any movement, it does not undergo any change. Within it is to be found the *Paramjyoti*, the self-effulgent light of the *Atma*. It is due to this all-pervasive light of the *Atma* shining in and through the *Chidaakasha* that you are able to experience the *Chittakasha* and the *Bhutakasha*. If there were no *Chidaakasha* there would be no subtle and no gross worlds for you, no *Chittakasha* and no *Bhutakasha*. Therefore, you have to base your life on the *Chidaakasha*, while at the same time, you must use the *Bhutakasha* to reach the *Chittakasha* and the *Chittakasha* to reach the *Chidaakasha*.

"In the phenomenal world also, you have to discover the common element that underlies all the states of experience, and unifies the *Bhutakasha*, the *Chittakasha* and the *Chidaakasha*. You can associate these three *akashas* with the three states of consciousness. You can think of the waking state (conscious state) as the *Bhutakasha*, the dream state (subconscious state) as the *Chittakasha*, and the deep sleep state (unconscious state) as the *Chidaakasha*. Beyond these three states, interpenetrating them and common to all of them, is a fourth state, the *Turiya*, that is, the superconscious state, the transcendental state. *Sushupti*, the deep sleep state, will not provide you with the permanent experience of real bliss. It is only after you come back to the waking state from deep sleep that you feel you have enjoyed peace. But in the *Turiya* state, the superconscious state, you will be able to enjoy true *ananda*, eternal bliss, and remain fully conscious of it always.

"Shankara described sleep as a state of *samadhi*. What is the meaning of *samadhi*? *Samadhi* is ordinarily mistaken to be an emotional state in which a person acts abnormally, as if in a state of high excitement or trance. You think that *samadhi* is something different from the waking, dream or deep sleep states. But truly, *samadhi* is something common to all three states. The meaning of *samadhi* is inherent in the word itself. *Sama* and *dhi* are the two syllables constituting the word *samadhi*. *Sama* means the same, and *dhi* refers to thinking. Therefore, *samadhi* means thinking with equal-mindedness. To be equal-minded in cold or in heat, in profit or loss, in praise or censure - that is *samadhi*.

"Therefore, a person who is immersed in *samadhi*, whose mind is in equanimity, will always be in a state of bliss, whether he is in the *Bhutakasha*, the waking state, the *Chittakasha*, the dream state, or the *Chidaakasha*, the deep sleep state. Everyone yearns for such a beatific state - to attain which, a great deal of spiritual practice is necessary. And you also have to earn the grace of the Lord. To earn His grace you must develop the quality of equal-mindedness, and practise the various virtues which are pleasing to Him.

"In the state of *turiya* you are able to see everything everywhere, and to enjoy bliss supreme. Whose is the light that illuminates this bliss state and permits you to experience this unmitigated joy? That light is the effulgence that emanates from the *Atma*. It is this light which illuminates all the other states as well, and enables you to see them. In the *Vedas*, the *Rishis* have spoken of this *turiya* state. They said, "We are able to see a state which transcends the others, including the darkness of the dreamless state. Beyond the dreamless state is the supreme light of the *Atma* which illuminates the waking, the dream and the deep sleep states. To understand this a little, consider an example from the waking state. When you close your eyes for a minute, what exactly are you seeing? You'll say that there is nothing there, only absolute darkness. But then the question arises, 'Who is it that is seeing this darkness?' Because you see it as darkness, you describe it thus; then there must be a light of consciousness which enables you to see even this darkness. That is the light of the *Atma*, the *Atma-jyoti* It is only through this transcendental light that all the other lights are shining.

"It is because of this *Atma-jyoti* that the eyes are able to see; it shines from inside and illuminates all beings and all objects, as well as the external sources of light, such as the sun and the moon.

"The *Vedas* have declared that the mind is the receptacle for storing the *atmic* energy. It is this inexhaustible source that provides the temporary flow of pleasure when some pleasing object is perceived.

"All the joys and pleasures which you enjoy in this world are only temporary, and are just reflections of the immeasurable joy which is inside.

"All the worldly joys, which you think to be so permanent, will give you a great deal of trouble in the end, and lead you to grief. Therefore Krishna told Arjuna, 'Pay attention only to the basic truth; then the manifestations will not bother you.'

"Therefore, Arjuna, Krishna said, 'control your senses and your mind, and recognize the defects that are inherent in all the objects of the world. Then you can live happily anywhere'. The *Vedanta* has never taught that you must give up your family or give up your worldly duties. Use all the senses in a proper and ethical way, appropriate to the time and the circumstance. It is in this context that the Bhagavad-Gita has taught discipline by setting limits to all your activities." (1)

"The *Atma* is everywhere, but for the purpose of sitting in meditation, the life principle can be considered as being ten 'inches' above the navel and at the centre of the chest. An 'inch' in this measurement is the width of the thumb at the first joint." (2)

"No one knows exactly when the *Vedas* were collated in their present form. Bala Gangadhar Tilak surmised that it must have happened about thirteen thousand years ago; others bring the date down to six thousand years, but all agree that it was at least four thousand years! And Buddha is a historical figure, who lived about two thousand five hundred years ago. Christ was born 1999 years ago, and Islam was formed six hundred years later. So chronologically as well as logically, the inference is correct, that the *Vedic Dharma* is the grandfather, Buddhism is the son, Christianity the grandson, and Islam the great-grandson. If there is any misunderstanding between them it is but a family affair. The ancestral property of which all are co-sharers is the same." (3)

"The *Vedas* come from certain fundamental sounds and their variations. The slightest modification of the sound changes the meaning of what is said. No written language is able to represent all of the *Vedic* sounds. It is impossible to write many of the words. The *Vedas* are God's breath and can be transmitted from person to person only by voice. In all of India there are only a handful of people who can recite the *Vedas* correctly. Some attempts have been made in recent years to write the *Vedas* and print them in books. The effort is wasted." (2)

References :

1. Sri Sathya Sai Baba, *Discourses on the Bhagavad-Gita,* compiled and edited by A. Drucker, First Indian ed. 1988, pp.111, 131-132,150-155
2. J. S. Hislop, *Conversations with Bhagawan Sri Sathya Sai Baba*, pp. 43-44,177
3. *Sathya Sai Speaks,* Vol. VII, Second American Printing, 1985, pp. 117

4. THE FOUR BODIES AND THE FOUR STATES OF CONSCIOUSNESS

"Man has three bodies: the gross body (*sthula deha*), the subtle body (*sukshma deha*) and the causal body (*karana deha*). The gross body has its characteristics - height, weight, girth, proportion, name, caste, sect, nationality. It is a pot, a container, it is devised, designed; it disintegrates, it is destroyed. It cannot be 'you'.

"The subtle body is like the water in the pot; that, too, is poured by someone. It does not originate therein; it is not an essential part of it; it is not its *dharma*. So it, too, is not 'you'.

"The causal body is affected by attachment and detachment, the world and its objects, through reaction and reflection. So it, too, cannot be 'you'. You are beyond all three. You are not limited by these three containers. Some aver that there is a fourth body, the super-causal body (*mahakarana deha*). This body is pure consciousness unmixed with any elemental principle, the Eternal Witness, the Self-luminous, the *Atma*. This is the primal cause that activates the other three. It is on par with the fourth state of consciousness (*turiya*).

"The gross body is connected with the waking state, the subtle body with the dream state, and the causal body with the deep sleep state of consciousness." (1,2,3,4)

"In the waking state, the senses have free play? The gross body is most active then. In the dream state, the senses subsist in their subtle form. The mind revels in its fancies then. In a dream, the subtle body is active. It creates many attractive and astounding scenes and incidents for its own edification. In the deep sleep state, the mind along with the subtle aspects of senses are submerged in the ego or the causal body." (5)

"The different kinds of lives and living organisms are infinite in number. Nevertheless, reality has three main aspects: namely, the empirical reality, the illusory reality and the absolute reality.

These three categories of human existence correspond to three levels of consciousness, viz. *jagrata,* or the consciousness of wakefulness, *svapna,* or the subconsciousness of dreams, and *sushupti,* or the unconsciousness of deep slumber. Spiritual life is more real than mundane life; mundane life is more fundamental and more real than the dreams of the subconscious mind. The surf comes from waves and waves come from water; likewise, consciousness follows subconsciousness and consciousness follows superconsciousness." (6)

"When I appear in a dream it is to communicate something to the individual. It is not a mere dream as is generally known. Do not think that these incidents you experience in your dream are extensions of your imagination. I am giving answers thereby to all your doubts.

"Here I must tell you one thing. Which dreams are real? Dreams relating to God are real. You see Me in the dream, I allow you to do *namaskaram* (the homage of prostration), I bless you, I grant grace..... that is true; that is due to My will and your *sadhana* (spiritual discipline). If the Lord or your *guru* appears in a dream, it must be the result of *sankalpa* (God's will) and not due to any of the other reasons which cause dreams. It can never happen as a result of your wish." (7)

"There are four states of consciousness: *jagratavastha,* the wakeful state, is the state of normal consciousness, and is concerned with the gross world of matter. It brings empirical knowledge of the phenomenal world acquired through sensations and perceptions. It has nineteen means of knowing. These consist of the *karmendriya* (the five organs of action), the *gnanendriya* (the five organs of perception), the five *pranas* (vital energies), *manas* (mind), *buddhi* (intellect), *chitta* (consciousness) and *ahamkara* (ego). In the *jagratavastha* these nineteen aspects of sensational or empirical knowledge are integrated. It is essentially this knowledge which yearns for the pleasures of the material world.

"*Svapnavastha,* the dream state of consciousness, has the subconscious faculty of recognizing and getting glimpses of the holy experience of Divinity and sancity. It is concerned with the subtler aspects of human knowledge and experience. It carries with it the subtler impressions of the experience of the *jagratavastha*." (8) "In the dreaming stage all the nineteen aspects, which we have mentioned earlier, still appear as subtle forms with a subtle phase.

"Both the waking state and the dreaming state are somewhat on the same footing and are equally important." (9) "The occurrences of the past and present, the things seen in the past and now, past and present experiences, all these are experienced by man in the form of dreams. Moreover, the consequences of activities in previous lives, which have become part of his spirit but are not known to him, are also experienced in dreams." (13)

"*Pragna* and *turiyavastha* assume different characteristics. *Pragnavastha* is a transcendental state of consciousness in which the dichotomy between grossness and subtlety disappears in superconsciousness. It is *pragna*, or consciousness of Divinity. In *pragnavastha*, the differentiating and diversifying faculties of the mind become inoperative. That is why it is said that *pragnanam* is *Brahman* (God). To help man reach this summit of Divinity, Krishna has expounded in the *Bhagavad-Gita* the *sadhana* of *dhyana*, the path of meditation. In *pragnavastha*, all mundane desires and dream-wishes are sublimated into the bliss of spiritual experience. The lambent light of *pragnana* shines steadily in this state of higher consciousness." (8) "In *pragna*, the state of deep sleep, there is no connection whatever, through the gross form or through the subtle form, with the material world. The deep sleep state is quite distinct and separated from the nineteen facets already mentioned." (9)

"The *turiyavastha* is the highest state of consciousness in which the essential nature of the *Atma* is experienced. *Shantam* (tranquillity), *shivam* (goodness), and *advaitam* (non-duality) are experienced by the *sadhaka*. *Turiyavastha* is a pure, tranquil and steady state of superconsciousness in which all discriminating and differentiating *guna* (attributes) are transcended and dissolved in the eternal and absolute reality of *Brahman*.

"The *Omkar* is the fusion of the three primal sounds, A, U and M. These three letters represent respectively the *jagrata*, the *svapna* and the *sushupti* states of consciousness. They also symbolize Brahma, Visnu and Maheshvara (Shiva). This Trinity represents the three personified realities corresponding to the aforementioned three states of consciousness." (8)

"There is the inert body. There is the supreme consciousness. And, between the two, there is the mind which is also inert, but which appears to be alive because it is infused with consciousness." (10)

"Man is a triune composite of body, mind and spirit (*Atma*). As a consequence, he has three natures in his make-up: a low, animal nature, a human nature, replete with worldly knowledge and skills, and the genuine nature of man, namely, the Divine *Atmic* nature." (11)

"Five sheaths encase the *Atma* and cloak its splendour from itself." (12) "The *annamaya kosha*, the material sheath, is the gross body. The subtle body consists of the next three sheaths, the vital (*pranamaya kosha*), the mental (*manomaya kosha*), the intellectual (*vignanamaya kosha*). The causal body is the bliss sheath (*anandamaya kosha*)." (1,2)

References :

1. Sathya Sai Baba, *Sanathana Sarathi*, January 1984 pp. 6
2. *Voice of the Avatar*, Extracts from the *Divine Discourses of Bhagawan Sri Sathya Sai Baba*, Part I. Compiled by D. Hejmadi, M.Sc., Second Edition 1981, pp. 56-57
3. Bhagawan Sri Sathya Sai Baba, *Prasnothara Vahini*, 1984, pp. 2-4
4. *Pathway to Peace*, Prasanthi as learnt at the Lotus Feet of Bhagawan by N. Kasturi pp. 62-66
5. Sathya Sai Baba, *Sanathana Sarathi*, January 1983, p. 81
6. Bhagawan Sri Sathya Sai Baba, *Summer Showers in Brindavan* 1979, pp. 52
7. Tumuluru Krishna Murty, *Digest, Collection of Sri Sathya Sai Baba's Sayings* 1985, pp. 89

8. Bhagawan Sri Sathya Sai Baba, *Summer Showers in Brindavan*, 1979, pp. 99 - 100
9. Bhagawan Sri Sathya Sai Baba, *Summer Showers in Brindavan*, 1977, pp. 133 - 134
10. J. S. Hislop, *Conversations with Bhagawan Sri Sathya Sai* Baba, pp. 180
11. Bhagawan Sri Sathya Sai Baba, *Vidya Vahini, 1984*, pp. 21
12. *Sathya Sai Speaks*, Vol. II, pp. 24
13. Sathya Sai Baba, *Sanathana Sarathi,* September 1991, pp. 234

NOTE: See scheme at the end of chapter 12

5. THE FIVE SHEATHS AND THE CHAKRAS

"The five sheaths, or *kosha*, can be thought of as various bodies interpenetrating each other in a successively more subtle way, each one finer than the previous one. The grossest sheath is the food, material, muscular sheath *(annamaya kosha)*, which comprises the physical body. Next is the vital, nerve-centred sheath *(pranamaya kosha)*, which relates to the life-breath and physical energy. Next is the mental, imagination-centred, symbol-dealing sheath *(manomaya kosha)*, which is a subtle body relating to the lower mind; then comes the reason-based, logical, intellectual sheath *(vignanamaya kosha)*, which is a still finer body associated with the higher mind and the intuition. The last sheath is the blissful, intuition-centred, experience-based sheath *(anandamaya kosha)*, the subtlest of all the bodies - beyond all aspects of mind, where only the veil of ignorance remains to hide the *Atma*." (1,2,3)

"In the *annamaya kosha*, that is to say, when man is established in the physical, and in the *pranamaya kosha*, when he is in the nervous and vital spheres of activity, he feels that life is fulfilled by means of food, recreation and a contented comfortable existence. When he rises up into the *manomaya kosha*, his imagination opens further vistas, and he gets glimpses of the glory and majesty of the Divine, which makes him adore and revere it. The next *kosha*, the *vignanamaya kosha* then steps in and makes him inquire into the validity of the experiences and leads him on to the fifth *kosha* the *anandamaya*, the stage of bliss, with the confirmation of the hypothesis of the Divine that the intellect framed. This liberates man from fear and doubt. Wisdom alone can grant full freedom. Just as the end of culture is progress, and the end of knowledge is love, so the end of wisdom is freedom.

"God can be realised only through love. Love is expansion and expansion is divine life. Sow Love; it blossoms as compassion and tolerance; it yields the fruit of peace *(shanti).*" (4)

"The undue importance now attached to the satisfaction of sensual desires must diminish as the result of your association with sacred books and saintly personages. You know that the dream world is a fantastic world of nonsense, where fifty years are compressed into five minutes and where weird incidents and things are taken as actually present and experienced. But let me tell you, that from the stage of realisation even the waking stage, wherein you analyse the dreams and declare them as invalid, is equally without validity. Therefore, have a sense of values, a scale of values rather. Give everything, everyone their worth or its worth, not a whit more.

"Five sheaths encase the *Atma* and hide its splendour from itself. Make all these pure and shining. The *annamaya kosha* must be purified by good, clean, pure food; the *pranamaya kosha* by calm, steady breathing and equanimity; the *manomaya kosha* by holy thoughts and emotions, untouched by attachment to the senses and unaffected by joy or grief; the *vignanamaya kosha* purified by contemplation on the reality, and the *anandamaya kosha* by becoming immersed in the ecstasy of God-realisation." (5)

"The *Upanishads* say that man is a spark of Divine Love, encased in five sheaths, the *annamaya kosha* (gross, material, food component), the *pranamaya kosha* (vital air, breath), the *manomaya kosha* (the mental, emotional, volitional), the *vignanamaya kosha* (rational, discriminatory, intellectual) and the *anandamaya kosha* (blissful, equanimous, well-balanced). It is the fragrance of that Divine Love that emanates from him as love towards things, beings and ideas. That love is ever urging and surging towards expression, enlargement and enveloping. But the tangles of fear, greed, egoism and aggrandizement do not allow the spark to grow and illumine the sheaths as well as the world around." (6)

"The *annamaya kosha* builds itself on food material, grows out of food and decays when there is no food. The next layer that gives strength and protects the external human body is the *pranamaya kosha*, or an inner layer. This part of the body is called the *maya deha*. The *pranamaya kosha* is dependent upon the heat created in the body and enables it to flow in the body and, thereafter, blood starts flowing into the blood vessels.

"The next layer is called the *manomaya kosha*, related to the mind. If the *manomaya kosha* is not there, then the *pranamaya* and *annamaya kosha* cannot exist. The *manomaya kosha* is responsible for all kinds of thoughts and desires. One's mind is really a bundle of desires. To some extent, this mind or the *manomaya kosha*, helps and becomes a support to the *pranamaya kosha*. The next layer is the *vignanamaya kosha*. The *vignanamaya kosha* has the function of enabling man to obtain the discriminatory power by which he may distinguish between good and bad. If there is no *vignanamaya kosha*, the other layers, *manomaya kosha, pranamaya kosha* and *annamaya kosha*, remain lifeless not being able to function. This *vignanamaya kosha* enables us to learn the nature of matter and how it functions. We shall here give an example by which we can understand the inner meaning. This is a table and is made of wood. I am making an attempt to hit it. When I describe this act of mine, I say that I have hit the table with my hand. This is not a full description. The table has also hit my hand equally strongly. The quality in you, which enables you to recognize the conduct of the table in this act, is the *vignanamaya kosha*. This *vignanamaya kosha* enables us to recognize whatever reactions and 'resounds' exist in all the material world.

"We can take another example for this. When we open our eyes and take an external view, we see many people and so many heads. We ask if it is the eye which enables us to see all this or whether it is the light in the eyes that enables us to see all the heads? No, the light that exists outside the eye is helping the eyes to see all this. It is the joining together of the light that is present in your eyes and the light that is present outside your eyes that enables you to see all the things. It is only when both are present that we can see the form of man. In this manner, the inner vision and the outer vision are together responsible for our vision. This is the function of the *vignanamaya kosha*.

"Truly, if we are perceiving all creation with our eyes, this creation is being seen because of our eyes. There is no creation separate from our eyes. What we see in the world are all reflections of the forms that are formed inside by our own inner vision. The thoughts and ideas which emanate within oneself have been called *vignana*.

"All these things have for their source the life-giving treasure. This has been referred to as the *anandamaya kosha*. We can conclude that all the four superficial *kosha*, the *annamaya*, the *pranamaya*, the *manomaya* and the *vignanamaya kosha*, all arise from the base, the *anandamaya kosha*. The spirit, *Atma*, which is the basis of all these things, is *ananda*, which is at the root of all these other *kosha*." (7)

"Great sages, like Vasishtha and Vishvamitra, by observing silence, could enjoy and have the vision of the *anandamaya kosha*, and they set good examples for the world.

"If anyone utters any word, we say by way of explanation that the word is coming from one's throat. This is not true. With one's throat one can utter a sound but one cannot utter a word. The word does not come from the throat but starts from the *muladhara chakra*, goes up to the *agneya chakra* and it then touches the *Atma* and gets its true and proper tone from the base of the *Atma*, and only then comes out as a sound. Here, in the *pranamaya kosha*, and the *manomaya kosha*, there are certain strings. These strings can be touched at certain places where there are bridges on these strings. Because those are being touched, sounds are produced and those sounds go to your heart. Then the sound will emanate as a word. The bridges on these strings come to the notice of the mind. People who know how to play on a *veena* can understand these steps easily." (8)

"In the science of *kundalini yoga*, the vital energy of man is lying dormant, like a coiled snake at the bottom of his spinal column in the lowest chakra, the *muladhara chakra*. The basic wheel is awakened and aroused so that it courses up through six more wheels (*chakras* - centres of superior consciousness) until it reaches the *sahasrara chakra* or thousand-petalled lotus wheel, at the very top of the skull. The passage for the *kundalini* is through the *sushumma* nerve in the centre of the spinal column. The worship of the snake, ridiculed as superstition, is the symbolic counterpart of this great *yogic sadhana* which confers vigour and vitality." (9)

"The *kundalini* energy is *prana*. It is imagined as rising up the spine by the practice of *pranayama*. The practice of *pranayama* is dangerous unless all the circumstances are exactly correct. It is not necessary and I advise against it. The area between the ninth and twelfth vertebrae is especially sensitive. An injury there can result in paralysis. Meditation as described by Me is the royal path, the easy path. Why bother with other practices?" (10)

"During meditation you have to adopt a comfortable posture and to sit straight so that the *kundalini* power is afforded unhampered movement. The *kundalini* power is present in man in the *muladhara chakra* as a Divinely radiant power. Its upward flow to the *sahasrara chakra*, or the thousand-petalled lotus, through the intermediary centres called the *svadhishthana*, *manipura*, *anahata*, *vishuddha* and *agna chakras*, corresponding respectively to the regions of the navel, stomach, heart, larynx and the *bhrumadhyasthana*, or the region between the eyebrows, takes man to various levels of consciousness and to spiritual awakening." (11)

"It is stated that Krishna was wedded to sixteen thousand *gopikas*. Who are these *gopikas*? They are not milk-maids in physical form. In the human head there is a lotus with a thousand petals. Each of these petals has sixteen *kalas*. The Lord is described as the embodiment of the sixteen *kalas*. As the Lord of the *sahasrara* (thousand-petalled lotus), He presides over the sixteen thousand *kalas* which are present in this lotus. The *kundalini* power, which starts at the bottom of the spinal column, rises and merges with the sixteen thousand entities in the *sahasrara*. This is the esoteric significance and the meaning of the role of the Divine within the body. Oblivious of this inner meaning, people indulge in misinterpretations and perverse expositions." (12)

"The *muladhara chakra* is the embodiment of *prakriti* (nature principle). Therefore it is related to the *annamaya kosha*. It is the *prithvi tatva*, or the earth. The purpose of the *muladhara chakra* is to keep the body erect and in good condition. This is something which protects the body.

"The *svadhisthana (svadhvaya) chakra* at the point of the navel is the guardian of the *pranamaya kosha*, the vital facet of the person. It is the *agni* (fire) principle, the spring and source of warmth in the body, that which maintains the processes of digestion and protection from environmental change.

"The *manipuraka chakra* is the next highest on the spinal scale. It is the *jala tatva* (water) principle, that helps the circulation of blood into the heart and out of it, from all parts of the body. This *chakra* is also related to the *pranamaya kosha*.

"The *anahata chakra* is in the region of the heart. It embodies the *vayu* (air) principle which is in charge of the breathing process, inhalation and exhalation, vital for life and activity. It also vitalises the spinal force and passes over the frets of the inner *veena*. This *chakra* is related to the *manomaya kosha*.

"The *vishuddha chakra* is in the pit of the throat, near the pituitary gland. It represents the *akasha* (ether, space) principle and promotes sound, or *shabda*. This chakra is related to the *vignanamaya kosha*.

"The *agna (agneya) chakra* on the mid-brow spot is the embodiment of *vigana* – the splendour of awareness – for when this *chakra* is reached, man glimpses the truth, is transformed and becomes translucent. This *chakra* is related to the *anandamaya kosha*. The *agneya chakra* makes you feel your existence. Not only this, it enables you to recognize your true form. This works in the field of *pragnana*. It enables you to fix the five vital airs in you and enables the aspect of five *prana* to shine. The purpose of the *agneya chakra* is to enable you to control the five *prana*. *Pragnana* is the higher knowledge, the pure unsullied vision of the wise, the higher learning, the act of controlling the inner feelings and the many layers of consciousness. It is only a step away from the final realisation, when the *sahasrara chakra* on the crown of the head is attained. That is the consummation of all *sadhana,* of all search. The *sahasrara chakra* has the important function of being the very base of all the vital points in you. This enables your *Iccha shakti* to function. The *Iccha shakti* refers to the capacity in a human being to transform what exists in each *chakra* into the aspect of *Atma.* (13, 14, 15, 16, 17)

"The *Vedas* describe the force of life as what we see when lightning comes in the clouds, and it is between the ninth and twelfth rings of the spinal column. A man can live after losing his leg, after losing his hand, but if his spine is broken, he cannot live. In the spinal column, what exists between the ninth and the twelfth rings is the essence of life. This is called *anahata chakra*. The passage of air through this *anahata chakra*, while breathing in and breathing out, sustains life.

"When the *Rishis* did not know this basic truth, that life really exists between the ninth and twelfth rings of the spinal column, they were trying to control each one of the *chakras*, starting from the *muladhara* and going right up to the *pragna*. They were performing *sadhanas* by which they could understand and control each one of the rings of the spinal column. We should recognize that by wisdom one receives two kinds of *pragna*. One relates to the world and the other relates to the spirit. The one that relates to the world enables you to understand what you see around you and how the material world goes on. We should take this to mean that, even before we understand the form and the meaning of external things, they are already contained within us. This knowledge, which relates to the *Atma,* that with which you have already seen and known is in some form within you, and it is now being seen as an external thing.

"I am now looking at this piece of cloth, but the form of this piece of cloth, has already been imprinted in my mind even before my eyes see the cloth. Thus, that which establishes the true form of what already exists as inner knowledge, is the first kind of *pragna*.

"The second type of *pragna* is that which enables you to see the aspect of *Atma* in all living beings as one and the same. This has been proclaimed by the *Rishis* in the saying, *Pragnanam Brahma*. This aspect of *pragnana*, which is identical with *Brahman*, is present in every individual. For man to promote himself and his knowledge, control of senses and control of mind are very necessary, but they are not easily achieved. What we should do today is to see that the mind does not take the wrong path but is diverted to the right path." (13)

"*Atma* is identical with *Brahman* and *Brahman* is identical with *Atma*. You cannot ascribe a time for *Atma* to come or go and thus place limitations on it. It is permanently present everywhere and it has neither good qualities nor bad qualities. It is present as the smallest thing in small things, and as the biggest thing in infinitely large things.

"Like the burning power of the fire and the shining strength of the sun, *Atma* is all-knowing. It has no sorrow, it has no attachment, it has no special sensations, like any of the five senses which man experiences. It is present in all living things. It endows all living beings with an amount of wisdom called *pragnana*.

"*Atma* is not visible from outside. *Atma* is neither visible nor invisible. It has no special form attached to itself. It is all-pervading. This cannot be something which is either seen or not seen, either experienced or not experienced. It is something which is and something which is not - neither manifested nor unmanifested. It is above all this and beyond all description or even comprehension." (18)

"The *Atma* is of the nature of *sat* (being) - *chit* (awareness) - *ananda* (bliss). It transcends the *sthula*, *sukshma* and *karana deha*. It is the witness of the waking, the dream and the deep-sleep stages. How then is it to be seen? By *Atma* unravelling the five sheaths that cover the personality, by negating each of them and experiencing not this and passing beneath and beyond to the substratum of the *Atma* (soul), the *Brahman* (God), which all the while appeared varied and manifold. Anything misplaced in the home must be searched for in the home itself. How can it be recovered by a search in the woods? *Brahman*, covered by the five sheaths, must be searched for in the five-sheathed body, not in the woods of *shastric* lore. Though *Brahman* cannot be discovered in the *Shastras* (Scripture), they tell you of the five sheaths *(pancha kosha)* and of their identification marks and characteristics and, so, by the exercise of the intellect, it is possible to reach the *Atmic* truth.

"But one fact has to be emphasised. The *Atma* principle is beyond the reach of even the most profound pandits who have learned the *Shastras*; it is understood only by direct experience. That is why it was said of old, that even the person who has had the vision of truth has to approach a *guru*. Without the guidance from such a teacher, the *Atma* cannot be grasped. Even Narada had Sanat Kumara as his *guru* and King Janaka had Shuka, and other saints had other *gurus*. When one has the grace of the Lord, the *guru* becomes superfluous, He makes everything known. Maitreyi, the consort of Yagnavalkya, the unlearned Leela and Chudala are examples to show that, without prolonged study of the *Shastras*, women in the past learnt the *Atmavidya* from the *guru* and attained success. Of course, whatever else a person may have, if he is blessed with the grace of the Lord, he can certainly have a vision of the *Atma*, however deficient he may be in generally accepted qualifications." (19) "*Dharma* comes from *annamaya kosha*. *Prema* comes from *pranamaya kosha* and *manomaya kosha*. *Prema* comes out of the mental and bliss sheath. *Shanti* comes from *manomaya kosha*. *Sathya* comes from *vignanamaya kosha* and *ahimsa* from *anandamaya kosha*." (20)

References:
1. Sathya Sai Baba, *Discourses on the Bhagavad Gita,* Compiled and Edited by A. Drucker, First Indian edition, 1988, pp. 111
2. *Voice of the Avatar,* Extracts from the Divine Discourses of Sathya Sai Baba, Part I, Compiled by D. Hejmadi, Second Edition, 1981, pp. 57
3. *Sathya Sai Speaks,* Vol. VII, Sec. 2nd Printing, 1985, pp. 29

4. *Sathya Sai Speaks,* Vol. VII, Sec. 2nd Printing, 1985, pp. 411-413
5. *Sathya Sai Speaks,* Vol. II, 1963, pp. 24-25
6. *Sathya Sai Speaks,* Vol. VII, 2nd Am. Printing, 1985, pp. 345 edited by N. Kasturi, pp. 62-65
7. Sathya Sai Baba, *Summer Showers in Brindavan,* 1977, pp. 125-127
8. *Sai Avatar,* Vol. III, pp. 90-91
9 *Sathya Sai Speaks,* Vol. IX, 1985, pp. 37
10. Tumuluru Krishna Murty, *Digest, Collection of Sri Sathya Sai Baba's Sayings,* pp. 164
11. Sathya Sai Baba, *Summer Showers in Brindavan* 1979, pp. 111-112
12. Sathya Sai Baba, *Sanathana Sarathi,* January, 1990, pp. 10
13. Sathya Sai Baba, *Summer Showers in Brindavan,* 1977, pp. 231-233
14. *Sathya Sai Speaks,* Vol. X, pp. 117-118
15. *Pathway to Peace, Prasanthi as learnt at the Lotus Feet of Bhagawan* by Prof. N. Kasturi pp. 62-65
16. *Sai Avatar,* Vol. III, pp. 91-93 H.S. Youngs, *Translations by Baba,* 1975, pp. 118
18. Sathya Sai Baba, *Summer Showers in Brindavan* 1977 pp. 56
19. Sathya Sai Baba, *Vidya Vahini,* 1984, pp. 62-63
20. Sathya Sai Baba, *Sanathana Sarathi,* May 1993, pp. 129-130

NOTE: See scheme at the end of chapter 12

6. PURUSHA AND PRAKRITI: MALE AND FEMALE

"*Purusha* signifies the shining and self-effulgent *Brahman* (God). *Purusha*, or the soul, is simply the manifestation of the Divine. The bounties of nature should be enjoyed only with the benediction of *Param Atma*. *Brahman*, which represents complete growth in all respects, has been represented as the characteristic of *Purusha*. The word *Purusha* refers to one who has experienced completeness or fullness." (1,3)

"*Prakriti* has no beginning. She is timeless. She cannot survive without the company of *Purusha*. She can be compared to a pious wife. Her beauty is beyond all description. Her strength is enormous. She can push anyone into the confusion of family when they forget God. She can cause trouble even to very able and great people. *Prakriti* communicates a lesson to us that there can be no pot without mud, there can be no ornament without gold, there can be no cloth without yarn, and there can be no world without *Brahman*.

"It is erroneous to separate *Prakriti* from *Paramatma* and regard them as distinct, and worship nature alone. We should not be subservient to nature, but make it subservient to us. Nature is not anybody's property. It is not even the property of all the people put together. Nature belongs to God. Therefore, if you want to keep nature under control, you will have to do so only after earning God's grace. If, after acquiring God's grace, you undertake to conquer nature, she herself will yield to you. Today, by neglecting and forgetting the Lord, and believing that nature is the only thing that is important, we are attempting to use nature unsuccessfully for selfish purposes." (2)

"Unfortunately today, as a consequence of scientific and technological progress, humanness has declined and man considers the world as intended only for his enjoyment. As a result, the powers of nature are being used in a manner which poses a great threat to the world. This world has not been created merely for our enjoyment. Abusing the resources of nature and forgetting his own basic human nature, man is going against the purpose of creation. Many natural catastrophes are entirely due to man's behaviour.

"Earthquakes and volcanic eruptions, wars, floods, famines and other calamities are the result of grave disorders in nature. These disorders are traceable to man's conduct. Man has not recognised the integral relationship between humanity and the world of nature. Man is a part of the human community. Mankind is a part of nature. Nature is a limb of God. Man has not recognised these interrelationships." (10)

"*Purusha* and *Prakriti* are the two eternal entities involved in creation. *Purusha*, the masculine entity, is imperishable and permanent; *Prakriti*, the feminine entity, is perishable and impermanent. While *Purusha* is the eternal reality of Divinity, or the cosmic witness, *Prakriti*, or primal matter, is given a motherly connotation. Thus, *Prakriti* is also referred to as *Bhumata* (mother earth), *Lokamata* (mother of the world), *Jaganmata* (mother of creation), and *Vishvamata* (mother of the universe). Likewise, *Prananatha* (Lord of life), *Lokanatha* (Lord of the world), *Jagannatha* (Lord of creation) and *Vishvanatha* (Lord of the universe) are the various names given to the masculine entity, *Purusha*.

"In order to understand *Prakriti*, we must know the essence of femininity. *Stri* in Sanskrit means woman. This word *stri* consists of *sa*, which stands for *satvaguna* (purity); *ta* which stands for *tamoguna* (inertia) and *ra* which stands for *rajoguna* (activity). The essence of femininity, thus, is the conglomeration of these three *gunas*: the *satvic*, the *rajasic* and the *tamasic*.

"Politeness, humility and forbearance are *satvic* qualities; shyness, fear and indolence are *tamasic* qualities; and aggressiveness, wilfulness, and envy are *rajasic* qualities. Generally, *satvic* and *tamasic* qualities are found to be predominant in woman. Men and women are both the conglomeration of their *gunas* - *satva*, *rajas* and *tamas* - and are subject to the universal laws of *Prakriti*." (3)

"*Prakriti* has not the strength by which to bear its burden. In this context, the features of *Prakriti* have been given the name *abala*, or one without strength. In common parlance this word connotes a woman. An individual who is weak and who has no strength is called *abala*, or woman. Every *jiva* (individual) who is part of the created world is in this sense, a weakling or a woman. Hunger, anger, jealousy, ego are all common to men and women. Sorrow as well as pleasure are experienced in the same manner by men and women. The difference is only in name and form, but all other qualities are the same in men and women. Therefore, if we look at people from the point of view of qualities and ignore names and forms, all are women on earth." (1) It is improper to say that women are weak and men are strong.

"Every individual has to submit to *Prakriti*, the female aspect of the universe. *Shakti* is the essence of female energy which man cannot afford to ignore. The *Bhagavad-Gita* has repeatedly stressed the element of femininity in the universe." (3)

"Motherhood is the most precious gift of God. The principle of motherhood is intimately associated with God, who has created the entire universe, Who has provided its sustenance, and Who is granting man every thing he needs" (Digest 2, p. 220-221)

"The patron deities of learning (*Sarasvati*), of wealth (*Lakshmi*), and of wisdom (*Parvati*), are all women.

"A woman is like a field, while man is just like a seed. If we do not have a field, the seed cannot sprout. For all life on earth, woman is responsible. Great people, great saints and even great Divine *Avatars* have come into the world because of the help given by woman functioning as a mother. Thus, the strength of a woman is really very sacred. The *gopikas* were such that they provided lustre to womanhood. Whether in the matter of patience, or forbearance, or friendship, they showed exemplary conduct.

"Women are the bulwark of spiritual culture. But, as is evident from the attitude and behaviour of educated women of today, they are fast succumbing to the flimsy attractions of froth and frippery, cheap and shoddy literature and sensual films.

"The mother seeks love, craves for gratitude, thirsts after sympathy. She values feeling, not external display. The Divine Mother, too, is moved by the same feeling. She does not appreciate demonstrative trappings like matted hair, rosaries, marks on the forehead or sacerdotal robes. She values sincerity, yearning, virtue, compassion, love.

"Every child has five mothers and owes its loyalty to these five that fill its life with meaning and purpose. The *deha-mata* (the mother who gave birth to its body), the *go-mata* (the cow that gives it milk and the bullock that is the partner in growing its food throughout life), the *Bhu-mata* (land that in return for seed offers grain a hundredfold), the *desha-mata* (region inhabited by a society that stamps its ways of living, lines of thinking and ideals and goals) and *Veda-mata* (the heritage of spiritual treasure). The first mother has to reveal to the child the glories of all the other four and so her status is crucial, her responsibility is pivotal.

"The woman comes first. We say Sita Rama, Parvati Parameshvara, and not Rama Sita or Parameshvara Parvati. That is why, in a woman, *Paramatma* is found with seven types of strength and with sixteen different *kalas*. Because of this Divine content in a woman, she can take to the path of spirituality with ease. In order to show to the world this exemplary behaviour of woman, the *gopikas* were given a proper place (in the folk tales).

"Women, who are the repositories of *shaktisvarupa*, are in no way inferior; how full of fortitude, patience and *prema* is their nature! Their self-control is seldom equalled by men. They are the exemplars and the leaders for men to tread the spiritual path. Pure selfless love is inborn in women" (1).

"*Prakriti* is like *kshetra* or a field, and *Paramatma* is the *Kshetragna* or the Lord of the field. *Kshetragna* contains in Himself the *kshetra*. If, from the word *kshetragna* we remove the word *kshetra*, the syllable *gna* remains. *Gna* stands for *gnana* and wisdom. Thus, a person who is a part of *Prakriti* becomes its master by acquiring *gnana* and cognizes the eternal reality of *Pursha*. He realises that the universe is a combination of the *kshara* (destructible) and the *akshara* (indestructible). He sees the indestructible as immanent even in the destructible world. He develops *ananya bhakti*, or one-pointed devotion. He transcends the man-made barriers of caste, creed and religion. He becomes dear to God." (3)

"The *Atma* is neither male nor female, it is not possible to impose these distinctions on it. They are merely physical attributes, pertaining to the body."[4] "Sex is but a vesture worn by the soul for the role of life on earth."[5]

"The female principle is spoken of as the illusion imposed upon Himself by the Lord, as the energy with which He equipped Himself out of His own will. This is *maya*, the female form." (6) "For having a dream, the cause is your sleep. If there is no sleep, you won't dream. Just as for a dream sleep is the cause, so also for creation, *maya* is the cause." (7) "The *Atma* is the universal cause, because it is the universal see-er. The see-er is the cause of all the delusion in this world; the see-er creates silver in the mother-of-pearl; the varied scenes of the dream-world are the creations of the see-er. So, too, for the multiplicity of things experienced during the waking stage, the *Atma*, who is the see-er, is the instrument. What the *Atma* does is to superimpose upon the external, evanescent object its inherent bliss, and thus envelop that object with a certain attractiveness. Objects are taken to be pleasure-giving but they are not really so; they only add to grief." (8)

"To regard *Radha* of the *Bhagavata Purana* as an ordinary woman, to regard *Krishna* as an ordinary human being, a man, and to regard the relationship between them as no more than between a man and a woman, as people generally understand it, is very wrong! The relationship is the sacred relationship that exists between God and His creation. It is not possible to separate Radha and Krishna from each other, because *Prakriti* and *Paramatma* are identical with each other. It is one single entity. Without *Prakriti*, or creation, there is no Krishna; without Krishna, we cannot see creation. This oneness of Radha and Krishna has been referred to in the Bible as the 'Kingdom of God'.

"*Prakriti* consists of earth, water, fire, air and ether, mind (*manas*), intellect (*buddhi*) and ego (*ahamkara*). Beyond this *Prakriti*, however, there is a higher realm known as *Paraprakriti*.

"Every person must grasp the meanings of *Prakriti* and *Paraprakriti*. It is through *Paraprakriti* that man becomes Divine. *Prakriti* binds man to the world. *Paraprakriti* divinises him. *Prakriti* is concrete, corporeal and tangible. *Paraprakriti* is abstract, incorporeal and intangible." (9)

"*Paraprakriti* is neither *sthula* nor *sukshma* it is *chaitanya* (consciousness, Divine nature), indwelling in the *jivi* (individual). *Jada* (inert matter) and *chaitanya* are the two essentials for the whole creation. They are the same as *Prakriti* and *Purusha*." (7)

References :

1. Tumuluru Krishna Murty, *Digest, Collection of Sri Sathya Sai Baba's Sayings,* pp. 198, 233, 330, 331
2. *Sai Avatar,* Vol. III, pp. 46 - 47
3. Sathya Sai Baba, *Summer Showers in Brindavan,* 1979, pp. 146 - 149
4. Sathya Sai Baba, *Sathya Sai Vahini,* pp. 93
5. *Sadhana, The Inward Path,* Quotations from the Divine Discourses of Bhagawan Sri Sathya Sai Baba, 1976, pp. 81
6. Sathya Sai Baba, *Dharma Vahini,* 1985, pp. 25
7. Tumuluru Krishna Murty, *Digest, Collection of Sri Sathya Sai Baba's sayings,* pp. 19, 186
8. Sathya Sai Baba, *Jnana Vahini,* 1984 pp. 52 - 53
9. *Sai Avatar,* Vol. III, pp. 114 - 115, 123, 148
10. Sathya Sai Baba, *Sanathana Sarathi,* December 1992, pp. 289 - 290

7. MAYA OR ILLUSION

"*M*aya, by means of its power of cloaking real nature and imposing the unreal over the real, makes the one and only *Brahman* appear as *jiva* (individual), *Ishvara* (God) and *jagat* (universe), three entities where there is only one!" (1)

"Krishna said, 'Listen, Arjuna, between Me and this universe there moves *maya*, called delusion. It is indeed a hard task for man to see beyond *maya*, for *maya*, too, is Mine. It is of the same substance; you cannot deem it separate from Me. It is My creation and under My control. It will turn in a trice even the mightiest among men, head over heels! Arjuna, do not take *maya* to mean an ugly thing descended from somewhere else; it is an attribute of the mind; it makes you ignore the true and the eternal *Paramatma* and value instead the attributeful created manifold multiplicity of names and forms. It causes your error of believing the body to be the Self, instead of the embodied (the *deha* instead of the *dehi*). *Maya* is not something that was and will disappear; nor is it something that was not, but later came and is. It never was, or is, or will be. *Maya* is a name for a non-existent phenomenon. But this non-existent thing comes within view! It is like the mirage in a desert, a sheet of water that never was or is. He who knows the truth does not see it; only those ignorant of the ways of the desert are drawn to it. They run towards it and suffer grief, exhaustion and despair.'

"*Maya* is the cause of all this *jagat* (universe), but it is not the cause of God. I am the authority that wields *maya*. This *jagat*, which is the product of *maya*, moves and behaves according to My will. So whoever is attached to Me and acts according to My will, cannot be harmed by *maya*. To overcome *maya*, the only method is to acquire the *gnana* of the Universal, and to rediscover your own universal nature. For then you attribute the limits of life on that which is eternal and it is this which causes *maya*. Hunger and thirst are the characteristics of life. Joy and grief, impulse and imagination, birth and death are all characteristics of the body. They are not the characteristics of the Universal, the Atma.

"Maya dare not approach anyone who has taken refuge in Me. For those who fix their attention on *maya*, it operates as a vast oceanic obstacle. But for those who fix their attention on God, *maya* will present itself as *Madhava!* The hurdle of *maya* can be crossed either by developing an attitude of oneness with the infinite God or an attitude of complete surrender to the Lord. The first is called *gnana yoga*, the second is named *bhakti yoga*. All men do not get an inner prompting to overcome *maya* by surrendering their all to the Lord. It depends on the merit or demerit accumulated during many births." (2)

"Affection for the body, attachment toward possessions of any kind, egoism that breeds the conflict of you and me, the bonds that grow between the individual and his wife, children and property all these are consequences of the primal illusion, *maya*. That illusion is basic, mysterious, and wondrous. Maya establishes her domain over all beings and things, all species of living creatures. The ten *indriyas* (five senses of perception and five senses of action) have each its presiding deity, and *maya* perceives the objective world deriving pleasure therefrom, through their instrumentality. Every item and particle of such pleasure is *maya*-made and therefore, illusory, evanescent and superficial.

"Maya has two forms: one type is called *vidyamaya* and the other is *avidyamaya*. The *maya* called *avidya* (ignorance) is very vicious; she causes boundless misery. Those drawn by it will sink into the depths of flux, the eternal tangle of joy and grief. The *maya* known as *vidya* (knowledge) has created the cosmos, under the prompting of the Lord, for she has no innate force of her own. Only while in the presence of the Lord can she create the three-stranded cosmos *(prapancha)*. The three strands are *satva*, *rajas* and *tamas*. The instant the individual discovers and knows that it is but the image of the Supreme, and that the distinction between the Supreme and itself has no basis in truth, *maya* will disappear like fog before the risen sun." (3)

"There are three steps in the progression of philosophic enquiry, or *vedantic* thought in India. They are the *dvaitic* (dualistic), the *visishta-advaitic*, or special-*advaitic* (special no-twoness) and the *advaitic* (non-dualistic). It is not possible to advance beyond these three steps by any human endeavour.

"*Advaitic* thought is beyond reach of the common man, it is not so easily comprehensible. To conceive of it with the intellect is also hard. To experience it, a powerful faculty of penetration is needed. Therefore, it is best to start with the dualistic, or *dvaitic* step, and experience it as the reality behind things; then the second stage of *visishta advaitam* is rendered easier to reach.

"The dualists posit that the cosmos is a vast machine designed and operated by God. The *Visishta-advaitins* declare that it is a phenomenon that is interpenetrated and imbued with the Divine. But, the *advaitins*, or non-dualists, assert that God is not outside the cosmos, that He became the cosmos (*jagat*) and that He is All That Is. There is nothing except God, no other, no second. This truth has to be accepted by all. This is the highest truth. To say that God is the *Atma* and the cosmos is as the body which He operates and lives in, is not correct. To assert that the *Atma* (God) is eternal and changeless but the cosmos which is His body can be subject to change and transformation is also not satisfying.

"What does it signify when it is said, God is the *upadana-karana*, the proximate cause of the cosmos? Proximate cause means the cause which produced the effect. The effect is the cause in another form. It cannot be separated from the cause. Every effect that we notice is but the cause that has assumed a new form. The cosmos is the effect, God is the cause - these statements only stress the fact that the cosmos is God in another form.

"Men, or individualised beings, are not separate from *Brahman*, or the Universal Absolute. Nor is there any need to assert that they are not separate. The relation between *Brahman* and *jiva* (individual) is not one of identity or one-ness; it is one of cause-effect. Until liberation is attained, the particular is distinct, is separate. When liberated, since the cause of individualisation is absent, the *jiva* is one with *Brahman*. Separation and oneness of *jiva* and *Brahman* are, in turns, the consequences of the delusion of bondage and the awareness of freedom.

"What now appears as the cosmos is really God; this is the vision that the true *sadhaka* (spiritual aspirant) has when he succeeds in his endeavours. The universe, *jagat*, appears to have emanated, as being experienced as such, and as disintegrating. These three are just superimposed ideations upon the One modificationless Reality, just like the snake superimposed upon the rope at dusk. This ideation is *maya*, for it hides and reveals at the same time. *Maya* cannot be said to be unreal. The rope appearing as a snake is known again as rope when the snake disappears. But, the universe does not disappear in the same manner. Its existence cannot be explained away. It is a phenomenon that is unique; we cannot compare it with any other. We cannot dismiss it as unreal or accept it as real. It is *sat-asat*, not *asat*. That is to say, real-unreal, not unreal.

"It persists for some time and is therefore real. It does not persist for all time and is therefore unreal. *Maya* is neither invalid nor valid. The universe appears to each in accordance with the point of view or the angle of vision. It has no independent existence apart from the ideations that are projected by and from the observer. Its support and sustenance is *Brahman*. *Brahman* is the unaffected Cause.

"The *jagat* can be conceived of as a picture of which the plain canvas is *Brahman* and the colours spread on is *jagat*, the appearance immanent on the canvas. The human figures are dark. The *jiva* is the experiencer of pain and grief through his involvement with the *jagat*. He is the seen, the observed. *Brahman* is truth; *jagat* is the play, the pantomime, the sport. It is the manifestation of the Will that is latent in *Brahman*. To recognise the Will behind the play is the attainment of liberation." (4)

References :
1. Sathya Sai Baba, *Jnana Vahini,* 1984, pp. 45
2. Sathya Sai Baba, *Geetha Vahini,* pp. 116 - 118
3. Tumuluru Krishna Murty, *Digest, Collection of Sri Sathya Sai Baba's Sayings,* pp. 187
4. Sathya Sai Baba, *Sathya Sai Vahini,* pp. 3 - 59, 218 - 221

8. DHARMA FOR MEN AND WOMEN

"For our spiritual life, *dharma* (righteous living, right conduct) is the basis. *Dharma* is universal. *Dharma* is the foundation for the welfare of humanity. God is the embodiment of *dharma*. His grace is won by *dharma*. He is ever fostering *dharma*. He is ever establishing *dharma*. He is *dharma* itself. When the river of *dharma* runs dry, or when it is clogged up by greed and hate, the *Divine Avatar* comes to let in His torrent of grace and restore its fresh, free flow. When *dharma* fails to transmute human life, the world is afflicted by agony and fear, tormented by stormy revolutions. When the effulgence of *dharma* fails to illumine human relationships, mankind is shrouded in the night of sorrow. Disaster now dances madly on the world stage, because right is neglected and there is disbelief in the essentials of a *dharmic* life. *Dharma* protects those who protect *dharma*, *dharma* destroys those who try to destroy *dharma*." (1, 2)

"*Dharma* is the moral path; the moral path is the light; the light is *ananda* (bliss). *Dharma* is *satya* (truth). *Satya* is the law of the universe. *Dharma* is the course, the path, the law. It leads one to universal love and unity.

"People refer to various duties, rights and obligations, but these are not basic *satyadharma*; they are only means and methods of regulating the complications of living. They are not fundamental. All these moral codes and approved behaviour are prompted by the need to cater to two types of creatures and two types of natures - viz., male and female. They connote *Prakriti* and *Paramatma*, gross and subtle, inert and conscious, the all-pervading duet. All this creation came about by the inter-relation of the inert and the conscious, did it not? So, too, all the various mores have emerged on account of this bifurcation. All this ramification and elaboration of *dharma* is due to this: the male and the female.

"Therefore, the chief *dharma* for practical progress in the world is the moral conduct and behaviour of these two; whatever any great teacher might teach, it cannot go beyond these two distinct natures. The *purushadharma* for the male, and the *stridharma* for the female, are the important applications of *sathyadharma*. Other codes and disciplines are accessories, tributaries like the streams that meet the *Godavari* when it is coursing ahead. They are related to various circumstances, situations and statuses that are temporary; you have to pay attention to the main river and not to the tributaries. Similarly, take the major male and female *dharmas* the chief guides of living, and do not give the minor accessory *dharma* any decisive place in the scheme of living.

"A wife endowed with virtue is really a brilliant jewel. Chastity is the ideal for womankind. With the strength that derives from that virtue, women can achieve anything. Modesty is essential for women. Humility, purity of thought and manners, meekness, surrender to high ideals, sensitivity, sweetness of temper — the peculiar blend of all these qualities is modesty. A woman must plant the seedlings of the fear of sin and the fear of the Lord in her heart and cultivate the charms of humility.

"It does not matter how bad or low the husband is, the wife must, through love, bring him round and correct him, and help him gain the blessings of the Lord. It is not correct to feel that her progress alone matters and she has no concern for his improvement or upliftment. She must feel, on the other hand, that the welfare of the husband, the joy of the husband, the wishes of the husband, the salvation of the husband, these are the panacea for her also. Such a woman will receive the grace of the Lord automatically, without special effort; it will be showered upon her; the Lord will always be by her side and be kind to her in all ways. By her virtue she will ensure the salvation of her husband.

"Observance of *dharma* is the sign of manhood. Man should honour his wife as the mistress of the home and act in accordance with her wishes. Then only can he deserve the status of man. Name and fame, honour and dishonour, vice and wickedness, good and bad are all equal and uniform for both men and women. Both are equally bound by the rules of *dharma*." (3)

"The highest *dharma* is for each one to follow his *sva* (own)- *dharma* boldly. As regards this problem, there is a conflict between religion and morals. '*Gaana karmano gatih,*' — it is difficult, fraught with danger, says the Lord, speaking of moral discipline. Which act is legitimate, which not? Which act is sanctioned by morals, which not? Persons have struggled and are struggling to decide these. But Krishna has mentioned the types of acts which are worthy, in the shlokas: '*Manmanaa bhava Madbhakto mad yaajee Maam namaskuru. Maamevaishyasi satyam te, pratijaane priyo si Me. Sarva dharmaan parityajya Maamekam sharanam vraja; Aham tvaam sarva paapebhyo mokshayishyaami maa shuchah:*' Fix thy thought on Me; be devoted to Me; worship Me; do homage to Me; thou shalt reach Me. This Truth do I declare to thee; for thou art dear to Me. This is my teaching, My grace. This is the path to come to Me. Give up all *dharmas*; surrender to Me; do not grieve; I shall liberate you from the consequences of all your acts.

"Of course, it is hard to effect this full surrender. But, if man makes even the slightest effort towards it, the Lord Himself will confer the courage to pursue it to the end. He will walk with him and help him as a friend; He will lead him as a guide; He will guard him from evil and temptation; He will be his staff and support. He has said, '*Svalpamapyasya dharmasya traayate mahato bhayaat*' - this course of action, if followed even to a small extent, will save him from terrifying fear." To follow *dharma* is itself a source of joy; it is the path least beset with hurdles. That is the teaching of the Lord.

"This *dharma* is not laid down or recommended for the extraordinary among men. It is within the reach of all, for all have the hunger for God, all have the discrimination to discover that there is something basic behind all this change. Even the most heinous sinner can quickly cleanse his heart and become pure by surrendering to the Lord in anguished repentance.

"Therefore, the Lord's command is that each should pursue the special *dharma* laid down for him; each person should plan his life according to the spiritual foundations of his culture; he should give up the objective vision and listen to the voice of God." (4)

"Marriage is like milk and sugar. Men are the milk, women are the sugar. Marriage is a sacred bond and it is a promise you are making to each other because the wife is half of the husband and the husband is half of the wife. Half plus half is not two but one. It is to kill the ego that two souls are brought together. Marriage means your life, a whole lifetime together, not just a few days or a few weeks, or a few years. Marriage is a training ground for fostering trans-sensual love. Today there is a tendency for separation, not coming together. Life is full of troubles and challenges. We should not separate ourselves because of these but rather face them together. Now when trouble comes, even if it is small, it separates us. That should not be the tendency, one should give ones heart to the other." (1)

"Married life and being a *grihastha* will not bar your way to realisation. Look upon the wife and children as a sacred trust and serve them in that spirit. Prepare yourself for a celibate and spiritual discipline from the age of fifty." (5)

"Mutual understanding is very important for marriage. Now understanding is actually forgotten and one tries to adjust, therefore adjustment is the main problem. The most important thing is to understand. Then adjustment becomes something very easy later on.

"No abortion! The soul enters the body on or after the fifth month. No, no! Even before the fifth month abortion is bad.... mind control, use mind control." (6)

"The *Ramayana* lays down ideals for all relationships in life, and for the realisation of the highest aim of human life. Nowhere else can be seen such a variety and quantity of moral dicta and their practical applications. If only the *Ramayana* is studied closely and observed in daily practice, mankind can attain peace and prosperity in all fields. (7)

"The *Ramayana* exemplifies the amity and harmony which should prevail among the members of a family. It extols the glory of ideal brotherhood, noble friendship and the greatness of love and affection. The *Ramayana* holds out Rama as an embodiment of ideal qualities. As a son, friend, husband, master and ruler, He was an ideal without equal.

"Who was Ravana? Ravana is described as a demon with ten heads. These ten heads are the six vices, namely, desire, anger, greed, infatuation, pride and jealousy, *manas* (mind), *buddhi* (intellect), *chitta* (will) and *ahamkara* (ego). Since these ten are present in every human being all men are Ravana indeed ! Whoever beheads all these ten heads in fact becomes a Rama. It is God alone who can behead these ten heads ! When a man surrenders himself to God, all these ten heads will go and he will merge in Rama." (8) "Sita is the embodiment of all the *dharmas* that are found in the world. The main characteristics of Sita are chastity, patience and virtue." (9)

"The *Ramayana* happens in everyone's heart. It does take place systematically and in the same sequence. In the Ramayana of actual life, *Atma* is Rama, *manas* is Lakshmana, *Brahmagnana* is Sita; and when that Sita is lost, Rama falls into the forest of existence; there, in that forest, there are despair and discrimination. If we associate ourselves with Hanuman, or courage, we can go across the sea of delusion with the army of zest, strength and steadfastness represented by Jambavan, Angada and other *vanaras* (monkeys). As soon as we cross it, we can destroy the *rajasic* quality and the *tamasic* quality symbolised by Ravana and Kumbhakarana; the *satvic* quality, or *Vibhishana*, can then be crowned; *Anubhavagnana*, or Sita is then attained. This union of *jada* (inert matter, creation) and *chaitanya* (consciousness), that is, of Sita and Rama, is the *ananda* (bliss), *jivanmu.' hi* (salvation) for the soul." (10)

References :

1. Tumuluru Krishna Murty, *Digest, Collection of Sri Sathya Sai Baba's Sayings*, pp. 80 - 184
2. Sathya Sai Baba, *Dharma Vahini*, 1985, pp. 1-2
3. Sathya Sai Baba, *Dharama Vahini*, 1985, pp. 26,31, 37,43
4. Sathya Sai Baba, *Geetha Vahini* pp. 7-9
5. *Sadhana, The Inward Path - Quotations from the Divine Discourses of Bhagawan Sri Sathya Sai Baba*, 1985, pp. 82
6. J. Jegathesan, *Sai Baba and the World Journey to God*, Part 2, pp. 88, pp. 248-249
7. Sathya Sai Baba, *Ramakatha Rasavahini*, Part II, pp. 64
8. Sathya Sai Baba, *Sanathana Sarathi*, August 1992, pp. 183 - 184
9. Sathya Sai Baba, *Summer Showers in Brindavan*, 1972, pp. 117
10. *Sandeha Nivarini Dialogues with Bhagawan Sri Sathya Sai Baba*, pp. 83 -84.

9. THE FIVE ELEMENTS AND THE FIVE PRANAS

"The whole cosmos is made up of the five basic elements (*pancha bhutas*), space (ether), air, fire, water and earth. Their qualities are represented by sound, touch, form, taste and smell. *Akasha* (space or ether) provides the initial impulse. It is comparable to an infinite container. The other four elements are contained in it. These elements vary in their order of subtlety. Water is subtler than earth and is more expansive and lighter than earth. Fire is subtler than water and air is subtler than fire and more pervasive. *Akasha* is subtler than air and is all-pervasive. Each of these elements is covered by a *kosha* (sheath).

"*Akasha* is activated by what is called *atigati*, very high-speed motion (or vibrations). These vibrations, by their movement, give rise to air. The movement of air results in fire (or heat). It is a scientific fact that friction causes heat, as in the case of the rubbing together of palms. To generate heat, air is necessary. When the heat cools off, water is produced. Fluids solidify into earth. Hence, the starting point for the five elements is *akasha*. These elements have come into existence to sustain the universe and demonstrate the omnipresence and omniscience of the Divine." (1)

"The Divine is present in each of the five elements in a specific form. In space the Divine is present in the form of sound as *AUM*. *Vayu* (air) carries the life-principle, the anima, the *prana*. Air is not needed when there is no life in a thing. *Prana* is the image of the air principle. Air has the power to sustain life. This power is represented by hydrogen and oxygen in the atmosphere. Oxygen has this Divine life-sustaining potency. The Divine is thus present in air in the form of the *prana* (life-giving breath). This is a matter of daily experience for everyone. When somebody faints, the people around him are cleared so that he may have more air and breathe more freely. This is a recognition of the presence of the life-energy in air.

"In *agni* (fire), the Divine is present as an alarm-signaller. Even when a fire is mild, people are careful. Consciously or otherwise, when we have to deal with fire, we develop a sense of cautiousness. Fire is luminous with vigilance, warning, wakefulness and attention (*jagrata*).

"In *jala* (water) the Divine is present as *pragna* (integrated awareness). The Scriptures declare: *Pragnaanam Brahma*, integrated awareness is *Brahma*. This *pragna* arises out of water. When a person becomes unconscious, water is sprinkled on him to restore consciousness. A cup of cold water can restore a person to activity.

"The fifth element is *prithvi* (earth). In earth, *chaitanya* (consciousness) is present. The potencies present in the five elements – *pragna-shakti* (integrated awareness), *jagrata-shakti* (the awakening or warning potency), *chetana-shakti* (consciousness), *shabda-shakti* (the potency of sound) and *jiva-shakti* (life-sustaining potency) are all different forms of divine power. Those who are engaged in the *angavati sadhana* regard the five elements as manifestations of the *Paramatma* (Supreme), and offer worship to them." (2, 3)

"The human body is a product of the five elements, the *pancha bhutas*. From *Brahman* originated *yatna* (effort) and *mahat* (cosmos); from these was born *akasha* (space); from *akasha* was born *vayu* (air); from *vayu, agni* (fire); from *agni, jala* (water) and from *jala, prithvi* (earth). Each element has again become fivefold and has gone into the composition of the body. The element space became the cogniser : *manas, buddhi, ahamkara* and *panchakam*. They are recognised as the inner senses. The five forms of the element air are *samana, vyana, udana, prana* and *apana*. In the body they are called *pancha prana* (the five vital airs). The element fire became the sensory organs: the ear, the skin, the eye, the tongue and the nose. They are called the *gnanendriyas*, the organs of knowledge. The element water became *shabda* (sound), *sparsha* (touch), *rupa* (form), *rasa* (taste) and *gandha* (smell). The element earth became the vocal organs, hands, legs, genitals and excretory organs. They are called the *karmendriyas*, the organs of action." (4, 5)

"The body is composed of cells, which are made up of atoms. The atoms are physical phenomena. They are fundamentally *jada*, or composite and without feeling. The *vedantins* speak of a subtle body, separate from this gross body. That, too, is physical. It is the centre of subtle skills and force. It is in this body that all the subtle mental feelings and agitations take place. Every force can work only through one medium or another which is physical. The same power that operates the gross body works through the subtle processes of thought. They are not two different entities. One is the subtle form of the other, that is all.

"What is the source of these powers? If we delve deep, we will find that there are two things in nature, *akasha* and *prana*. *Akasha* is the source of all the gross and subtle material one encounters. When *prana*, or life-force, contacts it, due to the impact, the *akasha* principle transforms itself into either gross or subtle, in varying proportions. *Prana*, too, is omnipresent, like *akasha*; it can also penetrate everywhere and everything. Like the blocks of ice that water becomes and that float on water and that move about on water, *prana* acts on *akasha* and bodies appear. *Prana* is the force that moulds *akasha* into various forms. The gross body is the vehicle of the *prana* that it has shaped out of *akasha*. The subtle body is of the form of thought, feeling, etc." (6)

"There are five vital energies, or *pranas*, which vitalize all bodily functioning. One of these is related to breathing, another to excretion, a third to circulation, the fourth to digestion and the fifth to the upward flow which energizes the higher centres." (7)

"The body derives its vital force from the sun. There are five types of life-breaths (*pranas*). The five *pranas* are known as *prana, apana, vyana, udana* and *samana vayus*. The *prana* comes from the sun, the *vyana* comes from air (*vayu*). The *apana* comes from earth (*prithvi*). *Udana* comes from fire (*agni*) The *samana* comes from space (*akasha*). Because of these five life-breaths functioning in us, we are able to live healthily. There are seventy two thousand blood vessels in a human being. The *vyana vayu* blows through the entire circulatory system. When the air is polluted the seventy two thousand blood vessels get polluted and the effect of this on the *apana vayu* leads to cancer and heart-attacks. Man needs pure *vyana vayu* for good health." (8)

References :
1. Sathya Sai Baba, *Sanathana Sarathi*, November 1988, pp. 229 - 293
2. Sathya Sai Baba, *Sanathana Sarathi,* April 1982. pp. 90
3. Sathya Sai Baba *Sanathana Sarathi,* August 1988, pp. 200 - 201
4. Sathya Sai Baba, *Prasnothara Vahini*, 1984, pp. 1 - 2
5. H. S. Youngs, *Translations by Baba,* 1975, pp. 71
6. Sathya Sai Baba, *Sathya Sai Vahini,* pp. 45 - 46
7. Sathya Sai Baba, *Discourses on the Bhagavad Gita*, compiled and edited by A. Drucker, First Indian Edition, 1988, pp. 112
8. Sathya Sai Baba, *Sanathana Sarath,* July 1983, pp. 157

NOTE: See scheme at the end of chapter 12

10. MASTERY OF THE SENSES

"To lead a purposeful and worthy life, you have to recognise the true meaning of the body, the senses, the mind and the intellect, and know how to use them intelligently and effectively. All the troubles of mankind are due to the fact that ninety-nine percent of the people lead lives without understanding this truth. The body, the senses, the mind and the intellect are only instruments for the individual and have no consciousness of their own. The body is inert. The body is only a temporary resthouse for the spirit. *Vedanta* declares: "The body is only a shrine for the eternal Spirit inhabiting it." It is necessary to know what enables the body, the senses, the mind and the intellect to develop or to deteriorate." (1)

"Krishna said, 'Arjuna! Your body is a chariot and your senses are the horses; your mind acts as the reins and your intelligence (*buddhi*) the driver.' It is only when the mind follows the *buddhi* that inner vision is developed. Inner vision leads to the experience of the bliss of the *Atma*. External vision, however, subjects man to untold suffering." (2) "The order of control based on the increasing order of subtlety ought to be as follows: the body, the sense organs, the mind, the *buddhi* and the *Atma*, each of them controlling the preceding one. This means that the *Atma* should hold sway over the rest of them.

"The role of the senses is remarkable. The wonders performed by the Divine defy description. But the part played by the senses is even more marvellous and mysterious. Strange, unpredictable and indescribable, indeed, are the ways of the sense organs. The senses are subtler than the body. Although the faculties of speech, touch, sight, hearing and taste as well as wind, bile and phlegm exist in the body, the senses exercise extraordinary and equal control over all of them. Joy and sorrow, heat and cold, etc., are experienced only when the sense organs come in contact with external objects. Without the sensory objects, the senses cannot function even for a moment. All the activities of the senses are oriented towards objects in the environment. It is not possible for us to comprehend or describe the myriad facets of sense organs and their activities.

"The senses are also called by the name *maatraah*, which means measuring instruments. Which is the sense organ that measures or decides the taste of an object? It is the tongue. Which organ is capable of declaring whether a picture is attractive or ugly? The eye alone is the measuring rod of this purpose.

"In the *Kathopanishad*, the senses are described as horses yoked to the chariot of the body. What is the inner significance of naming the senses as horses (*ashva*)? *Ashva* means that which is always restless. It is common knowledge that a horse, whether it is standing or running or even sleeping, moves some part of its body all the time, whether the tail, the leg, the back, the nose, or the jaws.

"The term *maatraah*, as applied to the senses, has yet another meaning. It indicates that the limit to what can be experienced by each sense organ has been prescribed by the Lord Divine. For instance, the eye can only see, it cannot hear. Everyone, therefore, should make use of the sense organs with due regard to the functions and limits prescribed for each of them.

"For example, the tongue has been given to man to consume wholesome food which promotes his health as well as to speak gently and sweetly so as to give joy to others, and to communicate his innermost thoughts and feelings to others. The tongue, which has been bestowed on us for such edifying purposes, is being grossly misused nowadays. It is being used for consuming drugs and narcotics, eating animal food, smoking, indulging in abuse of others, carrying tales, back-biting, and speaking harsh words that hurt others, etc. Through such perverse use of the tongue, Divine injunctions are violated by setting at naught the ordained limits. Consequently, man has to experience numerous troubles.

"Control of the senses must be the primary aim of men, not the fleeting pleasures of sense-objects, which give a little momentary joy followed by endless misery. The senses are extremely powerful. They are the root cause for all the joys and sorrows of mankind. You should, therefore, try to understand thoroughly the nature and role of the senses and harness them to your best advantage. Since the sense organs are highly potent, the first and foremost task for man is to bring them under his control in order to lead an ideal life. Because young people today have lost control of their senses, all their actions and behaviour are devious. They do not know how to sit properly in the class-room, how to walk about, how to read, how to sleep and how to behave towards their parents, teachers, elders and friends. They betray their lack of concentration even while talking to somebody, by casting their looks hither and thither. While sleeping they should stretch their body straight and not curl themselves up like coiled wire, in a bundle.

"Today, young people do not know how to sit properly while reading or writing, etc. They sit with their backs bent and drooping like eighty-year-old people. This causes various ailments and leads to premature old age. While walking or sitting, you must be straight as a rod, keeping the spine erect. There is a physiological reason for this. A very important nerve, the *sushumna naadi*, runs through the spinal column, from its base in the *muladhara chakra* to the *sahasrara chakra* at the top of the head. If it gets bent, serious results follow." (3)

"You can see without the eyes, hear without the ears, speak without the tongue, smell without the nose, touch without the body, walk without legs; yes, experience without even the mind. For, you are pure essence itself; you are the Supreme Self. You have no awareness of this truth; hence, you are drowned in ignorance. You feel you are the senses only and, therefore, you experience misery. The five senses are all bound up with the mind; it is the mind that separately activates the senses and is affected by their reactions. Man reads through the mind-associated eye and so he fails. But, the *gnani* has the *divya chakshus* (the Divine eye) for he has the Divine vision; he can hear and see without the aid of the senses." (4)

"Of all the sense organs, the tongue has an overriding importance and influence. Mastery over this one sense organ will enable one to master with ease all the other sense organs." (3) "The main door leading to *yoga*, union with God, is control of the tongue; this must be exercised both in the area of taste and in the area of speech. The *Gita* has declared that without control of the tongue it is impossible to follow the path of devotion and enter the mansion of *yoga* which leads to God. Each sense organ given to human beings has one particular use, but the tongue is endowed with a double power: it has both the power of speech and the power of taste. In the *Gita*, the Lord cautions you to be very careful in using your tongue; He praises the devotee who has attained complete control over his tongue, for such a one will soon develop a pure and steady heart, and feel the constant presence of the Lord. To gain such control, devotees have been practising a number of special disciplines, such as observing silence, controlling their diet, or maintaining a complete fast.

"Fasting promotes health for the physical body; in the mental realm, it gives joy and bliss. Unlimited and unregulated food is very harmful for devotees. Indulging in a variety of tasty food is likely to lead the devotee into the torpidity and inertia of *tamoguna*. To think that you can go on enjoying all the tasty dishes and pleasures of food, while at the same time trying to please God and enjoy the nearness of God, is extremely foolish. These two, indulging in food and gaining the nearness of God, are not compatible. Therefore, right from the beginning, you must make a determined effort to keep the tongue under control. Once you gain mastery over the tongue, the other sense organs will also come under control automatically. Because man has not been able to gain control over his tongue, he is afflicted with numerous doubts, emotional turmoils, contradictions and confusions. Control of the tongue refers not only to food but also to speech. You must recognize that there is nothing more powerful than the power of words. For this reason, you must keep your tongue strictly under control.

"Many sages have described how the tongue always longs to enjoy good things, and how everything will be easy once you gain control over it. Another word used for describing this control is silence. Silence does not merely refer to restraint of the tongue. Not only should you exercise silence in speech, but you should also be silent in thoughts. Your mind should remain free of all thoughts; that is true silence." (5)

"The inner conversation and the controversial chatter continues from morning till night, until sleep overtakes the mind. It causes ill-health and the early setting in of old age. The topics on which the chatter is based are mostly the faults and failings of others and their fortunes and misfortunes. This perpetual dialogue is at the bottom of all the miseries of man. It covers the mind with thick darkness. It grows wild very quickly and suppresses the genuine worth of manhood. The talk that inhabits the mind during the waking stage persists even in dreams and robs man of his much needed rest." (6)

"By the use of appropriate words, it is possible to transform the entire mind of an individual. Unfortunately, many scientists do not believe this. In the Scriptures you will also find statements that point out how words are extremely powerful and can destroy the world itself. There it is said that if you were to cut a tree, it could still sprout; or if a piece of iron were broken in two, a blacksmith could make the two pieces come together again by heating and pounding them until they were one. But if you were to break a heart by venomous words, it would not be possible to ever make it whole again. Words can cause endless troubles and they can also give boundless joy. Therefore, you should be most careful that the words you use do not hurt or give pain to others.

"If you were to physically slip and fall there might be a small injury that could cause you some inconvenience for a while; but there would be no grave consequences resulting from this in the long term. There might only have been a small wound, which you can easily have dressed, and which would soon heal. But if your tongue were to slip and you were to hurt the mind or the heart of another person with harsh words, it would create a wound in that person which could not be cured by any doctor in the world. Therefore, you should never use words which are likely to hurt another's feelings. One day, the words which you have used will come back to you. So, use always sweet and good words.

"I quite often tell the students, 'Dear students, you should not talk too much. The Divine energy which is in you will be wasted in the process. By engaging in too much talk your memory power will get lost and weaknesses will develop in your body. Premature old age will be the final result. Besides that, you will also earn a bad name.' The most common cause of premature old age and senility is this talk, and more talk, and still more talk. All this talk is not good. You have to observe silence. From birth, you have never developed the habit of silence. You have to develop it now. Actually, the two functions of the tongue are closely related. Too much talk leads to unnatural hunger. When the talker feels more hunger he will, of course, eat more food. On account of this excessive food, feelings arise which express themselves in still more talk. In this process, controlling the senses becomes an almost impossible task. Especially in this *Kali* Age, the tongue can easily be sanctified by repeating the holy names. Instead of wasting your precious Divine energy and your precious time in idle talk, let the tongue constantly sing the praises of God and repeat His name. Sing the name of the Lord! That is the proper way to spend your life, saturating your very existence with the glory and holiness of His presence." (5)

"Modern man has no idea of sense-control. He has no conception of self-restraint. He leads the life of a libertine. This kind of licentious living can only result in degradation and ruin. The aim of sense-control is to achieve one-pointed concentration. It helps also to steady the mind. Without mental steadiness man becomes dehumanised." (7)

References :

1. Sathya Sai Baba, *Sanathana Sarathi,* November 1988, pp. 292
2. Sathya Sai Baba, *Summer Showers in Brindavan,* 1979, pp. 75-76
3. Sathya Sai Baba, *Summer Showers in Brindavan,* 1990, pp. .39-42, 55-56, 59-62
4. Sathya Sai Baba, *Jnana Vahini,* 1984, pp. 39
5. Sathya Sai Baba, *Discourses on the Bhagavad Gita,* compiled and edited by A. Drucker, First Indian edition 1988, pp. 39, 42-46
6. Sathya Sai Baba, *Vidya Vahini,* 1984, pp. 84
7. Sathya Sai Baba, *Sanathana Sarathi,* August 1989, pp. 210

11. CONQUEST OF THE MIND

Mind alone is the cause of man's rise and fall in life
Mind alone is responsible for man's bondage or liberation
This mind alone makes man forget his reality and land himself in hell!

"Man is a combination of body, mind and *Atma*. These three together constitute the steps on man's ascent to the highest stage. The body is the instrument for action. The mind is concerned with cognition. The changeless and permanent reality is the *Atma*. Thus, doing, knowing and being are the triune manifestations of the human personality. Although the body, mind and *Atma* have different names and characteristics, their harmonization and unification help man to raise himself from the human to the Divine level. On the contrary, their alienation from one another, degrades him to the animal level.

"The word *antahkarana*, inner instrument, is used in the everyday worldly context as well as in the spiritual parlance. What is its form, its nature, its role, its importance and its destination? When we inquire along these lines, it will be found that mind itself assumes the subtle form of the *antahkarana*, consisting of four aspects, namely *manas* (mind), *buddhi* (intellect), *chitta* (memory), *ahamkara* (ego), the last three being the subtle aspects of the mind. The particular name is given based on the functions performed.

"When the mind is engaged in wavering thought processes, it is called *manas*. When it is busy in the process of enquiry and discrimination between right and wrong, it is named as *buddhi*. When it functions as a repository of memories, it is known as *chitta*. When it identifies itself with the physical body, assuming the doership of various activities, it goes by the name of *ahamkara*, ego. Thus, it may be seen that the mind, although basically one, displays these varied forms on account of the different roles assumed by it. In fact, the mind alone is the cause of all things. '*Manomulam idam jagat,*' say the Scriptures. It means the whole cosmos is nothing but a projection of the mind.

"Man derives his name from the possession of the mind. As a man thinks, so he becomes. Man means mind, and mind means man. The mind is only a bundle of thoughts. Thoughts give rise to acts, and what we enjoy or suffer in this world are the consequences of these acts. Thoughts are highly potent. They survive the death of man. Hence it is essential to keep out bad thoughts from our minds. It is bad thoughts which separate man from man and make them forget their common Divinity. When men realise that the *Atma* in everybody is one and the same, there will be no room for differences. The peace of the individual as well as of the world depends on the mind. Hence the need for proper disciplining of the mind.

"Man today is creating all sorts of trouble for himself due to wrong thoughts. No one else should be blamed for his pleasures or pains, gains or losses. Mind is the root of the tree of *samsara*, the cycle of birth and death, and the manifested universe in general. To destroy this tree, an axe should be laid at the root itself. In other words, the mind should be destroyed by diverting the thoughts to enquiry on the *Atma*, the real Self, or the real (I). Based on the differences of nature of the mind, different colours are attributed to it. For instance, the mind filled with anger is red in colour. A selfish mind is wheat brown. An egotistic mind is of the orange hue, while the mind dedicated to God is pure white. Today the world is riddled with fear. Whether at home or out in the streets, or while travelling in a train, bus or plane, people are haunted by fear. The root cause for this ubiquitous fear is the absence of pure and sacred thoughts in the minds of men.

"The mind is a priceless possession. It is God's greatest gift to man. The Scriptures have declared that the mind alone is responsible either for man's bondage or for his liberation. The mind is like a clean mirror. It has no intrinsic power of its own to directly experience the sense-objects except through the appropriate sense organs. For instance, it can see only through the eyes and hear only through the ears but can neither see nor hear by itself independently. Consequently, the offences committed by the senses are reflected in the mirror of mind. No blame attaches to the mind *per se*. It is the association with the wayward senses that pollutes the mind. According to the Scriptures, the mind is subject to three kinds of pollution: *mala*, *vikshepa* and *avarana*.

What is *mala*? Man commits many offences, knowingly or unknowingly, not only in this life but he committed them also in previous lives. The imprint of these acts is carried by the *chitta*, memory, life after life, like the dust accumulating on the surface of a mirror day after day. Thus the mirror of man's mind is covered in such dirt, which is technically named as *mala*. On account of this *mala*, man is unable to see clearly the reflection of his real identity in the mirror of his mind. Hence, it is necessary to clean the mirror of the impurities covering it. This cleaning is done by regulating one's food and other living habits including recreation. The complete removal of *mala* cannot be done in a day or a month. This requires persistent and prolonged practice.

The second distortion of the mind, called *vikshepa*, is due to the constant wavering of the mind, like the movements of the reflected image in a mirror that is kept moving or shaking frequently. To control this waywardness of the mind, one should undertake various spiritual practices, like meditation, prayer and the nine modes of devotion mentioned in the Scriptures, viz., *shravanam*, listening to the Lord's stories, *leelas* (divine plays), *mahimas* (glory); *kirtanam*, singing His glories; *smaranam*, remembrance of His grace; *pada sevanam*, service to the Lotus Feet; *archanam*, worship; *vandanam*, salutation, reverence towards nature and all life; *daasyam*, master-servant relationship; *sakhyam*, companionship; *Atma nivedanam* offering oneself to the Lord, i.e., self-surrender.

Avarana may be likened to a thick cloth covering the mirror of man's mind, which does not permit any reflection whatsoever of the image of the Self. This cloth is made up of the *arishadvarga*, the gang of six internal enemies of man, viz., *kama* (desire), *krodha*, (anger), *lobha* (greed), *moha* (attachment), *mada* (pride), *maatsarya* (jealousy, envy). Out of the six, pride may be considered the worst enemy. Pride is of eight kinds: pride of money, learning, caste, affluence, beauty, youth, position or authority, and *tapas* (spiritual pride). The best means to remove this thick cloth of *avarana* is to develop love for all. Love is God. Live in Love. All that you have to do to achieve purity in thought, word and deed is to follow these five injunctions.

Think no evil, think what is good.
See no evil, see what is good.
Hear no evil, hear what is good.
Speak no evil, speak what is good.
Do no evil, do what is good." (1)

"Without the mind, there can be no object or feeling or emotion. No mind, no matter! The mind revels in name and form; it imposes name and form and thus helps in creating things and experiences. It cannot contact or operate upon anything without name and form. That is why the mind is helpless when meditation has to be done on the nameless and the formless.

"The mind of man is not an organ that can be identified physiologically; it cannot be touched or operated on by doctors or surgeons. It is an intangible bundle of resolutions and hesitations, of desires and doubts, of wishes and wants, of pros and cons. The mind is the puppet of the food that is consumed by man. The quality of the food determines the direction of the desire that diverts the mental flow. That is why in the *Gita*, as well as in all scriptural texts, *satvic* food is recommended for the upward seeking individual. The mind is very truly characterised as a monkey! Why, it is even more wayward than a monkey, for it jumps from one perch to another that is miles away in space and centuries away in time in less time than a wink! The mind jumps from one desire to another, and entangles us in its coils. The wind gathers the clouds from the four quarters; similarly, the mind brings into your consciousness the disappointments of many hopes.

"The mind expresses itself through attraction and repulsion, *raga* and *dvesha*, affection and hatred, towards the external world. How to overcome *raga* and *dvesha*? By discrimination, by inquiry, by reasoning.

"Will-power motivated by God is the active force available for your upliftment. This is called *sankalpa bala*. Develop it by concentration and *japa*. The mind must be compelled to submit to the dictates of the will. Now, you are easily led astray by the vagaries of the mind. That is why I say, WATCH ! W is for watch your Words; A is for watch your Acts; T is for watch your Thoughts; C is for watch your Character; H is for watch your Heart." (2)

"Thoughts come from food and environment. If you have *satvic* food and desire only good things and atmosphere around you, only good thoughts will come to you. Where do thoughts go? They go nowhere, because thoughts do not flow through the mind. The mind goes out and grasps, and gets itself engaged in thoughts. If the desire is for God, the mind does not go out. The best way is not to become involved in the problem of 'How to get rid of thoughts?' See all thoughts as God. Then only God-thoughts will come." (3)

"The mind wills, yearns, prompts and insists on effort and action. This process is called *sankalpa*. These are like commands. The face is moulded by the mind. Every single *sankalpa* or thought accepted and acted upon is a line which affects its shape. The mind travels quicker than sound, far quicker than even light." (4)

"There are three states relating to the mind: *shunyatva* (emptiness), *anekagrata* (simultaneous pulls of multiple thoughts) and *ekagrata* (one-pointedness). These three states arise from the three *gunas*. While *tamoguna* (indolence) brings about a blankness in the mind, *rajoguna* (the quality inducing animated action) provokes the mind into wandering hither and thither. *Satvaguna*, the quality that promotes the sacred aspects in human life, stills the mind into one-pointed contemplation. Thus, it is only those who cultivate *satvaguna* who can undertake meditation with ease. The human mind is activated into dynamic equilibrium by the three *gunas* of *satva rajas* and *tamas*." (5)

"The desires that cling to the mind are the blemishes that tarnish man's inner consciousness. Control the senses, do not yield to their insistent demands for satisfaction. When the senses are negated, the mind disappears, delusion dies and liberation is achieved." (6)

"To bring the mind under control we have to free ourselves from the entire process of mental agitation. Agitations are the very nature of the mind. When desires are eliminated the mind will go. If the mind goes, the sense of separateness (ego) will go. It has been said that the destruction of the mind is the means to the realization of the Divine. The cessation of the mind can be brought about by the gradual elimination of the desires, like the removal of threads from a cloth. Finally the desires have to be consumed by the fire of *vairagya* (renunciation).

"Look upon life as one long railway journey. In this journey it is not good to carry heavy luggage. There are stations on the way, like suffering (*aarthi*), the desire for objects (*arthaarthi*), the yearning for understanding (*jignaasu*), and Self-realization (*gnani*). The less luggage one carries, the more easily and quickly one can get through various stages and reach one's destination. The primary requisite, therefore, is the eradication of desires." (7) "The fickle nature of the mind acts as an impediment to man's spiritual progress, and therefore, it is imperative that every spiritual aspirant gains control over his mind if he were to drench himself in the delight of his *Atma*." (1)

"The mind spins a cocoon for the *jivi* to be imprisoned in. *Karma*, which is the activity of *maya*, or ignorance, encloses the individual in its grip; it is the husk that makes the paddy seed grow and yield more paddy plants and more grains of paddy. Remove the husk and there is no more sprouting. *Maya* is like the ghost of a tribal woman which once possessed a great *pundit* in a Himalayan hermitage. The unfortunate *pundit* sang and danced like any *pahadi* damsel; he swore and cursed in the *Paisachi* dialect and everyone in the hermitage became ashamed of his company. At last, when the ghost was exorcised and the *pundit* was freed, he became his original self - he remembered nothing of his pranks and blabberings. Man is similarly possessed by the ghost of *maya*. The ghost has to be driven out. The mode of exorcism of this ghost is taught by the *guru* or the *Gita*. Do not despair, it can be driven out. Confidence adds the required courage and strength. Do not doubt or give vent to despair." (8)

References :

1. Sathya Sai Baba, *Summer Showers in Brindavan* 1990, pp. 69-87
2. *Voice of the Avatar, Extracts from the Divine Discourses of Sathya Sai Baba,* Part I, Compiled By D. Hejmadi, M. Sc., Second Edition, 1981, pp. 61-67, 74
3. Sathya Sai Baba, *Sanathana Sarathi,* March 1974, pp. 11 - 13
4. Sathya Sai Baba, *Sanathana Sarathi,* April 1986, pp. 187 - 188
5. Sathya Sai Baba, *Summer Showers in Brindavan* 1979, pp. 69 - 80
6. *Sadhana, The Inward Path,* Quotations from the Divine Discourses of Sathya Sai Baba, 1985, pp. 163
7. Sathya Sai Baba, *Sanathana Sarathi*, January 1984, pp. 17 - 19
8. *Sathya Sai Speaks, Vol. II*, pp. 215 - 216

12. THE MANAS, THE CHITTA, THE BUDDHI AND THE AHAMKARA – I

Purity of mind is the pathway to progress
Purity of mind means mighty power
A pure mind is like a precious pearl in the sea

See no evil, speak no evil,
Hear no evil any time, anywhere in the world
Remember always the picture of the three monkeys
What I say is truth indeed! (1)

"There are twenty-four bodily principles: the five organs of action (*karmendriya*), the five senses of perception (*gnanendriya*), the five sheaths (*kosha*), the five vital energies (*prana*) and the four aspects of the mind; the lower or thinking mind called the *manas*, the intuitive intellect and faculty of discrimination or discernment which is called the *buddhi*, the sense of personal self or ego called the *ahamkara*, and the seat of feelings and recollections called the *chitta*. All these together, along with the *Atma*, which is their basis, make up twenty-five. The twenty-four bodily principles are really just manifestations of your ignorance. It is these twenty-four principles that constitute the illusion which makes you appear a separate being." (2)

"The mind is called *karana* (an instrument). The senses are instruments which are used to contact nature and gather information about objects. Mind is the overall instrument which controls and directs the senses. It is called the *antahkarana*, the inner instrument. Higher than the mind is the *buddhi* (intellect), which analyses and categorises the impressions gathered by the mind through the senses. The *buddhi* is subordinate to *chitta* (consciousness) and the ego, or the I-sense, which is fundamental to the individual." (3) "In the human being, the *antahkarana* (the inner instrument) is made up of the mind, the intellect, the will and the ego. The ego is linked to the life principle *(prana)*. It is encased in the *vignanamaya kosha* (the sheath of integrated awareness). The mind is linked to the *chitta* (will), and is encased in the *manomaya kosha* (the mental sheath). Thus, between the individual soul and the *prana* (vital principle), the mind functions. The life principle functions between the mind and the body. The *buddhi* (intellect) functions above the level of the mind. The *prana* (vital principle) is surcharged with *agni* (heat). It is their combined presence in the body that accounts for heat in the body.

"The mind should not be treated as something trivial. Man comprehends the world through the mind and hence its workings should be completely watched. Because the mind is located between *buddhi* (the intellect) and *prana* (the vital principle) - both of which are filled with the fire principle - it tends to melt. The presiding deity for the mind is the moon. The moon represents coolness and fluidity. Fluids like water have a tendency to flow down and find their level. Fire, on the contrary, has the tendency to go up. The mind, because of its watery nature, tends to move downwards, to become interested in petty things. Efforts have to be made to make the mind aim upwards.

"It should be remembered that the mind, the intellect, the will and the ego are made up of the five elements, which are all emanations from the Supreme, the *sath-chit-ananda* (being-awareness-bliss). This is the primal source from which they have emanated, like innumerable sparks from a fire." (4) "*Manas* exists in the cupola, *buddhi* in the tongue, *chitta* in the navel and *ahamkara* in the heart. (5)

Chitta is the internal mental consciousness. The general nature of the *chitta* is to waver and hesitate and flutter in its search for happiness and peace. When the *chitta* gives up the attachment to external objects, when it is saturated with repentance for past foolishness, when it is filled with remorse, renunciation and understanding, when it directly fosters the development of head and heart, then truly it becomes fit to join the ideal. Whatever ideas and pictures it may form, instruct it to find only God in those creations of the mind-stuff. Treat your *chitta* as a little boy. Never deal forcibly with the *chitta*, for it will yield easily to tenderness and patient training. During both the waking and the dreaming stage, as well as during all the process of mental spinning and weaving of colourful pictures by the imagination, the *chitta*, has to be watched and trained. It must be made to flow, single-pointed and steady like water from a sluice, towards *Brahman* and *Brahman* only." (6) "The waking state and the dreaming state are both of the nature of illusion. In both, we have the *vasanas* (desires, impulses, instincts) operating. The *jagat* (universe) is the stable illusion; the dream is the unstable illusion." (5)

"One important object of work is purification of the heart, or *chitta*." (7) "The heart is the consciousness. The heart that women talk about is the subconscious mind mixed up with their desire." (8) "The heart can be compared to the sky, the mind to the moon, and the intellect (*buddhi*) to the sun. The thoughts that are generated in the mind are like the clouds that pass away." (9) "When the clouds of ignorance, the fog of egoism and the smoke of attachment hover in the inner, the sun of intelligence is hidden and things look murky and are mistaken. The sun is always associated with wisdom and intelligence." (10)

"You have been told previously that, according to the *Upanishads*, the human body is a chariot — the sense organs being the horses, with the mind as the reins. However beautiful the chariot may be, however dependable the horses, however firm and secure the reins, all these are of no use if there is no charioteer. So also, however efficient the body, the senses and the mind may be, they serve no purpose in the absence of the charioteer, namely, *buddhi*, intellect. In life's journey, the intellect is of supreme importance. It is called *nischayatmika buddhi*, which means, that the *buddhi* has the decision-making capacity. In daily life, many difficulties, problems and disturbances arise from time to time. For overcoming all these obstacles, *buddhi* is our mainstay. Without the intervention of the *buddhi*, none of our problems can be solved. "*SamshayaAtma vinasyati*," says the *Gita*, which means that a man filled with doubts will perish. Because the *buddhi* destroys doubts, the *Gita* affirms, "*Buddhi grahayam atindriyam*," *buddhi* can grasp that which is beyond the grasp of the sense organs.

"*Antarvaani*, the inner voice is another name for the *buddhi*. Man is guided by this inner voice in the conduct of his life. Whenever problems arise, he awaits the directives of the inner voice. If satisfactory answers are not forthcoming from his inner voice, man can have no satisfaction in life. In other words, his satisfaction with the external world is a function of his satisfaction with his inner world represented by the inner voice. Sometimes you hear people saying, "my conscience is not satisfied; or my conscience does not approve of this." Here conscience refers to the inner voice. So, when you are exhorted to "Follow the Master," the Master stands for your conscience. Only when you follow the dictates of your conscience can you reach the right destination.

"The name *vignana* is also sometimes attributed to the *buddhi*. But it is not correct, because *vignana* means the so-called scientific or mundane knowledge which helps man to discover facts relating to the objective or phenomenal world, whereas *buddhi* is concerned with the subtle realm of the inner world. Hence the role of the *buddhi* should be correctly understood.

"Off and on, the *buddhi* tends to be covered by *ahamkara*, the ego sense. In this context, one should remember that the senses are subtler than the body, the mind is even more subtle than the senses, and the *buddhi* far more subtle than the mind. The *Atma*, of course, is subtlest of all. In the light of this fact, when we say that *ahamkara* is able to envelop *buddhi*, it means that *ahamkara* is subtler than *buddhi*. Thus, *ahamkara*, being extremely subtle, is all-pervasive and permeates all our actions. This is why man is unable to transcend *ahamkara* and experience the *Atma*, the Self.

"The *ahamkara* which veils the *buddhi*, and which leads one to the wrong identification of the body with the Self, must be removed before one can realise the *Atma*. The *buddhi* is very close to the *Atma* and, therefore, it is well located to receive ninety percent of the *Atmic* energy and illumination. The mind derives its power from the *buddhi*, the senses from the mind, and the body from the senses. In this process of the flow of power from the *Atma* to the body in stages, there occurs a gradual quantitative and qualitative diminution of the power.

"The purity of the *Atma* gets gradually contaminated as it passes through the *buddhi*, the mind and the senses, and finally reaches the body. Nevertheless, it is possible, through effort, to minimise this quantitative and qualitative deterioration by sanctifying and purifying the *buddhi* and by facilitating the direct influence of the *buddhi* on the body. In the *Taitiriya Upanishad*, which is one of the most important among the ten principal *Upanishads*, the *buddhi* is described as a bird. *Shraddha* (faith) is the head of the bird. Its right wing is *ritam* (the cosmic rhythm), and its left wing is *satyam* (truth). The main body of the bird is *mahat tatva* (the great principle), its tail is called *yoga*. The *buddhi* in its complete form is thus composed of five constituents and is extraordinarily powerful.

"Today's man has *shraddha*, no doubt, but only in securing the fruit and not in the labour required for getting it. He does not have the spirit of work in him. The advances in science and technology have made man a lover of comfort and ease with no interest in hard work. There is nothing wrong with science, as such. It is the improper use of science that is leading man astray. What is needed today is to pay attention to love and spiritual advancement along with scientific progress. The difference between science and spirituality is brought out vividly, albeit succinctly, by the two simple equations: 'The spirit of love is spirituality; splitting of love is science.' " (1)

" Most intellectuals today, not realising the supremacy of the *buddhi* and only relying on their intelligence, are ignoring their inherent Divinity. *Buddhi* is the Divine element in man, which is always shining effulgently. The *Gita* declares: The *buddhi* transcends the senses (*atheendriyam*). It is related to the Divine. What passes for the intellect today is divorced from the Divine and is not *buddhi* in its real sense. This intellect is limited in its capacity and is motivated by self-interest. Hence the power of discrimination of the *buddhi* is used by man for selfish purposes. All actions are based on self-interest (*swa-artha*) and not on higher values (*para-artha*). Actions which are free from self-interest lead to *taarakam* (liberation). Actions based on self-interest lead to *maarakam* (mortality). The difference between these two should be properly understood. All actions based on the *Atma-bhaava* (the *atmic* feeling) lead to liberation. All worldly actions are self-destroying (*maaraka*)." (18)

"When the pleasure-giving objects are transient, and when the body that enjoys the pleasure is also impermanent, how illogical it is to expect permanent happiness from the conveniences and comforts offered by science and technology! If you want permanent happiness, you have to purify your *antahkarana* and develop universal love by following the spiritual path.

"Today we are witnessing rapid and radical changes in almost every field of life: political, economic, social, scientific, etc. However, there is no mental, ethical and spiritual transformation. This is because no effort is made to understand the nature and role of the human mind. The food consumed by man provides the source of origin, sustenance and development of his mind. After digestion, the grossest part of the food is thrown out as excreta. The subtle part becomes blood and flesh, while the subtlest part assumes the form of the mind. So the nature of the mind depends on the quality and quantity of food consumed. While the gross body or the *annamaya kosha* (food sheath), is chiefly derived from food, the subtle part of the water we drink contributes to the *pranamaya kosha* (life sheath). The grosser part of the water goes out as urine. The food sheath and the life sheath provide the basis for the other three sheaths, namely, the *manomaya kosha* (the mental sheath), the *vignanamaya kosha* (the intellectual sheath), and the *anandamaya kosha* (the bliss sheath). This shows the paramount importance of food and drink in moulding and developing the human personality.

"The correct meaning of *ahamkara* (ego) is the mistaken identification of oneself with the body. Everyone is a victim of *ahamkara* in the sense of considering oneself to be the body. It is this *ahamkara* that shrouds the *buddhi* and misleads it onto the wrong path."

"*Buddhi* may be considered as the resound, reflection and reaction of the *Atma*. On the other hand, *medha shakti* (the power of worldly knowledge) corresponds to *maya shakti* (the Divine power of delusion)." (1) "The mind generates *sankalpa* (thought, resolution) which is checked and allowed to remain by the intelligence (*buddhi*). The *buddhi* alone has the power to make decisions and to discriminate between the good and the bad." (9) "The mind (*manas*) is preoccupied with distinctions and differences. The *buddhi* is concerned with oneness. The *buddhi* reveals the unity that underlies the diversity. (11) "Sharpen the intellect, then the unity in nature will become evident. The most revered and the most popular *mantra* in the *Vedas* is the *Gayatri*. It seeks the grace of the source, of all Light, to foster one's intelligence, and nothing more." (12)

"*Tamasic* food is deadening the intellect (*buddhi*)" (15). "The intelligence has to be kept sharp, clear and straight. There are four directions in which the intelligence guides man:

1. *Svartha sukha buddhi*: This indicates the fully egoistic nature, where the individual does not care for even his wife and children, but is eager to fulfil his own needs first and foremost.
2. *Svartha parartha sukha buddhi*: This allows some consideration for the happiness of others also. Birds feed their young and undergo great exertion to bring them up.
3. *Parartha buddhi*: Those who have this seek for others as much happiness as they seek for themselves. They are prepared to

"Buddhi, endowed with the power of discrimination and objectivity is superior to the mere intellectual ability which is termed medhas The worth of a human being is based on hi buddhi. The more the buddhi develops the better is one as a man." (Digest 2, pp.53).

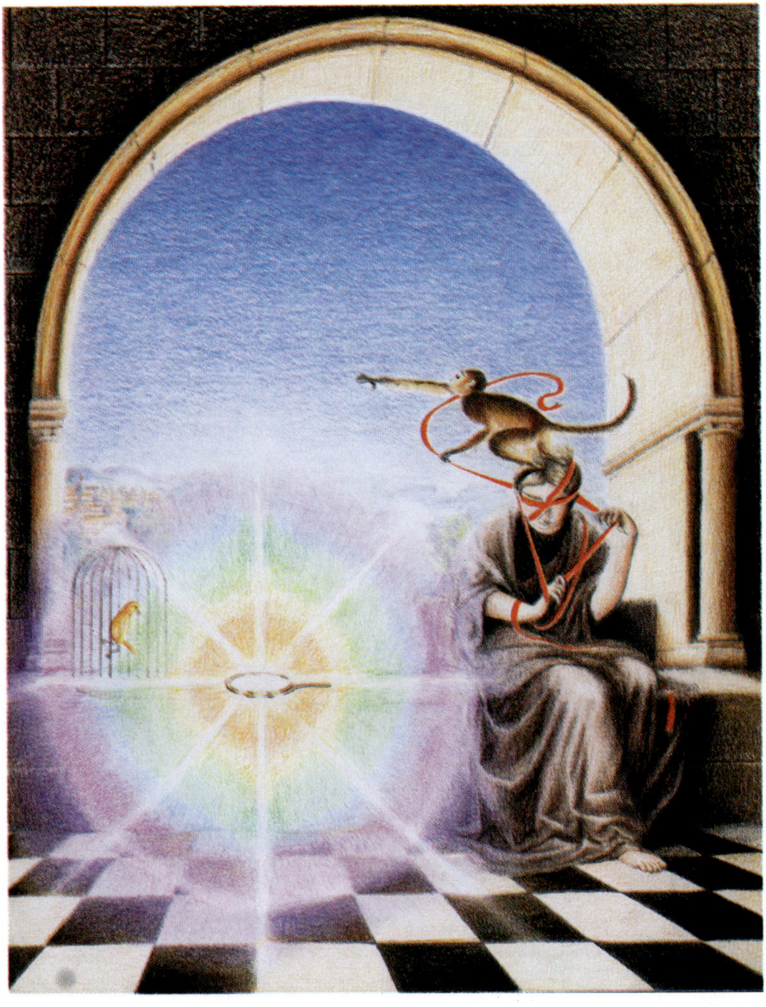

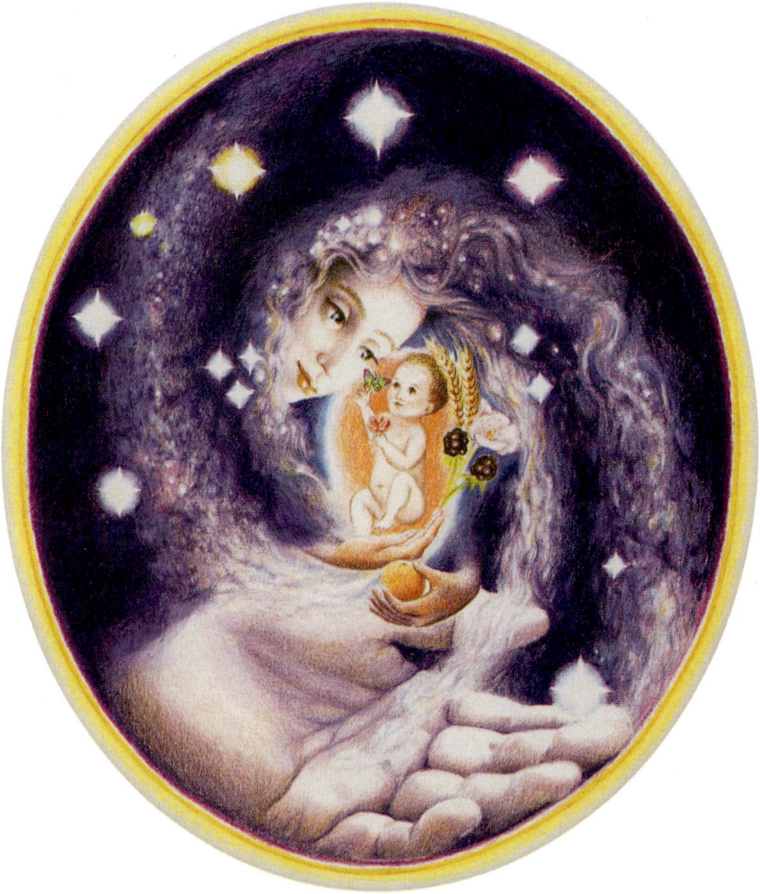

undergo any trouble to secure for others too, what they feel will grant them happiness.
4. *Adhyatmic buddhi:* This leads man ever on the path of renunciation and service, for they alone lead to spiritual advancement." (13)

"Though Rama resides in our own heart, Sita, i.e. our *buddhi*, is divorced from Rama. Why? Because the ten *indriyas* have taken Sita away to the golden Lanka of the sense-world. So we have to restore Rama Rajya in our hearts, by rescuing *buddhi* from the senses and making her sit side by side with Rama." (14)

"The ego in man sets him against all else; silence it and all become one's kith and kin. The ego is the first sprout from the seed of ignorance, which is not a positive acquisition, but only the absence of knowledge. When knowledge shines, inner and outer natures are both seen as Divine. There is nothing that is not IT. When this is experienced, love floods the heart and flows towards all. There is no independence: there is only interdependence, for all waves are equally dependent on the sea beneath. Egoism is the seedpot of greed, envy, anger, malice, conceit and a host of other down-dragging tendencies. They cloud the intelligence, they divert the attention from truth and make the false appear real, the real as distorted or false. So it is essential to cleanse the mind of these through regular *sadhana*, to tune the little will to the infinite will of God, so that it becomes merged in His glory. Scholarship and skill, however deep and varied, have no cleansing power. They only add the alloys of pride and competition. Learned men are not necessarily good, nor are men with spiritual powers over nature above pride, envy and greed.

"When man fails to use his attainments for the welfare of others, he becomes a *narakaasura*, hellish demon. But when in a competitive race for individual glory, he spends billions on getting to the moon and bringing rocks from its crust, instead of feeding millions who starve down below and promoting the prosperity of backward nations, he is only condemning himself. Even the best of things can be misused by men. Ravana, Shishupala, Kamsa, and other demonic persons mentioned in the Indian *Puranas* and epics, had vast scholarship, enormous economic and military power, and even immense *yogic* and occult skills won by years of austerity, and disciplined living. But they could not earn one skill - the skill to suppress the ego, and so, they became too obstinate, too obstructive and too dangerous to be allowed to live and prosper.

"The ego is most easily destroyed by *bhakthi* (devotion), by dwelling on the Lord and by rendering service to others as children of the Lord." (16)

"The root causes of man's bondage are *abhimana* (affectation) or *mamakara* (attachment or the possessive sense of mine) and *ahamkara* (egoism). Both *ahamkara* and *mamakara* are the result of consuming improper food. Bad kind of food, or food earned by foul means, will plunge a man in ignorance in several ways and suppress pure thoughts from arising in him. He will forget what to talk to whom, when, where and how. You must realise that food is mainly responsible for your feeling of *raga* and *dvesha* (attachment and hatred), as well as for *ahamkara* and *mamakara*, (I and mine). Regulating your food habits is extremely important for the healthy functioning of mind and the intellect." (1)

"The *ahamkara* (ego), is the exterior I. The *Atma* is the inner I, the real I. Persons who do not know this distinction confuse themselves and assert that I is applicable to the *dehatma*. But this is wrong. The body is a tool, it is an object; it is the seen and not the see-er.

How can the ego, identified with it, be the *Atma*? This ego is also of the seen category. It is absent in sleep and plays false in dreams. Truth has to persist unaffected, in the past, present and future. That which is absent in two states, how can it be true?" (17). "One may have a dream that one is a child, that one attends school, makes friends, marries, is a father and has a career - a sequence of events that covers forty-five years of one's life. The dream may occur at 3.15 a.m. and be over by 3.17 a.m. In two minutes of dreaming time the dreamer has experienced events that extend through forty-five years of waking time. When the waking state is transcended, it also is seen to be a dream, and a lifetime in the waking state has taken only a few moments in the transcendental state. The waking state is seen to be a dream, and the dream state, a dream within a dream. The dream state is unreality in truth; the waking state is truth in unreality; and the transcendental state is truth in truth. The I in the dream state is taken to be the mind. And the I in the transcendental state is God." (18)

"The causal body is of great importance to all of us, for in this state, man can bring under his control *manas, buddhi, chitta and ahamkara*. The causal body is made of the two principles of *chitta* (reflexive mind) and *pragna* (constant integrated awareness). Man has to travel from the gross body to the super-causal body crossing the causal body in between. Man is the repository of all powers, for all powers are encased in him. There is nothing that man cannot understand in the world as he is endowed with infinite and marvellous powers." (19)

Bibliography:

1. Sathya Sai Baba, *Summer Showers in Brindavan*, 1990, pp. 88–95, 101, 104
2. Sathya Sai Baba, *Discourses on the Bhagavad Gita,* Compiled and edited by A. Drucker, First Indian edition, 1988, pp. 112
3. *Sathya Sai Speaks,* Vol. VII, Sec. Am. Printing, 1985, p.370
4. Sathya Sai Baba, *Sanathana Sarathi,* November 1988, p. 293
5. Sathya Sai Baba, *Sandeha Nivarini,* 1985, pp. 38, 109
6. *Sadhana, The Inward Path,* Quotations from the Divine Discourses of Sathya Sai Baba, 1976, pp. 131–133
7. Sathya Sai Baba, *Sanathana Sarathi,* August 1985, pp. 204
8. J. S. Hislop, *Conversations with Bhagawan Sri Sathya Sai Baba,* pp. 10–107, 117–118
9. Sathya Sai Baba, *Summer Showers in Brindavan* 1979, pp. 74, 116
10. Sathya Sai Baba, *Geetha Vahini* pp. 164-165
11. Sathya Sai Baba, *Sanathana Sarathi,* April 1983, pp. 81

12. *Sadhana, The Inward Path,* Quotations from the Divine Discourses of Sathya Sai Baba, 1976, pp. 142
13. Tumuluru Krishna Murty, *Digest, Collection of Sri Sathya Sai Baba's Sayings,* pp. 147
14. *Lessons for Study Circle,* 1982, pp. 91
15. Sathya Sai Baba, *Sanathana Sarathi,* April 1976, pp. 44
16. *Voice of the Avatar,* Extracts from the Divine Discourses of Sathya Sai Baba, Part I, Compiled by D. Hejmadi, M.Sc., Second Edition 1981, pp. 113–118.
17. Sathya Sai Baba, *Sathya Sai Vahini,* pp. 188
18. Sathya Sai Baba, *Sanathana Sarathi,* December 1992, pp. 308
19. Sathya Sai Baba, *Summer Showers in Brindavan,* 1993, pp. 3, 41

NOTE: The two schemes form a unity and are from the writer. They put things together and show levels.

AKASHA universe	DEHA body	TRIMURTI trinity	State of conciousness
BRAHMAN PARAMATMA Divine principle	MAHAKARANA DEHA supercausal body	ATMA soul, spirit	TURIYAVASTHA transcendntal superconcious
CHIDAKASHA causal universe	KARANA DEHA causal body	higher mind supermind	PRAGNAVASTHA SUSHUPTI deep sleep state unconscious state
CHITTAKASHA subtle universe of themind mental world (5 subtle elements)	SUKSHMA DEHA subtle body mental body (5 subtle elements)	mind	SVAPNAVASTHA dream state subconscious state
BHUTAKASHA gross, physical universe (5 elements)	STHULA DEHA gross, physical body (5 elements)	body	JAGRATAVASTHA waking state conscious state

KOSHA sheath	19 bodily principles	CHAKARA centre of consciousness	human values element
		SAHASRARA on the crown of the head	
ANANDAMAYA KOSHA pragna, equanimity, intuition, superintellectual, bliss sheath	CHITTA in the navel, internal mental consciousness, (heart), memory, will, feeling	AGNA (AGNEYA) between the eyebrows	AHIMSA PREMA
VIGNANAMAYA KOSHA reason-based, logical, intellectual, discriminatory (right-wrong sheath)	AHAMKARA ego, in the heart BUDDHI in the tongue, inner voice, conscience, intuitive intellect unifying, internally oriented	VISSHUDDHA larynx	SATYA AKASHA (ether, space sound)
MANOMAYA KOSHA mental, emotional, volitional, imagination-centred, symbol-dealing sheath	MANAS in the cupola, lower mind, thoughts, pros and cons, desires, doubts, preoccupied with differences externally oriented	ANAHATA heart, essence of life between the ninth and twelfth ring	SHANTI PREMA VAYU air (breathing)
PRANAMAYA KOSHA vital, nerve-centred sheath, breathing, physical energy	5 PRANAS 5GNANEN DRIYAS senses of perception	MANIPURA stomach	PREMA JALA water (blood)
		SVADHISTANA navel, guardian of pranamaya kosha	AGNI fire (heat)
ANNAMAYA KOSHA food, material, muscular sheath	5 KARMEN DRIYAS organs of action	MULADHARA kundalini PRAKRITI (nature)	DHARMA PRITHVI earth

13. THE MANAS, THE CHITTA, THE BUDDHI AND THE AHAMKARA – II

"The 'I' principle is present everywhere. It began with the Divine itself. The first word was *aham* ('I'). Even the *pranava* (Om) came after *aham*. Before all creation, *aham* alone existed. That aham became the may. The sense of duality arises when the 'I' (*aham*) assumes a specific form and name" (1). In the *Atma* the *aham* abides as a subtle entity. When the *aham* acquires a form, it becomes *ahamkara* (ego). To identify the *aham* with the corporeal form is *ahamkara*, the ego feeling." (2)

"The ego is associated with the three *gunas: satva, rajas* and *tamas*." (3) "The ego is the core of the personality." (4) "That which is attached to the body and fees as 'I' is the *Jiva*, The *Jiva* is outward-faced. What is the relation between the *Jiva* which says 'I' and the senses and the body? There is body, the mind, etc. The 'I' is separate from the body, the mind, etc. The 'I' simply superimposes on jiva, that is itself, the body-consciousness, and the internal behaviours of the mind, etc. The atma observes everything and its shadow the jiva, which is deluded by the association of the body-consciousness, plays this drama through all its acts." (5)

"Every human being has three bodies (*tripuras*, three cities). The gross body, the subtle body and the casual body. The three puras are the body, the mind and the heart." (2)

"During the phases of dreams, man turns into himself. The individual is busy with his memory and the plans and projects the mind has played with. The dream has validity for the dreamer, it absorbs light from the deeper levels of consciousness; it reveals the latent through inner luminosity. In the dream state, only the four internal senses - the mind, the buddhi, the chitta (subconscious mind) and the ahamkara - function. They constitute the antahkarana (the psychosomatic energy)" (1).

"Men are accustomed to treat the mind as part of the body. This relates only to the sensory activities of the mind. This mind

(*Manas*) is made up of thoughts and doubts. But the mind that is associated with the divine atma transcends the body. Consequently, it is only when the ordinary thought processes are extinguished that the divinity within can be experienced." (2) "Manas or mind is but a bundle of thoughts, a complex of wants and wishes. As soon as a thought, a desire or a wish raises its head from the mind, buddhi must probe into its value and validity, is it good or bad? Will it help or hinder? Where will this lead or end?" (6)

"*Manas* grasps the object; *buddhi* examines arguments for or against; *chitta* understands the object by means of these; *ahamkara* changes the decision for or against and by attachment., slackens the hold of gnana." (5) When desires and plans, wishes and yearning roll along, we call it *chitta*. When the white cloth is dirty, it is mind (*manas*) and when the whiteness is restored, it is *chitta*. The *chitta* is the source and support of the resolutions. All resolutions, delusions and plans are the produce of *chitta*. They originate there and are registered there." (7)

"Man's worth has declined today because he does not recognize the importance of the *buddhi*. The form is human but the thinking is at the animal level. The buddhi is superior to the more intellectual ability which is termed medhas." (6) "The *medhas* is related to the instruments of perception and action (*indriyas*). The *medhas* is described as the control-room; it controls the indriyas. The *buddhi* is not related to the body and transcends the *indriyas*." (2)

"Human intelligence is restricted. It can deal only with facts discoverable by the senses and experiences related to these. It an act only in the area of the visible, the viable. But the intellect (buddhi) subjected to the processes of cleansing and sharpening in the Vedic way can serve us by presenting a picture of the full truth of the objective world." (8) "The *buddhi* should not be confused with medhas which refers to the possession of worldly talents, intelligence and cleverness, without having self-knowledge." (6)

"There is a vital difference between medha-shakthi (intelligence) and *buddhi*. Intelligence exists as physical entity in man. It is the centre of the nervous system. A kind of control-room for man. The *buddhi* is not related to the physical body or to the physical phenomenal world. By its relationship to the atma, it has divine attributes." (9)

"Another name attributed to *buddhi* is *vignana* (confirmed knowledge). *Vignana* helps to decide the truth relating to external objects. As the *buddhi* investigates internal processes also and comes to decisions on them, it is not entirely correct to describe it as vignana. *Vignana* relates to the phenomenal objective world. *Buddhi* relates to the subtle realm of the internal. Hence the role of the intellect (*buddhi*) has to be correctly understood.

"The eleven *rudras* - the five organs of perception, the five organs of action and the mind - turn the buddhi towards sensuous objects and thrust the individual in the sea of samsara (wordly life)." (6)

"The bird of buddhi, in addition to *shraddha* (faith), has *satya* and *rita* as two wings. *Rita* represents the triple purity - of thought, word and deed - that transcends time and space. The bird's tail is *yoga*. It is through *yoga* that balance is maintained early only when it is governed by *satya*, *rita* and *yoga*. *Yoga* here means control of the senses. What is *mahat tatva*? It is the recognition of the *buddhi* of the true nature of the Self (*Atma*). The buddhi could be described as an image of the atma, a reaction and an echo of the *Atma*." (9) "Man's most precious and sacred gift from God is the intellect (*buddhi*). Use the mirror of the *buddhi* to recognize your true Self." (2)

When the mind is free of the dirt and impurities of the sense - organs, it is described as *chitta*. When it is associated with the sense-organs, it is *manas*, the impure mind (6).

"Man commits many offences, knowingly or unknowing, not only in this life, but also to backlog from previous lives. The imprint of these actions is carried by the chitta (memory) life after life, like the dust accumulating on the surface of the mirror day by day. It is necessary to cleanse this mirror of the impurities covering it. This cleansing is done by regulating one's food and other living habits including recreation. This requires persistent and prolonged practice." (6) *Chitta* is concerned with contemplation." (2)

"The *buddhi* and the *ahamkara* are the most important places. There will be no misery when these two are made pure." (5)

References:

1. *Discourses by Bhagavan Sri Sathya Sai Baba*, Compiled by Tajmool Hosein and Kuntle Mathura, Volume 2, Ace Printerey, Tunapuna, Trinidad, 1989. pp. 1.36, 58.
2. *Discourses by Bhagavan Sri Sathya Sai Baba*, Compiled by Tajmool Hosein and Kuntle Mathura, Volume 4, (1991-1992) Ace Printerey, Tunapuna, Trinidad, 1993(1991-1992). pp. 148, 171-172, 262, 377.
3. Bhagavan Sri Sathya Sai Baba, *Summer Showers in Brindavan*, 1973, pp. 216.
4. D. Hejmadi, M.Sc., De Stem van de Avatar (*Voice of the Avatar*), Holland, 1995, pp. 138
5. Bhagavan Sri Sathya Sai baba, *Sandeha Nivarini*, 1985, pp. 38-39, 54, 106.
6. Tumuluru Krishna Murty, Digest 2. *Collections of Sri Sathya Sai Baba's Sayings*, India, 1994, pp. 53, 202, 212, 264, 274.
7. M.N. Rao, *Our God and Your Mind*, M. Srininvas, Prasanthi Nilayam, India, 1992, pp. 278.
8. Bhagavan Sri Sathya Sai Baba, *Sathya Sai Vahini*, pp. 152-177.
9. *Discourses by Bhagavan Sri Sathya Sai Baba*, Compiled by Tajumool Hosein and Kunti Mathura, Volume 3, Ace Printery, Tunapuna, Trinidad, 1991, pp. 189, 262, 265,

14. KNOW THYSELF

O Gudakesha! Conqueror of sleep, Arjuna!
I am the Atma residing in all beings
I am also the beginning, the middle and the end of all beings.

"In the above verse of the *Gita*, Krishna tells Arjuna, 'I am the *Atma*, the Self, residing in all beings; I am also the beginning, the middle and the end of all beings.' That is to say, that the entire cosmos consisting of moving and non-moving objects, is only the *Atma*. Nothing exists other than the *Atma*, or the Self. What today's man needs to do is to constantly contemplate on the Self, to realise the Self, to be firmly established in the Self and to experience the bliss of the Self.

"*Atma* is also known as awareness. It is this awareness that is responsible for the 'I' consciousness in all beings, which is called *aham*. When this *aham* identifies itself with the body, it becomes *ahamkara*. This is the false I, and not the real I. What hides the *Atma* is always the mind. The clouds which are formed due to the sun's heat hide the sun itself. Likewise the mind, which is the offspring of the *Atma*, hides the *Atma* itself. As long as the mind is there, man cannot hope to understand anything about the Self, not to speak of realising and experiencing the bliss of the Self. That state in which one is established in the Self at all times and under all circumstances, is called *Sakshatkara* (Self-realisation).

"The first sound that emanated from the Self was 'I' The entire creation began only after the emanation of this 'I' sound. If there is no 'I' there is no (I) creation. The terms 'I', *Brahman*, *Atma* or Self are all synonymous. The I without mind is the *Atma*, or the Self, in its pristine purity. The 'I' associated with the mind is the false self, or *mithya Atma*. There is only one *Atma*, or Self, and that is the 'I'.

"The paradox, however, is that to experience his own reality, man is undertaking several *sadhanas* or spiritual practices. All such practices undertaken for seeking the Self are activities in which man engages himself during the state of *agnana* (ignorance) only. You will not find the *gnani* (the realised one) doing such *sadhana*, because for him, there is no distinction such as the means and the end. If man is practising *sadhana*, it is merely for his mental satisfaction. Such practices, when pursued for mental satisfaction, will only serve the purpose of strengthening the mind instead of destroying it, as recommended in the teachings of *Vedanta*. If at all you want to do *sadhana*, the only right approach to it is to dispel the *anatmabhava* (the false notion of the 'non-self'). If, instead of doing this right thing, you go on worshipping three million gods and goddesses, disregarding the common truth taught by all the Scriptures of the world, that there is only one God, or if you pursue all sorts of so-called *sadhanas* to attain Self-realisation and liberation, what does it indicate other than your mental aberrations, hallucinations and delusions?

"It is important to recognise that as long as the mind is there, desires will not leave you. As long as you have desires, the false notion of 'I' and 'mine' will not leave you. As long as the feeling of 'I' and 'mine' is there, *ahamkara* (your wrong identification with the body) will not leave you. As long as *ahamkara* does not leave you, *agnana* (ignorance) too, will not leave you. In effect, it means that there is no way other than the annihilation of the mind to attain *Atmagnana* (knowledge of the Self), or *Atmadarshan* (vision of the Self), or *Atmananda* (bliss of the Self), whatever you may choose to call it.

"The right kinds of *sadhana* for seeking the *Atma* are only those that are directed toward the destruction of the mind. Because of his identification with his body, man is being helplessly tossed hither and thither in various ways by his ego. 'I am doing this; I am enjoying that; I have conquered this,' thus saying to himself, man is lending strength day by day to his sense of *kartritvabhava* (doership). Remember that success and failure do not depend on your efforts, or *sadhana*, and such other activities. You are simply inflating your *ahamkara* (ego) by deluding yourself that you have been able to achieve things by your own effort. Look around and see the many instances where the best of efforts have not been crowned with success, while, with little or no effort, victory has come unsought in the case of many others.

"You become frustrated because your self-reliant efforts have not been crowned with success. While, with little or no effort, you can surely win success by dedicating all your activities to the Divine, by considering them as the Lord's work, and by undertaking them with unwavering faith in God. All things happen according to the *Daiva sankalpam* (Divine Will). By your own effort you cannot achieve anything. You should have the firm conviction that nothing happens due to human effort. Proof of this assertion need not be sought for in some far-off place. It can be found right within your own body. For instance, what effort are you making for the ceaseless beating of your heart or for the incessant breathing of your lungs? Does the digestion of the food eaten by you take place because of your will? Are you able to live because you want to live, or die because you want to die? Does your birth take place according to when and where you desire? If you ponder deeply along these lines of thought, you will discover that your feelings of *ahamkara* and *mamakara* ('I' and 'mine') are being unduly fostered by your false sense of doership and enjoyership.

"Today we are preoccupied with various activities just for our mental satisfaction. But the mind never knows any satisfaction, whatever we may do and for however long. Mind alone is *maya*. Mind alone is desire. Mind itself is *avidya* (ignorance). Mind alone is *prakriti* (nature). And mind alone is delusion. Deeply immersed in this *bhrama*, how can you hope to attain *Brahman*, without getting rid of your *bhrama* ? Seeing your own shadow, you are trembling with fear! You are afraid of your own feelings and imaginations! However, reality is One, *ekam sat,* and that is *Atma*.

"There is some mighty power, unknown to me, different from me and far away from me, thinking thus, some people resort to meditation. There is some secret and sacred Divine power distinctly separate from me and I must acquire it, imagining thus, some others observe many vows, perform several rites and undertake various austerities. All this is sheer ignorance. As long as you think there is anything different from you, so long are you submerged in ignorance, there is nothing in the universe other than, or higher than, you. To think otherwise or to try to prove otherwise is nothing but your *manobhranti* (mental delusion), resembling a dream.

"In your dream you see many sights and experience various things, but for how long are they real? Only as long as your dream lasts. When the dream ends, they are all unreal. Similarly, your hardships, losses, worry and sorrow, etc. are real only as long as your mind is under delusion. Once the delusion leaves you, they will all be unreal. They will then turn out to be castles of myths created by your mind. Relying on the false 'I', you are rejecting the real 'I'. You are boosting your *ahamkara* by thinking continually that you are the body.

"If only we can understand one small but subtle truth, we can expand the horizons of our thoughts and feelings to any extent. There is nothing other than the Self in the universe. All the things you see as existing in the phenomenal world are but reflections of the One Self. *Atmagnana* (Self-knowledge) reveals itself after the annihilation of the mind. You see the phenomenal universe only as long as you have not crossed the threshold of the mind. Once you go beyond the mind, you will experience nothing but the Self.

"*Bhakti* is the best means to experience *Atmagnana* and to enjoy *Atmananda* (the bliss of the Self). What is *bhakti*? It is constant contemplation on the Self. *Bhakti* and *gnana* are not two different things. *Bhakti* itself is *gnana*. And *gnana* itself is *bhakti*. They are closely inter-related and interdependent. The singular bond that unites *bhakti* and *gnana* is *prema* (Divine Love). With this sacred cord of *prema*, you can bind the Lord Himself.

"All the differences you find in the world are only reflections of your mind. Whether you love someone or hate someone or ridicule somebody, they are all merely your own reflections. If you give up these reactions, resounds and reflections of your mind, which appear to you in the phenomenal world, and get hold of the spiritual heart called reality, then all these differences in thoughts, feelings, actions, etc. would disappear. God does not have thoughts and feelings of any kind. But He appears to respond suitably according to the thoughts, feelings, attitudes, and actions, like worship, prayer, etc. of the devotees. He has no likes and dislikes. Nor is He angry with some and pleased with some others. He does not have moods that change from time to time in respect of the same person or different persons, as is imagined by many of you. Of course, as a result of putting on a body, the Divine, *Avatars* also appear to have such reactions, resounds and reflections, but it is only to set an example to others and to help them to reform themselves, so that they may make the needed progress on their spiritual journey. God does not differentiate or discriminate between 'high' caste and 'low' caste, between the young and the old, between men and women, between people of one country and another, etc. These are all mundane differences pertaining to the phenomenal world but have nothing to do with Divinity.

"Living in this vast universe, you must develop broad thoughts and feelings to understand the nature of the infinite *Atma*. Spirituality should not be approached from a narrow standpoint. Doing worship, *bhajans* (devotional singing), meditation and the like are considered by many as signs of spirituality. But all these are only mental aberrations and serve to give only mental satisfaction to the practitioners. You praise God, saying, 'Lord, you are my mother, my father, my friend," and so on. But why all this mumbo-jumbo or gibberish? Why not simply say, 'You are I, I am You,' and be done with it? You should visualise and realise the unity of the body and the *hridayam* or *Atma*.

"Spirituality means merger with God. You are not different from God. You are God, God is you. If you are firmly established in this faith, you need not undertake any other *sadhana* or spiritual practices. There is only one God who appears to have assumed all the names and forms of all gods and goddesses, as well as of all beings in the entire universe. You should have unshakeable faith in the unity of Godhead and assert, 'I am you, you are I; we are not two, but one.'

"Your mind is the cause of your inability to understand the real nature of this world. The characteristic of the mind is *pravritti* (external orientation). Man is wasting his life, night and day, for acquiring external things like houses, lands, vehicles, wealth and other so-called properties which, in fact, are not 'proper ties'. Is it for the sake of these trifles that man is born? No, No, No. To realise God is his foremost task in life. Man must realise God, feel God, see God and talk to God. This is realisation. This is religion.

"According to one of the most important mantras in the *Veda*, immortality can be obtained only by *tyaga* (renunciation), and not by good actions, progeny or wealth, etc. But what exactly is renunciation? It does not mean giving up one's wife and children, or house and other properties. What actually is your bondage? It is the delusion of your identification with the body. You must give up the false idea that you are the body and imbibe the truth that you are the *Atma*. Then alone can you achieve *moksha* (liberation). *Deha virakti* (detachment from the body consciousness) will free you from the grief of bondage, and *daiva asakti* (attachment of God) will give you the bliss of *moksha* (liberation and merger with God).

"How to get rid of *deha bhranti* (body consciousness)? Not by giving up food and drink, reducing the body to a skeleton and courting death, but by asserting with faith that I am not the body. The body, the senses, the mind and the intellect are all my instruments. You must give up your body consciousness, just like removing your soiled clothes.

"You are the very embodiment of bliss. Bliss is your very nature. But it is a tragedy that you are unable to recognise it and to experience it. This bliss is veiled by likes and dislikes, the sense of 'I' and 'mine', hesitation and doubt, pleasure and displeasure, etc. Attachment and hatred are the thick clothes which shroud the bliss in you. When you get rid of attachment and hatred you can discover your own real nature. How strange and foolish it is that despite yourself being the very embodiment of bliss, you are searching for bliss elsewhere! Although everything is within you, you are unfortunately running after petty desires and silly sensual pleasures in the phenomenal world. What is the reason for this mad race? Ignorance of the truth that you are yourself the source of all bliss.

"Lured by the momentary sensuous worldly pleasures, man is unable to seek, to understand and to enjoy the supreme Divine bliss. The sages have named the *Atma* as *ananda* and described it variously as eternal bliss, supreme bliss, absolute bliss, bliss of wisdom, bliss transcending all the pairs of opposites, pure bliss, unshakeable bliss, bliss that is beyond the grasp of the mind, bliss which transcends the three *gunas*, and so on. When such a priceless treasure of bliss is readily available within you, why should you foolishly run after this phenomenal world which brings trials and tribulations, sufferings and sorrow?" (1)

"The *Atmic* power that vibrates and shines in the food sheath is known as bodily consciousness; the *Atmic* power that functions in the vital sheath is called nervous consciousness; the *Atmic* power that activates the mental sheath is known as mental consciousness; the *Atmic* power that shines in the intellectual sheath is termed as intellectual consciousness. The power that pulsates the bliss sheath is called 'Pure Divine Self' (*Pavithra Purushaartha*). This is also known as 'all infinite Will'. It is this infinite Will which protects the world. It is pure ecstasy.

"The *Vedanta* declares that he who knows himself, knows all. You should make the right endeavour to know yourself. You can know yourself by developing inner vision, rather than outward vision. All sensory activities like sound, smell, touch and taste are only external activities. We delude ourselves into thinking that these activities are real, and ruin ourselves ultimately. It is by harnessing the mind that we will be able to realise the Divinity within.

"In every man there is mind, supermind, higher mind, illuminated mind and overmind. Man remains only man as long as he rests in the mind. He should attain the state of *amanaska*, where the mind is extinguished. *Amanaska* is one who travels beyond the physical mind and enters into the realms of the supermind. The body is the source of all doubts and debilities. The supreme quality that everyone should cultivate is *Atma visvasa* (Self-confidence).

"The mind manifests its influence in the state of *jagrata* (waking) and *svapna* (dream). The mind comes to a standstill in the state of deep sleep. Here the mind shines as super-intellectual consciousness. In this state mind ushers in the state of supermind. The supermind enjoys a state of serenity without delusion. It is when we attain this state of steady and unruffled serenity that we can reach the lofty heights of the overmind.

"While the ordinary mind triggers action in the waking state, it is the supermind which activates the dream state. The joy derived in the deep sleep state is attributed to the higher mind. This is associated with the causal body, which is of great importance to all of us for in this state, man can bring under his control *manas*, *buddhi*, *chitta* and *ahamkara*. The causal body is made of the two principles of *chitta* (reflexive mind) and *pragna* (constant integrated awareness).

"The *mahakarana* is responsible for all that happens in the universe. It is the illuminated mind, the power that illuminates everything in the world. To experience this cosmic principle we need a Divine form. This is the superdivine Self. It is called *Purushatva*, which is, in fact, the overmind. The super-causal body, also known as the overmind, is self-resplendent, self-luminous and self-radiant. Man has to travel from the supermind to the overmind to understand Divinity. How can we reach this overmind? The *Vedic* injunction is: 'you should always be a *yogi*; you should practise *yoga* at all times and in all places.' " (2)

References :
1. Sathya Sai Baba, *Summer Showers in Brindavan, 1990,* pp. 115 - 127, 140 - 142, 147 - 152
2. Sathya Sai Baba, *Summer Showers in Brindavan, 1993*, pp. 2 - 3, 9, 19 - 20, 24, 41, 45 - 46

PART II

HEALTH, FOOD AND SPIRITUALITY

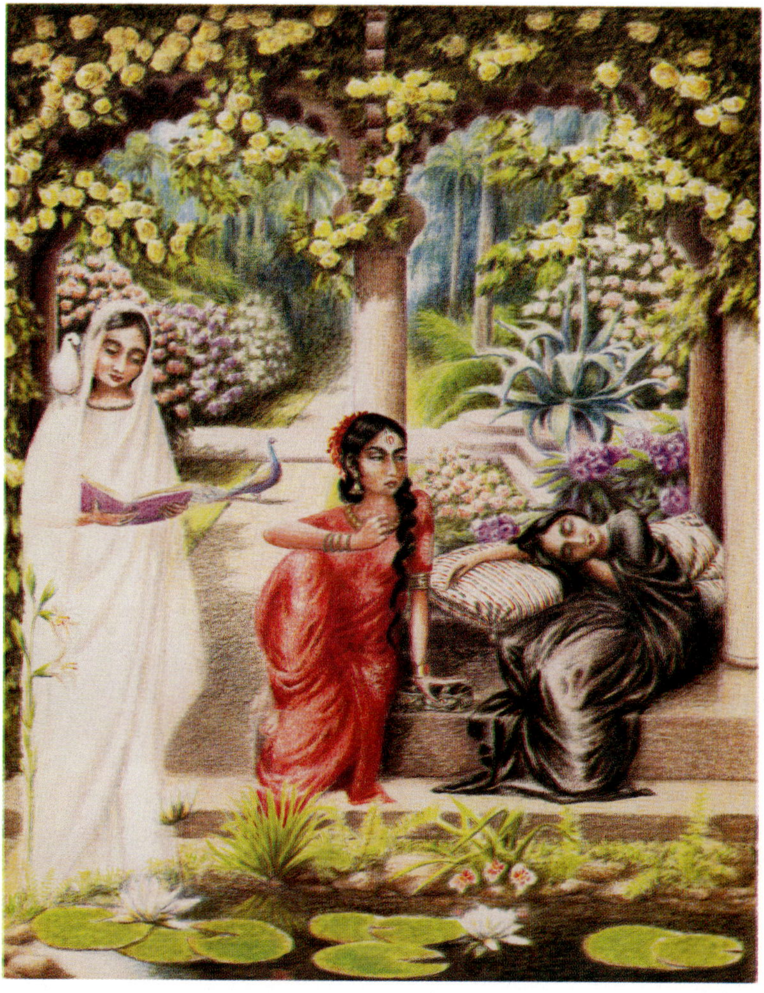

15. THE THREE GUNAS

"To bring out the Divine aspect in nature and make it manifest, all things have been endowed with certain *gunas* (qualities). They are *satva, rajas* and *tamas*. To endow nature with these qualities, certain intermediaries are necessary. These have been described as *Brahma, Vishnu* and *Maheshvara*. *Brahma, Vishnu* and *Maheshvara* are not entities with forms. The Trinity represents, the deified expression of the three qualities. The *puranas* have misrepresented *Brahma* as a four-headed deity engaged in cosmic creation. This is not correct. In fact, the Trinity represents the three *gunas*.

"*Ishvara, Vishnu* and *Brahma* symbolise the heart, the mind and the faculty of *vak* (speech). The combination of all the three represents the *Atma*. Hence, each of the three should be revered as the one supreme *guru* in three forms.

"What is the role of the *guru*? It is the total removal of the darkness of ignorance. As long as there are the three *gunas*, there can be no freedom from darkness. It is only when one transcends the three *gunas* that one attains the state of the *guru*. Alternatively, when one realises the unity of the three *gunas*, the message of the *guru* is comprehended. The import of the unity of the three *gunas* is indicated in the *Gita* declaration: '*Mamatma sarvabhutatma*.' (My *Atma* is the in-dwelling spirit in all beings).

"It is on account of the varied functioning of the three *gunas* that the process of creation, growth and dissolution takes place. The three *gunas* are the primal source, the basis and the life-breath of the universe. They are responsible for the manifestations and transformations in nature. The permutations and combinations of three *gunas* in varying proportions account for infinite diversity in the cosmos.

"Three colours have been ascribed to the three *gunas*. It is commonly believed that *Vishnu* represents the *satvaguna*. It is not so. The *satvaguna* is really the attribute of *Ishvara*. It is not subject to *maya*. In the state of *yogic* sleep (*yoga nidra*), it acquires the *chit shakti* (the power of awareness) and appears as *shuddha Atma* (the pure Absolute). Hence *satva* represents the *Ishvara* principle. Its colour is white.

"The *rajoguna* manifests itself in likes and dislikes. It used to be associated with *Brahma*. But this is wrong. It is a quality associated with *Vishnu*. *Vishnu* bears the name, *Vishvambhara*, one who protects and rules over the universe. As a *raja* (ruler), he has the *rajoguna*. The colour of *rajoguna* is red.

"Then there is *Brahma*. The *rajoguna* has been attributed to *Brahma*. This is incorrect. *Brahma* represents *tamoguna*. *Tamoguna* is associated with *murkhatwam* (irrationality) and the darkness of *andhakara* (ignorance). It is filled with *mamakara* (the sense of possessiveness) and *abhimana* (attachment). These two impulses account for creation. If there were no sense of 'I' and 'mine', the creative process would not go on. These two are the insignia of *tamoguna*, which is represented by the black colour.

"White, red and black are the most important colours. All colours are merged in these three. Likewise, there are in the world people with *satvaguna*, *rajoguna* or *tamoguna* who are distinguished by one or other of the three colours." (1)

"The entire cosmos consisting of living and inanimate objects is permeated by the three *gunas*. Man should strive to understand the principle that transcends the three *gunas*. To start with, the *pancha bhutas* (the five subtle elements of space, air, fire, water and earth) emerged from the *Atma*. Each of the five subtle elements is constituted of the three *gunas*. Under the influence of these three *gunas*, the five subtle elements evolved into the five gross elements and the entire cosmos through the process of *panchikritam* (fusion by permutation and combination).

"The cosmos is permeated by the three *gunas*, *satva*, *rajas* and *tamas*. At first the nature of creation due to the *satvaguna* has to be clearly understood. The *antahkarana* (the inner instrument) in human beings represents the total *satvic* quality of the five elements. *Akasha* (space) is the first among the five elements. From *akasha* emerged what is known as *shuddha satva* (pure *satva*). This accounts for the human form. The *satvic* aspect of *akasha* accounts also for the emergence of the organ of hearing, the ear. The second element is air. The skin is the product of the *satvic* component of air. The eye is the organ representing the *satvic* principle of the fire element. The individualised *satvic* aspect of the fourth element, water, is the tongue.

"The nose represents the individualised *satvic* aspect of the fifth element, the earth. Thus the *satvic* components of these five elements account for the five faculties of *shabda* (sound), *sparsha* (touch), *rupa* (sight), *rasa* (taste) and *gandha* (smell). As each of these faculties has emerged from only one particular element, the five faculties are distinct in every person and perform different functions without any overlap.

"While each of the sense organs is limited functionally to its specific role, the *antahkarana* combines the functions of all the five organs, because it is the cumulative product of all the five elements. This alone has the capacity to experience all the perceptions of the five *gnanendriya* (senses). Do these organs of perception function externally or internally? The answer is that they perform a dual role, both internal and external. If only the physical organ, the ear, is present, but the faculty of hearing is absent, the ear cannot hear. If the faculty of hearing is present, but there is no ear to receive sounds from the outside world, the faculty is of no use. It is the combined operation of the five *gnanendriya* (external organs of perception) and the corresponding invisible internal sense centres in the brain, that account for the functioning of the human personality. For example, if you want your voice to reach a vast audience, you should have the microphone near you and the loudspeaker further away. A loudspeaker without a microphone or vice versa cannot serve the purpose.

"While the combined operation of the five elements in their *satvic* aspect is seen in the *antahkarana*, the collective functioning of the five elements in their *rajasic* aspect expresses itself as the *prana* (life-force). Among the five elements, in their individual expression of their *rajasic* quality, *akasha* (space) is represented by the *vak* (voice). *Vayu* (air) finds expression in the hand. *Agni* (fire) expresses itself in its individualised *rajoguna* as the foot. The fourth and fifth elements (water and earth) find *rajasic* expression in the two excretory organs in the body.

"In this context, you must take note of some significant facts in the functioning of these elements. In its *satvic* aspect, *akasha* (space) expresses itself as ear. But the same *akasha*, in its *rajasic* aspect appears as the *vak* (faculty of speech). It may be inferred from this that *akasha* has two children, the ear representing *satva* and the voice representing *rajas*.

"The ear, which is the first child of *akasha*, receives the sounds coming from outside. The second child, namely voice, sends its reaction from the inside to the outside in the form of words. Likewise, the skin is the first child of *vayu* in its *satvic*. Aspect. The second child, in its *rajasic* aspect, is the hand. For instance, the skin recognises an ant crawling on the body. Immediately, the hand tries to remove it. It will be seen from these examples that the *satvic* quality is concerned with receiving impressions from outside, while the *rajasic* quality is concerned with casting them out by way of reaction. In other words, the five *gnanendriya* originating from the *satvic* receive stimuli from outside, and the five *karmendriya* derived from *rajas* respond to the stimuli. In the world today what is happening is the exact opposite. What is *rajasic* is being taken in and what is *satvic* is being rejected. In the natural scheme of creation, what should be received is that which is *satvic* and what should be rejected is all that is *rajasic*.

"The primary quality of *Prakriti* (nature), is *satva*. *Prakriti* is called *stri* made up of the three syllables *sa, ta* and *ra*. The significance of this term is: first of all, you have to take in what is *satvic*, secondly *ta* implies developing some *tamasic* qualities, like submission, humility and modesty. *Ra*, representing the *rajoguna*, implies that there are occasions in life when some firm resolutions and stern actions have to be taken. The *rajasic* quality comes last and it means that *rajasic* acts have to be done as a last resort, when they are unavoidable. In the cosmic process, it is the *satvic* quality, the *sa-kara* or the syllable *sa*, that comes first. Hence the duty of everyone is to develop the satvic quality in every aspect, in thoughts, attitudes, words and deeds.

"The next aspect to be understood is that under the influence of *tamoguna*, the five subtle elements evolve into the five gross elements by the process of *panchikritam* (fusion through permutation and combination). This highly complicated process may be illustrated by the following example for easy understanding. Suppose the five elements come together as five individuals, each having a one rupee coin. Now, each of them exchanges his one rupee coin for one half-rupee coin and four two-*anna* coins. A two-*anna* coin is equivalent to one eighth of a rupee. Then, *akasha* retains half a rupee and distributes among the other four elements one eighth of a rupee each. The second element, *vayu* (air), also does likewise, retains half a rupee for itself. Fire, water and earth also follow the same procedure. As a result of this redistribution, each has one *rupee*, but its composition is affected by the exchanges among the elements, with parts of their respective nature. Originally, each element was whole by itself. The process of mixing has resulted in the presence of all five elements. This means that, ultimately, each element is composed of half its original nature, the second half consisting of one eighth of each of the other four elements. For example, the composition of earth is $1/2$ earth + $1/8^{th}$ space + $1/8^{th}$ air + $1/8^{th}$ fire + $1/8^{th}$ water. Similar is the composition of the other four elements. In relation to the human being, the process of *panchikrita* makes man a mixture of the five elements and creates diversity from unity. These have been described in spiritual parlance as *shodasa kalas* (the sixteen aspects). What were these sixteen aspects? They are the five *gnanendriya* (organs of perception), the five *karmendriya* (organs of action), the five elements, and the mind. Every human being has these sixteen constituents, although the sixteen *kalas* are attributed only to the Divine. The implication is that each one has to realise his divinity." (2)

"When the *Atma* is reflected in the *satvic* mode, the image becomes *Ishvara* (God); when reflected in *rajas*, it becomes *jiva*, or individual being; and when reflected in *tamas*, it becomes matter." (3)

"To grasp the significance of a Divine Incarnation, it is imperative that we rise above the *rajasic and tamasic gunas*. Only *satvaguna* can lead us through the path of true devotion to the lotus feet of the Divine. To remove *rajas* and *tamas*, and to promote *satvic* nature, a favourable environment and *satsang*, or the company of good people, are essential.

"The mental make-up of a person can be judged from the way in which he maintains his immediate surroundings . For example, a person whose room is full of pictures of his relations, friends and political leaders can at once be understood to be one dominated by *rajoguna*. He is one who attaches undue importance to human relationships and adores worldly power and wealth, ignoring God. Similarly, if the room is full of ugly and obscene pictures, the individual is essentially *tamasic* in nature. Both these categories are unfit to follow the sacred path of meditation. A third category, with pictures of God and holy figures adorning the walls of their rooms, converting their rooms into shrines, as it were, are the *satvic* people, those who are rightfully qualified to undertake meditation.

"Pictures and people do leave indelible impressions and exercise considerable influence on the minds of men." (4) "God exists in all the created *gunas*, but the *gunas* themselves do not exist in God, and therefore, we can correctly describe Him as being above the *gunas*." (5) "The *satvaguna* has as its unmistakable concomitants, splendour, wisdom, bliss, peace, brotherliness, sense of sameness, self-confidence, holiness, purity and similar qualities. Only he who is saturated in *satvaguna* can witness the image of the Atma within. It is when the *satva* is mixed with the *tamasic* and *rajasic* that it is rendered impure and becomes the cause of ignorance and illusion. This is the reason for the bondage of man. The *rajasic* quality produces the illusion of something non-existent being existent! It broadens and deepens the contact of the senses with the external world. It creates affection and attachment and so, by means of the dual pulls of happiness and sorrow (the one to gain and the other to avoid) it plunges man deeper and deeper into activity. These activities breed the evils of passion, fury, greed, conceit, hatred, pride, meanness and trickery.

"And the *tamasic* quality? Well, it blinds the vision, and lowers the intellect, multiplying sloth, sleep and dullness, leading man along the wrong path, away from the goal. It will make even the seen 'unseen'! One will fail to benefit even from one's actual experience when immersed in *tamas*. It will mislead even well-known scholars, for scholarship does not necessarily confer moral stamina. Caught in the tentacles of *tamas*, the *pundits* cannot arrive at correct conclusions. Even the wise, if they are bound down by *tamas*, will be affected by many doubts and misgivings and be drawn towards sensory pleasures to the detriment of the wisdom they have gained. They will begin to identify themselves with their property, their wives and children, and such other worldly things. They will even confuse untruth with truth and truth with untruth! Note how great a trickster this *tamas* is!" (6)

"The first stage in spiritual *sadhana* is to put an end to the *tamasic* quality. The *tamoguna* is characterised by *murkhatvam* (foolish obstinacy). A *tamasic* person lacks intelligence and is inclined to indulge in meaningless questioning and argumentation. It is essential to get rid of such tendencies. Every issue should be deeply studied and the conclusions should be digested. Only then will the experience be rewarding. Endless verbal debates over every trivial matter should be avoided. Such controversies result only in provoking bitterness instead of harmony. They do not serve to reveal the truth. The *tamasic* person is incapable of perceiving the truth and cannot realise the Divine. He will be caught up in the endless cycle of birth and death.

"The person with *rajoguna* is one who is excessively happy when he gets what he desires. His ego gets inflated thereby. When his desires are not fulfilled, he develops hatred. Thus, for the *rajasic* person, whether the desires are fulfilled or not, the effects are not good. He is consumed by anger and bitterness. *Rajasic* qualities make a person hot-blooded and hot-tempered."

"The third quality is *satva*. Even this results in a form of bondage. It becomes a redeeming quality when all pure and meritorious actions are done as an offering to the Divine." (7) "The three *gunas* are bonds; man is bound by them, like a cow whose forelegs are tied together, whose hind legs too are bound and whose neck and horns are bound by a third bond. The threefold *gunas* are such threefold bonds. How can the poor beast move freely when it is bound so? The *satvaguna* is a golden rope, the *rajoguna* is a copper rope and the *tamoguna* an iron rope: all three bind effectively in spite of the difference in the cost of material. As bonds, all three are obstacles to freedom of movement.

"Man suffers from two types of ills, physical and mental; the one caused by the disequilibrium of the three tempers of *vata*, *pitta* and *sleshma*, and the other caused by the disequilibrium of the three *gunas: satva, rajas* and *tamas*. One peculiar fact about these two types of illnesses is that the cultivation of virtue cures both. Physical health is a prerequisite for mental health and mental health ensures physical health. An attitude of generosity, of fortitude in the presence of sorrow and loss, a spirit of enthusiasm to do good, to be of service to the best of one's capacity, these build up the mind as well as the body. The very joy derived from service reacts on the body and makes you free from disease. The body and the mind are so closely inter-related.

"The mind is the puppet of the food man consumes. The quality of the food determines the direction of the desire that diverts the mental flow. That is why in the *Gita*, as well as in all spiritual texts, *satvic* food is recommended for the upward seeking individual. Mind means desire, *sankalpa* something sought for. When the Formless desired form, the universe arose; so mind is the creative principle, the *maya*, that desired the very first desire 'to be many'. When it is now fed on *rajas*, or passion and emotion, activity and adventure, it gallops into the world and plunges into desire. It brings man deeper into the morass. When it is fed on *tamasic* food, which dulls, inebriates, blunts reason and induces sloth, the mind is callous, inert and useless for uplifting man." (8)

"The food man partakes of these days is essentially *rajasic* and *tamasic*. This is the reason why there is cruelty and unrest in the minds of men. Their physical health, too, is poor. Today, a boy of sixteen would have passed through all the physical experiences that a man of sixty would have gone through. Such is the deplorable condition of our youth."(4) "The food decides the *guna*, the *guna* seeks the food congenial to it; thus the vicious circle moves on." (9)

"Love assumes three forms according to the three qualities, *tamas*, *rajas* and *satva*. Love based on physical relations is considered by the *Shastras* as *tamasic* and as the lowest of the three types of love. It manifests itself as attachment to one's own kith and kin, or possessions, and is confined to a narrow circle.

"The second category of love combines self-centred love with love for others for the purpose of gaining one's ends. These persons pretend to have love for their superiors, or people in power, and thereby seek to achieve their aims. They adore men of affluence or power and, by their obsequious service to them, they try to win favours from them. This is *rajoguna prema* (love that is prompted by self-centred urges).

"The third category is pure *stavic* love. In contemporary conditions, this type of love is rare. People filled with *satvic* love recognise that the same Divine is present in all beings, and consider that without love towards all beings, life is meaningless. By their universal love, they proclaim the truth about the omnipresence of the Divine. Their vision is spiritual, as they see the Divine in all beings. Such persons are as fearless as lions which roam about without any fear of danger from anywhere. The person with bodily vision behaves like sheep, steeped in fear." (10)

"Happiness and misery are the consequences of the attributes one cultivates and fosters, the three chief ones being *satvic*, *rajasic* and *tamasic*. The *satvic* is marked by light, clarity, wisdom, balance, tolerance. The *rajasic* is marked by activity, ambition, passion, emotion. The *tamasic* is marked by indolence, ignorance, inactivity, sloth, dullness. When *satvic* predominates, one is happy; when *rajasic* predominates, one is discontented; when *tamasic* qualities are supreme, there can be no joy and no happiness." (11)

"Man struggles variously to attain *ananda*, which is the height of happiness, the embodiment of joy. It is sought in three different ways, according to the innate quality of the seeker - the *satvic*, the *rajasic* and the *tamasic*. The *satvic* path is poison in the early stages and nectar while coming to fruition. It involves firm control and regulation of the senses of cognition and action. This will be very hard to accomplish. But, as one progresses in practice, the joy increases and bliss is attained. How can such a goal be secured without undergoing hardships? The Scriptures say: 'Happiness cannot be won only through happiness. Happiness can be won only through misery. Pleasure is only an interval between two pains.' To achieve the *satvic* happiness that is positive and permanent, man must perforce take on trials and tribulations, loss and pain.

"Now about the second type, the *rajasic*. In the early stages, this path is nectarine, but later it slides into misery, for the happiness was derived through the senses, from objects of the external world. The pleasure soon reveals itself as unreal, false and exhausting. Once the process starts, it drags on with no rest. Man becomes too weak to pursue the goals of *dharma*, *artha*, *kama*, and *moksha* which are laid down for him. His intellect, imaginative skill, intuitive faculty, all are rendered lame. Man might even lose his humanity. The blind pursuit of objective sensual pleasure has today resulted in this very calamity. Lastly, we have the *tamasic* path. People who prefer this way of life are unconcerned with the problems of the world, they sleep away their lives, deriving joy in sloth and darkness. Of these three paths towards the goal of *ananda*, man must accept the *satvic* road, whatever the hardship, the loss, the misery, the anxiety and the labour.

"The system of caste is founded on attributes and activities. The world was in the very beginning predominantly *satvic* in nature, and as a consequence, all were only *Brahmins*. Later, through the adoption of various vocations and the development of various inclinations and preferences, types of people were demarcated as castes. The one and only *Brahmin* class of *Rishis* and sages, had later to be sectionalised in the interest of social justice and harmony when the qualities of character varied.

"In the *shanti parva* of the *Mahabharata*, Sage Bhrigu has elaborately answered a question raised about this development by sage Bharadwaja. It runs as follows: '*Brahmins*, fond of worldly pleasures, affected by egoism, subject to anger, lust and other passions have *rajoguna* mixed with their innate *satvic* nature, and so, they are classified as *Kshatriyas*. In fact, all *Brahmins* cannot be predominantly *satvic* in nature, nor can all of them be devoted to pure ritual activity. Those who do not adhere to the *satvic* ideal of truth, and who evince the qualities of *tamoguna* mixed with *rajasic* traits, those who are mostly both *tamasic* and *rajasic* were classed as *Vaishyas*. The rest, who spend their lives in occupations involving violence, who do not practise cleanliness and who are bogged down in *tamasic* means of livelihood, were classed as *Shudras*. Thus, the *Brahmins* denoted various castes and ensured the safety and security of human society. This is the assertion of the Scriptures, the *Shrutis*.'

"Those endowed with pure *satvic* characteristics are *Brahmins*, those with *rajasic* qualities and, as a result, equipped with courage and heroism, are *Kshatriyas* who can protect mankind from harm. Those who have neither valour nor heroism but are proficient in persuasive talents and the tactics of commerce, and are eager to use these skills in proper methods, are *Vaishyas*. In this class, *rajoguna* and *tamoguna* are blended. The others who have no inclination for undergoing asceticism or acquiring scholarship, who do not practise *sadhana*, who have no physical stamina or mental courage necessary for battle, who do not possess the special skill needed for trade and commerce, are *tamasic* in nature, and so engage themselves in *tamasic* professions. These are the *Shudras*. They fulfil themselves by their labour through which they contribute to world prosperity and peace.

"The four castes are only limbs of one body, they are not separate entities. There is no basis to consider that one is superior and another inferior. Each performs its function so that the body can be healthy and happy, so that each can win the highest state of consciousness from its own role. So the ancient *Vedic varna* organisation, based on such broad ideals, was taken to be the Divine plan. The plan witnessed the truth that the four castes were the four limbs of the one Divine Cosmic Person, or *Purusha*.

"But, this holy and profoundly significant *varna* organisation fell into the hands of unintelligent selfish men with restricted outlooks and narrow ideals; they expounded it in writing as their fancy dictated. Thereby they brought about great harm to the world. As a result, the system is interpreted today as a plan designed by the majority to suppress the minority! Caste is the Cosmic Person Himself manifesting as human society. It is the visible form of the Lord, charming in every limb. It is a great pity that this truth is not widely recognised.

"In a general way, predominantly *tamasic* natures are grouped as *Shudras*; but, among them, have we not many who are of pure *satvic* quality? Among those who are grouped as *Brahmins*, the pure *satvic* type, have we not many who are predominantly *tamasic*? Therefore, the *Vedic* religion of Bharat has clearly laid down that appearance alone, or birth in a particular family alone, cannot decide caste; it has to be determined on the bases of character and occupation. The castes are not based on race or birth, but on innate nature and tendencies, and the profession adopted and pursued. All sparks are fire. There is only one caste, humanity." (13)

"The *Ramayana* has a deep undercurrent of significant meaning. *Dasaratha* means he who rides in a chariot of ten — the five *karmendriya* (senses of action) and the five *gnanendriya* (senses of knowledge), that is to say, man. He is tied up with three *gunas*, or three wives. He has four sons, the four *purushartha*: *dharma* (Rama), *artha* (Lakshmana), *kama* (Bharata) and *moksha* (Shatrughna). Lakshmana represents the *buddhi*, or intellect, and Sita is *Sathya* (truth). Hanuman is the mind, and it is the repository, if controlled and trained, of courage. Sugriva, the master of Hanuman, is discrimination." (9) "The three *Rakshasa* chiefs are personifications of the *rajasic* (Ravana), *tamasic* (Kumbhakarana) and the *satvic* qualities (Vibhishana)." (14)

References :

1. Sathya Sai Baba, *Sanathana Sarathi,* August 1988, pp. 198 - 200
2. Sathya Sai Baba, *Summer Showers in Brindavan 1990*, pp. 106 - 110
3. Sathya Sai Baba, *Sathya Sai Vahini*, pp. 154
4. Sathya Sai Baba, *Summer Showers in Brindavan* 1979, pp. 87 - 89
5. Sathya Sai Baba, *Summer Showers in Brindavan* 1974, pp. 86
6. Sathya Sai Baba, *Jnana Vahini* 1984, pp. 14 - 15
7. Sathya Sai Baba, *Sanathana Sarathi*, February 1988, pp. 36
8. *Sadhana, The Inward Path,* Quotations from the Divine Discourses of Sathya Sai Baba, 1976, pp. 214 - 215, 220 - 222
9. Tumuluru Krishna Murty, *Digest, Collection of Sri Sathya Sai Baba's Sayings,* 1985 pp. 112 - 240
10. Sathya Sai Baba, *Sanathana Sarathi,* September 1989, pp. 241
11. Sathya Sai Baba, *Sanathana Sarathi*, January 1974, pp. 337
12. Sathya Sai Baba, *Sanathana Sarathi,* May 1981, pp. 116 - 117
13. Sathya Sai Baba, *Sathya Sai Vahini*, pp. 213 - 218
14. Sathya Sai Baba, *Ramakatha Rasavahini, Part I. The Inner Meaning.*

	SATVAGUNA	RAJOGUNA	TAMOGUNA
Trinity	Maheshvara	Vishnu	Brahma
Colour	White	Red	black
Qualities	truth, love, righteousness, equanimity, non-violence, wisdom, beauty, goodness, bliss, brotherliness, clarity, tolerance, purity, patience, perseverence, self-confidence, harmony, unity, faith, devotion, holiness.	activity, aggression, production of illusions, wilfulness, emotionality, ambition, power, lust, anger, jealousy, pride, malice, hatred, greed, adventure, conceit, trickery, likes and dislikes, unrest, haste, quick temper.	passivity, depression, ignorance, fear, attachment, ego, possessiveness, meaninglessness, lack of vision, lowering of the intellect, obstinacy, argumentativeness, stupidity, dullness, sloth, indolence, sleepiness, submission, cruelty.
Paths	poison in the early stages and nectar while coming to fruition.	in the begining nectarine, later sliding into misery.	unconcerned with the problems of the world, darkness, heedlessness.
Kinds of love	unselfish, unconditional, divine love (prema).	love for superiors, people in power and rich people.	based on physical relations, attachment to one's own kith and kin or possessions, confined to a small circle.
Time	4 a.m. - 8 a.m. 4 p.m. - 8 p.m.	8 a.m. - 4 a.m.	8 p.m. - 4 a.m.

16. THE HEART OF THE BHAGAVAD - GITA

" 'Krishna! You say that the *daivic* (Divine) and *asuric* (demonic) natures of man are the consequences of acts and feelings impressed upon the individual in previous births. Since it is impossible to escape from such impressions, what is the fate of those who are condemned to carry this burden with them? Are there any means by which this can be avoided? Or can their consequences be mitigated? If such exist, please tell me about them so that I may save myself thereby,' enquired Arjuna in order to draw out from the Lord the remedy for all mankind.

"Krishna gave an immediate answer. 'There is no paucity of means. Listen. There are three types of *gunas: stavic, rajasic* and *tamasic.* They are based on the *antahkarana,* the inner consciousness. That too, is dependent on the intake of food. You are what you feed on: your activities shape your nature. So, at least in this birth. by regulating *ahara* and *vihara* (food and activity), man can overcome the *asuric* (demoniac) tendencies that tend to prevail upon him. He can promote *satvic* tendencies through planned self-effort.' This advice was tendered lovingly by the Lord to the eager inquirer, Arjuna.

"Arjuna was thrilled with joy when he heard that man has the means of saving himself; he longed to inform himself further. Krishna showered grace through His enchanting smile and condescended to reply. 'Arjuna! Food is the chief formative force. The soiled mind dulls the brilliance of moral excellence; how can a muddy lake reflect clearly? The Divine cannot be reflected in the wicked or vicious mind. Food makes man strong in body; the body is intimately connected with the mind. Strength of mind depends upon strength of body too. Moral conduct, good habits, spiritual effort, all depend upon the quality of the food; diseases, mental weakness, spiritual slackness, all are produced by faulty food.' 'Krishna!' Asked Arjuna, 'pray, tell me the constituents of *satvic, rajasic* and *tamasic* foods.'

" 'Arjuna! Food, to be *satvic*, should be capable of strengthening the mind as well as the body. It should not be too salty, too hot, too bitter, too sweet or too sour. It should not be taken while steaming hot. Food which fans the flames of thirst should be avoided. The general principle is that there should be a limit, a restraint. Food cooked in water should not be used the next day; it becomes harmful. Even fried articles should be consumed before they develop unpleasant odours. *Rajasic* food is the opposite of *satvic*. It is too salty, too sweet, too hot, too sour, too odorous. Such food excites and intoxicates.'

" 'Lord, excuse me if I appear impertinent; I ask with a desire to know, that is all. By merely a change in food habits, can character be changed from one *guna* to another? Or, has something more to be done to supplement the purification process? Tell me, if there is anything more.'

" 'My dear brother-in-law! If transformation of character were so easy, wickedness and vice, so characteristic of the *danava* nature, could have been wiped off the surface of the earth in a trice. Of course, there are some more things to be done. Listen. There are three kinds of purities to be observed: purity of provision, purity of the vessel in which the food is prepared, and purity of the persons serving the prepared food.'

" 'It is not enough if the provisions are pure and of good quality. They should have been procured by fair means; no unfair, unjust, untrue earnings should be used for one's maintenance. These are fouled at the very source. The source as well as the course and the goal must all be equally pure. The vessel must be clean, free from tarnish. The person who serves must not only be clean in dress, but clean in habits, character and conduct. He should be free from hate, anger, worry and indifference while serving the dishes; he should be cheerful and fresh. And he must be humble and full of love. While attending upon those who are eating, he should not allow his mind to dwell on wicked or vicious ideas. Mere physical cleanliness, or charm, is no compensation for evil thoughts and habits. The *sadhaka* who has to secure concentration has to be careful about these restrictions. Otherwise, during *dhyanam* the subtle influences of the wicked thoughts of the cook and the servers will haunt the *sadhaka*. Care should be taken to have only virtuous individuals around. Outer charm, professional excellence, reduced wages, these should not be allowed to prejudice you in favour of harmful cooks and attendants. Examine carefully their habits and their character.

" 'The food you eat is an important constituent of the physical and mental stuff with which you have to struggle in the spiritual field. Purity of mind can be and has to be supplemented by bodily purity, as well as purity in its important function, speech. That is the real *tapas*: physical, mental and vocal.

" 'The mind should be free from anxiety and worry, hate and fear, greed and pride. It should be saturated with love for all beings. It has to dwell in God. It has to be restrained from pursuing objective pleasures. No lower thought should be allowed to creep in; all thoughts must be directed towards the elevation of the individual to higher planes. This is the proper *tapas* of the mind, or *manas*.

" 'Now, for physical *tapas*. Use the body and its strength and capabilities for the service of others, for the worship of the Lord, for the singing of His glory, for visiting places hallowed by His name, for regulated exercises in breath control, for holding the senses away from deleterious paths, and for treading the path of God. The service of the sick and the distressed, the observance of moral codes and such beneficial acts must make it sacrosanct.

" 'Vocal *tapas*, too, has to be engaged in. Avoid talking too much; desist from false statements; do not take delight in back-biting and in scandal-mongering; never speak harshly; speak softly and sweetly; speak with the memory of *Madhava* ever in the background of the mind. Of these three, physical *tapas*, mental *tapas* and vocal *tapas*, even if one is absent, the *Atmic* effulgence (*Atma jyoti*) cannot radiate light. The lamp, the wick and the oil are all essential for a light; the body is the lamp; the mind is the oil, and the tongue is the wick. All three must be in good order.

"'Some pious people consider that acts of charity are also physical *tapas*. It is good that they think so. But, when doing charity, one has to do so after pondering over the place, the time and the nature of the recipient. For example, charities for schools should be given at places where there have been no schools until then; hospitals have to be established in areas where diseases are rampant; hunger has to be appeased where famine conditions have been caused by floods or droughts. The nature and condition of the recipient have to be considered while imparting teaching of *dharma* and *Brahmavidya* and while doing service of various kinds. The charitable act that removes from a person the deficiency that is most harmful to his progress is called *satvic*.' 'Arjuna interrupted Krishnaa, 'May I ask a question here? Charity, however done, is charity, is it not? Why do you distinguish them by *satvic, rajasic* and *tamasic*? Are there any such?' Krishna answered, 'Of course there are. Among those who donate to charities, most are anxious to get name and fame; that is the motive for the act. They are after something in return for what they offer. Very few desire the grace of the Lord, and nothing else. Gifts made with that one end in view, to receive the grace of the Lord, are *satvic*. Gifts made expecting something in return, like fame and publicity, esteem and power, or made in a huff, or made reluctantly under pressure, these are to be classed as *rajasic*.

"'Charity should be given with reverence and faith. It should not be just thrown in the face of the recipient. Nor should it be given to an undeserving person or at an inopportune moment. Food for the overfed is a burden, not a boon. Hospitals in places that are inaccessible are as good as charity thrown away. Such benefitless and wasteful charity is called *tamasic*. While engaged in *daana*, or charity, one has to be very vigilant. You should not scatter it to whomsoever pleads for it; nor can you shower it on all kinds of places. Be careful that you remember the three types mentioned by Me and then do as seems most proper. The gift you make must not be for name or fame; it should have no motive of pomp or publicity; it should be purposeful and useful. In all acts, the *satvic* attitude is best. This attitude must permeate all acts, seeing, hearing or speaking.'

"Arjuna, who was listening with head bent and with great concentration to all this, drinking in the sweetness of the Lord's countenance, asked Him thus, 'What exactly is true listening and true seeing? Please tell me this in some detail. I can then follow the instruction.' He prayed to Krishna in such a pleading tone that the Lord smiled kindly at him.

"Krishna patted Arjuna on the back. He said, '*Satvic* listening is listening to the stories, experiences and messages of sages and saints who aspired to God and who realised Him. *Satvic* seeing is seeing the worshippers of the Lord, seeing portraits of saints and sages, attending festivals in temples, etc.

" '*Rajasic* seeing is seeing scenes of luxury, pictures of sensuous joy, of pompous pageantry, of the exhibition of power and status and display of egoistic authority. Taking delight in the description of sensuous scenes and incidents, in the demonstration of power and authority, in the assertion of might and prowess, these are to be classified as *rajasic* listening. Others take delight in listening to gruesome adventures, stories of wicked ogres and vicious deeds. Such are *tamasic* individuals. They admire cruelty and horrifying scenes and they take pleasure in keeping such pictures before them. They worship demonic, bloodthirsty gods, and they revel in the lore of ghosts and evil forces.'

"Dear Readers! This is the heart of the teaching of the *Bhagavad-Gita*. The body and life in it are based on food and are sustained by food, *anna*. So, food decides the level of attainment, high or low. Nowadays, emphasis is not being laid on discipline and regulated *nishta* (behaviour), but only to the *nashta* (food). However great and learned a person may be, however much he pays attention to the teachings of the *Vedanta* and takes care to spread them, if he neglects the strict code laid down for the food that is the very basis of the body and its functions, he cannot succeed.

"The *Padartha Sudhi* (purity of the provisions), *Paka Sudhi* (of the cook), *Patra Sudhi* (of the container) and of what has been prepared, these are not attended to. They feel content when their stomachs are filled and hunger is appeased. The first temple they visit when dawn breaks is the restaurant, where *idli* and *sambar* are offered to the *Atmarama*. How can such gourmands have concentration? Purity in cooking, purity of provision, and purity of service, how can these be guaranteed in restaurants? Who pays attention to these? Without doing this, people complain aloud that they do not have success in concentration, and suffer greater confusion! The desired effect will be secured only when the proper causes function well. When bitter things are cooked how can the final dish be sweet?

"*Ahara* and *vihara* (food and recreation) should both be very carefully regulated according to the *Gita*, but little heed is paid to its teaching, nor is it considered essential. There are people everywhere who swear by the *Gita*, who expound it for hours together and who preach it, but very few put its teachings into practice. The verses fill their heads but they are powerless to meet the one hundred twelve reverses of life, with philosophical cheer. *Ananda* and *shanti* can be secured only when food and recreation are cleansed and purified.

"Darkness and light cannot co-exist, *kama* and Rama cannot be in the same place together, they are like fire and water. How can one escape an evil reaction if the *Gita* is held in one hand and hot tea or coffee or a lighted cigarette or *beedi* or a pinch of snuff is held in the other? Some even justify their unregulated lives by declaring that whatever is eaten, however eaten, wherever eaten, the stuff is rendered pure and acceptable on account of the raging fire of *gnana* which they have in them!

"How can a bitter fruit be transformed into a sweet one even if it is dipped in a series of holy rivers? How can people who only speak on the *Gita* be saturated with the sweetness of its message? What really happens is that those who listen to such hypocrisies lose even the little faith they have in our Scriptures and become hardened disbelievers.

"How can a person who feels helpless to restrict and regulate his food habits be trusted to restrict and regulate his senses? If he cannot limit and control his feeling, how can he limit and control the senses? Can the nose which falls down during a cough survive a sneeze? How can one who is too weak to climb stairs, climb to heaven's heights? When a man is a helpless victim of coffee or cigarettes or snuff, how can he muster strength and courage to overcome the more powerful foes: anger, lust and greed? When he cannot renounce dirt, how can he renounce desire? Become master of the tongue and then you can master sex. They are firmly interconnected, as close as the eyes and the feet."

Sathya Sai Baba, *Geetha Vahini*, pp. 238 - 246

17. FOOD AND CHARACTER

"The Mohammedans call God Allah,
The Christians call Him Father, Son and Holy Spirit,
And the Hindus call Him Shiva, but there is only one God.
The Almighty is also called Paramatma (Universal Soul).
The peoples' inner yearnings express themselves in different names.
The names may be different, but there is only one Almighty God.
He is the one who disposes of the destiny of all people,
Regardless of the name that they choose to give Him.
He is the giver of all life, prosperity, health, experiences;
In short, He is the giver of all. God is One, believe this.

"Humanity is an inseparable Oneness. Still we see that men have differences of opinion, that there are constant conflicts between different religions, that there are tensions between the castes, and that one country is the enemy of another. What is the cause of all these conflicts? This question can be asked, for nowadays this question is very important, and has great relevance.

"You will discover that every object around you is composed of *sat* (being), *chit* (consciousness) *ananda* (bliss), *rupa* (form) and *nama* (name). The last two of these are form and name; these two are given to nature. All in nature changes constantly and only has a temporary form and name. There is no permanence in nature. Nothing in nature has a fixed name or form. *Sat, chit* and *ananda* are Divine attributes, Divine characteristics. In the language of the *Vedanta*, these three Divine attributes are called *asthi, bhati* and *priya*. These three Divine attributes are unchangeable and permanent. The last of the three is bliss, *ananda*.

"The word *ananda* has a great meaning for man. The acquisition of this bliss is the goal and fulfilment of the life of man. There are three types of bliss: the first is the type which is derived from knowledge and teachings (*vidyananda*). *Vidyananda* supports life. The second type of bliss concerns bodily existence, with nature, in this world (*vishayananda*). Man hastily tends to look for material and bodily pleasures, whereas they are not so enthusiastic in their search for *vidyananda* and neglect this bliss. *Vidyananda* and *vishayananda* are not permanent. Both their forms of bliss are supported on the foundation of *Brahmananda* (Divine bliss).

"We speak of warm water, but warmth is not a quality of the water; it is fire that gives the water warmth. Just like heat and water, the first two forms of bliss are not associated with *Brahmananda*; *Brahmananda* is closely linked to God (*Brahman*).

"Another example, *laddus* are made from flour of lentils. This flour is not sweet. By mixing sugar with the flour, it becomes sweet and we are left with *laddus*. People think that bliss is a result of their own efforts. This is not true, because bliss is not attached to the bodily existence. It is the Divine bliss that man experiences through his body that makes him happy. In all times of peace and happiness, it is this *Brahmananda* that you are experiencing. The main cause of your happiness is the bliss of God, it is His will. Happiness and peace are manifestations of God.

"The first goal of man in life must be to find Divine bliss. You must not search for temporary happiness, but for true lasting happiness. The stars are proud because they give light and make you happy, but they only sparkle because of the darkness. But, how long can the stars remain proud? Until the moon appears. When the moon appears, she becomes filled with pride, feeling that she is the one who sheds light in the darkness. When the sun rises in the heaven, the moon is knocked off her pedestal. At the moment of the rising of the sun, the moon has to bow her head; the sun ends the ego of the moon and stars.

"In the same way, we remain striving for the joy of *vidyananda* and *vishayananda* as long as we do not possess divine bliss. We attach much importance to these two forms of bliss. Still, they are only worldly capacities. All feelings concerning material things are temporary. These feelings pass quickly, but we should not ignore them. We have come to this world, so we should at least respect these two forms of bliss, until we come to possess Divine bliss. We pay attention to the starlight and moonlight until the sun rises. Afterwards, we pay them no further attention. *Brahmananda* is the basis of *vidyananda* and *vishayananda*.

"What do we have to do to obtain Divine bliss? Which *sadhana* (spiritual practice) should we engage in? What is the reason for our taking all the conflicts around us to be true? All people are equally subjected to life, birth and death and belong to the same genus, isn't that so? What is the cause of all the conflicts and differences? People have always wanted to know the answer to this question. Why are there demons on the one hand, and immortals on the other? There are certainly not many who inquire along these lines. Once we know the cause we shall probably become successful in our efforts.

"The cause of all these conflicts and differences is *aharam* (food). The food that you eat causes all these differences, as it is the food that you eat that determines what you are ultimately.

"There are three qualities in the food that you eat; *satva*, *rajas* and *tamas*. Some people eat only *satvic* food, others just *rajasic* food, while others eat *tamasic* food. Some eat a combination of *satvic* and *rajasic* food, while others eat a combination of all three types. We can detect these food-combinations in man's behaviour. So we can speak of *satvic*, *rajasic* and *tamasic* behaviour, and what the people eventually become explains all the differences of opinion and conflicts. Because everyone does not eat the same food, they do not all reach the same level of understanding. The food that people eat results in differences of opinion. To compare the example of two people's behaviour we can use two brothers, sons of the same mother. Even in this case, the difference in their behaviour is determined by the different food they eat.

"Ravana and Vibhishana had the same mother, but Ravana was not given to the same thoughts and holiness that Vibhishana was given to. The reason for this was the fundamental difference in the food they ate. Two people can only have a good understanding with each other if they eat the same types of food as their fundament.

"There can never be good contact between two people if one eats only *satvic* food and the other only *rajasic* food. Temporarily, they may be able to hang on to a superficial relationship but, eventually, they will separate. A lasting friendship can only exist when both people eat only *satvic* food. Water can be mixed with water, but not with oil. The mutual relationships between *satva*, *tamas* and *rajas* can be compared to the relationship between water and oil.

"If you wish to have a lasting relationship and friendship with God, your habits and thoughts must be *satvic* and fundamentally Divine in nature. God is by nature pure *satva*. If you want to have friendship with God, you must exert yourself to strenghten the *satvic* qualities in yourself, and your behaviour ought to reflect the *satvic* qualities, for God is by nature *satvic*. It is the food that determines the condition and form of the mind. And it is the mind that has to seek refuge in God.

"There are people who experience God's closeness for some time, but it is possible that these feelings of closeness do not last for a long time. The connection with God can only last as long as there are *satvic* feelings. If the *rajasic* nature in man tends to take over the guidance of the *satvic* nature, he will slowly lose his relationship with God. If his holiness and purity decrease he will certainly become separated from God. Such people remain looking for the causes of this separation. The person himself is responsible for the breaking of the relationship with God; God cannot be blamed for it. To make the relationship with God lasting and permanent, you must develop the *satvic* qualities in yourself.

"People of all times and of all quarters should strive to eat *satvic* food; only then will they be able to obtain the link of brotherhood with God. What exactly do we mean by *satvic* food? Flour, milk, fruit and beans are *satvic* food. Food that makes men happy, that is attractive, juicy, oily, nice, tasty and delicious can often be called *satvic* food. This food has a subtle element that we call *satvic* as it is concerned with vital strength. *Satvic* food can be associated with oil, not with fat!

"Now comes the question how much food should we eat. We should eat moderately. If we go to table effortlessly and with a light feeling, we should be able to leave the table with that same feeling. Then our food is really *satvic* food. People devoted to God should take one meal per day as a rule. One who eats three meals a day is a sick person (*rogi*). One who eats twice a day is a *bhogi* (enjoyer). One who eats just once a day is a *yogi*.

"Unfortunately, we see that most people show restraint neither in the number of meals that they eat each day, nor in the type of food they eat. They eat all that is available to them and all that comes on their path. They keep on eating for their pleasure and satisfaction.

"Anyway, the food that you eat must be healthy for you. Your health must not be damaged. Health is wealth. For spiritual exercises, good health is necessary. All rules and laws that you follow should protect your health. In fact, it is said that *dharma* (right behaviour, morality), *artha* (wealth, prosperity), *kama* (fulfilment of justified desires) and *moksha* (liberation from slavery), are there to protect health.

"What is *rajasic* food? *Rajasic* food is too salty, too sweet, too bitter, too sour or too spicy. One should not eat such food. Also food without oil, which is thus totally dry must not be eaten. Some people eat food that is very hot; this is *rajasic* food, it only strenghtens the *rajasic* qualities.

"What is *tamasic* food? If you have cooked food, you should not save it for other people; it becomes *tamasic* food. Heated food that has totally cooled down is *tamasic* food. Food that begins to smell is also *tamasic*. Do not keep cooked food one or two days, or longer, for it becomes *tamasic* food. Eat cooked food soon after it has been cooked. The longer you wait, the more *tamasic* the food becomes. Nowadays many devotees of God who go on pilgrimage select and collect imperishable food such as pop rice and food made of oil and the flour of pulses, but they do not understand that they eat *tamasic* food. *Tamasic* and *rajasic* food put the mind in slavery. The gross part of the food is excreted as faeces. The subtle part of the food takes the form of blood. The part between the subtle and the gross takes the form of muscles in our bodies. The part that you might call the essence takes the form of the mind.

"In the same way, the water that we drink should be pure. If the water is pure, the gross part of it is excreted as urine, and the subtle part forms *prana* (life, life-breath, life-force, essence of life). Water takes the form of life. Food takes the form of the mind. Now you understand how close the links are between the mind and the food that you eat and drink. That is why the spiritual aspirant should keep himself to strict rules and prescriptions concerning food. You will not be able to make progress in your spiritual discipline if you do not fully control your eating habits.

"Wine and meat give you lots of *tamasic* qualities. Meat promotes the demonic qualities in you. It is possible that soldiers in the army need this food, but *sadhakas* do not.

"Based upon the types of food that people eat, they may be split up into two types, the *amaras* (immortals) and the *asuras* (demonic people). Food that is very hot, spicy or sour can be compared to wine and meat. What you call pickling is literally laying the food in salt. The effect of the salt is worse than that of wine. I advise those with high blood pressure not to use salt, because adding salt pollutes the blood. So do not eat any salty, sour or strongly spiced foods. If a person eats such foods, he will have a tendency towards a certain kind of determination, not to go on the way to God, but to strenghten the demonic qualities in himself. Such people develop qualities like hatred and anger, and they thirst for revenge.

"There are six bad qualities: desire, anger, deceit, egoism, pride, and what is called, in Telugu, *matsarya*, which is jealousy, hatred and vengefulness. Maybe you have an element of egoism in you, or anger or hatred, but make sure that you never get any of the qualities of *matsarya* in you. Through these qualities, you will try to take revenge at the first and best opportunity and to separate yourself from other people. The quality of *matsarya* is a very bad quality. You can take the poison of a scorpion, a sharp sword or a snake, none of these are as bad and hostile as the qualities of *matsarya*. A person possessed with the qualities of *matsarya* is probably the worst of all creatures.

You can even find these qualities in people who you consider to be devotees of God, either because their wishes could not be fulfilled, or because perhaps God did not hear their prayers. Maybe God wanted to warn that person, and at the same time, make it clear to the person what he has done wrong; this can lead to the development of hatred and hostility in the heart of the devotee. The source of this hatred is the quality of *matsarya*; through this hatred the devotee separates himself from God. This vice of people is called the demon. Individuals with these qualities of *matsarya* are called *asuras* (malicious people) or demons. Here, demons does not mean a person with a deformed or ugly form, but someone who has demonic qualities. The foundation and cause of all of this is the quality of the food that you eat.

"Nowadays, people eat for the taste and not because they are hungry. Hunger is a sort of sickness. You may want to heal yourself from this sickness, but you go looking for food that tastes good, whereas you should be prepared to use any medicine that can cure your illness without taking into account the taste. Hunger is a type of sickness and food is the cure to heal this sickness. But, nowadays, the cure in the form of food has to appeal to our taste preferences. However, this leads to the cure losing its characteristic qualities. To make our food tastier, we add a little salt, Spanish pepper or tamarind, but in this way, we increase the negative qualities of food.

"You would expect that devotees who have exercised different methods of spiritual discipline over numerous years would have made progress, but the whole tragedy is as follows. This tragedy is like a barrel full of holes; this barrel is unable to hold anything. It is possible that you recite the names of God, or that you do concentration exercises, but seldom or never does it remain silent or peaceful enough. We make pilgrimages, we bathe ourselves in holy water, we visit great saints, we read books, we perform various different types of spiritual exercises, but our minds remain the same. The result of these activities don't reach our mind. It is evident that all your efforts have been of little value to your mind; otherwise, you would have been enjoying peace and comfort. The reason is that you have not changed the foods that you eat. *Sadhana* will not yield any results unless you change your eating habits. You will be successful in *sadhana* once you change your eating habits.

"We can read all the *Vedas*, all holy texts and other books, and visit all the holy places, but unless these activities are accompanied by the transformation of one's mind, we will not come face to face with the Supreme Reality. If we wish to become sure of the Supreme Reality, we will have to develop at least a few Divine qualities in ourselves. In the first place, we should not criticise others or do them harm. It is possible that you like another person or that you do not, but do not be critical of that person.

"Criticising and offending others is a great sin. What must we say of people who criticise God, when the criticising of our fellow-men is already such a big sin? Let us first free ourselves from the quality of criticising others. He who does not criticise his fellow-man is My devotee. Everyone is equal to God. That is what Krishna told Arjuna in the *Bhagavad-Gita*. This is the essence of what Mohammed told the Mohammedans. The word *Allah* comes from the word *Elah*. *Elah* means looking for surrender. If you surrender yourself to God, you become one with *Allah*. *Allah* means God. It is possible to give God every name, form and description. All different names and forms are names and forms of the same God. The names may differ, but it is the same God who is called. The names and forms that we give God are dependent upon our personal preference.

"If we wish to bring something holy into our system, we should first of all bring our heart and consciousness to a better condition; they must be cleansed and purified. We should then only allow pure and serene thoughts to enter our consciousness. At this moment, your head is full of thoughts. Is it possible to empty your head? If your head is empty, you can fill it with good, useful and fruitful thoughts. We have so many things in our heads. What we need is one interest that is focused on one point.

"For the eyes, sight is most important. For the ears, hearing is the most essential. For the nose, smelling is central. For the total human, love for God is the most important quality. It is this quality that distinguishes the devotee from other people; he thinks constantly of God, he is constantly immersed in thoughts of God. The true devotee concentrates on God incessantly and he subjects himself to God alone.

"Every organ of sense has a specific function. The function of the nose is to purify the air that is inhaled, so that the blood is provided with air that keeps the body healthy. This is the most important function of the nose. If you tax your nose by snorting, this will damage the *Kundalini shakti*, the spiritual energy present in all people. Every organ of sense must be obedient to certain rules and laws. Krishna has said, 'Oh tongue, you know what you should take, you know the sweetness of juice, do not divide yourself by running after things that, after having been investigated, show themselves to have no meaning at all. Instead of this, use your time to repeat the holy, lovely names of God; repeat *Govinda*, *Keshava* and *Madhava*. Eat the type of food that makes you healthy. Speak sweet and excellent words that give others encouragement. It was not intended that you should criticise and offend others, and eat everything that comes your way!

"And then we have ears. They were not given to you to listen to everything that those around you have to say; the intuitive discrimination (*buddhi*) warns the ears, 'Oh ear, do not spend all your time listening to everyone everywhere; you are more than willing to do that. But if the name of God is brought to your attention, you are inclined to become dissatisfied and disinterested.' Rama said the following about the ears: 'If your attention is taken by something in the world, by the conversations of those around you, for example, you listen very carefully not missing a single word, but when it concerns the name of God and when the name of God is sung, you are no longer interested. Oh ears, you are fully prepared to give all your attention to the criticism and gossip of other people, but you are not interested in anything at all concerning God. When God is discussed, you turn away!'

"The eyes can also be given a lesson. 'Oh eye, without bothering about any inconvenience, again and again you are totally prepared and keen to go out to see a film; this is fundamentally senseless and fruitless. You even go to the effort of obtaining binoculars to see better, but if you have to concentrate on God for just a second, you hesitate. If you go into a temple and stand before an image of God, you close your eyes, but you do not see God.' The eyes also behave strangely when an image of God is carried around in a procession or when Sathya Sai Baba comes out. The eyes do not want to see what is happening, so you not only shut your windows, you also shut yourself totally off! This behaviour is the consequence of demonic qualities and character traits, which are developed in your mind from the food that you eat. Such people may best be described as demons, or *asuras*.

"It is not only the food that determines who you are, but also your habits. When it rains, if you do not sow anything, you cannot expect a harvest. If you sow and there is no rain, you cannot expect a harvest either. You have to make sure that the rain and the seed come together. So sow directly before the rain comes; then you will be successful. In the same way, you have to make sure that your spiritual efforts come together with the grace that God pours out. The seed can only sprout if it rains. First of all, you have to sow, and then it has to rain. In the same way, you have to see to it that the food you eat and spiritual energy come together. If you do thus, you can be assured of the grace of God.

"There are devotees who put portraits of God on their walls, and pray to Him as a ritual. How quickly they say that He has not come. They begin their ritual prayer and expect God to come directly! They quickly become impatient. You can do *puja*, but you should wait calmly. With one drop of water, you do not get a full tank. With saliva alone you cannot quench your thirst. It is foolish to expect direct results when you have only just begun. All words we are speaking, all we are seeing, all we are listening to and our heart, should be totally filled with holiness; then we can hope to be successful. Firstly, we should be careful about the food we eat; the food should be pure. Also our behaviour should be blameless. The food and behaviour should come together.

"You can recite all the *Vedas*, study the *Vedanta* and exercise every spiritual practice, but keep it in mind that all this has to go along with the purifying of one's heart and consciousness, and this is where food is of overwhelming importance.

"Our body is like a bag of water, it is not permanent. Every second, every moment and everywhere you are uncertain what will happen. Every second, you should be prepared for the last moment and you should be constantly thinking of God. Many people say that they are happy and that all their comforts are provided for. It is certain that they do not understand the words they speak. This is foolishness. They say that they do not need anything else. This is the ultimate foolishness. And to speak the truth, you do not enjoy the comfort, but the comfort enjoys you. If you actually enjoy the comfort, you should experience the effect of it. Why do you become a bigger and bigger weakling? Because you do not experience anything. You have food to eat, clothes to protect you and a house to shelter you. And then the foolishness begins. You begin to think, 'I have a house, I have clothes to wear, I have food to eat and my house is full of happy, lively children.' In reality, all those things have you in their power and infringe upon your comfort. You are not conscious of this. On the contrary, you think that you understand and experience everything. You create your own picture of what you experience. However, it is not in accordance with your true nature. All these worldly pleasures and comforts are not able to offer you peace and comfort, they will only bring you more pain and misery.

"Only God can lead you to a higher stage in your evolution. It is an upward path that we must find, not a path that will lead us down. We have many negative qualities because of our ego and attachments. Remove the ego, cut off all attachments and choose the right food, control your eating habits and be successful in life. Eat *stavic* food, then your holy nature will express itself. The holy world comes out of *satvic* food. Do not criticise others. The *Bhagavad-Gita* gives us the very first rule: *Adveshta sarva bhutanam*, hate no being, criticise no one. You cannot always do someone a favour or be of service to him, but you can always speak in a friendly manner."

Sathya Sai Baba, Prasanthi Nilayam, July 15, 1983,
Sri Sathya Sai Baba Bhajanavli pre-recorded cassette, 20.
Translated from Telugu.

18. FOOD, HEALTH AND GOODNESS

"Health is the essential prerequisite for success in all aspects of life, for realising the four ideals that should guide humans, namely: moral living, prosperity, fulfillmet of beneficial desires and liberation from grief. Everywhere man seeks to live happily and peacefully, but happiness and peace are not won from worldly activities. The body that yearns to be happy and secure is subject to disease, decay and death. The Dweller, the Self within the body is, however, not born, nor does it die. It is the *Atma*, God. The body is the temple of God. Hence it is the duty of man to keep the temple in good condition.

"Health is necessary for gaining this world and the next, for earning worldly and other worldly progress to realise the very purpose for which the self has embodied itself in this human form, namely, to become aware of this source, *the Paramamata*. In order to attain this goal, the ideals of righteousness, prosperity, moral desire and realease from sorrow have to be practised with the help of the sound mind in a sound body." (1)

"Every activity of man is dependent on the energy he derives from the intake of food. The spiritual *sadhanas* he ventures upon, depend for their success on the quantity and quality of the food taken by the *sadhaka*, even during the preliminary preparations as recommended by Patanjali. The most external of the five sheaths that enclose the *Atmic* core, namely the *annamaya kosha*, has impact on all the remaining four, the *pranamaya*, the *manomaya*, the *vignanamaya* and the *anandamaya*. The *annamaya kosha* is the sheath consisting of the material flesh and bone built by the food that is consumed by the individual.

"Food is generally looked down upon by ascetically minded *sadhakas* and seekers and treated as something which does not deserve attention. But since the body and the mind are mightily interdependent, no one can afford to neglect it. As the food, so the mind; as the mind, so the thought; as the thought, so the act. Food is an important factor which determines alertness and sloth, worry and calm, brightness and dullness. The Scriptures classify food as *satvic, rajasic* and *tamasic* and relate these three types to the three mental modes of the same names." (2)

What are the main causes of ill health? Millions of living beings grouped as species dwell on earth; they sustain themselves by means of food secured from nature, as provided by nature. It is only man that is an exception. In order to cater to his palate and other senses, he changes the composition and characteristics of the things provided by nature and prepares, through the process of boiling, frying and mixing, concoctions which have no vitality in them. Birds and beasts do not adopt such destructive methods. They eat things raw and consume the strength-giving vital essence. So they do not fall victim to the many ills that man brings on himself. Plant a boiled pulse in the soil; it will not sprout. How, then, can it contribute life to the living? The vitamins and proteins that are valuable ingredients are destroyed while they are cooked to please the palate! The billions of cells in the body are so interdependent that when one is weakened or damaged all of them suffer. There is a limit and a balance which every limb and organ has to maintain. Insufficient or improper food will endanger this balance. An occasional cough helps to strengthen the lungs and to clear them of extraneous matter, but fits of coughing are signs of positive illness.

" 'Eat in moderation and live long.' This is the advice handed down through the ages by the seers of the past. This advice is seldom heeded. People fill themselves with such large quantities of food that they find it hard to rise from the eating platter. Ruining their digestive system by consuming heavy, rich foods, the affluent are proud when they host costly banquets. Those who know that physical health is the greatest treasure, take great care to eat only *satvic* food." (1)

"An intake of too much food is harmful. Simply because tasty food is available and is being offered, one is tempted to overeat.

We have air all around us but we do not breathe in more than we need. The lake is full but we drink only as much as the thirst craves for. But overeating has become a social evil, a fashionable habit. The stomach cries out, 'enough,' but the tongue insists on more, and man becomes the helpless target of disease. He suffers from corpulence, high blood pressure and diabetes. Moderate food is the best medicine to avoid bodily ills. Do not rush to the hospital for every little upset.

"Too much intake of medicines is also bad. Allow nature full scope to fight the disease and set you right. Adopt more and more the principles of naturopathy, and give up running after doctors. The type of food that you consume decides the degree of concentration you can command; its quality and quantity decide how much your self-control is lessened or heightened. Polluted air and water are full of maleficent viruses and germs and have to be avoided at all costs. There are four pollutions against which man has to be vigilant: of the body (removable by water); of the mind (removable by truthfulness); of reason (removable by correct knowledge) and of the self (removable by yearning for God). *Vaidya Narayano Harih*, the *Shrutis* declare, 'God is the doctor.' Seek Him, rely on Him, you will be free from disease. "(2)

"Uncooked food, nuts and fruits and uncooked raw pulses just sprouting are the best and are to be preferred. Use these at least at one meal, say, for the dinner at night. This will ensure long life. And long life is to be striven for in order that the years may be utilised for serving one's fellow beings." (1) "The coconut, offered to the gods, is a good *satvic* food, having a good percentage of protein besides fat, starch and minerals. Food with too much salt or pepper is *rajasic* and should be avoided; so also, too much fat and starch, which are *tamasic* in their effects on the body." (2)

"Evil thoughts cause ill health. Anxiety, fear and tension also contribute their share. All these result from greed - greed to have more things, power and fame. Greed results in sorrow and despair. Contentment can come only from a spiritual outlook. The desire for worldly goods has to be given up. One should not distinguish between 'my work' and 'work for God'. All work should be worship. Whatever the reward, it is the gift of God. It is for our lasting good. If this attitude is developed, suffering and pain can toughen us and help us to progress towards Divinity.

"It is through pain that pleasure is gained. Darkness enables us to appreciate light. Death teaches us to love life. Diseases which torment man are many in number. Of these, hatred, envy and egoism are the worst. Even doctors cannot cure them, for most of them suffer from these. One should develop equanimity and serenity if one desires to be free from these diseases. Do not seek to listen to vile and vicious stories. This tendency reveals a diseased mind. What is heard is imprinted, like a carbon copy, through the ear, on the heart. One is injuring oneself through indulgence in this evil habit.

"Anger is another enemy of good health. It injects poison into the blood stream and brings about a profound transformation which damages it. Two women who were neighbours turned into bitter enemies on account of a dispute over a very trivial incident. The cow belonging to one woman, while going on the road, dropped its dung in front of the other woman's house. The owner of the cow ran to collect the dung, while the other woman claimed that it belonged to her since it lay on her doorstep. From words they very nearly came to blows. Just then the other woman's little baby wailed from the cradle. She rushed in to feed the baby and while the child was drawing its food, she shouted most furiously at her neighbour. Her anger poisoned her blood so much that the child died while drinking her milk! Another cause of ill health is vice and vile conduct. People believe that a wicked person need not be a diseased person but most diseases are mental illnessess, fundamentally.

"Doctors have to deal with patients sweetly and softly and consider their profession as a calling dedicating them to their fellowmen. It is best to preserve one's health by good thoughts and good deeds. It is best to be vigilant about food habits. Coconut kernel, coconut water, sprouting pulses, uncooked or half cooked vegetables, and greens are good for health. Try earnestly to live long, without falling into the hands of medical practitioners. When they give you one injection, they keep another ready to counteract its reactions! While trying to cure one disease, they cause a dozen more. Moreover, the drugs they recommend are mostly spurious, since the manufacturers want to amass a fortune by hook or by crook. Most illnesses can be cured by simple living, simple exercises and by intelligent control of the tongue. Live long so that you can witness the career of the Divine Avatar for years and years." (1)

Reference :
1. *Sathya Sai Speaks,* Vol. XI, pp. 148 – 151
2. Sathya Sai Baba, *Sanathana Sarathi,* March 1980, pp. 62 - 63

19. A COMPREHENSIVE SATVIC DIET

The lambent light of the Atma shines with eternal effulgence.
It has neither birth nor death, nor beginning nor end.
Nor can it be destroyed.
It is the immortal witness, the beholder of all space and time.

Embodiments of Love!

"*Na shreyo niyamam vine*, said Krishna to Arjuna. An unregulated, unsystematic, undisciplined and disorderly life cannot experience joy, goodness or well-being. One who controls and regulates the actions of others is called *yama*. One who controls himself and regulates his own actions possesses the quality of *samyama*. Yama has no control over a person endowed with *samyama*. There should be discipline and regulation in life in accordance with self-imposed constraints. These self-imposed constraints constitute the *tapas* of an individual. An unrestrained life is an immoral life. The wind and the sea and also the other phenomena obey the universal laws of nature. The earth rotates round its own axis and revolves around the sun periodically. These uniformities in the universe are the laws ordained by God. They are obeyed by the macrocosm as well as the microcosm. The laws of nature ordained by God are necessary for creating and sustaining the universe, and for maintaining its dynamic equilibrium.

"Such self-imposed discipline is conducive to real *shanti* (peace of mind, poise, equanimity and stable equilibrium of the mind). Peace of mind is the most desirable thing in this world. It gives us physical and psychical euphoria. In order to achieve this *shanti*, an aspirant must develop a thirst for *gnana* or spiritual wisdom. He must also aquire the qualities of love, sympathy and compassion, and do selfless service for others. *Shanti* should not be regarded as a part-time virtue to be cultivated only during *dhyana*, or meditation. It is a constant state of inner tranquillity. It should become habitual and instinctive.

"*Dhyana* is also universal and eclectic. It is not restricted by the barriers of space-time. It is not governed by the dogmas of any particular creed. *Dhyana* is a way of life for the total Divinization of man. *Dhyana* and *shanti* are inseparable. *Dhyana* promotes *shanti* and *shanti* intensifies *dhyana*. The quality of Divinity is not limited to the icon that we worship. Some people experience the most profound peace of mind as long as they are in meditation. But, the moment they come out of the meditative state of mind they exhibit their demoniacal nature. It should not be so. The Divine attributes acquired during meditation should be cultivated and nurtured in everyday life.

"Mere medication will not cure a sick man. He must also control his diet for quick recovery from illness. There is no single panacea for great world-sorrow. Each individual has his own specific type of suffering. Nevertheless, meditation on God is an unfailing remedy for human suffering if it is supplemented with the practise of *dharma* and the strict observance of moral restraints. We are all interdependent. We must learn to share the joys and sorrows of other people. A practitioner of meditation must pray for the welfare of others as sincerely as he prays for his own welfare.

"A spiritual aspirant need not live in monastic isolation. He should practise universal compassion, which is nothing but an intense desire for the welfare of the entire humanity. Food plays an important part in the cultivation of universal compassion. Yesterday, I talked to you about the right type of food for spiritual aspirants. Today, I will deal with *satvic* food or the type of food necessary for spiritual progress. *Satvic* food enables the *sadhaka* to apprehend the omnipresent reality of Divinity. He progresses through the four stages of the life Divine. These four phases of spiritual advancement are *salokya*, *samipya*, *sarupya* and *sayujya*. *Salokya* is entrance to the field of theocentric reality. *Samipya* is proximity to the fundamental mental spiritual substance of the universe. *Sarupya* is the assimilation of the form of the deity. *Sayujya* is liberation and ultimate union with the Godhead.

"*Satvic* food is conducive to the progressive attainment of these four states of spirituality. Here, it is necessary to examine the implications of the concept of *satvic* food. Some people are under the wrong impression that *satvic* food should consist of only milk, yogurt, sweets and fruits. They believe that they will become *satvic* by consuming large quantities of these delicacies. They are absolutely mistaken. Excessive and immoderate consumption of milk and its products awakens and aggravates the *rajasic* and *tamasic* qualities in man. A diet extra rich in milk, curds and ghee cannot be called *satvic* because it leads to the development of the passionate nature of man.

"In this context, I have to expand on the nature of human knowledge, and the five gateways of perception. Man is endowed with the five sensory organs connected to the five faculties of *shabda*, *sparsha*, *rupa*, *rasa* and *gandha* (sound, touch, sight, taste and smell). The preservation and the development of these sensory faculties depend on the *satvic* food taken through the mouth. The type of *satvic* food that we take is determined by the fancies of individual taste. We feel satisfied when we take the right type of food through our mouths. But we forget that we absorb an incorporeal type of food through the other sensory organs also. The wholesome effect of *satvic* food will be nullified if we listen to bad talk, indulge in bad talk, look at bad things, come into physical contact with bad things, and smell bad things. Mind and body are tainted, contaminated and polluted by evil. Thus, *satvic* food alone is not enough for the spiritual regeneration of man. We should not speak of evil. We must avoid condemning others and praising ourselves. Self-adulation and self-glorification retard spiritual development. We must feed our sensory organs with wholesome food, wholesome sounds and wholesome sights. The tongue is meant to sing the glory of God. The ears are meant for feasting on the glorious manifestations of the Divine.

"Each organ of perception must be provided with its proper spiritual sustenance. Thus, *satvic* food does not mean the moderate consumption of milk, curds, ghee and fruits alone, but the enjoyment provided by noble thoughts, sacred sounds, holy sights, and spiritual discussions as well. We must develop *satvic* sight and spiritual vision. We must have *darshan* of the beauty of nature and the Divinity of idols in temples. We should avoid all distracting sights and sounds. We should not look at anyone with an evil eye. Evil thoughts develop an evil eye. The eyes are the windows of the heart.

"The heart should overflow with love and compassion. *Satvic* nature is developed by feeding the eyes with *satvic* sights. The sense of smell is also equally important. The olfactory sense should be satisfied with sweet smells. All obnoxious odours should be avoided. To create on atmosphere of holiness, sweet perfumes are used and fragrant incense sticks are burnt at the altars in temples. Foul smells destroy sanctity. The idea of holiness is always associated with sweet scents and perfumes. The tactile sensation, or the sense of touch, should be satisfied by coming into physical contact with the feet of holy men. Contact with evil men must be avoided. Their contact promotes bad thoughts.

"*Satsang*, or the company of the virtuous, is of supreme importance. *Satsang* leads to non-attachment. Non-attachment induces equanimity which, in turn, leads to liberation during life. With the aid of *satsang*, many things are achieved. We cultivate good habits and participate in pious activity. *Satsang* sanctifies the human body for becoming a temple of God.

"Thus, a comprehensive and balanced *satvic* diet must provide *satvic* satisfaction to all the sensory organs of the human body. The sensations of *shabda*, *sparsha*, *rupa*, *rasa* and *gandha* must be provided with *satvic* satisfaction by means of *satvic* discourse, *satvic* company, *satvic* sights, *satvic* food and *satvic* perfumes. A comprehensive *satvic* diet provides *satvic* gratification to all the sensory organs. Today, the idea of *satvic* food has been restricted to food consisting of fruit, milk and its products. We have already seen that immoderate consumption of such food has a deleterious effect on the human body.

"The spiritual technique of *dhyana* mentioned in the *Bhagavad-Gita* cannot be beneficial in the absence of comprehensive *satvic* food which should feed the entire body with *satvic* sights, sounds, smells and tactile sensations. Otherwise, it becomes a mere pose. Today, *dhyana* has degenerated into a fashionable pastime. The true meaning and significance of *dhyana* should be clearly grasped in order to avoid the pitfalls and dangers inherent in its faulty practice. Restraints are necessary for the welfare of human beings. Limited food and *satvic* food are essential for spiritual progress. Such food should give satisfaction to all the sensory organs. All rivers join the ocean.

"Likewise, the aim of all *sadhana* is the merging of the individual soul with the universal soul. God's grace is like the unlimited ocean. The water vapour symbolizes the *sadhana* (propitiation); the cloud is *satya* (truth); and the raindrops are *prema* (love). They collect together to form the stream of *ananda* (bliss) which joins the vast ocean of *anugraha* (Divine grace). Knowledge obtained directly from *shastras* and scriptures is like sea water. By exercising the faculty of discrimination, and by entering the meditative state of mind, the pure water of wisdom can be distilled from the saline sea water of scriptural knowledge. This knowledge is humanized by experience and divinized by selfless love. Bookish knowledge divorced from experience leads to fanaticism and intellectual arrogance. Knowledge by acquaintance is always superior to knowledge by description. Practice is better than precept. We must live the scriptural injunctions rather than merely talk about them. Self-imposed discipline is more effective than discipline enforced by an external authority.

"The quality and quantity of food that we take determine our thoughts and feelings. There is, indeed, an intimate connection between 'food, head and God.' *Satvic* food is conducive to self-realization and liberation from the dualities and relativities of the world. *Rajasic* food generates virulent thoughts. By consuming non-vegetarian food we develop brutal mentalities. Those who are practising meditation must abstain from meat. We should also remember constantly that *ahimsa*, or non-violence, is the supreme *dharma*. It is sin to kill innocent animals for the sake of filling our stomachs. We must remember that God dwells in all creatures. *Isa vasyam idam sarvam* (all this is pervaded by God), says the *Isa Upanishad*. The truth of this aphorism can be experienced through meditation.

"*Udaranimittam bahukrita vesham*, for the sake of the stomach, men don different guises. Like the chameleon, they change their colours according to the demands of the situation. They become opportunists and hypocrites. In the end, they try to justify their opportunism and rationalize their hypocrisy. They delude themselves by this policy of expediency and time-serving. Such people can never follow the path of meditation. It should not be supposed that the path of meditation is easy and artificial. If *dhyana* is easy, why should the great sages of our country have mortified themselves for the attainment of *moksha*?

"Some modern techniques of meditation claim to achieve *nirvikalpa samadhi* instantaneously. *Dhyana* is mistaken for temporary freedom from worries. If this sort of anaesthesia is needed, one can become tipsy by drinking liquor. *Dhyana* is not a state of inebriety or amnesia. *Dhyana* is a state of complete identification with one's *dheya*, or object of meditation. It is a state of total spiritual empathy. Today, many artificial and distorted methods of meditation are being popularized. Students must beware of them because they are all unprofitable and potentially dangerous.

"There are three *gunas*: *satva*, *rajas* and *tamas*. There are three eyes: the two physical eyes and the invisible spiritual eye. There are three times: the past, the present and the future. And there are three worlds. The unity of these triads is vouchsafed to the spiritual aspirant during his transcendental state of meditation. Then sin and sorrow are annihilated. *Sat-chit-ananda* (existence-consciousness-bliss) is experienced through meditation and complete self-surrender. This is the essence of *dhyana*. Today, a number of rites and rituals are being performed as part of *sadhana*. These are only aids to concentration. They are not of much use for true *dhyana*. Correct posture, the right type of food and the right place are only aids to *dhyana*, or concentration. *Satvic* food, *satsang*, etc., assist the *sadhaka* to some extent. They develop the habit of concentration. Our efforts should not end here. Concentration should be followed by contemplation and meditation.

"There should be an element of reciprocity in all human and personal relations. Love, sympathy, compassion and affection are always mutual. They cannot thrive in isolation. They atrophy and vanish wherever selfishness and jealousy manifest themselves. We must discharge our duties in a spirit of self-surrender, without consideration for wealth or recognition.

"*Prema* (love) is the greatest *sadhana* (spiritual activity). *Prema* is not mere reciprocal love, it is an extended and sublimated form of self-love. It is the extension of love to humanity and to the entire creation. The essence of *prema* as a *sadhana* lies in the cultivation of humanitarianism, universal compassion and altruism. Nobody can become a saint or a sage overnight.

"We must start early, drive slowly and reach the goal safely. Haste makes waste and waste creates worry. A true *sadhaka* must develop the qualities of patience and persistence in order to reach the ultimate goal of spiritual enlightenment."

Sathya Sai Baba, *Summer Showers in Brindavan, 1979*, pp. 91-98

20. A SEAWORTHY BOAT

"To many, it might appear strange that in this *ananda nilaya* (abode of bliss), there exists an *arogya nilaya* (abode of health) or hospital. They may wonder why prominence is given to bodily health in a place that is dedicated to the health of the spirit. But for attaining the four aims of human life, *dharma* (righteousness), *artha* (prosperity), *kama* (fulfilment of desires) and *moksha* (liberation from bondage), the basic requirement is health of body and mind. Disease means feeling uneasy, disturbed, on account of the upsetting of one's temper or balance or equilibrium, which affects the physical as well as the mental condition. This happens for two reasons: faulty food and faulty activities (faulty *ahara* or faulty *vihara*).

"It is wiser to prevent disease than to run after remedies after it has happened, or grown beyond control. Man does not attend to precautionary measures; he allows things to worsen and then disease is aggravated by fear, uncertainty and anxiety. There is an axiom believed in by the men of old which says, 'One meal a day makes a *yogi*, two meals a day make a *bhogi*, and three meals a day make a *rogi*.' A *yogi* is the contented God-centred man. A *bhogi* is the man revelling in sensual pleasure. A *rogi* is the man ridden by illness. Yes, the quantity of food intake of the well-to-do is now much beyond essential requirements. Overeating has become a fashion.

"Breakfast does not serve to break any fast, for there has been no fasting at all! It is as good as a full meal. Lunch is pressed in and consists of many dishes, chosen for the palate rather than to assuage hunger. Tea is tea only in name; it includes rather heavy fare, out of all proportion to the needs of the body. Dinner at night is the heaviest meal and includes the largest variety; and so, one goes to bed weighted with unwanted stuff, to roll from side to side in a vain effort to get a few minutes of sleep. The shortage of food grains is mainly due to bad and wasteful eating habits; it can be set right, and people can live longer and more healthily if only they eat the minimum, rather than fill themselves with the maximum. Regular prayers twice a day will give strength and courage, which can withstand illness.

"The grace of God will confer mental peace, and so, good sleep and rest for the mind. Feel that you are one hundred per cent dependent on God; He will look after you and save you from harm and injury. When you go to bed, offer thankful homage to Him for guiding and guarding you throughout the day. When a friend offers you a cigarette, or some one gives you a glass of water, you say immediately, 'Thank you,' how much more gratitude should you evince to God who watches you and wards off all harm threatening to overwhelm you. Activity must be dedicated to God, the Highest Good. Then it will provide health of body and mind.

"The body is a chariot wherein God is installed; it is being taken along in procession. Let us consider some points on which we have to be vigilant in order to avoid breakdowns on the road. Fast one day in the week. This is good for the body as well as for the country. Do not eat a dozen plantains, half a dozen *puris* and drink a quart of milk and call it a fast! Take only water, so that all the dirt is washed away. Do not crave for fruit juice or other liquids. Even physical machinery is given rest; they cannot run for ever, continuously. What then shall we say of this delicately organised human body! It is not a sign of culture to overvalue the body by overindulging in its whims. It is a sign of barbarism.

"The older generation in this land used to take a small quantity of rice soaked in curds as the first meal in the morning. It is good *satvic* food; or they drank some *ragi* gruel, which is equally good. Cattle and dogs have better eating habits. If a dog has fever, it will refuse food; but man ignores even the warnings of the doctor and eats on the sly! Through dieting alone, birds and beasts set their health aright! But man lives on tablets and pills and injections, after venturing into forbidden realms, so far as eating and drinking are concerned. Drink large quantities of water, boiled and cooled, not during meals, but some time before and after. Only the healthy person can afford to forget the body and dedicate his thoughts to God, and derive *ananda* therefrom. The mind is the eleventh sense and, like the other ten, one must reduce it to the status of an obedient instrument in the hands of the intellect. Eat at regular intervals, according to a well established time-table. Move about and fill the day with activity, so that the food is well digested.

"Develop biting hunger before sitting down for a meal. Wait until you get the call before you load the stomach again. The rich are under a great handicap in this respect. And so are women, who are petted so much that they feel physical work to be demeaning! Illness is the inevitable result of idleness and indulgence; health is the inevitable consequence of a tough hard life. If everyone decides to carry on all personal services themselves, rather than depend on servants or helpers, their health will definitely improve and hospitals will have much less work. Keeping the mind fixed on God and having good ideas also helps health. Keep the eye, ear, tongue, hands and feet under restraint. Do not read enervating exciting stuff. Do not attend film shows which exhaust or inflame the mind. Do not lose faith in yourself, you are the Divine encased in the body. Contentment is the best tonic. Why inflict on yourself the disease of greed and consume tonics to get strength, and to hanker after further things? Use the body as a boat to cross the ocean of life with devotion and detachment as the two oars.

"Do not spend much thought on the body; some people worry always about health. Be in the sun; let the sun's rays penetrate into the home, let them fall upon the body for some time, let them warm and illumine clothes and food; that will suffuse them with health. There are some who are puzzled at the sight of a hospital here. They imply that everything here should be done through some miracle or in a strange and inexplicable manner! It also implies that no one who has come here should fall ill or die. I have no desire that you should live, nor fear that you may die. It is you that decide your condition. All have to die sooner or later. Death is but the casting off of old clothes. When even Divine Avatars leave the body after the clothes have become old, when even they leave the body after their task is fulfilled, how can mortal man be saved from inevitable dissolution? The hospital is for those who believe in doctors and drugs. It is faith that matters, that cures. It also serves to accommodate those who are too ill to move about, and yet come here for cure. Those who are in the hospital can also hear the *pranava*, the *sankirtan* and the *bhajan and* benefit by the spiritual vibrations that fill the air in this *Prashanti Nilayam*."

References:
Sathya Sai Baba, Prasanthi Nilayam, October 12, 1969,
Sathya Sai Speaks, Vol. II, 2nd Am. Printing, 1985, pp. 110 - 114

21. LIMITS (MITI) AND PROGRESS (GATI)

"Jonnalagadda Sathyanarayanamurthy thrilled you so much, since he spoke softly and sweetly in his charming style. He has returned from Russia, where there is too much rush, to this quiet place, this *Nilayam* of *Prashanti*. This is an occasion connected to physical ills, their cure and prevention, and so I shall confine My remarks to them.

"Man has two varieties of troubles: the physical due to the imbalance between the three humours, *vata*, *pitta* and *sleshma*, and the spiritual, due to the imbalance of the three *gunas*, *satva*, *rajas* and *tamas*. Sathyanarayanamurthy gave some pathetic instances of the sufferings caused by indifferent and ignorant doctors. I also agree that it is wise to adjust one's living so intelligently that there is no need to approach any doctor. Illness is due to the neglect of some simple rules of healthy eating and drinking and due to the damage caused to the system by evil habits and stupid cravings. Man ruins himself by greed and lust, worry and fear; he falls an easy prey to his insatiable thirst for a happy life. He does not know the source and spring of happiness, that it lies within himself; he believes he can get it in plenty and quickly by running after the mirage of fashion and fancy, excitement and entertainment. He thinks that floating on the roaring, raging torrent of the world helps, but that only gives him unbearable tossing and nausea.

"Joy is a subjective feeling, it is not inherent in the objective world. You are the witness separate from the scene; you are the seer, not the seen, *drashta* not the *drig* or the *draya*.

"The screen is *satya* and the images that flit across it are *mithya*. When you see a film you do not see the screen as a screen; you forget its existence and you think that there is just the picture and nothing else as its base. But the screen is there all the time and it is only the screen that makes you experience the picture. *Narayana* is the screen and *prakriti* is the film; when the play is on,

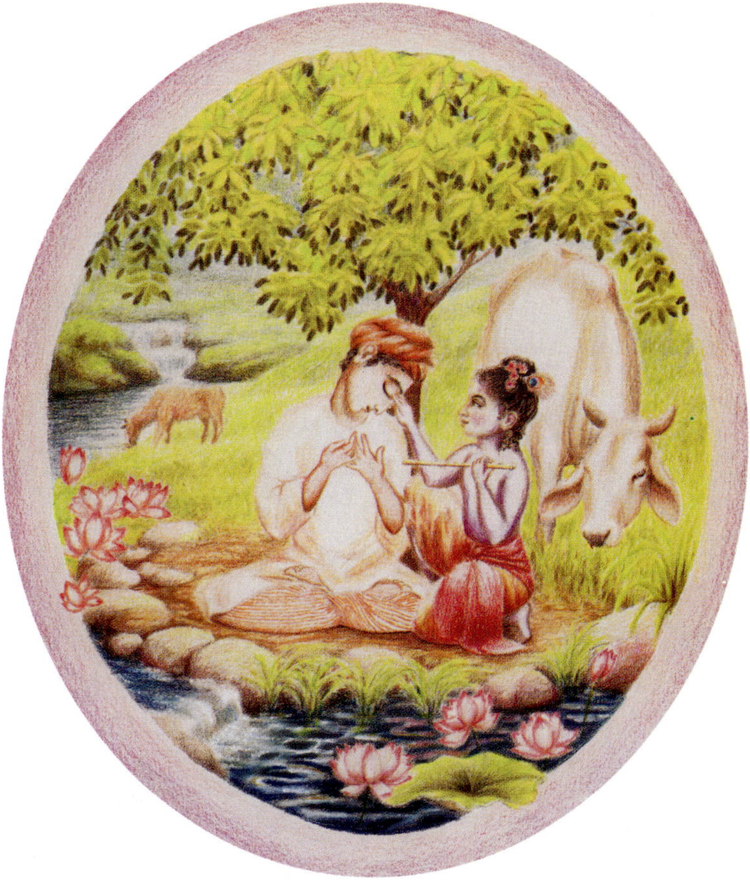

the screen is the *adhara* and *prakriti* becomes *Narayanamayam*. The screen is *satyam;* the story is *samsaram* (flood of change), for it has only some *saram* (reality)!

"*Surdas*, the blind singer, had as his ardent listener when he sang, Krishna Himself, sitting in front of him as a cowherd boy humming in appreciation; *Surdas* took Him to be a cowherd from the surrounding villages, though he sang that all beings are His forms. One day, Krishna revealed to him that He was the hero of his heart. He touched his eyes with His Divine fingers so that He could be seen! From His lips, he could hear the self-same strains of the flute which he was hearing all along, whenever he started meditating on the Lord. As a matter of fact, he was only trying all along to put that music into verse. He then declared that he did not care to see other things with the sight vouchsafed to him; he said the inner eyes were enough. The purified inner vision gives lasting joy and, therefore, unfailing health.

"To purify the *antahkarana*, *Vedas* and *Shastras* prescribe the proper processes; some people dismiss the *Vedas* and *Shastras* as so many shackles on thought and action, but they are 'bunds' (dams) which regulate the flow of feelings, emotions and instincts along safe channels.

"Coming more directly to the topic of physical ills, I must tell you that you must practise moderation in food, drink, sleep and exercise. Good food taken in moderate quantities at regular intervals, that is the prescription. *Satvic* food promotes self-control and intelligence more than *rajasic* and *tamasic*. So for spiritual aspirants, *satvic* food is very necessary.

"In one of the jails of this state, there was once a very pure soul devoted to spiritual ideals. Carefully practising *sadhana*, he had advanced very far in *dhyana* and *dharana*. One day, however, when he sat for *dhyana*, he felt very savage emotions surging up in him and was shocked to find that he could not, in spite of a tremendous struggle, suppress the hateful and murderous thoughts that took hold of him. He was rocked in agony and his *guru*, too, was upset at the turn of events. The *guru* probed into the history of his disciple rather deeply, but could not find any valid reason for the tragedy. At last, he found that a certain fanatic murderer had been the cook in the jail kitchen the day before the calamity, and his hateful homicidal thoughts had pervaded the food he cooked and which the *sadhaka* had consumed. There are subtle invisible thought-forms that can pass from one person to another through such means. Here, one has to be very careful about food, especially when one is proceeding Godward on the steep path of *yoga*.

"Sleep, too, should be regulated and moderate; it is as important as work and food. Remember also that dress is primarily for protection against heat and cold, not for vain display even at the cost of health. Virtuous conduct also ensures mental peace and that, in turn, saves you from many a physical and mental illness. If you overstep *miti* (bounds), you miss your *gati* (progress). Above all, do every act as an offering to the Lord without being elated by success or dejected by defeat; this gives the poise and equanimity needed for sailing through the waters of the ocean of life.

"It is the mind that builds up the body, strong and shining, or wastes it to skin and bone. For *manushya* to be strong, the *manas* has to be strong. Live always as the servant of the Lord within you, then you will not be tempted into sin or fall into evil. Get into the habit of living in the light of God. It is the habit that rehabilitates the fallen. Have the attitude of *sharanagati*, or else your destiny will be *sara-gati*. That is why Krishna said, *Manmanaabhava!* You may ride in a smart car of your own; but you are entrusting daily, without a second thought, the car and yourself and your family to the skill and presence of mind of your chauffeur. However, when advised to entrust your affairs to the Lord, *mayashakti* hesitates and declines! It refuses to surrender to *Mahashakti*. What are we to say about such absurd conceit? If you have *sharanagati*, you will be ever content and ever so happy and healthy. Then this hospital can be closed for want of patients; it would be well used to accommodate devotees and give them lodging!

"All that you eat, all that you see, all that you hear, all that you take in through the senses, makes a dent in your health. There are three types of reactions you usually have from the outer world and three types of men in whom one or the other predominates: the cotton which gets soaked in whatever it gets immersed; the stone which escapes from getting affected, and the butter which is changed by whatever it comes across, even a little warmth. The 'butter' men are moved by instant sympathy, either at another's joy or at his grief. Do not, like some mental patients, be always worrying about some little ailment or another. Have courage, that is the best tonic; do not give up before you have to.

"It is not a long life that counts - if you live on and on, a time may come when you have to pray to the Lord to take you away, to release you from travail. You may even start blaming Him for ignoring you and blessing other luckier people with death! By all means, worry about success or failure in achieving the real purpose of life. And then you will get as many years as are needed to fulfil that desire. Yearn, yearn, yearn hard - and success is yours. Remember, you are all certain to win; that is why you have been called and you have responded to the call to come to Me.

"What other task have I than the showering of grace? By *darshan* (seeing the form of the Lord and receiving His blessing), *sparshana* (contact with the Divine) and *sambhashana* (hearing a great person), you share in that grace. When that melts and this melts, the two can merge. Treat Me not as one afar, but as very close to you. Insist, demand, claim grace from Me; do not praise, extol and cringe. Bring your hearts to Me and win My heart. Not one of you is a stranger to Me. Bring your promises to me and I shall give you My promise. But first see that your promise is genuine, sincere; see that your heart is pure; that is enough.

References:

Sathya Sai Baba, Sathya Sai Hospital, October 10, 1961.
Sathya Sai Speaks, Vol. II, pp. 75 - 80

22. FOOD, HEALTH AND SADHANA

Good thoughts, good words and good deeds,
As also the tendency to listen to all that is good and desirable,
And to absorb only good and wholesome sights,
And good traits and good behaviour,
Only these confer good health and a good way of living,
This word of Sai is verily the path of truth.

Embodiments of Love!

"Now, in this world of ours, man is given over to enjoying and experiencing wealth beyond description. But, out of all the types of wealth that one can possibly come across, it is one's health, which you find is the most valuable possession. It is said, "Health is wealth." One who does not have good health cannot possibly succeed even in the least of ventures.

"It is one's health, again, which is the paramount requirement, both in this world and in the world beyond. One can have wealth and money beyond description, or one can have positions of authority and importance. But without health the person concerned would look upon these - the position, authority and wealth - as inconsequential. Only when he has health in the first place, would he be in a position to use the wealth for a good purpose.

"In order to discharge one's responsibilities of *dharma*, *artha*, *kama*, and *moksha* (the four *purusharthas*), one's health is vitally necessary. The first three of these *dharma*, *artha* and *kama*, belong to this world. But *moksha*, or liberation, comes to you in the world beyond. What is the primary aim and goal of one's life? It is this *kaivalya*, or liberation, which is man's goal, destiny and the very secret of his existence. You might have an important position, you might have wealth beyond your dreams, and you might hold responsibility and authority, but unless you are able to reach your destination, these are futile.

"Man is born with five sheaths, or *koshas*. These five are the *annamaya kosha*, the *pranamaya kosha*, the *manomaya kosha*, the *vignanamaya kosha*, and the *anandamaya kosha*. Of these five, three belong to your physical existence and two to the world beyond. It is not possible to distinguish between these two. What you are trying to seek in this world and the world beyond are closely interlinked, inseparable. We refer to God as *sat-chit-ananda* (existence-knowledge-bliss). Through the media of name and form, which are temporary and transient, you are able to experience *sat-chit-ananda*, which are lasting, eternal. The totality of one's existence on this earth consists of the coming together of the three sheaths: *annamaya*, *pranamaya* and *manomaya*. From this human plane of existence you transcend and rise above to become one with the Divine. For that, you need the assistance of the *vignanamaya kosha* and the *anandamaya kosha*.

"Unless you set this distant goal before you, this worldly existence will be meaningless. Why do you need to protect and safeguard your health? Not for your worldly existence, but for the sake of experiencing *Atmananda*. In this creation, there is any number of life forms. The different types of life forms have been classified into 8,400,000 species. Of these species of life forms, 8,399,999 types tend to eat food which is not cooked. They eat food which is natural and available in the world, and they enjoy perfect health. But of course, it does happen, that because of climatic variations and factors which are beyond ones control, some of these life forms do also fall ill.

"It is man alone who is subjected to the maximum amount of trouble. For him, any number of diseases is on the increase. The reason is that man does not like to eat food which is of God's creation, which is available in nature. He is a victim of his taste buds. Whatever is available in nature he transforms to suit his tastes, and he thereby kills the very essence of life contained in them. Because he now exterminates the life-giving forces in his food he is needlessly subjecting himself to an increasing amount of disease. If man were to seek to eat foods which are available in their natural state, he certainly would not be subjected to ever-increasing disease. Look at the head. If you ask the question, 'What is the cause of headaches?' It is not the head, which has to be faulted. It is the stomach, which has gone out of shape!

"It is this way for all the different organs that you have. It is the stomach, which is the key point. Whatever is given to the stomach, the stomach digests it and supplies the essence of it to all the organs. This power of digestion given to the stomach is, in fact, a God-given thing. That is how one reveres and worships Him. In fact, God resides in a being as this digestive force, which is what governs and runs all the life processes in the body. To such a God as this, what is it that you should offer and give? This God should be given that which is His own creation, not what is made by man. So, whatever is available in the natural state, as given to you by God in His creation, if you want to give that to your stomach, everything would be all right.

"What do we really mean by *ahara*, or food? We look upon things like rice, fruit, vegetables as food. Whatever you can possibly see in this world is food. And that foodstuff which experiences and partakes of the food is also a type of food. What follows is that 'food experiences food.' An animal or a beast is also a type of food. And this beast partakes of some other animal as its food. It is food eating food.

"The quality of *satvic* food is that it is full of *stavic* attributes and puts you on the path of *dharma* (right action). When you bring together these three seemingly different entities (*dharma, artha, kama*), you can secure the fourth, *moksha*. You find that the priests who preside over religious ceremonies, like weddings and marriages, when they keep chanting *mantras*, they make a reference to *dharma, artha* and *kama*. They do not utter the word *moksha*. The reason is, if you can really experience and fulfil what is to be done in regard to *dharma, artha* and *kama* in the right way, *moksha* will come to you of its own. We keep in sight *moksha* and forget all about *dharma*, *artha* and *kama*, so much so that we really do not do what we should in regard to this *dharma*, *artha* and *kama*.

"We do not discharge our responsibilities and obligations in the proper way with regard to the first three. We ask for *moksha*. How can it be ours? What is the quality of it? While following the path of *dharma*, you seek *artha*, or wealth. To tread the path of *dharma* and then secure *artha*, or wealth, in the proper way, you reach the third step, your desires and aspirations. Here also they should be saturated with the element of *dharma*.

"Wealth without *dharma* and desire without *dharma* cannot make you worthy of securing or wanting to secure *moksha*. If *dharma*, *artha* and *kama* have been discharged in the way they ought to have been, man would not have been subjected to the increasing volume of stress and disorders and various other ailments as he is now. The main thing which governs these three, is, again, food.

"We tend to eat food in excess and the kind of food, which leads us to mental derangement. There should be a limit placed on the food that one eats. If you exceed it, you are bound to suffer. To protect and safeguard the body, food is necessary. But even this food should be taken in accordance with the qualities required for the sustenance of the body. If you exceed that limit, then disorders will come to your body.

"Take, for instance, the heart. The heart has a capacity to pump blood to the rest of the body. It cannot exceed this function. You find that in God's creation the body requires a certain amount of power for its heart. Whenever you want to build your body beyond the means and limits of your heart, it cannot function. That is why there is an increase of heart disease. You want to build your bodies like boulders. What can your poor heart do? Even amongst educated people this disease is crippling. Even those doctors who specialize in heart disease become its victims. They exhort each and every one; "Health is wealth." But not when it comes to their own bodies!

"For instance, a person may have a problem with blood pressure. Hereafter, he gets diabetes. One can equate the two as twins: blood pressure and diabetes. One follows in the footsteps of the other. And here is a peculiar thing: if you take a medicine for diabetes, the blood pressure goes up. If you take a medicine for blood pressure, the diabetes goes up, because these two are a pair of opposites and they cannot be brought down and controlled through medicine. These diseases are such that once they creep in, it is very difficult for you to push them out. But how can you cure them?

"The golden principle, or formula is diet control! Keep a curb on your food intake and everything will be all right. You must reduce your weight. The body is like a mount, a heap. You sweep your house continuously for a month, collect all the dust till it becomes a heap. In the same manner, in this body which is inert, you are putting the dust of *idli, sambar, vadas, dosa* and food like that. Do not put in any of these for a week, and it will show a reduction in size. The body is like a tyre. You pump up the tyre and it becomes inflated. If you deflate a tyre, there is no inherent danger. But, if you go on pumping, there is always the danger that the tyre might burst! It is better to be safe.

"Blood pressure and diabetes, according to us, are commonplace diseases. This is a highly mistaken notion. These two are very dangerous. Both of these diseases affect and act on the heart. One of these tends to enlarge the heart, the other tends to enlarge the surroundings of the heart. Both these together would enlarge the heart. What causes the right amount of sugar in the blood? It is insulin. If insulin is on the decrease, the blood sugar increases. Because the blood should contain only a certain amount of sugar, a diabetes patient is injected with insulin. When the sugar comes down or goes up, the person can become unconscious. In order to keep a check on the sugar content of the blood, doctors generally advise a patient to eat food like wheat and other cereals. Whatever you eat becomes glucose in the body.

"In the southern part of India, people eat more rice. It is their custom. Once a person starts eating more and more rice, the glucose content increases. Therefore, doctors in the south advise one to eat wheat instead. Because the person is not used to eating wheat, he will not be tempted to overeat. A person in the north is normally given to eating wheat. The fact that they are used to eating wheat, does not make them free from diabetes. What kind of diet control should a northerner have? He should eat rice. He will eat less food then and the sugar content will come down. The main idea is that the amount of food you take should be limited.

"Excessive food leads to mental derangement. Limited amounts of food confer joy and happiness. Food and our personal habits can really confer longer life. Maybe certain circumstances beyond your control could lead you to distress, but otherwise there is no cause to be subjected to disease. What people are eating today has absolutely no innate power to sustain them. For the upkeep of the body you need vitamins and proteins.

"One vitamin gives you good sight, power to the eyes. Another purifies and strengthens the blood. A third vitamin strengthens the bones. Proteins are a must. Protein means 'that which protects you'. When you look at the protein content in food, that which is not cooked contains the largest amount. Take, for instance, pulses, like mung, *dhal,* soya beans. Indians proudly call gram 'Indian soya beans'. Here, the protein content is quite a lot. The way of eating them is to soak them in water and then, when they are chewable, eat them. They come to you in their richness. Because we are victims of our palate, of the tongue, of our tastes and whims and fancies, what do we do? Get rid of all the protein! Boil them! Subject them to various types of transformation by adding oil and various other ingredients. In the process, we deprive them of their basic content, deprive ourselves of what they can give us.

"Take fruit. In fruit there are vitamins. Or take vegetables. They can give you any amount of strength. But, what we have today can be called artificial vitamins. And through these artificial forms of vegetables, all types of diseases abound. Formerly, in villages, they used to have various crops of vegetables. The common practice, was to have manure in its natural state, in the form of cow dung, and it used to be given to these plants; you could get *bhindi*, lady's fingers, cucumbers and the like in their natural state. The size could have been small, but they were rich in nutrient content.

"Or, take for example a chilli plant. A chilli can be small, but it is enough to give its flavor to a potful of *sambar*. Today, you find the same chilli bloated up out of all proportion, a huge, big one. You get a large number of these chillies and put them in the *rasam*, a small tumblerful. Still, you do not get its taste! What is the reason? These plants are now cultivated with artificial manure, and they really do not have the innate strength which they ought to have.

"When you contrast the village with the city, the villagers have far less diseases than the city dwellers. Because those living in cities and towns can not breathe pure air, they cannot get pure water to drink, cannot get pure food to eat. The external pictures of what they get is certainly healthy. But what they actually offer is undesirable.

"The present fertilizers are full of defects. As a result, you find an increase in the number of cancer cases and heart complaints. To this day, there has been no doctor who has come up with a cure for cancer. What is the cause of cancer? Somebody might say eating betel leaf gives you cancer. A few others say cancer is the direct result of smoking beedies and cigarettes. And some might say that the air around you is polluted, so you get cancer. All said and done, what you must understand is, to a limited extent, these factors might be contributing in a small way. But they are not the primary cause of cancer.

"The main cause of cancer is sugar. In order to produce commercial sugar, a lot of chemicals such as powdered bone are used in the process. And this substance, as you ingest the sugar, might become lodged in any part of the body and create problems. You have got two types of blood corpuscles, white and red. The white ones get clogged up, blocked in a certain part, and in that can grow a cancer. Some people call it glaucoma. This glaucoma is a primary ingredient, assisting cancer. This glaucoma is the primary problem of sugar, this chemical, as such.

"Water, air, pollution, smoking, they cannot be the main cause. Sugar is the main cause. In the good old times, in what form was sugar eaten? Not this artificial, synthesized one, but as jaggery powder, a wholesome form. That was what was taken to add sweetness to dishes. But today, you find the superficial means being adopted, artificial things in everything you eat, all merely for the sake of making money. People have taken to any number of such dubious ways, and the result is increasing diseases.

"There was a Greek emperor called Alexander. He also made conquests in this country on more than one occasion, and he was extremely powerful and wealthy. But he was not content with what he had. He wanted to add more and more kingdoms to his own. On one such occasion, he made a trip to India, conquered it, and amassed great treasures. On his way back, he suffered a horrible disease. He had at his bidding a large number of doctors, boys, and orderlies, who would come running to his command. All the doctors came and, one by one and examined him. Then they started shedding tears, saying, 'There is nothing that can be done, nobody can possibly do anything for him!'

"At that endpoint of his life, a great realization dawned on Alexander. He said, 'During my lifetime I did not realize it, but after my death, this realization of mine should be proclaimed far and wide to all the people in all lands.' He summoned all his ministers, 'Ministers, in a few moments I am going to leave this body. And, according to my wishes, you must perform my funeral rites.' 'We will certainly do your bidding, O Lord,' they said. Then Alexander told them, 'After I die, you must transport my corpse, my dead body, to Greece. And there you must wrap the body in a cloth of white all around, except my two hands; let my two hands be raised up so that everybody may see them.' But the ministers said, 'But, Sir, this is against our custom and tradition. How are we going to answer the people if they ask, "Why have you done this? Put the hands of the king up like this?"'

"And then Alexander uttered his last words before breathing his last. He said, 'Here is the emperor of Greece, a mighty man without parallel, a wealthy man and one who could ask for anything. But what did he take at the end of his life? Nothing! He could not possibly take anything, and he is going away bare-handed! This is the message you must give my countrymen.' But, what do we do now? For the sake of wealth, we literally waste and fritter away our time and energy.

"In order to protect and safeguard our health, we have established hospitals in several places. But some may be assailed by this doubt: here is Swami who can cure every one of their diseases through His own power, through His own miracles. Why, then, establish these hospitals? What you feel is normally reflected externally. There may be some who have implicit and total faith in the *vibhuti* of Swami, who take it and are cured. But, there may be some who have intense faith in the form of medicine available only in hospitals. And there are also people afflicted with minor ailments and diseases, who could seek the help of doctors and be cured. For instance, you have a cold, you have a cough and immediately you put your hands up in prayer, 'Oh, Sai Baba, cure me of this cold; cure me of this cough!' It is all these seemingly insignificant and totally irrelevant things you keep asking to be cured of. You should get relief from them by going to a doctor!

"There are many innocent villagers. They do not even know they have a disease till they become alarmingly sick. For the sake of such people, we have established hospitals, not in towns or cities, but on their outskirts or in villages and other such places. These village folk who are innocent in the extreme have to be rendered this service. There are many among them who do not know the cause of the disease they are suffering from, and in their ignorance, they only go on increasing the disorder. It is a pity that there is no one to tell them what is wrong with them, nobody to examine them and tell them that what they have is a disease.

"Take for instance, the hospital, which has been established at Whitefield. It is a tremendous relief for the people in nearby villages. All our medicines are free. They need not spend any money, and whatever they want, it is theirs for the asking. Certainly, it has to be said that the doctors who are working in these hospitals are extremely fortunate. In this hospital in Whitefield, Dr. Rajeshwari spends a lot of time and spares no effort. And there are those others, her colleagues, nurses and other doctors, who also give her a helping hand, and with love and affection render service to the innocent country people.

"Because these people are devout devotees they do not charge anything. They do not take even a single *paisa*. No doctors are being paid by us here in Puttaparthi or there in Whitefield, because they feel this is a service they can render to Sathya Sai Baba. There are doctors who come from Sri Lanka and Uttar Pradesh, and various other places, who have come out of love and regard for the place and for Swami, and work motivated by the spirit of service. Because people from far and near come to this place to seek relief, we are establishing a new hospital here, with more than a hundred beds. There is also going to be sophisticated equipment and instruments to carry out tests to detect diseases like cancer, heart disorders, X-ray machines and various other super specializations.

"This is a way not merely of serving humanity at large, it is a medium where the doctors can fulfil themselves. These doctors are no ordinary beings. One could say they are very much like Narayana Himself, because they have in their hands the strength and capacity to cure and sustain a body. But Dr. Rajeshwari said that they are mere instruments in the hands of Sathya Sai Baba, and that He is the Divine Doctor. But, as you say it, you have the Lord in thought and you let your hands do the rest. Because you have the instruments of your hands, Sathya Sai Baba also gives you the strength and the required ability. I am hoping that in this world, as the world is today, that doctors should be motivated by the spirit of service and sacrifice, so that they may decrease and bring to an end, as quickly as possible, death due to disease.

"Embodiments of Love, what is the sum and substance of all that I have been saying to you? First, health is of paramount importance. Second, for what sake, for whom? That you might experience *ananda* of the *Atma*. Try to understand who you are, your own reality. If you cannot understand who you are, what is the use of your being alive in this world? Do not make a distinction between that which is this world and that which is beyond this world. Bring the two together and realize that you have to realize your own true nature, and experience Divine *ananda*. And what is given to man, Love, further it. Do not give any room to petty-mindedness, or a narrow outlook. And try to conduct yourself in a way that you do not injure or harm others. Only then will you be sanctifying yourself and your existence."

References:
Sathya Sai Baba, Prasanthi Nilayam, August 10, 1983, Translated from the Telugu, transcribed by Estelle Tepper, edited for Western readers by Diane Wells, June 1984.

23. SATVIC FOOD, RAJASIC FOOD AND TAMASIC FOOD

"If one is able to control one's senses, even if blind, one will reach the destination of *moksha*, that is, attain liberation. On the other hand, if one's senses are not controlled, even if one is the best of men, one will not be able to reach the Divine destination.

"You must learn to use the elements of nature in order to promote the well-being of man. Although everything in the world is God's creation, we must cultivate the wisdom to make the proper use of things. Our sense organs, for instance, also have to be used in the right way. Each particular organ has a distinctive feature. Amongst them, the one that has the sense of taste, the tongue, is a very important one. It is imperative that we keep it in check. Sometimes to satisfy our palate, we consume all types of food - not knowing that through it bad qualities like lust, anger, greed, attachment, arrogance and selfishness grow in us." (1)

"The physical part of the food that we consume serves the needs of the gross body. The subtle element in it goes to the mind. The subtler element enters into speech." (21) "The subtle parts of the food will appear as our mind. Thus, either for the distortions in our mind, or for the sacred thoughts that generate therefrom, the food that we take is mainly responsible. Good qualities like peace, forbearance, love and attachment to truth can only be promoted by taking good food. Indian culture, as contained in the *Vedas*, advises us that control of our sensory organs and living on *satvic* and good food are the paths for realisation of the Self and liberation thereof. This is the reason why, from time immemorial, in our Indian tradition, the *Rishis* ate *satvic* food and drank clear flowing water. They kept their minds perfectly clean and this is how they were able to understand the Divine spirit. You should make an attempt to control your tongue when you are young. If at this age, you do not control your tongue and all other sensory organs, you will have to face many difficulties in your later life.

"To rectify the world and put it on the proper path, we have to first rectify ourselves and our conduct. If at an advanced age, you try and control your desires and senses, you may or may not win God's grace. On the other hand, if, at this young age, you control your organs, there is no doubt whatsoever that you will gain God's grace." (1)

"We should not think that the importance being given to the aspect of food is unnecessary. For all types of *yoga* (*pranayama, niyama, pratyahara, samadhi,* etc.), the correct type of food is the most important basis. You may have some doubts as to why we should give so much importance to a minor matter, like the intake of food, when there are so many other important things. Without purity of mind, we cannot achieve even a small thing. By the unclean food that we take in, we expose our body to unnecessary ills." (8)

"Both *ahamkara* and *mamakara* (egoism and attachment) are the result of consuming improper food. Bad kinds of food, or food earned by foul means, will plunge a man into ignorance into several ways, and suppress pure thoughts from arising in him. He will forget what to say to whom, when, where and how. The following episode in the *Mahabharata* illustrates this point. Bhishma was a great *gnani* (man of wisdom), and also a man of great renunciation (*maha tyagi*). Sri Rama, the hero of the *Ramayana*, is famous for having obeyed his father's orders for only fourteen years. But Bhishma followed his father's commandments throughout his life. He got his name Bhishma, because of his great determination and strict observance of vows, unparalleled in human history. Such a great hero was very grievously wounded by Arjuna's arrows and, as a result, he fell down on the battlefield on the ninth day of the *Kurukshetra* War.

"According to his own grave determination even at that critical period at the end of his life, he lay on a bed of arrows. When the Pandava brothers, along with their spouse, Draupadi, approached their grandsire Bhishma to pay homage to him, he began expounding to them all the aspects of *dharma* from his bed of arrows. After hearing him for a while, Draupadi suddenly burst into laughter.

"All the Pandava brothers were very upset by Draupadi's unaccountable levity and, considering it an affront to the venerable Bhishma, frowned at her. Understanding their distress, Bhishma calmed them down with soft sweet words, and told them that Draupadi, being an exemplary woman in every respect, must have a valid reason to laugh. He then asked Draupadi to explain the reason for her laughter and thereby remove the misapprehension of her husbands. She replied, 'Revered Grandsire! The lessons of *dharma* which you should have taught to the evil-minded and wicked Kauravas, you are now teaching to my noble and virtuous husbands. This appeared to me both ironical and futile. Hence I could not refrain from laughing, although I knew it would seem impolite.'

"Bhishma then explained that he had served the Kauravas and lived on their bounty. He said, 'As a result of eating the food of such ignoble and vicious persons, my blood became polluted and all pure thoughts in me were thereby suppressed. Now that Arjuna's arrows have drained away that impure blood from me, the *dharma* that was lying buried deep in me is gushing forth, inducing me to communicate it to your husbands.' From this episode, students should realise what a crucial role is played by food in determining one's thoughts, words and actions.

"In this connection, it may not be out of place to mention that Draupadi was a *maha pativrata*, a paragon among women who worship their husbands as veritable representatives of God and serve them in that spirit; moreover, there is an esoteric meaning to her name. Draupadi does not merely mean the wife of five husbands, namely, the Pandavas. Every human being has within him or her, five husbands in the form of the five life-breaths: *prana, apana, vayana, udana* and *samana*. When it is said that Draupadi lived harmoniously with all her five husbands, the allegorical meaning is that she ensured the maintenance of harmonious equilibrium among her five life-breaths, which is the prerequisite for a balanced living. In the case of most people, one or more of these life-breaths become excited beyond the optimum limit, resulting in a loss of equilibrium and harmony among the five life-breaths, and a consequent lack of balance in life as a whole. Everyone should try to follow the example of Draupadi in the matter of leading a life full of contentment and harmony, as well as in being satisfied with simple but pure food." (2)

"The Kauravas, even while experiencing the fruits of their previous *punya* (good deeds) were engaged in *papakarma* (evil activities). The Pandavas, on the other hand, even while undergoing the suffering due to their previous *papakarma* (bad *karma*), were thinking and doing only *punya!* This is the difference between the wise and the unwise. The Kauravas were slaves of the appetites of hunger and sex, and the Pandavas did every act for the sake of the Lord, having *satya* and *dharma* as their charioteer." (3)

"In the body of man, the *Atma* is the husband and the inclinations are the wives. Every act, word and thought must subserve the needs of the emancipation of the individual. By the recognition of the sovereignty of *Atma*, the primal formless Absolute wedded desire, and mind was born. The mind wedded two wives, inner contemplation and outer activity. The first gave birth to five sons: *satya, dharma, shanti, prema,* and *ahimsa*, the five Pandava brothers. The mind became infatuated more with the second wife, and so she gave birth to a hundred, each one with a name indicative of badness and wickedness, the Kauravas. God was on the side of the Pandavas, and they won.

"The seventeenth chapter of the *Gita* clearly defines the nature and tastes of the three types of food eaten by man: the food that promotes love, virtue, strength, happiness and cordiality is *satvic*, that which inflames, arouses, intoxicates and heightens hunger and thirst is *rajasic*, the food that depresses, disrupts, and causes disease is *tamasic*. The company in which food is consumed, the place, the vessels in which it is cooked, the emotions that agitate the mind of the person who cooks it and serves it, all these have subtle influences on the nature and emotions of the person who takes in the final product! It is because the sages of India realised this that they laid down many do's and don'ts for the process of eating, as for the different stages of spiritual progress." (4)

"The quality and quantity of food that we take determine our thoughts and feelings. *Satvic* food is conducive to self-realization and liberation from the dualities and relativities of the world." (5)

"One must prefer *satvic* to *rajasic* foods. By drinking intoxicating stuff one loses control over the emotions and passions, the impulses and instincts, speech and movements, and one even descends to the level of beasts.

"By eating flesh one develops violent tendencies and animal diseases. The mind becomes more intractable when one indulges in *rajasic* food. It can never be remoulded if *tamasic* food is consumed with relish. When the mind is fed on *tamasic* food, which dulls, inebriates, blunts reason and induces sloth, the mind becomes callous and inert and useless for the uplifting of man." (6)

"*Tamasic* food deadens the intellect (*buddhi*). (7) "In the seventeenth and eighteenth chapters, the *Bhagavad-Gita* describes *satvic* food as that which has been offered to God. By frying or cooking, the *satvic* life-force that is present in natural food is destroyed. By eating such food, man makes himself liable to several types of diseases. Because man eats such cooked food, he also becomes distant from *sadhana*. It is because of this, that in ancient times, *Rishis* and devotees of God ate only uncooked food in its natural form." (8)

"Therefore, raw pulses just sprouting are to be preferred. Also nuts and fruits. The coconut, offered to the gods, is a good *satvic* food, having a good percentage of protein besides fat, starch and minerals. Food having too much salt or pepper is *rajasic* and should be avoided; so also too much fat and starch, which are *tamasic* in their effect on the body." (9) "Do not eat too much rice." (3)

"Uncooked food, nuts and fruits, germinating pulses are the best. Coconut kernel, coconut water, sprouting pulses, uncooked or half-cooked vegetables and greens are good for the health." (10) "The food types that you eat should be nourishing and nutritious. What people are eating today has absolutely no innate power to sustain them. For the upkeep of the body you need vitamins and proteins. When you look at the protein content in the food, that which is not cooked contains the largest amount. Take, for instance, pulses like *mung dhal* and soya bean. Here the protein content is quite a lot. The way of eating them is to soak them in water and then, when they are chewable, eat them.

"What do we do? Get rid of all the protein! Boil them! Subject them to various types of transformation by adding oil and various other ingredients. In the process, we deprive them of their basic content. You are now feeding the plants, the vegetables with artificial manure, and they really do not have the innate strength which they ought to have. The present fertilizers are full of defects. As a result, you find an increase in the number of cancer cases and heart complaints." (11)

"Flour, milk, fruit and beans are *satvic* food. Food that makes happy, that is attractive, juicy, oily, nice, tasty and delicious can often be compared to *satvic* food. This food has a subtle element that we call *satvic*, it is concerned with vital strength. *Satvic* food can be associated with oil, not with fat!." (12) "Roots, tubers and fruits are *satvic* food." (13) "Vegetables which grow above ground are more conducive to a good mental development than the roots which grow underground. Buttermilk is better than milk." (14)

"Some people are under the wrong impression that *satvic* food should consist of only milk, yogurt, sweets and fruits. They believe that they will become *satvic* by consuming large quantities of these delicacies. They are absolutely mistaken. Excessive and immoderate consumption of milk and its products awakens and aggravates the *rajasic* and *tamasic* qualities in man. A diet extra rich in milk, curds and ghee cannot be called *satvic* because it leads to the development of the passionate nature of man." (5)

"The older generation in India used to take a small quantity of rice soaked in curds as their first meal in the morning. It is good *satvic* food. Or they drank some *ragi* gruel, which is equally good. Drink large quantities of water, boiled and cooled, but not during meals, sometime before or after. Eat at regular intervals, according to a well established time table." (15) "If the *sadhaka* gets tired, then he can eat, at the end of the day's *dhyana*, a few groundnut kernels or almond seeds well soaked in water." (16) " 'Eat in moderation and live long.' This is the advice handed down through the ages by the seers of the past." (10)

"Fasting promotes health for the physical body; in the mental realm, it gives joy and bliss. Unlimited and unregulated food is very harmful for devotees. Indulging in a variety of tasty food is likely to lead the devotee into the torpidity and inertia of *tamoguna*."

"The *Gita* has emphasized the need for exercising extreme care in selecting the food you eat, constantly keeping in mind the importance of *satvic* food for helping you to maintain equanimity in all situations, so that you neither become elated when praise is showered, nor become depressed when criticism is heaped upon you. The *Gita* has also declared that there should be purity of the vessels and utensils used when cooking, and purity of the cooking process itself. The pots and pans used must be absolutely clean. Purity refers not only to physical cleanliness, but also to the way in which the implements and the articles of food have been acquired. You have to see whether these things have been acquired by proper means and honest work, or whether they have come through dishonest means. Articles which are acquired by improper means and used for cooking, will not only generate bad thoughts but will lead you down the wrong path.

"The next step is to inquire into the purity of the cooking process itself, by ascertaining the thoughts and feelings of the person who is cooking the food. There are three things mentioned that are to be carefully looked into and controlled. Normally, you pay attention only to the purity of the vessels and not the other two, namely, the purity of the person cooking and the purity of the food itself. You do not know the feelings in the mind of the cook and you do not know if the shopkeeper has acquired the articles you bought in the market by proper or improper means.

"Therefore, just before taking your food, you should pray and offer the entire meal to God, in order to cleanse and purify it. The prayer which is offered before food is not for the benefit of God, but it is for your own benefit; it will purify your food by evoking God's blessing. Before saying the prayer, the food is merely food; but once you offer it to the Lord, it becomes *prasadam*, consecrated food. This prayer removes all the defects and flaws in the vessels and in the articles of food, as well as removing any negative influence acquired during the cooking process." (17)

"Food, to be *satvic*, should be capable of strengthening the mind as well as the body. It should not be too salty, too hot, too bitter, too sweet or too sour. It should not be taken while steaming hot. Food which fans the flames of thirst should be avoided. The general principle is that there should be a limit, a restraint. Food cooked in water should not be used the next day; it becomes harmful. *Rajasic* food is the opposite of *satvic*, it is too salty, too hot, too bitter, too sweet, too sour, too odorous. Such food excites and intoxicates." (18)

"People can be healthy and live longer only if they eat the minimum they require rather than fill themselves up with maximums. The shortage of food grains is mainly due to bad and wasteful eating habits. Fasting for one day during the week is good for the body. Develop a biting hunger before you sit down to a meal, and wait for the call before you start loading the stomach again." (19)

"What is *rajasic* food? Some people eat food that is very hot, that is *rajasic* food, it only strengthens the *rajasic* qualities. Also food without oil, which is totally dry, must not be eaten." (12)

"Alcoholic drinks and meat-eating promote *rajoguna*." (8) After what men consider as a day of hard work, they go to clubs, where they become slaves of drink and ultimately ruin themselves, because 'First, the man drinks the wine, second, the wine drinks the wine and third, the wine drinks the man.' " (2)

"*Rajasic* food generates virulent thoughts. By consuming non-vegetarian food we develop brutal mentalities. Those who are practising meditation must abstain from meat. We should also remember constantly that *ahimsa,* or non-violence, is the supreme *dharma*. It is a sin to kill innocent animals for the sake of filling our stomachs." (5) "God is in every creature, so how can you give such pain? Sometimes when someone beats a dog he cries, he feels so much pain. How much more pain, then, in killing? Animals did not come for the purpose of supplying food to human beings; they came to work out their own life in the world. Dirty thoughts come with fish." (20) "Fish are *tamasic* items of food." (13)

"What is *tamasic* food? If you have cooked food, you should not save it for other people, it becomes *tamasic* food. Heated food that has totally cooled down is *tamasic* food. Food that begins to smell is also *tamasic*. Do not keep cooked food one or two days or even longer, for it becomes *tamasic* food. Eat cooked food immediately it has been cooked. The longer you wait, the more *tamasic* the food becomes. Wine and meat give you lots of *tamasic* qualities. Meat promotes the demonic qualities in you. Based upon the types of food that people eat, they may be split up into two types, the immortals (*amaras*) and the demonic people (*asuras*). The effect of salt is worse than that of wine. I advise those with high blood pressure not to use any salt, because adding salt pollutes the blood. Do not eat any salty, sour or strongly spiced foods. If a person eats such foods, he will have a tendency towards a certain kind of determination, not to go on the way to God, but to strengthen the demonic qualities in himself." (12)

"The main cause of cancer is commercial sugar." (11) "Too much medication is also bad. Allow nature full scope to fight the disease and set you right. Adopt more and more the principles of naturopathy, give up running around to doctors." (9)

"The water that we drink should be pure. If the water is pure, the gross part of it is excreted as urine, and the subtle part forms *prana* (life, life force, essence of life). Water takes the form of life. Food takes the form of the mind. Now you understand how close the links are between the mind and the food that you eat and drink." (12)

"A *satvic* diet does not mean simply the food we take through our mouth, but it also means the pure air we breathe in through our nose, the pure vision we see through our eyes, the pure sounds we listen to through our ears and the pure objects we touch through our feet. The intake must always be pure and blameless, *satvic*. The sound, the sights, the impressions, the ideas, the lessons, the contacts, the impacts, all must promote reverence, humility, balance, equanimity and simplicity. The place where one spends one's life also has subtle influences on character and ideals." (6)

"When we say that we should accept only *satvic* food, it refers to food that we accept through all the organs. Our eyes must accept only visions which are sacred and *satvic*. We should use our eyes to see only the sacred creation of the Lord. Next is the process of listening, or the food that we take in through our ears. We should not indulge in blaming others, criticising others and listening to unnecessary things. All this constitutes unsacred food. We should also not listen to things intended to ridicule others. We should be prepared to listen only to sacred thoughts of the Lord. We should not be prepared to listen to blame heaped on others.

"Then comes the process of smell, the food we take in through the nose. You should take in only sacred smells associated with Divine aspects. A good smell does not mean scent or perfume. Good smell connotes sacred smells associated with the Divine.

"Thus, through all the organs, we should try to take in only sacred and pure things.

"Next, is the sense of touch. Our ancients have prescribed that contact should be only with Divine aspects. When we sit down for *dhyana*, we use a small plank and sit on that so that there is no contact with the earth. It is not possible for us to realise what might happen through the contact that exists between us and the earth." (8)

"Allergy is produced by unpleasant smells, or when something intrinsically unwelcome is contacted and tasted." (6)

"Wherever there is dirt and an unclean atmosphere, there will be bad and filthy germs; while in a clean place, where the atmosphere is good and clean, there will be clean bacteria. When we touch an unclean body, there is the possibility of disease-causing germs flowing into us. Further, that unclean and unsacred body may communicate a part of its uncleanliness to us. One body and another are like magnets in this case. That is the reason why individuals who take to the path of *sadhana* should keep away from unclean surroundings and objects. It is in this context that our ancients have recommended that we should go and touch the feet of sacred and elderly people, so that the sacredness that is contained in their body can be transmitted to us." (8)

"Man does not realise that there is a vast unknown beyond the purview of the five faulty instruments of perception that he has. For example, from every being and thing, constantly and without intermission, millions of minute particles and millions of vibrations issue forth. Certain substances like camphor emit so much of these that a lump disappears in a few days. The bodies of others affect us by these emissions, and we, too, affect them in the same way. Naturally, the growth of the body is affected, as well as our health and strength by the contact or company we develop.

"Five types of baths are prescribed in the Hindu scriptures in order to maintain physical immunity from the emanations of others: mud-baths, sun-baths, baths in water, air-baths and ash-baths, where the body is given a coating of fine ash, or *vibhuti*, revered as the mark of Shiva. The ash guards the body from evil contacts and deleterious effects of the vibrations emanating from others; it also sanctifies and purifies the vibrations of the individual wearing the ash, for it reminds him always of the inevitable end of all that one feels as one's own, except only the Lord, who is the very Person Himself." (6)

SATVIC FOOD

Food offered to God	NOT	too much
that which puts you onto the path of *dharma*	"	too warm
	"	too salty
PURE, NATURAL, RAW, UNCOOKED FOOD	"	too sweet
raw biological fruit	"	too sour
raw biological nuts (soaked in water)	"	too bitter
coconut kernel and fresh coconut milk	"	too spicy
fresh biological roots and tubers		
fresh uncooked biological vegetables	EAT	moderately
(if necessary half cooked)	"	in silence
raw, biological ground kernels	"	at regular intervals
(soaked in water)	"	slowly
raw biological pulses, such as soya beans,	"	in a clean room
mung beans and lentils (soaked in water)	"	in good company
sprouting pulses	"	in the
little rice soaked in curds or water		right attitude of mind

ragi gruel
foods with natural oil content

one meal per day fast
one day during the week

a little raw milk (from cattle
tended with love and wisdom)
" " buttermilk
" " yogurt
" " curds
" " butter, ghee
buttermilk is better than milk

do not drink during
meals drink a lot of pure
water between meals

pure sights, sounds,
smells and touches
pure environment

PURE WATER

sufficient exercise
" rest and sleep
PURE AIR
" SUNLIGHT

RAJASIC FOOD

Food cultivated with fertilizers
and other chemicals

heated food dry food
without oil pepper

tamarind
drugs/medication
tobacco
alcoholic drinks
too much milk and milk-products
eggs
too much fruit

coffee, tea
salt

too much
too warm
too salty
too sweet
too sour
too bitter
too spicy

many books, films, magazines
and newspapers
sensuous scenes, exciting sights
aggressive sounds

TAMASIC FOOD

Food cultivated with
fertilizers and other
chemicals

heated food heated
food that has totally
cooled down (bread, etc.)
most industrial nutrition
artificial food

tamarind
drugs/medication
tobacco
alcoholic drinks
too much milk and
       milk products
too much fruit
meat, fish meat, fish
coffee, tea, chocolate
commercial sugar
pasteurized milk and
       milk products
fat
starch

meaningless questioning
and argumentation

many books, films,
magazines and newspapers
horrifying scenes
offensive smells

References :

1. Sathya Sai Baba, *Summer Showers in Brindavan,* 1973, pp. 131 - 138
2. Sathya Sai Baba, *Summer Showers in Brindavan,* 1990, pp. 102-104, 112
3. Sathya Sai Baba, *Prema Vahini,* 1985, pp. 60, 67
4. *Voice of the Avatar,* Extracts from the Divine Discourses of Sathya Sai Baba, Part I, Compiled by D.Hejmadi, M.Sc., Second Edition 1981, pp. 54 - 55
5. Sathya Sai Baba, *Summer Showers in Brindavan,* 1979 pp. 93 - 96
6. *Sadhana, The Inward Path,* Quotations from the Divine Discourses of Sathya Sai Baba, 1976, pp. 207 - 216
7. Sathya Sai Baba, *Sanathana Sarathi,* April 1976, pp. 44
8. Sathya Sai Baba, *Summer Showers in Brindavan,* 1978, pp. 189 - 193
9. Sathya Sai Baba, *Sanathana Sarathi,* March 1980, pp. 62 - 63
10. *Sathya Sai Speaks, Vol. XI,* pp. 149-151
11. Sathya Sai Baba, Prasanthi Nilayam, August 10, 1983, translated from the Telugu, transcribed by Estelle Tepper.
12. Sathya Sai Baba, Prasanthi Nilayam, July 15, 1983, Sri Sathya Sai Baba Bhajanavli prerecorded cassette, 20.
13. Sathya Sai Baba, *Ramakatha Rasavahini,* pp. 385
14. Ra. Ganapati, Baba: *Sathya Sai,* Part I, 1984, pp. 57
15. *Sathya Sai Speaks, Vol. VII,* 2nd. Am. Printing, 1985, pp. 112
16. Bhagavan Sri Sathya Sai Baba, *Dhyana Vahini,* 1988, pp. 55
17. *Sri Sathya Sai Baba, Discourses on the Bhagavad Gita,* Compiled and edited by A. Drucker, First Indian Edition, 1988, pp. 39-42
18. Sathya Sai Baba, *Geetha Vahini,* pp. 238-246
19. E. B. Fanibunda, *Vision of the Divine,* Pop. Edition Reprint, 1984, pp. 61
20. J. S. Hislop, *Conversations with Bhagavan Sri Sathya Sai Baba,* pp. 26-27
21. Sathya Sai Baba, *Sanathana Sarathi,* December 1992, pp. 308

24. PURIFICATION OF OUR FOOD

"Just before taking your food, you should pray and offer the entire meal to God, in order to cleanse and purify it. This prayer offered before taking food is not for the benefit of God, but for your own benefit; it will purify your food by evoking God's blessing. The prayer that can be used before eating is the twenty-fourth verse from the fourth chapter of the *Gita*, and the fourteenth verse from the fifteenth chapter of the *Gita*:

Brahmarpanam, Brahma havir, Brahmagnau Brahmana hutam;
Brahmaiva tena gantavyam, Brahma karma samadhina.

(Gita, "Chapter IV : 24")

"The act of offering is Brahman, the offering itself is Brahman, offered by Brahman in the sacred fire which is Brahman. He alone attains Brahman who, in all his actions, is fully absorbed in Brahman.

Aham Vaishvanaro bhutva, praninam dehamashritah;
Pranapana sama yuktah, pachami annam chatur vidham.

(Gita, "Chapter XV : 14")

"I am *Vaishvanaro*, the all-pervading cosmic energy lodged in the bodies of living beings. Being united with their in-going and out-going life-breaths, I consume all the different (four) types of foods.

"Before offering this prayer, the food is merely food, but once you offer it to the Lord it becomes *prasadam* (consecrated food). This prayer removes all the defects and flaws in the vessels and in the articles of food, as well as any negative influence acquired during the cooking process." (1)

"The purpose of our chanting the fourteenth verse of the fifteenth chapter of the Gita is to obtain success in worldly matters and to overcome the obstacles on the spiritual path. Here, the food we eat determines, in many ways, what we are going to get in future for ourselves. The food we eat determines the type of ideas that sprout in us.

"While taking our food, if we use exciting words, ideas related to the exciting words will sprout in us. The lesson we should learn is that when we take a bath, when we sit for *dhyana* (meditation), or when we take our food, we should not think of other activities and other ideas. Too much talk while we take our food also causes harm to us. We should not give room to any kind of talk when we take our food. With a happy heart and with a sacred word, we must undertake to utter this particular verse and then take our food. In this way, whatever has been offered to Brahman will become the *prasad* which comes to us as a gift of Brahman. The meaning of the verse is that God Himself, who is in a human form in you, is the one consuming the food. Therefore, this changes our food into food for God. The kind of food we eat will determine our ideas. For all our ideas it is our food that is responsible. If we eat *satvic* food seated in a clean place, we will have clean ideas through eating that food.

"There will thus be a good possibility of our receiving spiritual ideas. Even if there are lapses in the cleanliness aspect, namely the pot, the material used for cooking, and the process of cooking, if we offer the food to *Paramatma* before we eat it, then the food becomes clean. By thus offering to the Lord the food that we eat, we bring to it these different kinds of cleanliness, and so, our ancestors have told us that these are the steps which we must observe regarding our food. Today, when one is hungry, one does not care what one eats, in what restaurant one eats or what kind of food one eats. People will eat anything. Selfishness is growing while selflessness and help to others is diminishing. The heart is becoming harsher and harsher. Intelligence is on the rise but good qualities are diminishing. Thus all the agitation and lack of peace in the world may be traced to our own food habits. Wherever you may go, before you eat your food, you should remember the two verses of the *Gita* and the *Asatoma* prayer:

Asatoma sadgamaya,
tamaso ma jyotir gamaya,
Mrityor ma amritangamaya,
Aum shanti, shanti, shantihi.

"Lead me from untruth to truth, from darkness to light, from death to immortality, Aum peace, peace, peace." (2)

"From the transient world of decay lead me to the everlasting world of bliss. Let the effulgence of Thy grace illumine my being with truth. Save me from this cycle of birth and death and destroy the cravings of the mind which produce the seeds of (repeated) birth." (3)

"Before meals you may also chant the *Gayatri mantra:*

Aum,
Bhur bhuvah svaha,
Tat Savitur Varenyum,
Bhargo Devasya dheemahi,
Dhiyo yo nah prachodayat (3, 4)

"O Mother, Who subsists in all the three *kalas* (timepast, present and future), in all the three *lokas* (worlds: heaven, earth and the lower regions), and in all the three *gunas* (attributes: *satva, rajas* and *tamas*), I pray to Thee to illumine my intellect and dispel my ignorance, as the splendrous sunlight dispels all darkness. I pray to Thee to make my intellect serene and bright and enlightened.

"The *Gayatri mantra* is a universal prayer, enshrined in the *Vedas*, the most ancient scripture of man. The *Gayatri mantra* has in it the validity of the *Vedas*. It contains the essence of *Vedic* teachings. The *Gayatri mantra* is considered *Vedashara*, it is the essence of prayer, and prayer fosters and sharpens the knowledge-yielding faculty. As a matter of fact, the four *maha-vakyas*, or core-declarations, enshrined in the four *Vedas* are implied in the *Gayatri mantra*.

"Each of the four *Vedas* has a core axiom enclosed in it; *Tat tvam asi* (That thou art), *pragnanam Brahma* (consciousness is

Brahma), *ayam atma Brahma* (this Self is *Brahma*) and *Aham Brahmasmi* (I am Brahman). When all these are synthesised, the *Gayatri* mantra emerges.

"The *Gayatri* is described as *Chhandasam Mata*, the mother of all the *Vedas*. One meaning of *Gayatri* is that it is a *mantra* which protects or fosters the *gayas* or *jivis* (individuals). If chanted regularly, all the merit that would be obtained by the recital of the *Vedas* are earned. It is during the *satvic* period, from 4 a.m. to 8 a.m. and from 4 p.m. to 8 p.m. that the *Gayatri mantra* should be recited.

"This *mantra* is the embodiment of all deities. It is not related to any particular sect, caste or idol or institution. It is essential to recite the *Gayatri* at least three times during morning, noon and evening. This will serve to reduce the effects of the wrong acts one commits every day. It is like buying goods for cash instead of on credit. There is an accumulation of karmic debt as each day's *karma* (activity) is atoned on the day itself through reciting the *Gayatri mantra*." (3)

"The sound of a *mantra* is as valuable as its meaning. Even a poisonous cobra is quietened by music: *nadam*, sound, has that allaying property. The meaning of the *Gayatri mantra* is easy and profound. It does not ask for mercy or pardon; it asks for a clear intellect, so that the truth may be reflected therein accurately, without any disfigurement." (5)

"The sacred *Gayatri mantra* is an invocation addressed to the Sun for the improvement of the faculty of *buddhi*, or intelligence. The darkness of ignorance is dispelled by the incandescence of the light of the *buddhi*, like the glorious sun. 'Among the faculties, I am the *buddhi*,' proclaims Krishna in the *Bhagavad-Gita*." (6)

"Chant the *Gayatri* daily and it will lead you to the realization of the splendour of Brahman, by setting you free from the limitations which surround the three worlds, the three *gunas* and the triple aspect of time. The *Gayatri mantra* should be chanted in order to purify the mind and, like the sun's rays, it will dispel the darkness from within you. Children, right now is the golden time for you. Open your hearts and recite the *mantra* and you will be successful in life. Just as the trunk supports a tree, the *Gayatri mantra* supports the human system; without it, the tree of life would be sapless. If you chant the *Gayatri mantra* and also respect your parents as God, then the effects of both these will work together, fuse into one and produce a great effect on your lives by giving you splendour and brilliance." (4)

"The *Gayatri mantra* is usually chanted at dawn, midday and dusk. But God is beyond time. So, you need not be bound to the three points of time to recite the prayer. It can be said always and everywhere; only, one has to ensure that the mind is pure. I would advise you young people to recite it when you take your bath. Do not sing cheap and defiling songs. Recite the *Gayatri mantra*. When you bathe, the body is being cleansed; with the *Gayatri mantra* let your mind and intellect also be cleansed. Never give up the *Gayatri mantra*. You may give up or ignore any other *mantra*, but you should recite the *Gayatri mantra* at least a few times a day. It will protect you from harm wherever you are, in a bus or car, a railway train or plane, in a bazaar or on the road.

"Westerners have investigated the vibrations produced by this *mantra*. They have found that when it is recited with the correct accent as laid down in the *Vedas*, the atmosphere around becomes visibly illumined. So *Brahmaprakasha* (the effulgence of *Brahma*) will descend on you and illumine your intellect and light your path when this mantra is chanted. The goddess *Gayatri* is *Annapurna*, the Mother, the Force that animates all life. So do not neglect it." (7)

"*Gayantam trayate iti Gayatri*. Because it protects the one who recites it, it is called *Gayatri*. When *Gayatri* acts as protector of the life-force, She is known as *Savitri*. *Savitri* is the presiding deity of the five *pranas*. She protects those who lead a life of truth. This is the inner meaning. When one's intelligence and intuition are developed by recitation of the mantra, the activating deity is *Gayatri*.

When the life-forces are protected, the guardian deity is called *Savitri*. When one's speech is protected, the deity is called *Sarasvati*. Because of the protective roles of *Savitri*, *Sarasvati* and *Gayatri* in relation to life, speech and the intellect, *Gayatri* is described as *Sarvadevata-svarupini*, the embodiment of all deities." (3)

References:
1. *Sathya Sai Baba, Discourses on the Bhagavad Gita,* Compiled and edited by A. Drucker, First Indian Edition, 1988, pp. 41 - 42
2. *Sai Avatar,* Vol. III, pp. 98 - 100
3. *Bhajananamavali* (for overseas devotees), pp. 3 – 5, 26
4. *Vision of the Divine* by E.B. Fanibunda, Pop. Edition Reprint 1984, pp. 87
5. *Sathya Sai Speaks,* Vol. III, pp. 242
6. Sathya Sai Baba, *Summer Showers in Brindavan*, 1979, pp. 152 - 153
7. Tumuluru Krishna Murty, *Digest, Collection of Sri Sathya Sai Baba's Sayings,* 1985, pp. 118

25. HEALTH AND ILLNESS

"Really, all misery is caused by mankind itself, not by any extraneous agency. Having all the instruments of joy and contentment in one's possession, if man is miserable, it is due only to his perverseness, his stupidity. He has been warned over centuries by the scriptures of all cultures that he should give up greed and lust, give up the habit of catering to the senses, give up the belief that he is just this body and nothing more. And yet he does not recognize the illness that is torturing him. The disease is due to 'vitamin deficiency', as they say: the vitamins are *satya* (truth), *dharma* (right conduct, morality), *shanti* (peace) and *prema* (love). Take them and you recover; assimilate them into your character and conduct, and you shine with fine mental and physical health." (1)

"Moderation in food, moderation in talk, in desires and in pursuits, contentment with what little can be got through honest labour, eagerness to serve others and to impart joy to all, these are the most powerful of all the tonics and health preservers known to the science of health - *sanatana ayurveda*.

"For attaining the four aims of human life, *dharma* (righteousness), *artha* (prosperity), *kama* (fulfilment of desires), and *moksha* (liberation from bondage), the basic requirement is health of body and mind. Disease means feeling uneasy, upset due to the unsettling of one's temper or balance (equilibrium), and that affects the physical as well as the mental condition. This happens for two reasons: faulty food (*ahara*), and faulty activities (*vihara*). It is wiser to prevent disease than to run after remedies after it has begun or grown beyond control.

"People can live longer and be more healthy if only they eat the needed minimum. Regular prayers, twice a day, give strength and courage, which can withstand illness. Activity must be dedicated to God, the highest God. Then, it can provide health of body and mind. Even material machinery is given rest, they cannot run forever continuously. What then shall we say of this delicately organised human body?

"Fast for a day each week. That will be good for your body as well as for the country. Take only water so that all dirt is washed away. It is through dieting alone that birds and beasts set their health aright!

"Only a healthy person can afford to forget the body and dedicate his thoughts to God, and derive *ananda* (joy) therefrom. Illness is the inevitable result of idleness and pandering to one's ego; health is the inevitable consequence of a tough, hard life. Carry out all your personal chores yourselves, and your health will definitely improve. Contentment is the best tonic. Use the body as a boat to cross the ocean of life, with devotion to God and detachment from the world as the oars.

"Spiritual health is preserved and promoted by attention to the three *guna: satva, rajas* and *tamas*. Health is preserved and promoted by attention to the three humours, *vata* (wind), *pitta* (bile), and *kapha* (phlegm). The *tri-dosha* (triple-error) has to be avoided, that is to say, the three humours must not become vitiated or unbalanced. A healthy body is the best container for a healthy mind; illness makes the mind agitated and anxious. The material and the spiritual are the two pans in the balance; they have to be attended to in equal measure at least until a certain stage of progress is attained in spiritual development." (2)

"Man is the victim of many a pain; to those who identify themselves with the body, life is a series of troubles and miseries. But to those who know that the body is merely a vehicle, these troubles cannot cause anxiety. Bodily health is important, for ill-health affects mental poise and concentration. When the body is fit, mental functions, too, run smoothly; when the body suffers, the mind, too, becomes unsettled. So, this raft called body, which is the only means we have of crossing the sea of *samsara*, or mutability, has to be kept in good trim. Untruth, injustice, anxiety, all cause leaks and loosen the knots of the raft. The human raft is the most efficient, for it is built of *viveka* (wise discrimination), *vichakshana* (keenness of intellect) and *vairagya* (detachment), hard timber that can withstand the beat of the wave and the pull of the tide. If one does not make the best use of this opportunity, it may not come again for a long time. Devotion to God and morality are as important for physical health as they are for mental health. They free the mind from agitation, they feed it with joy and contentment, they quieten the nerves and help even bodily processes. Among the means to ensure health, spiritual discipline is the most important.

"You should not ever become entangled in the meshes of this world and its problems. Try to escape into the purer air of the spirit as often as you can, having the name of the Lord on your tongue. Of the twenty-four hours of the day, use six hours for your individual needs, six hours for the service of others, six hours for sleep and six for dwelling in the presence of the Lord. Those last six hours will endow you with the strength of steel." (1)

"When two people meet, it is considered good manners for each to inquire about the health of the other. This is true of people in the East and the West. You ask each other, 'How do you do?' regardless of the fact that both are every moment approaching death, nearer and nearer. Really speaking, both are undergoing *kshaya* (decline), not *kshema* (the security of health)! With each exhalation of breath, a fraction of our life-span escapes from our hold. So each should warn the other, remind the other, instruct the other, to use the available time to realise the God within the universe and within oneself.

"The body has to be maintained in good condition, for it is only when it is embodied in the form of his human tabernacle that one can realise God. The body is either strong or weak, an efficient instrument or an inefficient one, according to the food, recreations and habits of one's parents. When elders do not pay attention to these, the health of their children suffers. We have hospitals, dispensaries and clinics in every street now because disease has its hold on every family in every home. Even little children wear glasses, young people dye their hair, and many people wear dentures. The reason is that the atmosphere in the modern home is filled with artificiality, anxiety, envy, discontent, empty boasting, vain pomp, extravagance, falsehood and hypocrisy. How can anyone growing up in this corrosive atmosphere be free of illness? If the home is filled with the clean fragrance of contentment and peace, all its occupants will be happy and healthy. The elders have, therefore, a great responsibility towards the generation that is growing up." (3)

"The human body is the home of countless microbes, worms and various other parasites. No one can be free from these disease-inducing causes. But one can easily overcome this sorrow, by developing feelings of compassion towards all beings and thoughts which thrive on love and spread love. Illness, both physical and mental, is a bodily reaction caused by poisons in the mind. Only an uncontaminated mind can ensure continuous good health. Vice breeds disease. Bad thoughts and habits, bad company and bad food are fertile grounds where disease thrives. Health and bliss go hand in hand. A sense of elation and exultation keeps the body free from illness. Evil habits in which man indulges are the chief causes of diseases, physical as well as mental. Greed affects the mind, disappointment depresses man. Man can justify his existence as man only by the cultivation of virtue. Then he becomes a worthy candidate for Godhood. Virtue also confers freshness, skill and long years of youthfulness." (4)

"With the advance of a technological civilisation on our earth, various deadly, dangerous and mysterious diseases have appeared all over the world. Healthy habits like bathing, keeping the teeth clean, etc., are considered outmoded and uncivilised by youth. In the name of fashion, many insanitary and morbid practices are adopted. Smoking, drinking, sitting long hours in the midst of packed crowds in cinema theatres and subjecting oneself to all kinds of shocks and tensions lead to chronic damage both to the body and to the mind. Cancer, eosinophilia, tuberculosis, heart diseases, all these have increased as a result of such deleterious habits. Man has to be vigilant about his habits, his emotions, the impressions he gathers through his eyes and ears, the books he reads, the films he sees, etc.

"Simple living is the best prescription for health. The name of God is the most reliable and efficient medicine. Faith in God and in one's own *Atmic* reality guarantees, more than all the medicines in the world, continued health both physical and mental. Develop health both in body and mind. I am urging you to do this, for you have yet to witness and delight over many more *leelas* (Divine plays) and *mahimas* (miracles) of Swami, *leelas* and *mahimas* far surpassing those you have witnessed so far; and many more wonders, victories and triumphs among mankind. You can thrill and be in ecstasy witnessing them. So guard yourself well and carefully, and maintain good health and joyful hearts." (5)

"In this era of technology, it is becoming increasingly difficult to lead peaceful lives, Men are becoming the targets of various types of mental ailments. In countries on the frontline of civilisation, like America and England, people have lost the delight of natural sleep at night. They experience only artificial sleep induced by tablets they swallow. As a consequence of these and many other medicines taken to ward off other ills, they suffer more and more from diseases of the heart and blood pressure. In the end, they render themselves unhealthy wrecks. Such lives are highly artificial. People are sunk in fear and anxiety; mentally on one side and physically on the other they have no rest. Drugs, tablets, capsules and pills are produced by the million, but their general health has not improved. Besides, new varieties of illnesses have emerged and are developing fast. A few intelligent westerners have realised that their only refuge is *yoga*: they have confirmed their conclusion by means of experiments; they have taken to *yoga* with increasing faith." (6)

"In the past, illness was cured by simple remedies provided by nature, rest, regulation of diet and spiritual discipline. But now man lives in an age of tablets and injections. Do not believe that health is retained or maintained through doctors, nor can medicines guarantee it. Most illnesses are produced by faulty food habits and foolish ways of spending leisure." (7)

"When the mind of man is unattached to the ups and downs of life, but is able to maintain equanimity under all circumstances, then even physical health can be assured. The mental firmament must be like the sky which bears no mark of the passage of birds or planes or clouds. Illness is caused more by malnutrition of the mind than of the body. Doctors speak of vitamin deficiency; I will call it the deficiency of vitamin G, and I will recommend the repetition of the name of God, with accompanying contemplation of the glory and grace of God. That is the vitamin G." (8)

"The body is the temple of the Lord; keep it in good and strong condition. It is damaged by food and drink of the *rajasic* and *tamasic* types, and also by *rajasic* and *tamasic* behaviour, like anger, hatred, greed, etc., or sloth, sleep and inactivity. When you get violent and angry with anyone, quietly repeat the name of the Lord or drink a glass of cold water, or lie down until the fit of fury passes. While angry, you abuse another and he does the same. Tempers rise, heat is generated and lasting injury is done. Five minutes of anger damages the relationship for five generations, remember." (9)

"Do not stay near the person who has provoked your anger, because there is no limit to what anger may lead you to. Owing to anger and agitation the blood becomes heated. It takes three months for it to cool down. Within that period the nerves become weaker and even the blood cells are destroyed. Weakness is aggravated and the memory power is reduced. Old age sets in prematurely. All the aberrations that we witness today among man arise from anger. Our entire life is filled with anger. You must meet this by presenting a smiling face at all times. That will demonstrate the presence of Divinity. Happiness is union with God." (10)

"Anger is a great cause of ill-health, besides being dangerous for other reasons. It brings a long trail of camp-followers, each one adding its share to the final ruin. So, you must conquer this passion when it arises in the mind by reminding yourself of the omnipresence of God, of God as the inner motivator of all, of His being the director of this play called life. Try to think of something other than the circumstances that aroused your anger, do some *namasmarana*, lie down, go for a long walk, drink some cold water, struggle with yourself until you win. Do not fight with others; fight with your own urges. Stop anger at the threshold of the mind. Then the body's safety can be ensured. The best preventive of ill-health is the *ananda* that comes of unconcern." (3)

"The enemy takes delight in abusing you, and it is said in the *Puranas*, that as a consequence, he goes on diminishing and wiping off from your account the demerits you have to live out in misery. The faster and fouler his abuse, the sooner and better will your future prospects be brightened. The enemy absorbs your sins and their effects." (2)

"Fear, anger and affection are the closest comrades of attachment, the comrades dearest to its heart! They are, all four, inseparable companions, moving always together. This is why even *Patanjali* was forced to assert, 'Attachment runs after happiness.' And, what is it that grants happiness?

"The fulfilment of desire, is it not? Desire leads to hatred of those who thwart it, fondness for those who feed it, and the inevitable wheel of opposites, or likes and dislikes; there is no escape from this for the ignorant." (11)

"*Asuya* or chronic jealousy is the source of all mental and physical ailments in this world. In order to acquire mental equipoise and inner tranquillity, man should make his heart pure by purging his mind of this psychological mania called jealousy. Man must first humanize himself before attempting to Divinize himself. To feel jealous of others even in trivial matters suppresses the humanitarian instincts of a person. Men today waste all their time and energy in blaming others, without realising that to search for and find faults in others is the most grievous and ghastly sin. Arjuna was completely free from the deadly qualities of envy, jealousy and malice. That is why he acquired the appellation of Anasuya and deserved the nectarine message of the Bhagavad-Gita from Krishna." (12)

"Although man today has a surfeit of comforts and amenities, he is steeped in fear and worry. Despite all his attempts to ensure security, fear remains. All the convenient amenities do not confer peace of mind on him. Why is he haunted by this fear and lack of peace? It is because he entertains in his heart the fires of hatred, jealousy and the like." (13)

"Another method of avoiding illness is to diminish mental worry. Now, I find people increasing their worries, and getting anxious about things that they do not understand; nor can they correct them or reform them. Radio, newspapers and other means of communication or information cause so much fear and discontent, that worry and anxiety have increased and the mind of man is weakened. Parents talk about their anxiety in front of their children, and so they, too, start worrying. There was a six-year-old boy who came to Me the other day, weeping, because his father was involved in debt and was being pestered by his creditors. His father must have lamented in the boy's presence, 'Poor fellow! How am I to feed you and clothe you and pay your fees and buy books for you? I am sunk in debt.' The boy said that even in the classroom, he was worried about the father and his debts. You must not allow the boys to know about all this; their tender minds will be harmed by fear and anxiety. Their health also will be affected.

"Fear is the biggest cause of illness. When you have a slight temperature, you start imagining that it is the beginning of some serious fever. You say to yourself, someone whom you knew also had a slight increase of temperature which later became grave and led to complications, and so you become more prone to illness than formerly. Think rather of the instances where fever was prevented or overcome; think of the grace of the Lord that restores and saves. Resolve that, relying on His grace, you shall be free from illness from this moment. Transfer the faith that you have in medication to God; put your trust not in medicine but in Madhava (God).

"I am astounded at the number of people resorting to tablets and tonics. Resort to prayer, to *sadhana* (spiritual discipline), *japa* (continual repetition of the name of God) and *dhyana* (meditation). They are the vitamins you need; they will restore you. No tablet is as efficacious as the sacred name of Rama. I shall give you *vibhuti* and that will cure you. The hospital is for those who have faith in drugs and doctors. But, what can drugs and doctors do without the grace of God?

"Desires, disappointments, despair, all these also cause diseases. For many illnesses, filling the mind with the thought of God is the curative dose. For the rest, regimented diet, sleep, pastimes and activities are effective cures. Give the body the attention it deserves, but not more. Some people advise that you should cultivate disgust towards it; but that is not beneficial. Tend it as an instrument, use it as a boat, as a raft. Disgust is not a desirable attitude towards anything in creation. Everything is God's handiwork, an example of His Glory, His Majesty." (8)

"Regulate your food habits, restrain the greed of the tongue. Eat only *satvic* food (conducive to equanimity); engage yourselves in *satvic* recreations. Then you can be free from physical and mental ill-health. Bear calumny, loss, disappointment, and defeat boldly and with equanimity; then no mental depression can overwhelm you. I must tell you that I am happy when someone among you is subjected to suffering, for that is a chance given to you to demonstrate your intelligence and sense of values." (2)

"Bad thoughts, bad emotions and bad habits contaminate the blood and lead to blood pressure, defects, heart attacks, etc. Fear is the most prolific cause of illness. Doctors, too, very often create fears which bring about what they warn us against. If they intimate that a person's heart is getting weaker, they only hasten the process. The words instill fear, fear leads to greater weakening.

If you are strong in faith and believe that you have a Divine guardian, you can resist such fears and escape the consequence."(14) "In the beginning, sports and athletics were intended mainly to promote health and experience joy. Today these objectives are being forgotten. Everything is being commercialised. Self-interest is getting predominant. Consequently, peace and happiness are being lost." (15)

"Limiting birth by artificial means is an absurdly wrong step. This is like chopping off the head, since the door is too low and you do not want to enter with a stoop. What you have to do is to discover means of growing more food, by, as an example, utilising the vast resources of underground waters. Artificial means of preventing conception will promote licentiousness and bring down on the country bestial promiscuity. Those who encourage these dangerous tactics should rather encourage sense-control and self-restraint through *yoga* and seva (service), methods advocated in the scriptures by sages who knew the calamities that are the consequences of irresponsible fatherhood and frustrated motherhood. The innocent, ignorant victims can be educated to master their lower urges and sublimate them into more beneficial channels. Without mental preparation and determination these artificial methods may cause ill-health, insanity and other complexes.

"Through the media of films, books, music and the behaviour of elders, young minds are excited and aroused into self-indulgence. Through the campaign of family planning, they are persuaded to adopt means by which they have no responsibility for the consequences of that indulgence. This is, indeed, burning the future strength and progress of the nation at both ends. The best method of family planning is the ancient one: making man realise through sadhana his innate divinity." (2)

"The units of the Sathya Sai Seva Organisation are engaged in enthusiastic service of health and education. To improve and maintain the health of the people, continuous education on the principles and practice of hygiene and environmental cleanliness is essential. Education is the most effective safeguard against physical and mental ill-health. So these two activities are closely interrelated." (16)

References :
1. *Sathya Sai Speaks*, Vol. IV, pp. 210, 212, 215
2. *Sadhana, The Inward Path,* Quotations from the Divine Discourses of Sathya Sai Baba, 1976, pp. 78, 207 – 212, 218 - 221
3. *Sathya Sai Speaks,* Vol. VI, pp. 89 - 90
4. Sathya Sai Baba, *Sanathana Sarathi,* August 1980, pp. 176
5. Sathya Sai Baba, *Sanathana Sarathi,* November 1978, pp. 218-219
6. Sathya Sai Baba, *Sathya Sai Vahini,* pp. 182
7. *How to maintain health till we breathe our last,* An humble presentation from Haryana and Chandigarh Sri Sathya Sai Seva Organisation on the auspicious occasion of the Commemoration of 60th Birthday Anniversary of Bhagawan Sri Sathya Sai Baba, 1985, pp. 2
8. *Sathya Sai Speaks*, Vol. V, pp. 52 – 54, 58
9. *Sathya Sai Speaks*, Vol. I, pp. 88
10. Sathya Sai Baba, *Sanathana Sarathi,* April 1985, pp. 87
11. Sathya Sai Baba *Jnana Vahini,* 1984, pp. 19
12. Sathya Sai Baba, *Summer Showers in Brindavan,* 1979, pp. 140
13. Sathya Sai Baba, *Sanathana Sarathi*, September 1989, pp. 235
14. Sathya Sai Baba, *Sanathana Sarathi*, January 1977, pp. 249
15. Sathya Sai Baba, *Sanathana Sarathi*, February 1990, pp. 31
16. Sathya Sai Baba, *Sanathana Sarathi,* October 1976, pp. 180 - 183

26. KARMA, SUFFERING AND GRACE

"Our present condition and circumstances are decided by deeds performed in previous lives. Similarly, the conditions in which we have to spend the future are determined by what we are doing now. Between one life and another, one death and the next, the individual either progresses or regresses, expands or shrinks. Like a frail ship caught in a stormy sea, man climbs the froth-rimmed peak of some gigantic wave and the next moment, he is hurled with terrific speed into the deepest trough. The rise and the fall result inevitably from his deeds, good and bad.

"Every child comes into the world bearing the burden of unrequited consequences accumulated in previous lives. It does not drop from the lap of nature like a streak of lightning from the clouds. It is born in this world in order to experience the beneficial and the malignant consequences that are the products of its own acts in past lives. This is the explanation for the differences that are evident among men. This is the principle of *karma*.

"Among men, each one is himself the cause of his fortune, good or bad. He is himself the builder, the architect. Fate, destiny, pre-determination, the will of God, every one of these explanations is toppled by the principle of *karma*. God and man can be reconciled and affiliated only on the basis of this *sutra* or principle of *karma*. When man realises that God has no share in causing his suffering, and that he is himself the sole cause of it, that no blame attaches to any other person, that he is the initiator as well as the beneficiary, the cause and the effect of his acts, that he is free to shape his future, then he approaches God with a firmer step and a clearer mind." (1)

"The law of *karma* is not an iron law. By dedication, by purification, which invites benediction, its effects can be modified, and its rigour mitigated. Do not despair, do not lose heart." (2)

"*Prarabhda karma* is that which we are presently undergoing and experiencing. *Sanchita karma* means all the past *karma*. *Agami karma* refers to *karma* that will follow in the future. If we perform *karma* (activity) in such a way, as if we were performing all actions for the pleasure and for the satisfaction of God, in worship and dedication to Him, no *prarabhda* will trouble us. We need not be afraid of either *prarabhda* or *sanchita*. If we think that the effect of the *prarabhda karma* is inescapable, then what is the use of worshipping God? Even though the *prarabhda* might still be there, the grace of God will certainly remove to a large extent the bad effects of it. We can become beneficiaries of God's grace, we need not be afraid of either *prarabhda* or *sanchita* or *agami*." (3)

"Death should arouse no fear. It should not be regarded as inauspicious. You should not run away from the problem, imagining that death happens only to others, and that it will not happen to you. Neither should you postpone reflections on death, judging that they are inappropriate now, and profitless. For inquiry into death, is really inquiry into one's own reality. This truth has to be recognised." (1) "Death involves certain developments that weaken and extinguish (bodily) life. It does not affect the *Atma*, the *Atma* has no death. It cannot be destroyed. Therefore, one should not fear death. Death is but another stage of life. However long one suffers from illness or however severe the injury, death can happen only when time signals the right moment." (4)

"The duration of life is under the control of He who gave life, the Creator. It does not depend on the calories of food consumed or the quantity of drugs injected, or the abilities of the physician who prescribes the medicines. The chief causes of ill-health and death are fear and loss of faith. If one concentrates on the *Atma* - which is changeless and possesses no characteristics, no subtraction or senility, no decline or damage man can conquer death. Therefore, the most effective prescription is the injection of *Atma-vidya* (knowledge of the *Atma*, the soul as one's real Self).

"Death stalks its prey everywhere at all times, with relentless determination. It pursues its victims into hospitals, hill-stations, theatres, aeroplanes, submarines, in fact, no one can escape it or take refuge from its hold. God alone is the giver of life, the guardian of life and the goal of life. Do not contemplate upon death, it is just one incident of life. Contemplate on God who is the master of all life, God who is the indweller of your physical frame. Be aware of Him all through life and offer all your activity - breathing, talking, walking, earning and spending - to Him, for it was by Him and through Him that you were able to do all these things.

"To fall ill and to call in a doctor is something unnatural, debasing. Once you have offered yourself to God, it must go well with you. There can be nothing ill in you." (5) "Bhishma taught the world that the time of death was more important than the time of birth. More than being born on an auspicious day, it is an aspiration to die on an auspicious day and time as well. If one dies like that, one's rebirth will be a good one. The inner meaning of a good birth is to enable one to have a good death. We must recognise the truth that all the *sadhana* that we do, we do not for the sake of a pleasurable life but for a good and peaceful death." (6)

"Generally, man seeks only happiness and joy - under no stress will he desire misery and grief! He treats happiness and joy as his closest well-wishers and misery and grief, as his direct enemies. This is a great mistake. When one is happy, the risk of grief is great, the fear of losing his happiness haunts man. Misery prompts inquiry, discrimination, self-examination and fear of worse things that might happen. It awakens you from sloth and conceit. Happiness makes one forget one's obligations to oneself as a human being. It drags man into egoism and the sins that egoism leads one to commit. Grief renders man alert and watchful.

"So misery is a real friend. Happiness spends out the stock of merit and arouses the baser passions, so it is actually an enemy. Really, misery is an eye-opener; it promotes thought and the task of self-improvement. It also endows one with new and valuable experiences. Happiness draws a veil over experiences that harden a person and make him tough. So troubles and travails are to be treated as friends, or at least, not as enemies. It is best to regard both happiness and misery as gifts of God. That is the easiest path for one's own liberation.

"Not to know this is basic ignorance. A person so ignorant is blind. Really, happiness and misery are like the blind man who must always be accompanied by one who sees. When the blind man is welcomed, you have inevitably to welcome the man with eyes, for he is the constant companion of the blind man. So, too, happiness and misery are inseparable, you cannot choose only one. Moreover, misery highlights the value of happiness. Happy living is only of short duration; the joy of liberation is eternal, unshakable." (7)

"People who suffer are being tested, but it should not be called so. It is grace. Those who suffer have My grace. Only through suffering will they be persuaded to turn inward and make the true inquiry. And, without turning inward and inquiring, they can never escape misery."(10) "Open your heart to pain, for it is God's will wrought for your own good." (11)

"When a *yogi* practising *nishkamakarma* (desireless activity, renunciation of the fruit of action) dies, his words (the essential material for thoughts) enter the mind; the mind enters the *prana*, or life-force, and the *prana* merges into the *Atma*. The *Atma*, when it liberates itself, rushes to *Suryaloka*, the region of the solar principle, the *Surya*. From there, it reaches the region of Brahma, *Brahmaloka*. Having reached that region, the individualised *Atma*, or *jivatma*, has no concern with *Prakriti* (nature). It will exist there till the end of time. It will experience boundless delight. It will have all powers except the power of creation.

"When *yogis* who practise *sakama karma* (acts done with the ambition to reap and enjoy the fruit) die, their words merge into their minds, their minds merge in their *prana*, and the *prana* thereafter merges into the *jivi*, and the *jivatma* travels to the region of the moon principle, *Chandraloka*. That is to say, the *loka* of the presiding deity of the mind, suggesting that they have to enter again the realm of the mind with all its agitations and turmoils of wants and wishes. In *Chandraloka,* such *jivis* will experience some satisfaction and delight, up to the point that the consequences of their good acts last.

"That is why it is said in the scriptures *Ksheene punye, martyalokam vishanti,* (when the acquired merit is spent, they enter again the world of mortal men). The *jivatma* encases itself in a body equipped with sense organs, etc., appropriate to the earned consequences of the deeds of the previous body, and starts another life-career. The residence of the soul in *Chandraloka* is what the Hindus refer to as the time spent as a *Deva* in heaven, or as an angel according to Christian and Islamic religions. The name *Devendra* given to the Lord of these *Devas* is an indication of a position of authority. Thousands have risen to that position. According to the *Vedas,* when the highest good is observed, that person is elevated to the position of *Devendra*-hood. The soul raised previously to that position will descend to the earth and resume its career in human form. Just as on earth monarchs change, in heaven, too, rulers cannot escape rise and fall. The residents of heaven, too, are subject to the law of ups and downs. It is only *Brahmaloka* that is free from birth and death, ups and downs. This is the basic doctrine of *Bharatiya* thought - its eternal nectar, administered to humanity.

"The word hell *(naraka)* can nowhere be found in the *Vedas.* The concept of hell is foreign to the spiritual thought of Bharatiyas (Indians). The idea of hell and the various descriptions of hell are all later additions in the *Shastras* and *Puranas.* The authors of these texts believed that religion is incomplete if it does not posit hell. They laid down diverse tortures as part of hell, but they laid down one limit to the pain that hell inflicts. They declared that there can be no death in hell. The purpose for which hell was created was only to incite fear among the people in order to make them desist from sin. But, *advaita (Vedanta)* does not posit heaven or hell. It is concerned only with bondage and liberation, ignorance and illumination. It is known as *Vedanta*. There is no faith higher than that which *Vedanta* stands for."(8, 9)

"*Naraka* means hell, the name appropriate to one who believes he is the body and therefore toils to cater to its needs and its clamourings."(6)

References:

1. Sathya Sai Baba, *Sathya Sai Vahini*, pp. 23, 92 - 93, 101 - 102.
2. *Sathya Sai Speaks*, Vol. IV, pp. 399.
3. Sathya Sai Baba, *Summer Showers in Brindavan 1972*, pp. 145 - 148
4. Sathya Sai Baba, *Vidya Vahini*, pp. 24
5. *Sathya Sai Speaks*, Vol. VI, pp. 300-301
6. Tumuluru Krishna Murty, *Digest, Collection of Sri Sathya Sai Baba's Sayings*, 1985, pp. 65, 202
7. Sathya Sai Baba, *Geetha Vahini*, pp. 30 - 31, 38
8. Sathya Sai Baba, *Sathya Sai Vahini*, pp. 50 - 52
9. Sathya Sai Baba, *Geetha Vahini*, pp. 163 - 165
10. Diana Baskin, *Divine Memories of Sathya Sai Baba*, 1990, pp. 240
11. P. Mason and R. Laing, *Sathya Sai Baba, the Embodiment of Love*, 1975, pp. 232

27. THE DOCTOR'S PROFESSION

"Health and happiness go together. Happiness is a vain dream if health is absent. The *Shrutis* declare that health is the most basic necessary quality for human life, since without it one cannot realise any of the four goals of life - *dharma* (right doing), *kama* (right desiring), *artha* (right earning) and *moksha* (final release). A sound mind needs a sound body.

"Virtue is the panacea for both the diseased body and mind. The virtuous person can be both healthy and happy. How is virtue to be cultivated? Through service to living beings (*seva*). Virtue must flow through the triple channel of love, mercy and detachment in order to feed the roots of *seva*. In order to urge humans on to the path of mutual sympathy, compassion and concrete service, they have been endowed with the instinct of gregariousness. Man is a social animal. Humans find solitary living unnatural and miserable.

"Doctors are the most important class of *sevakas* in the present conditions. When *seva* is rendered with love, intelligence and earnestness, it leads persons nearer and nearer to Divinity, for it draws unto itself the grace of God. This is the reason why scriptures elevate doctors or *vaidyas*, to the status of God. *Vaidya Narayano Harih*, 'The doctor is Narayana, he is Hari.' He is Hari, the remover or destroyer, since he destroys hurdles on man's path to *sadhana*. If the doctor is full of love and compassion, God works through him.

"Doctors, therefore, have to endeavour to become the receptacles of Divine power during the healing process. How can they heal when they are themselves ill in body or mind? When their minds are innocent and contented, a smile will spontaneously shine on their faces, and their words will be sweet and tender. The manner and mien of the physician are more effective in drawing out the latent sources of strength in the patient than the most powerful drug. The behaviour, the voice, the mien of the doctor count for fifty per cent of the cure, the drugs and their efficacy manage the other half.

"*Ayurveda* has to be studied with as much awe and veneration as the *Vedas* at the feet of the *guru*. It has to be practised with as much devotion and dedication as *vedic* ceremonies and recitations. The *Veda* or knowledge that can confer *ayu* (life) is *ayur-veda*. It can prolong life, preserve and protect it from hazards.

"*Ayurveda* deals not only with curing illness, but also with its prevention. Absence of mental ease and equanimity leads to what we correctly call dis-ease. One sacred duty of the doctor is to advise people on how to preserve health and prevent disease. He has to be vigilant in society in order to discover and then suppress every tendency of *ahar* and *vihar* (feeding habits and social entertainments) by which diseases are developed. The dress worn by people, the houses they live in and the areas where they are situated, have to be tidy and clean. The food that is taken has to supply all elements needed to keep the body strong enough to resist illness.

"The current belief is that medicine is to be valued for its validity during illness. Its use ends with the cure. But this point of view has to change. Medicine is used to see that one does not fall ill, not to raise him up after he falls, just as the purpose of truth is to live in such a way that one is not subjected to another birth." (1)

"*Ayurveda* is the *upa-veda* (sub category) of *Adarvana Veda*. The Indians have neglected the supreme science of *ayurveda* down the ages, though this science transcends all the three times. It is necessary to understand the difference between allopathy and *ayurveda*. While allopathy is an external science, *ayurveda* relates to the inner feelings. The doctors have to integrate the essence of these two. Allopathy is objective while *ayurveda* is subjective. While integrating the two the heart is important. The subject is more value-oriented than the object. The object is marked by the external vision whereas the subject is marked by the inner vision. These two sciences are intimately related.

"Ayurveda affirms that purity of mind is most essential for one's health. But allopathy affirms the view that the destruction of disease-causing germs alone can secure good health. Allopathy does not take into account the role of the mind and Self in the cure of diseases. The science of allopathy is based more on experimentation and investigation. But *ayurveda* is based on experience-based knowledge. Allopathy believes in the use of antibiotics to ensure quick cure. But it has serious reactions. Though it cures one disease it causes other diseases as well.

"The main causes for sickness are *vata, pitta and sleshma*. *Vata* (wind) causes 36 diseases, *pitta* (bile) causes 93 diseases and *sleshma* (phlegm) causes 96 diseases. If the three factors are in a state of equilibrium there will be no disease. But the imbalance of the three causes diseases. Moderation is the golden rule for good health. Even the existence of germs in moderation is important. In allopathy they kill the germs. But all the germs should not be killed. We should see that they are not in excess. *Ayurveda* prescribes *til* oil for *vata,* ghee for *pitta* and honey for *sleshma*. But these three should be in moderation. Moderation is the law of nature.

"What is the reason for heart disease? Hurry, worry and curry (fat) are the causes of cardiac diseases. Heart diseases are more among non-vegetarians. Fat causes the rise of cholesterol which in turn causes heart ailments. When hurry and worry also join, blood pressure shoots up, with the consequent rise of blood sugar as well. Blood pressure and diabetes follow each other like twins. Both act on the heart, one inside and the other outside. The absence of sufficient exercise is also a cause for cardiac disease. Today all the five elements of nature are polluted. This pollution has caused diseases never heard of before. We should travel in vehicles less and less to control pollution. riding bi-cycle is a good exercise and ensures sound health.

"It is good for doctors to develop more devotion towards God than towards money. It is not possible to live in this world without money. But we should have money also in moderation. It is necessary that for all the knowledge the doctors receive, they should serve free. Sacrifice is the mark of education. Because you find absolute selfishness in medical science and other branches of sciences, we run into so many hazards in the world. Doctors should educate the ordinary people about the various reasons for heart ailments. Whenever people think of heart disease, they think of operation. You should not entertain the word operation as far as possible. We should try to cure patients by using drugs, without performing operations. Doctors should make every effort to cure the disease without operation. The word operation creates fear. We should develop confidence in them to remove fear." (2)

References :
1. Sathya Sai Baba, *Sanathana Sarathi*, September 1980, pp. 200 – 201
2. Sathya Sai Baba, Intern. Cardiac Speciality Symposium (February 1993)

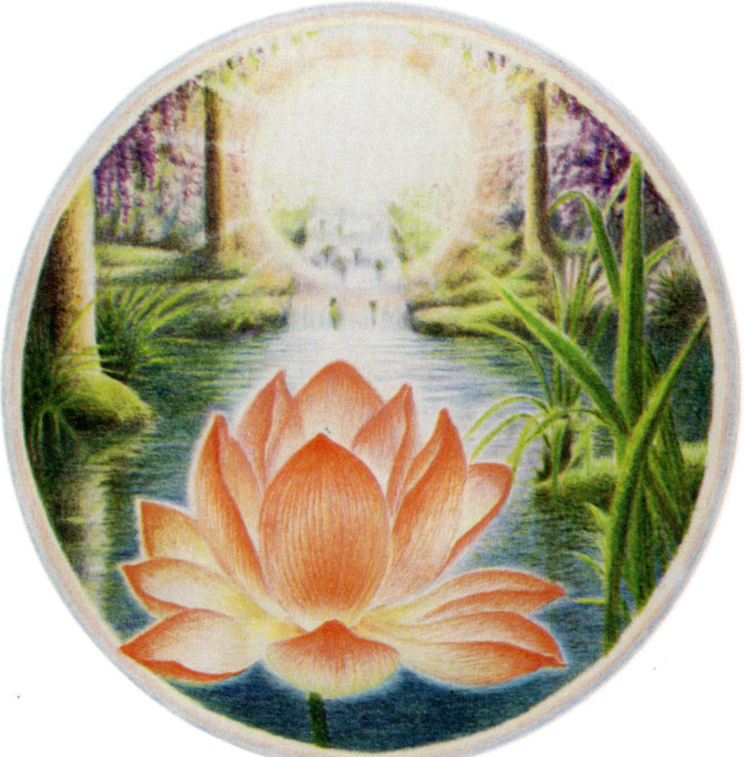

PART III

YOGA

28. BHAKTI YOGA, KARMA YOGA AND GNANA YOGA

"That is the real *sadhana* (spiritual discipline), the basic *sadhana*: the withdrawal of the senses from the objective world. Train the mind to dwell on the inner equipment rather than the outer attractions. Use the mind to cleanse the feelings, impulses, attitudes, tendencies and levels of consciousness." (1)

"What are the requisites for *sadhana*? First, faith that can stand the ridicule of the ignorant, the cavilling of the worldly, the laughter of the low-minded. Second, do not worry about ups and downs, loss or gain, joy or grief. Third, reason out and become convinced of the truth, that all is *Brahman*. Fourth, be steady in *sadhana*, and never waver once you have resolved upon it." (2)

"You feel the presence of God when silence reigns. In the excitement and confusion of the market-place, you cannot hear His footfall. He is *Shabdabrahma*, resounding when all is filled with silence. That is why I insist on silence, the practice of soft speech and minimum sound. Talk softly, talk little, talk in whispers, sweet and true. When you want to place a heavy thing on the ground, place it with care, do not drop it from a height and make a great noise. Do not drop your bed from a height; bend and place it slowly where you want to spread it. Examine each act of yours and see that you execute it with minimum noise. Transact all dealings with minimum speech. Do not shout to a person standing far away, go near him or beckon to him to approach you. Loud noise is sacrilege upon the sky, just as there are sacrilegious uses of earth and of water. This is the reason why we have certain disciplines at Prasanthi Nilayam, which you are all expected to follow. Maintaining silence as a step in *sadhana*, which you learn here and practise wherever you go, is the most patent of these rules.

"The realisation of the reality through *sadhana* is an arduous enterprise, as fraught with calamity as playing with fire or duelling with tigers or battling with barbarian hordes. One has to be alert, vigilant and fully trained to meet all emergencies. Many quail before its impossible demands. The *Upanishads* have compared the aspirant's path to a razor's edge." (3)

"Without self-confidence no achievement is possible. If you have confidence in your strength and skill, you can draw upon the inner springs of courage and raise yourselves to a higer level of joy and peace. For confidence in yourselves arises through the *Atma*, is your inner reality. The *Atma* is peace, it is joy, it is strength, it is wisdom." (1)

"O People! you are by nature ever full. You are indeed God moving on earth. Is there a greater sin than calling yourselves sinners? When you accept the appellation, you are defaming yourselves. Arise! Cast off the humiliating feeling that you are sheep. Do not be deluded into that idea. You are *Atma*. You are drops of *amrit*, immortal truth, beauty, goodness." (4) "*Sat* (existence), *chit* (consciousness), *ananda* (bliss), *paripurna* (complete), *nitya* (perpetual); Brahman is described by these five arrtibutes. Through an understanding of these Brahman can be grasped." (5)

"Those who strive through activities and achievements to establish Divine union are *karma yogins*; those who follow the *prema* path are the *bhakti yogins*; those who strive to manifest their latent powers and canalise them are the *raja yogins*; those who adhere to logical analysis and rational interpretations and attain intuitive perception are the *gnana yogins*. In *Bharatiya* spiritual history, these four types recur again and again." (4) "There is no distinction between *bhakti* and *gnana*. I will not agree that *karma*, *bhakti* and *gnana* are separate. I do not even like to classify one of these as first, the other as the second and next as the third. I will not accept a mixture of all the three or even a *samuchchaya*, a merger of the three. *Karma* is *bhakti* and *bhakti* is *gnana*." (6)

Bhakti yoga is congenial to those who are emotionally oriented. It is the path for those capable of filling their hearts with love. The urge is to have God as the beloved. The *bhakti yogi's* activities will be different, for they relate to incense-burning, gathering flowers for worship, building shrines and temples where he can install and adore symbols of beauty, wisdom and power."

(4) "For the sake of human satisfaction, you give a name and a form to the Lord, but, in reality, He does not have any form at all. Yet, He will take on that form so that you can worship Him, and feel awe, reverence and love for Him, and thereby satisfy your spiritual aspirations. It is for your own satisfaction that you give names and form to God and use these to worship Him

"Everywhere you look, the attributless Divine has taken on attributes. God is present everywhere, but without the help of a name and a form you cannot comprehend the attributeless and formless Divine. *Narayana* is everywhere, but before you can have that realization, you have to develop your love and devotion for God with form. Therefore, in the beginning you enter the *bhakti* path on the lowest rung and worship the Lord with a name and a form. Then steadily, inch by inch, you rise to a higher state. You withdraw your mind from the external world and worship the formless Divine until, finally, you realize your own reality. That is Self-realization.

"These days, many choose not to even recognize God; instead they prefer to rely only on their own limited strength and to be impressed only by human achievement. They are prepared to bend low before a village officer or a petty government official, but they refuse to show humility and obedience to the all-powerful cosmic Personality, who is the master of all creation. God, who is the origin and cause of everything in creation, is being treated improperly." (7)

"*Bhakti*, the path of devotion, is the easiest path for everyone. It does not call for mastery of the scriptures. It does not enjoin performance of rituals and sacrifices. The elusive quest for unity in diversity is avoided. By cultivating love of God, the senses naturally come under self-discipline. Those who are well-versed in the *Shastras* are good scholars, but they hardly practise what they preach. What matters is practise and not scholarship. Knowledge without action is a useless burden. One must strive to put into practise at least one or two of the things learnt from the spiritual field.

"The most important goal for man is to put into practise the doctrine of Divine Love. The principle of love is the greatest unifying force which unites all spiritual practices, all creeds, all the goals of life and all the scriptures. The foremost path for the spiritual aspirant is the path of complete surrender to the Lord to earn His love and grace." (8) "It is only when God is regarded as a friend and a companion that He is much pleased. By addressing Him as; 'Oh my dearest Friend, my beloved One, the Darling of my heart,' you can give Him the greatest joy." (9) "Of the various types of *bhakti*, *namasmarana* (remembrance, repeating the names of God) *bhakti* is the best.

"In the *Kali Yuga*, the Divine Name is the way to save oneself. If every *sadhaka* considers the name of the Lord as the very breath of his life, and has complete faith in good deeds and good thoughts, if he will develop the spirit of service and equal love for all, then there can be no better path for liberation."(6) "The name of the Lord must always be pronounced with joy, thankfulness, exultation, awareness of its uniqueness and splendour. Say it with love. Say it with sincere yearning." (3)

"A special merit of *namasmarana* is this: other *sadhanas*, like *yoga* and *tapas*, may awaken *siddhis* (occult powers) in the *sadhaka* who, blinded by pride on that account, is likely to forsake the Lord and even let go the victory and the spiritual strength won by that *sadhana*. No such dangers beset one on the path of *namasmarana*, which develops *prema* (love) in the devotee. Through *prema*, *shanti* is achieved. Once *shanti* (peace of mind) is achieved, all other benefits are attained automatically.

"When you are depressed by what appears to be loss or calamity, engage yourselves in *namasmarana*, that will give you consolation, courage and the true perspective of the event or situation. Practise it at all times and in all circumstances with love and devotion, that is the remembrance of the name of the Lord. That name is the thunderbolt which pulverizes mountains of sin. The name of the Lord must dance on your tongue forever. When the name dances on the tongue, the latter will speak only soft and sweet words, giving pleasure to others. The tongue guards the human heart." (10)

"You, too, must pass your days in song. Let your whole life be *bhajan*. Believe that God is everywhere at all times and derive strength, comfort and joy, singing in your heart, in His presence, the glory of God. Let melody and harmony surge up from your hearts and let all take delight in the love that you express through that song. Some people do question the propriety of calling on God by means of such a multiplicity of names. But each name is indicative of only one aspect of Divinity. Every name is but a facet, a part, a ray of the Supreme. (11) You are carrying a huge load of worry all day; keep that aside for an hour every evening and spend that time with God who can make your shoulders strong and your burden light. You will relish the *bhajan* as you make it a daily function, like eating and sleeping." (12)

"Bhajans are best held on Thursday evenings and Sunday evenings but that is not an unbreakable rule, for it is not the day of the week that counts, it is the heart that must be ready and eager to imbibe the joy and share it." (13) "In a congregation, *bhajans* should not evoke a sad and sagging mentality. There should be no slackness or sloth in the melody and rhythm. Vibrant speed is a must to hold the attention of the rest. It is indeed true that the Almighty appreciates devotion more than musical demonstration. Still, when there is group-singing, if somebody goes off key, and disturbs the unison, it diverts the others' harmony. So, it is desirable that those who cannot sing in harmony or keep the beat, do not take the lead in singing. On the other hand, musical gymnastics and hard-to-follow tunes should also be avoided." (14)

"Singing one's intense yearning for God, enjoying the experience that the adoring of Him brings, helps to purify the atmosphere. Man is today forced to breathe the air polluted by sounds that denote violence, hatred, cruelty and wickedness. Therefore, he is fast losing sight of the high attainments that are in store for him. The vibrations of the *nama-sam-kirtans* can cleanse the atmosphere and render it pure, calm and ennobling. No man can escape from the effects of the pollution in the air he breathes. The sounds that we produce, with good intent or bad, spread throughout the air around us. The sounds produced at radio stations pass through the atmosphere and reach our homes when we tune in. The vibrations travel vast distances and affect the nature of those who take them in. The atmosphere affects also the food man consumes. The pollution in the atmosphere is imbibed by the plants, the plants supply the food. The food shapes the character and behaviour of the person. When the environment is clean and free from evil vibrations, food is pure and the person develops a tendency to be loving and simple."(11)

"It is the law of *karma* that rules the movements of stars, the planets, the galaxies and other heavenly bodies in space. The same law directs and controls all that happens in all the worlds. It is inscrutable in its very essence. No one can penetrate into time or space when there was no *karma*. What, why, when and how events do happen is beyond the capacity of man to predict with accuracy. *Karma* is generally known to mean 'work', but transactions and actions of all kinds can be designated as work.

"There are no levels of work, such as low or high. All work is holy if it has to be done for the upkeep and upliftment of life. This is the reason why *karma* is praised as sacrosanct and highly desirable, and as imbued with meritorious or deleterious consequences." (15)

"Understand that the activities of the limbs, the senses, the intelligence, the feelings, the emotions and the mind are all *karmas*. When one has a right to engage in *karma*, one has a right also to its fruit; no one can deny that or refuse this right. But the doer can, of his own free will and determination, refuse to be affected by the result, favourable or unfavourable. The *Gita* shows the way: 'Do, and deny the consequence.' The desire for the result of your action is a sign of *rajoguna*; the giving up of action, if you cannot benefit by its fruit, is a sign of *tamoguna*. To engage oneself in *karma*, to know that the result will follow, and yet not to be attached to it or become concerned with it, that is the sign of *satvaguna*.

"Krishna taught, 'O Arjuna, give up all attachment and engage in acts as if they are each a *yagna* (sacrifice) dedicated to the Lord." (16). "Without becoming attached, without being aware of whom the *karma* you perform helps or how, the lesson that *karma yoga* teaches is: do the *karma* (deed), as *karma* (deed), for the sake of the *karma* (deed). Why does the *karma yogi* fill his hands with work? That is his real nature; he feels that he is happy, while doing work. That is all. He does not bargain for a result: he is not urged by any calculation. He gives, but never receives. He knows no grief, no disappointment; for he has not hoped for any benefit." (4)

"When an action is performed without desire and without any feeling of egoism, then it may be called *karma yoga*. Remove your egoism. Drive it away. Remove your desire for the fruit. When you perform action with this attitude, it becomes a *yagna*, it becomes work in the spirit of true sacrifice, it becomes *tapas* (penance), and it becomes *yoga*. All three of these, *yagna*, *tapas* and *yoga* convey the same idea. Every action performed by man should be sanctified in this way. Even inhaling and exhaling are actions; without performing *karma* (action) man cannot live for even a moment in the world. But *karma* associated with the ego is always narrow and harmful; therefore, perform all actions with only the feeling of sacrifice in your heart.

"Whether the result will be good or bad, beneficial or harmful, depends on the type of acts you perform. The acts themselves depend on the feelings you have. The feelings, in turn, depend on the thoughts you harbour. And the thoughts depend on the food you consume. Therefore, you have the sequence of food leading to thoughts leading to feelings leading to actions which lead, ultimately, to results. In this context you see the need for taking in pure *satvic* food." (7)

"Every being has three varieties of instruments to acquire knowledge, and through that knowledge, wisdom. First is 'instinctive'; this is very strong, active and advanced in animals. This is the earliest, the lowest and, therefore, the least beneficial of the three. The second is 'rational', the instrument that seeks the cause and the effect thereof. This is most evident in man. Instinct operates only in the limited field of senses and sensory experiences. In man the instinctive knowledge is largely subordinated by the rational instruments. The limits of the instinct are very thin; reason can range over vastly wider fields. In spite of this, reason, too, is capable of only a very poor performance; its reach is restricted. It can proceed only a certain distance. It cannot venture further. The road that logic takes is not straight. It is more circular, returning again and again to the place where it started.

"Take for example, our knowledge of the objective world, of the elements and energies that compose it. That which urges and prompts the objective world and its components does not stop with just that much. It absorbs also that which is immanent, outside the objective world. And so, the extent that reason can spread over and explain is, like the 'consciousness' that is imprisoned in the tiny molecule, compared to the vastness and grandeur of the transcendent Fullness.

"For us to go across the boundaries of reason into this full, free realm of intuition, certain spiritual exercises and disciplines are essential. They can be grouped under the name, God-propelled *gnana*. For we have only three stages of *gnana* : *sahajagnana* (derived from the senses of action and perception), *yukti-yuktagnana* (knowledge derived by the process of discrimination and evaluation), and *Ishvarapreritagnana* (God-induced knowledge, gained through grace by inner vision or intuition).

"The first of these is the knowledge possessed by animals, the second is characteristic of man, and the third is the special treasure of high-souled individuals. It is possible for everyone to foster, cultivate and develop the seedlings of this third *gnana*, for the capacity is latent in all. Another fact also has to be borne in mind. The three are stages of growth, and so, not three mutually exclusive types of knowledge. The *Ishvarapreritagnana* will not contradict the *yukti-yuktagnana*; it will only bring to light what is unmanifest in the *yukti-yuktagnana*. The later stage only confirms and elaborates the previous ones.

"The *gnana yogi*, too, yearns to merge into the centre, the core of reality, away from the tangle of apparent diversity. He exerts himself to become the Truth, not just to become aware of it. Of course, as soon as he is aware of it, he becomes It. He cannot tolerate the thought that he and truth are separate and distinct. The *gnana yogi* is vigilant against the temptations held before him by his senses and, turning them aside, he approaches the Divine and seeks strength and solace there. He realises that the power and energy that vitalise the tiniest of the tiny and the vastest of the vast is the same Divine Principle. His actions, thoughts and words reveal this vision which he has experienced.

"The knowledge has to be digested through actual experience. This is the crucial test. It is not enough if the intellect nods approval and is able to prove that Godhead is all. The belief must penetrate and prompt every moment of living and every act of the believer. *Gnana* should not be merely a bundle of thoughts or a packet of neatly constructed principles. The faith must enliven and enthuse every thought, word and deed. The self must be soaked in the nectar of the *gnana*.

"In this world there are several branches of learning, like physics, music, literature, art and mathematics. Of all these forms of knowledge, self-knowledge is sovereign. Without its attainment one cannot enjoy any peace. Though one may gain renown and recognition in the world, one will not experience happiness without self-knowledge. Knowledge of the soul, knowledge of God and spiritual knowledge, all these expressions connote that wisdom which promotes full awareness of soul and God. Self-knowledge is that knowledge, by acquiring which, everything else is known.

"A person with self-knowledge can indeed be acclaimed as all-knowing. Some people relentlessly seek spiritual knowledge at the expense of secular learning. This is not desirable. They miss both and wander aimlessly between the two; such a predicament, too, is undesirable. Secular learning should not be neglected." (17) "Because one can progress very fast if one keeps close to the wise person who has realised the truth, one must, in unconditioned renunciation and sincere earnestness, follow the instructions of the teacher and the *Shastras*." (18)

"Regard the heart as a vast field. Use the mind as a plough. Treat the qualities (*gunas*) as oxen. Use the intelligence (*viveka*) as a whip. With these aids, cultivate the field of your heart. What is the crop that is to be grown in it? Truth (*satya*), right conduct (*dharma*), peace (*shanti*) and love (*prema*) are the crop. Devotion (*bhakti*) is the rain, meditation (*dhyana*) is the manure, bliss (*Brahmananda*) is the yield."(19) "In the playground of our spiritual heart, on one side are the *arishadvargas* (the six bad qualities, vices). These six bad qualities are *kama, krodha, lobha, moha, mada* and *matsarya*. That is, lust, anger, greed, attachment, arrogance and jealousy. On the other side are the six other players, *satya, dharma, shanti, prema,* along with two others, *ahimsa* and *purnatva*, that is, non-violence and fullness. These two sets of contestants have the ball of life right between them." (20)

"If you want happiness and if you want peace, you must give love. Only through love will you find true happiness. Only through love will you find inner peace. Therefore, develop your love, live in love. Love lives by giving and forgiving." (7) "*Prema* (love) is the basic principle of human nature. That short two-syllabled word has immeasurable potentiality. Too often, it is confused with the affection of the mother for the child, the attachment between husband and wife, the dependence of friend on friend, or the relationship of teacher and pupil. In every one of these, a trace of an egoistic need can be discerned. Love untainted by ego is genuine love. It is all-inclusive, pure, full and free. Love can emerge from the heart and brighten with delight only after anger (the mastiff), pride (the boar) and the ego-sense (the buffalo) are put out of operation and removed from the heart. So long as these beasts occupy the heart, man cannot escape being a beast." (21) "How is *prema* to be cultivated? There are two methods: firstly, consider always the faults of others, however big, to be insignificant and negligible. Consider always your own faults, however insignificant and negligible to be big, and feel sorry and repentant. By these means, you avoid developing the bigger faults and defects, and you acquire the qualities of brotherliness and forbearance.

"Secondly, whatever you do, with yourself or with others, do it remembering that God is omnipresent. He sees and hears and knows everything. Whatever you speak, remember that God hears every word; discriminate between the true and the false and speak only the truth; whatever you do, discriminate between the right and the wrong and do only the right. Endeavour every moment to be aware of the omnipotence of God." (22)

"You peep into space at the stars, but leave your inner sky unexplored. You peep into other's lives and pick faults and talk ill of them; but, you do not care to peep into your own thoughts, acts and emotions and judge whether they are good or bad. The faults you see in others are merely projections of your own; the good that you see in others is a reflection of your own goodness."(23)

"What is the way to God? All that you have to do to achieve purity in thought, word and deed, is to follow these five injunctions:

"Think no evil, think what is good; see no evil, see what is good; hear no evil, hear what is good; speak no evil, speak what is good; do no evil, do what is good." (24)

"There are some people who are attracted to various systems and methods, like *hatha yoga* and *kriya yoga*, which claim to help people to realise the Self. None of these can make you realise God. Only the discipline of love can lead you to God. These *yogas* may calm the mind's agitations temporarily, and may improve health and prolong life for a few more years, but that is all that they can do." (25)

References:

1. *Sathya Sai Speaks,* Vol. VI, pp. 36, 109
2. *Sathya Sai Speaks,* Vol. III, pp. 243 - 244
3. *Sathya Sai Speaks,* Vol. V, pp. 251, 253, 255
4. Sathya Sai Baba, *Sathya Sai Vahini,* pp. iii, 61 - 62
5. Sathya Sai Baba, *Upanishad Vahini,* pp. 77 - 78
6. Sathya Sai Baba, *Prema Vahini,* 1985, pp. 9, 72
7. *Sri Sathya Sai Baba, Discourses on the Bhagavad Gita,* Compiled and edited by A. Drucker, First Indian Edition, 1988, pp. 1 - 4, 10, 222 - 223
8. Sathya Sai Baba, *Sanathana Sarathi,* April 1989, pp. 87 - 88
9. Sathya Sai Baba, *Sanathana Sarathi,* November 1989, pp. 282
10. *Namasmarana, A Universal Sadhana,* Compiled by Dr.Brahmanand Mavinkurve, pp. 4 - 7, 23 - 24
11. *Bhajananamavali* (for overseas devotees), pp. 7 - 10
12. *Sathya Sai Speaks,* Vol. X, pp. 81
13. *Sathya Sai Speaks,* Vol. VI, pp. 237 - 238
14. Tumuluru Krishna Murty, *Digest, Collection of Sri Sathya Sai Baba's sayings,* pp. 38
15. Sathya Sai Baba, *Sathya Sai Vahini,* pp. 133, 135 - 136
16. Sathya Sai Baba, *Geetha Vahini,* pp. 39, 46, 83
17. Sathya Sai Baba, *Sathya Sai Vahini,* pp. 65 - 69, 169 - 170
18. Sathya Sai Baba, *Jnana Vahini,* pp. 1
19. *Sathya Sai Education in Human Values,* Taken from discourses given by Sathya Sai Baba, Compiled by Lorraine Burrows, 1988, pp. 20 - 21
20. Sathya Sai Baba, *Summer Showers in Brindavan,* 1972, pp. 59
21. Sathya Sai Baba, *Sanathana Sarathi,* June 1985, pp. 159
22. Sathya Sai Baba, *Prema Vahini,* 1985, pp. 19
23. *Sathya Sai Speaks,* Vol. VI, pp. 58
24. Sathya Sai Baba, *Summer Showers in Brindavan,* 1990, pp. 86
25. *Sadhana, The Inward Path,* Quotations from the Divine Discourses of Bhagavan Sri Sathya Sai Baba, pp. 57

29. DHYANA YOGA

"The word *dhyana* is interpreted by many people in many different ways. They also prescribe different kinds of meditation and cause some confusion in the minds of aspirants. *Dhyana* stands for the *sadhana*, or the practice, by which the *sadhaka* meditates upon God and thereby unifies the three constituents, namely: the object of meditation, God, the person who is meditating, the 'I' or the individual, and the process, the meditation itself. The combination and oneness of these three is *dhyana*." (1)

"Many people think that concentration is the same thing as meditation, but there is no such connection between concentration and meditation. If one wants to drive a car, unless one has concentration one cannot drive it on the roads. All the usual functions, like walking, talking, reading, writing, eating, all these things we do only as a result of being able to concentrate.

"We must rise from being below the senses (that is, the state of concentration) to the senses (that is, the middle position called contemplation); and from there we must rise above the senses, that is called meditation. Between concentration and meditation there is a border area which covers both, and that is the area of contemplation. To be in that state of contemplation is to free yourself of worldly attachments. If you break away from all worldly attachments, all routine attachments in the world, then you will enter the region of contemplation. When you have completely broken away all your attachments, you break through this area of contemplation and you get into the area of meditation. These steps can also be described as starting from self-confidence, and then getting self-satisfaction and self-sacrifice, and the last step is self-realisation.

"The ultimate step of self-realisation depends upon the base of self-confidence. You must therefore develop as a first step confidence in your own self. Without having and developing confidence in your own self, if all the time you talk of some power being with someone and some other power being with someone else, if in this way you travel all the time and depend upon power which is with someone else, when are you going to acquire any power and confidence in your own self?

"Peace and bliss are within you, they are not something which is external to you." (2) "*Dhyana*, or meditation, is the seventh in the series of steps leading to the eighth *samadhi*, or conquest of the mind. Unless you have secured a strong foothold on the six previous steps, you will slide back from *dhyana*, even if for years you may try to stick to it. The first step is to control the senses, the second is control of the emotions and impulses. The third is mastery of balance, equipoise; the next is the regulation of breathing and movement of the vital airs; the fifth is the prevention of outer influences from deviating the mind; the next is the one-pointed attention to one's own progress; and then, we come to real *dhyana*, or meditation, to one's real Reality, which easily leads to its realisation in *samadhi*. Without the preliminary rungs, you cannot hop straight on to the seventh! And then skip onto the eighth!" (3)

"To cure an illness without resorting to drugs, *dhyana* is the only remedy. Even the capacity to discriminate and analyse will increase, and by means of that, illness, however serious, can be overcome." (4) "Meditation on God is an unfailing remedy for human suffering if it is supplemented with the practice of *dharma* and the strict observance of moral restraints." (5)

"The *sadhaka's* mission is to practise *dhyana* without deviating from the path. The rest is all His grace. It does not depend upon the number of days or the length of time. Some may require many births; others may realise the goal in a few days even. Worry about the discipline needed for the *sadhana* but not about its fruition. The reality, the realisation of the reality, these have no steps or limits. Do not yield to all sorts of delusions or desires for this stage and that. Stick to the goal and the journey. Never give up the discipline of the (chosen) *sadhana*. Do not change the time of *dhyana*. With one aim and an unchanging attitude, strive to attain it. That will vouchsafe the fruit. That will bless you with the bliss. Do not be led away by what others say about their imaginary experiences. For you, nothing can be as genuine as your own experience. Therefore, first attempt to gain undeviating concentration, *ekagratha*; let that be your one aim." (6)

"There are three states relating to the mind, *shuyatva* (nothingness), *anekagrata* (severality, multiplicity; simultaneous pulls of multiple thoughts) and *ekagrata* (one-pointedness). These three states are referred to and arise from the three *gunas* in man. While *tamoguna* (indolence) brings about blankness in the mind, *rajoguna* (the quality inducing animated action) spurs the mind into wandering hither and thither. *Satvaguna* (the quality that promotes the sacred aspects of human life) stills the mind into one-pointed contemplation. Thus, it is only those who cultivate *satvaguna* that can undertake meditation with ease." (7)

"Time, like man, has three qualities: *satva*, *rajas* and *tamas*. The day is divided into three parts. The four hours between 4 a.m. and 8 a.m. in the morning and between 4 p.m. and 8 p.m. in the evening have the *satva* quality. The eight hours between 8 a.m. and 4 p.m. are *rajasic*. The eight hours between 8 p.m. and 4 a.m., mainly used for sleep, are *tamasic*. The eight hours of the day from 8 a.m. to 4 p.m. are employed by all beings, including animals and birds, in the discharge of their day-to-day duties and are regarded as *rajasic*. When the four *satvic* hours of the morning, 4 a.m. to 8 a.m., are used to engage oneself in good actions, like worship, virtuous deeds, and keeping good company, one is sure to raise oneself from the human to the Divine level." (8)

"For meditation to be most effective it should be performed at a fixed time and at a fixed place everyday, and according to a well-regulated procedure. Sometimes this routine may be upset, as, for example, when you have to go on a journey, it may not be possible to perform meditation at the usual place, or according to the normal procedure. Nevertheless, one must ensure that at the appointed hour every day, the meditation is performed steadfastly. If the meditation is done at the correct time everyday, the mind will take the subtle body to the usual environs and make the individual go through the prescribed regulation inwardly, thereby cutting away any possible feelings of alienation that could crop up at unfamiliar places.

"The ideal time for engaging oneself in meditation is *Brahma muhurta*, that is, the period commencing at 3 a.m. and ending at 6 a.m., early in the morning (sometimes in a narrower band, from 4.30 to 5.15 a.m.)." (9) "*Brahma muhurta* literally means the time of *Brahman*. You must choose a fixed time for meditation during the *Brahma muhurta* and meditate regularly at the same time every day.

"Adopting a comfortable posture, you have to sit straight so that the *kundalini power* is afforded unhampered movement. The *kundalini* power is present in man in the *muladhara chakra* as a Divinely radiant power. Its upward flow to the *sahasrara chakra*, or the thousand-petalled lotus, through the intermediary centres called the *svadhisthana, manipura, anahata, vishuddha* and *agna chakras*, corresponding respectively to the regions of the navel, stomach, heart, larynx and the *bhruhmadhyasthana*, or area between the eyebrows, takes man to various levels of consciousness and spiritual awakening.

"During meditation the *sadhaka* should neither shut his eyes completely nor open them wide. He should gaze at the tip of his nose with half-closed eyes and concentrate on the Divine radiant power at the *agna chakra*. In this blissful mood he has to keep his hands in the *chin mudra*, with the thumb and index finger joined at their ends, the other three fingers of both the hands kept apart. The thumb represents *Brahman*. The forefinger represents the *jiva*. *Chin mudra* is symbolic of the proximity of *Brahman* and *jiva*. The *jiva*, in combination with its *gunas*, is conditioned by time. God, however, is beyond time and, therefore, all *gunas* vanish when a *jiva* and God become one.

"The purpose of *dhyana* is to unite the *jiva* with *Ishvara*. The essence of *Trimurti* is the integral unitive reality of *jiva* (man), *Ishvara* (God) and *Prakriti* (world). The Divinity of the individual and the oneness in diversity can be visualised by adopting the *chin mudra* during meditation.

You have to try to experience in meditation the oneness of the *Sarvatma* (cosmic soul) and the *Ekatma* (individual soul) *Ekagrata* (one-pointedness) for a single moment does not amount to *dhyana* (meditation). Meditation is sustained concentration and identification with the *dhyeya* (the aim of meditation). If you give food to a dog continuously for ten days at a particular time, it will come regularly and punctually every day thereafter. A dog's loyalty is well known. Faith is very important. In fact, *Vishvasa* (faith) is like our *shvasa* (life-breath). In other words, faith is our '*elan vital*'. Life without faith is living death. In the beginning, meditation may be easy and interesting. The first few steps will be encouraging. But when you begin to ascend the higher steps of the stairway of *dhyana*, unforeseen obstacles will crop up. However, one should not become disheartened by these unexpected hurdles. They must be taken in their stride with courage and conviction. A person should not undertake the *sadhana* of *dhyana* without a strong will to do so." (5) "A half-hour in the morning and a half-hour in the evening is enough for sitting in meditation." (2)

"When we want to be in meditation, we should try and put ourselves in what is called a *padmasana* (lotus-position). You should not sit on bare ground. You should sit either on a wooden plank or on a mat, or something like that. Not only that, you should not sit on a bare wooden plank. You should spread a piece of cloth over it. In the beginning, you should attempt to make a start with a wooden plank which is above the ground at least by half an inch. There are some reasons for taking a wooden plank. The reasons are that the earth has got the power of conduction and diffusion. When you sit in meditation, the current of Divine strength is passing through your *dhyana*, on account of the earth's attraction, you should not be disturbed. Therefore, you have got to have a plank.

"We should take all the precautions that are necessary by insulating ourselves from the earth and by preventing the power, or the strength, in you from flowing away or dissipating itself into the earth. That is why our ancients have taught us that we should sit on a plank. The practice of getting up at 4.30 a.m., at the *Brahma muhurta*, is also a very good habit." (10)

"To sit straight is important. Between the nineth and twelveth vertebrae is the life-force. If the spine is injured at this point, paralysis occurs. If the body is in a straight position, as if it were wound around a straight pole, the life-force can rise up through the straight body and bring the quality of intense concentration to the mind. Moreover, just as a lightning rod attached to the roof of a building attracts lightning, in like fashion, a perfectly straight body provides a conductor, so to speak, for Divine power to enter the temple of your body and give you the strength to accomplish your task and reach your goal. As another example, the Divine power is always here, just as radio signals are here. But to hear the radio music, there must be an antenna. Further, if the tuning device is not properly adjusted, there will just be some sound but no music. In like fashion, the Divine power, which is always present, may flow into you if the meditation is correct and the body straight." (11)

"Before you start your *dhyana*, your meditation, chant *Soham*, inhaling *So* and exhaling *Ham*. *Soham* means 'He is I'; it identifies you with the Infinite and expands your consciousness. Harmonise the breath and the thought. Breathe gently, naturally; do not make it artificial and laboured. It must flow in and out, soft and silent. If you have some flour on your palm, hold it near your nostrils; it should not flutter in the least. Your breath has to be as soft as that! The faster the breathing, the sooner you are burnt up, the shorter becomes your life span! Slow breathing quietens and calms the emotions. The mood of relaxation produced by this *Soham* recital is a pre-condition for a beneficial session of meditation.

"The mind must be allotted some difficult piece of work to hold it down. This work is called *dhyana*. Keep the mind above the upper lip, between the two nostrils, right in front of the bridge of the nose. Inhale through the left nostril, closing the right with the right thumb. As the breath goes in, it utters *So* (meaning He); then exhale through the right nostril, closing the left nostril. As the breath goes out, it utters *Ham* (meaning I). Inhale and exhale slowly and deliberately, conscious of the identity of He (the Lord) and I (yourself) which it asserts, until the breathing and the awareness grow into an unnoticed process. Keep the mind as a watchman, to note the incoming and outgoing breaths, to listen with the inner ear to the *Soham* that the breath whispers, and to witness the assertion of your being the Divine, which is the core of the universe. This is the *dhyana* that will bring triumph.

"When this *Soham dhyana* has stabilised itself in you, you may start to steady in your mind the form, or *rupa*, of your *Ishtadevata*, the God of your choice. Picture the form from head to foot, taking at least fifteen to twenty minutes to do so, dwelling on each part of the body and imprinting it clearly on the heart; then, proceed from foot to head in similar way. This will help to fix the form on the altar of your heart." (12)

"The name of God and His form are the reverse and obverse of the same coin. Recite the name and the named one will be before you. Picture the named one and the name will leap to your lips. *Nama*, i.e. the name (of God) and *nami*, i.e., the named or the form, should have constant and continuous contact in the devotee's mind." (13)

"When your mind wanders away from the recital of the name, take it on to the picture of the form. When it wanders from the picture, lead it to the name. Let it dwell either on that sweetness or this. Treated thus, the wayward mind is easily tamed. The imaginary picture you have drawn will get transmuted into the *bhavachitram*, or emotional picture, dear to the heart and fixed in the memory. Gradually, it will become the *sakshatkara chitra*, when the Lord assumes that form in order to fulfil your longing. This *sadhana* is called *japasahita dhyana*, and I advise you all to take it up, for it is the best form of *dhyana* for beginners." (2)

"I will never force you to take up a particular name or form of the Lord as your *Ishtam*. The Lord has a million names and a million forms, and He wants faith and attachment to be evoked in you by any one of them, as you recite the names or contemplate the forms."(14) "In this *Kali yuga*, the name is the path for saving oneself." (2)

"As regards the technique of *dhyana*, different teachers and trainers give different forms of advice. But I shall give you now the most universal and the most effective form. This is the very first step in spiritual discipline. Set aside for this, at first, a few minutes everyday and later go on extending the time as and when you feel the bliss that you will certainly receive. Let it be in the hours before dawn. This is preferable, because the body is refreshed after sleep and the peregrinations of daytime will not yet have impinged on you.

"Have a lamp or a candle with an open flame, steady and straight, before you. Sit in the *padmasana* posture or any other comfortable *asana*, in front of the candle. Look on the flame steadily for some time and, closing your eyes, try to feel the flame inside you, between your eyebrows. Let it slide down into the lotus of your heart, illumining the path. When it enters the heart, imagine that the petals of the lotus open out one by one, bathing every thought, feeling and emotion in the light, and so removing darkness from them.

"There is no space for darkness to hide. The light of the flame becomes wider and brighter. Let it pervade your limbs. Now those limbs can never more deal in dark, suspicious and wicked activities; they have become instruments of light and love. As the light reaches up to the tongue, falsehood vanishes from it. Let it rise up to the eyes and the ears and destroy all the dark desires that infest them, leading you to perverse sights and puerile conversation. Let your head be surcharged with light and all wicked thoughts flee therefrom. Imagine that the light is in you more and more intensely. Let it shine all around you and let it spread from you, in ever-widening circles, taking in your loved ones, your kith and kin, your friends and companions, your enemies and rivals, strangers, all living beings, the entire world.

"Since the light illuminates all the senses everyday, so deeply and so systematically, a time will soon come when you can no more relish dark and evil sights, yearn for dark and sinister tales, crave for base, harmful, deadening toxic food and drink, handle dirty demeaning things, approach places of ill-fame and injury, or frame evil designs against anyone at any time. Stay on in that thrill of witnessing the light everywhere. If you are adoring God in any form now, try to visualise that form in the all-pervasive light. For light is God, God is light.

"Practise this meditation as I have advised regularly everyday. At other times repeat the name of God (any name fragrant with any of His many majesties), always taking care to be conscious of His might, mercy and munificence." (15)

"The light is first moved into the heart which is conceived as a lotus, the petals of which will open. The *jyoti* (light) is then moved to other body parts. There is no particular sequence. But, important is the final body station, which is the head. There, the light becomes a crown enshrining and covering the head. There the light is then moved outside, from the particular to the universal. Move the light among relatives, friends, enemies, trees, animals, birds, until the entire world and all its forms are seen to have the same light at their centre as has been found within oneself. The idea of moving the light into the universal stage, the idea of universality is that the same Divine Light is present in everyone everywhere. To impress this universality on the mind, we do the spreading of the light outside one's own body. One should understand that what comes about in meditation, as one moves deeply into it, is not the thinking of the light, but the forgetting of the body and thereby the direct experience that the body is not oneself. This is the stage of contemplation when the body is totally forgotten. It cannot be forced. It comes about by itself and is the stage that naturally follows correct concentration. Vivekananda said that in meditation he was unable to find his body. Where was his body? He could not find it.

"Spreading the light into its universal phase, sending the light into every other body and, when one is so concentrated in it that one is no longer conscious of the body, that is the stage of contemplation. As contemplation deepens, the stage of meditation comes about of its own volition. It cannot be forced. If the meditator remains conscious of himself, that he is engaged in meditation then he is not meditating, but is still in the preliminary stage, at the beginning of concentration.

"These are the three stages: concentration, contemplation and meditation. When contemplation deepens it moves naturally into meditation. Meditation is entirely above the senses. In the state of meditation the meditator, the object of his meditation and the process of meditation have fallen away - there is only one, and that One is God. All that may change has fallen away and *Tat tvam asi*; 'That thou art', is the state that exists. As one gradually returns to one's customary and habitual state of consciousness, the *jyoti* is again placed in the heart and kept lighted there throughout the day." (11)

"How is meditation to be done? The first step is *dharana*. Twelve *dharanas* amount to one *dhyana*. Twelve *dhayans* equal one *samadhi*. Dharana is steady concentrated viewing of any object for twelve seconds. You have to look at any object, a flame, a picture or an idol, for twelve seconds only, but with total concentration, without blinking the eyelids. This is *dharana*. Practising *dharana* is a preparation of *dhyana*. The duration of *dhyana* is twelve *dharanas*. This means *dhyana* should last 144 seconds or two minutes and twenty-four seconds. Dhyana does not call for sitting in meditation for hours. Proper *dhyana* need not last more than two minutes and

24 seconds. It is only after *dharana* has been practised well that one can do *dhyana* well. Twelve *dhyanas* equal one *samadhi*. One *samadhi* is 28 minutes 48 seconds, very much less than an hour. If *samadhi* is prolonged, it may prove fatal. These are the disciplines that *yogis* practised.

"These disciplines are not explained in any of the *Shastras*. If you want to attain *samadhi* in the proper way, you should start with *dharana*. Start practising *dharana* for twelve seconds a day from now on. This is very important for students. In the past, *yogis* like Aurobindo and Ramana Maharishi practised these disciplines. Ramana Maharishi used to go up to the terrace and concentrate on a particular star for twelve seconds. In that state, the mind also was still and steady. By continuing this practise of *dharana*, you develop the capacity to perform *dhyana* for two minutes and twenty-four seconds. Continuing the practice of *dhyana* in this way, you develop the capacity to be in a state of *samadhi* for 28 minutes and 48 seconds. The correct meaning of *samadhi* is the state in which the intellect has achieved equanimity.

"This will enable you to sharpen your minds and develop the keenness of your intellect. Likewise, *dhyana* is an extremely easy process. *Samadhi* is even more easy. But because of an improper understanding of the methods, aspirants become caught up in difficulties. Through *dharana*, control of the senses is achieved; purity of mind is also secured. The more you develop your purity, the more youthful you will be. No illness will affect you. *Dhyana* means absorption in thought. It should be centred on only one specific subject. This is described in *Vedantic* parlance as *salokyam*. This means concentrating your thought on what you desire, whatever is the object or the subject. *Sa* comprehends every aspect of Divinity. *Salokyam* means absorption in thoughts of Divinity.

"There are different types of meditation carried out today. But all these types are only petty - minded approaches. In the very first instance, control your mind. Only through controlling your mind can you reach *dhyana*, meditation. Today, closing the eyes and sitting in a meditation posture is considered meditation. That is only a disease. Students must therefore develop the power of *dharana*. In *dharana* practice you should have only one form. You can keep an object in the mind for twelve seconds. Concentrate your vision on that. There is also an internal method of practising *dharana*. When you close your eyes, a small dark spot appears before the inner eye. If you want to look at that particular black spot it keeps running away. If you can make it stand still, then you are able to meditate. That develops real meditation." (18)

"Seeing all sorts of things and hearing all kinds of sounds during *dhyana* is delusion. It handicaps progress. Delusions implant conceit and disperse concentration. The distraction of sights and sounds is no sign of *dhyana*. Do not allow the mind to wander onto them; never lose sight of the Divine form which you have pictured for yourself. Be convinced that these are but obstacles designed to scatter your attention away from the Divine form. If you permit these sights and sounds to creep in, the original form will be dimmed, your *ahamkara* (ego) will increase, and you will lose your way.

"If you fix your attention on the sublimely beautiful form of the Lord and concentrate on that alone, you will receive His grace in that very form in various ways. While doing so, many a disturbance might intervene. You should not be deluded; be on your guard, never forget the auspicious form. Picture to yourself that all creation is immersed in it.

"You can have an idea of the stage you have reached if you examine daily how you are able to concentrate, how far you have subdued the wandering nature of the mind, and how deeply you taste the Divine form; that is all. The stage reached cannot be cognised. What you receive and at what time, depends on His grace." (6)

"A *sadhaka* will have several types of experiences during meditation. When he is absorbed in Divinity he listens to many kinds of sounds. He develops a sort of extrasensory perception. He listens to the sounds of musical instruments like the *veena*, *mridangam* and flute. These sweet strains of music are symbolic of *Sakara Brahman*. They are the first results of *dhyana*. During the preliminary stages of *dhyana*, all sensory organs become hypersensitive. This acute sensitivity enables the *sadhaka* to respond to extraordinary sights and sounds. In course of time, this faculty of hypersensitivity or extrasensory perception develops into the highest faculty of listening to the Voice of Silence itself.

"There is *shabda* in *nishabda* (the sound in soundlessness; the Voice of Silence). It is the primordial sound of *Ishvara's Pranava*. The *sadhaka* listens to the repetition and reiteration of the primal voice of *Aum*. He experiences the ineffable and inexplicable bliss of the *turiya* state of super consciousness.

"During profound meditation, some *sadhakas* feel that their bodies have become very heavy and are unable to move freely. Some others experience a feeling of extreme lightness and levitate upwards. Some *sadhakas* have a sensation of trembling and shivering. The tenacious and steady-minded *sadhaka* will not be unnerved by these supernormal experiences. He will continue his *sadhana* unhampered by his fantastic experiences.

"Ramakrishna Paramahamsa went through all these stages of *dhyana*, from *sakara* to *nirakara* (from form to formlessness). During his spiritual evolution, the Divine Mother revealed Herself to him as *Kali*. But the *Atma* is formless. That is why the *sadhaka* is advised to leave behind him all forms and names and strive for the experience of the Formless Brahman. The Absolute Brahman without form and attributes gives the highest spiritual ecstasy. He experiences perfect bliss. This superconscious state of meditation transcends all dualities. It is a state of unitive knowledge of the Brahman. It is everlasting and transcends all attributes and feelings." (16)

"It is not possible to have this bliss permanently. The longest one can be in that state is twenty-one days, after which the body drops off or one has to give up that state."(17)

References :

1. Sathya Sai Baba, *Summer Showers in Brindavan,* 1973, pp. 219 - 220
2. Tumuluru Krishna Murty, *Digest, Collection of Sri Sathya Sai Baba's Sayings,* 1985, pp. 56, 189, 191, 201
3. *Sadhana, The Inward Path,* Quotations from the Divine Discourses of Bhagavan Sri Sathya Sai Baba, pp. 140
4. Sathya Sai Baba, *Dhyana Vahini,* pp. 52
5. Sathya Sai Baba, *Summer Showers in Brindavan,* 1979, pp. 92, 111 - 113
6. *Sandeha Nivarini,* Dialogues with Sathya Sai Baba, pp. 99 - 101
7. *Sai Avatar,* Vol. III, pp. 142
8. *Bhajananamavali* (for overseas devotees), pp. 3 - 5
9. *Translations by Baba,* Compiled by H. S. Youngs, 1975, pp. 35
10. Sathya Sai Baba, *Summer Showers in Brindavan,* 1972, pp. 132 - 133
11. J.S.Hislop, *Conversations with Bhagavan Sri Sathya Sai Baba,* pp. 181 - 182, 187
12. *Sathya Sai Speaks,* Vol. VII, 2nd Am. Printing 1985, pp. 38, 381 - 382
13. *Namasmarana, A Universal Sadhana,* Compiled by Brahmanand Mavinkurve pp. 15 -16
14. *Sathya Sai Speaks,* Vol. II, pp. 12
15. *Sathya Sai Speaks,* Vol. X, pp. 274 - 275
16. Sathya Sai Baba, *Summer Showers in Brindavan,* 1979, pp. 102 -103
17. E .B. Fanibunda, *Vision of the Divine,* 1984, pp. 98
18. Sathya Sai Baba, *Sanathana Sarathi,* August 1989, pp. 207 - 209, and Am. report discourse, June 29, 1989.

30. SEVA SADHANA : SPIRITUAL ENDEAVOUR THROUGH SERVICE

"Society is the coming together of people. Cooperation among the people of a society motivated by spontaneity and by pure intentions is the hallmark of *seva* (service). *Seva* can be identified by means of two basic characteristics: compassion and willingness to sacrifice. History informs us that in all countries and in every age, man has been and is a social animal. Man is born in society, he grows in and through society, and his life ends in society, itself. Man's songs and speech, his duties and diversions, are all determined by society. Society for man is like water for fish: if society rejects him or neglects him, he cannot survive. What a single individual cannot accomplish a well-knit group or society can achieve. A man walking alone will feel tired and miserable at the end of five miles but, walking with ten others as a group he would find the five miles a pleasant stroll. He arrives refreshed and strong.

"Social living contributes to increased happiness and more efficient effort among birds and beasts. They are able to defend themselves from enemies, secure food and shelter, migrate to places at great distances when they act as a group. Even ants have learnt that immense benefits are derivable from group activity and social organisation. Monkeys also live in groups for greater security and happier lives. Let me tell you that nothing is impossible to achieve if an organised society is set on achieving it. Even liberation from material entanglement *(moksha)* can be won through serving and promoting the progress of society. Through the sense of unity, the willingness to sacrifice, and the softness of compassion, all objects can be gained.

"The first lesson in *seva* has to be learnt in the family circle itself: comprising father, mother, brothers, sisters. One must engage in loving service and prepare for the wider *seva* that awaits outside

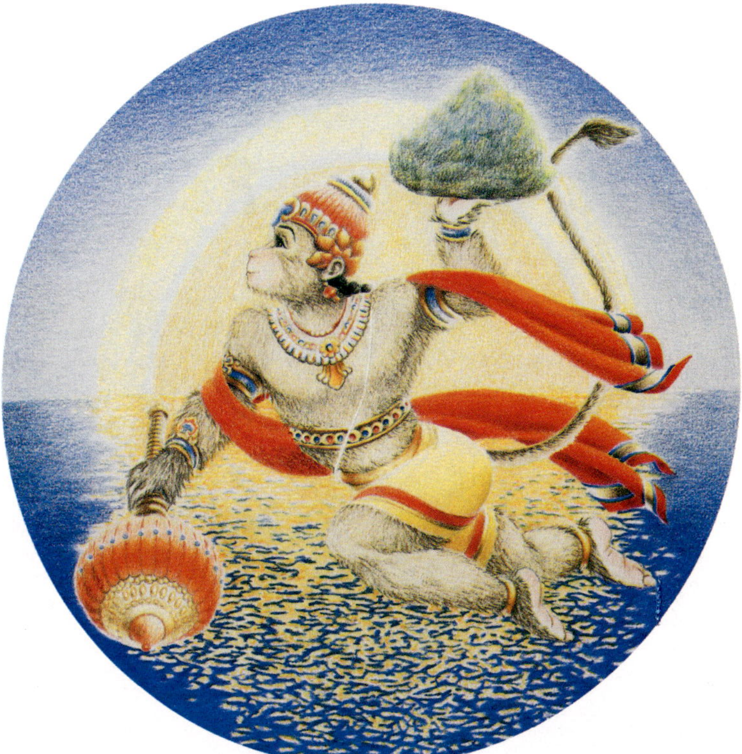

the home. The character of each individual member determines the peace and prosperity of the family; the character of each family is the basic factor that decides the happiness and joy of the village or the community. And, the nation's progress is based on the strength and happiness of the communities which are its components. So, for the welfare of the country and of the entire world, the spirit of service, vital enthusiasm, constructive imagination, pure motivation, and unselfish alertness are all urgently needed.

"During the battle of Kurukshetra, which climaxed the *Mahabharata* story, Krishna served as the driver of Arjuna's chariot throughout the day on the field, and when dusk halted the battle, he led the horses to the river, gave them a refreshing bath and applied healing balms to the wounds suffered by them during the fierce fray. He mended the reins and the harness and rendered the chariot battle-worthy for another day. The Lord set the example for the devotees to follow. He teaches that service done to any living being is offered to Him only, and is accepted by Him most joyfully. Service rendered to cattle, to beasts, to men is laudable *sadhana*.

"Many do such things now as social service, not as a *sadhana* in a full-hearted manner. The *sadhana* spirit is not found in the activity. Through *seva sadhana*, Hanuman attained identity with Rama, as the river attains identity with the sea. Arjuna, too, considered every act as *sadhana* to attain the grace of Krishna, for Krishna directed him to fight on, ever keeping Him in memory, *Mamanusmara yuddhyacha*. You, too, should keep God ever in your mind as the pace-setter, whether you are serving patients in the hospitals, cleaning a drain in the bazaar, or providing help to those who live around you. That is *tapas*, that is the highest form of *sadhana*. More than listening to a hundred lectures or delivering them to others, offering one act of genuine *seva* attracts the grace of God.

"The body has to be used to serve others. Activity is its main purpose. Krishna says, 'I have no need to be engaged in work but I work in order to activate the world.' More *ananda* can be won by serving others than can be had by merely serving oneself. Offer service to someone in need with a full heart, and experience the *ananda* that results. It need not be something big, it can even be small and unnoticed by others. It has to be done to please the God within you and him. We require today those who take delight in selfless service, but such men are rarely seen. One has to eliminate the ego totally. Even a trace of it will bring disaster. However long you may do *dhyana*, however constant your *japa*, a little ego will render them barren of result. *Bhajan* done with egoistic pride will be as harsh as the crow's caw. So try to avoid the ego marring your *sadhana*, even to a small extent.

"The Sathya Sai Organisation has laid down *seva* as *sadhana*. Service helps you to remove your ego. So do not pay heed to what others might say when you engage in service activities. When you are doing good acts, why hesitate, why feel ashamed, why fear? Let compassion and sacrifice be your two eyes; let egolessness be your breath, and love be your tongue. Let peace reverberate in your ears. These are the five vital elements you have to live upon. God will not ask you, when and where did you do service? He will ask, with what motive did you do it? What was the intention that prompted you? You may weigh the *seva* and boast of its quantity. But God seeks quality, the quality of the heart, the purity of the mind, the holiness of the motive."

References:
1. Sathya Sai Baba, Seva Dal Conference, November 19, 1981
2. *Sathya Sai Speaks,* Vol. XI, pp. 191 - 195

31. EDUCATION FOR TRANSFORMATION

"What we need today is not a new system of education, nor a new social order, nor even a new religion. What we need today are noble and high-minded men and women." (1)

"The present-day education develops the intellect and skills but does little to develop good qualities. Of what avail is all the knowledge in the world if one has not got good character? It is like water going down the drain. It is no use if knowledge grows while desires multiply. It makes one a hero in words and a zero in action.

"Man's achievements in the field of science and technology have helped to improve the material conditions of living. What we need today, however, is a transformation of the spirit. Education should serve not only to develop one's intelligence and skills, but also help to broaden one's outlook and make one useful to society and the world at large. This is possible only when cultivation of the spirit is promoted along with education in physical knowledge. Moral and spiritual education will train a man to lead a disciplined life. Education without self-control is no education at all. True education should make a person compassionate and humane. It should not make him self-centred and narrow-minded. Spontaneous sympathy and regard for all beings should flow from the heart of one who is properly educated. He should be keen to serve society rather than be preoccupied with his own acquisitive aspirations. This should be the real purpose of education in its true sense.

"Education should instill in the student fear and faith. Fear does not mean timidity. It is fear of sin and faith in God which have to be promoted. One should feel that one will forfeit the respect and regard of the community if one commits a sinful or immoral act. The student should learn to avoid unrighteous conduct. Students should be taught to love their mothers and their motherland with deep devotion. Devotion to one's country is one form of devotion to God. One who has no love for his mother, his motherland, his mother tongue and his religion will be leading a meaningless life. The educational system is beset with many problems. It has failed to promote in the young such qualities as love, forbearance and fortitude. Instead, it serves to encourage the animal nature in students. There is no place in it for cultivating human values, such as truth and righteousness. It does not imbue the student with a sense of humility, which is the hallmark of the right education.

"Parents are keen to educate their children, but they are not concerned about the kind of education they are given. Education should help to make students the embodiment of human values such as truth, love, right conduct, peace and non-violence. Academic knowledge alone is of no great value. It may help one to earn a livelihood. But education should go beyond the preparation for earning a living. It should prepare one for the challenges of life morally and spiritually. It is because human values are absent in 'educated' persons that we find them steeped in anxiety and worry.

"Who is responsible for the deplorable state of education today, for the lack of discipline among students and the absence of moral values among the educated? It is not correct to blame the students. Teachers do not understand the needs and impulses of students, and the students, for their part, have no great regard for teachers. The management of educational institutions and the educational administrators do not understand the problems of teachers or the real needs of students. The parents, the teachers, the administration and the government are all to blame.

"In the world there is nothing as sacred as *gnana*, the highest knowledge. There is nothing more precious in the world than true education. It reveals the Divinity that sustains the universe and promotes the welfare of mankind materially, mentally and socially. Only through education do we understand creation and the truth of humanity. Those who realise the nature of the Divine can know the relationship between nature, society and the infinite potential of man. Instead of being subject to nature, man can acquire through education the knowledge to utilise the forces of nature. Thereby the highest bliss (sat-chit-ananda) can be experienced.

"In today's educational system, the spiritual element has not found place. This cannot be true education. Education must proceed primarily from the spirit to nature. It must show that mankind constitutes one Divine family. The Divinity that is present in society can be experienced only through individuals. Education today, however, ends with the acquisition of degrees. Real education should enable one to utilise the knowledge one has acquired to meet the challenges of life and to make all human beings happy as far as possible.

"Born in society, one has the duty to work for the welfare and progress of society. The knowledge gained from education is being misused today solely to obtain and enjoy creature comforts and sensuous pleasures. This education has served to develop some kinds of intellectual abilities and technical skills, but has totally failed to develop good qualities. Society today is steeped in materialism because of its preoccupation with mundane pleasures.

"Education does not mean imparting of verbal knowledge. The knowledge that is gathered in schools and colleges should be capable of being used for service to society and helping to improve the conditions of one's fellowmen. The place where true teachers and students are gathered should be filled with serene peace and orderliness. Students, whose hearts should be soft and compassionate, have become hard-hearted and violent. Humility, reverence, compassion, forbearance, sacrifice and sense-control, are the qualities which reveal the outcome of true education.

"Science and technology have made astonishing progress, but humanity is going on the downward path. There are undoubtedly many brilliant scholars and scientists in the world today. But science alone is not enough. There must be the discrimination to devote the uses of these scientific discoveries for the right purposes. Science without discrimination, human existence without discipline, friendship without gratitude, music without melody, a society without morality and justice, cannot be of benefit to people.

"What is the reason for the decline in human character and the growth of violence and hatred? There is a marked increase in bad qualities, evil actions and cruel traits among human beings compared to the past. If the reasons for this growth are examined, it will be found that it is due to the continued predominance of the animal instincts in man. How else can we explain the fact that in fifty five hundred of recorded history, there have been as many as fifteen thousand wars? Even now, men are not free from the fear of war. It is these wars that have progressively dehumanised mankind and eroded all regard for human values. The constant fear that at any moment one may lose one's life in some conflict or the other has an oppressive effect on the mind. This is mainly responsible for men losing their zest for living. It is not external wars alone that are responsible for this. The general climate or conditions in which men live also contributes to fear and uncertainty.

"Men are becoming increasingly selfish and self-centred. How can such egocentric persons derive happiness from society or contribute to the happiness of society? Increasing numbers of persons are seeking education not for learning, but for acquiring the means to gratify their desires. Education today has nothing sacred about it. Students have no steadiness of mind, not even for a moment. Men today are concerned solely with their rights, and have no regard for their duties, obligations and responsibilities. Universities today have become factories for turning out degree holders and are not real centres of knowledge.

"Man can make genuine progress only when the idea that education is for earning a living is given up. The link between education and jobs should be totally snapped. Education should be for life, not for a living. Only one who realises this truth is a truly educated person. In ancient times this truth had been recognised by the sages of India, who preserved the nation's cultural heritage. Knowledge does not mean mere book lore. It is not the transference of the contents of books to the brain. Education is intended for the transformation of the heart.

"Man today is proud of the little knowledge he has acquired about the physical world, and boasts that he knows all about the universe. True knowledge is that which establishes harmony and synthesis, between science on the one hand, and spirituality and ethics on the other. It should be realised that whatever scholarship one may possess, whatever position or reputation one may have, without righteous conduct all these are meaningless. Right conduct is the only thing that really matters. What you do determines what you get. Hence you must concentrate on right conduct. Give up narrow feelings. Broaden your outlook. True education can be summed up in one word: love, all-encompassing love. A life without love is worse than death.

"Education today is a process of filling the mind with the contents of books, then emptying the contents of one's mind in the examination hall and returning empty-headed. True education consists in the cultivation of the heart. What you learn should become a part of your whole being. Only then will you have a sense of fulfilment and establish complete harmony between thought, word and deed.

"Today, the world needs people who lead such integral lives. In my view, the cultivation of human values alone is education. Whoever tries to understand the human values of truth, right conduct, peace, love and non-violence properly, who practises these values and propagates them with zeal and sincerity, only that person can be described as a truly educated person. All are entitled to acquire the knowledge of human values. It has been mentioned that these values should be practised by people at home, in the factory and at the office. But this is not enough. Everyone should practise truth, right conduct, peace, love and non-violence.

"We rejoice when schools and colleges rise numerically in every country of the world, without realising that what is happening through them is the worsening of the sickness of the community. Unrest, fear and anxiety are increasing as a result of improper and incomplete education. Education can yield peace and prosperity only when, along with technical skills and objective information, students are equipped with moral ideals, righteous living, and spiritual insight. Now the educational process does not concern itself with these values. It even works counter to them. It is quite unwilling to emphasise righteous living. It lays no stress on morals. As a consequence, the products of this process, who have no sense of values, gradually enter the professions and positions of authority in the administration of nations and rise up in time to higher levels. The world has come to the brink of disaster as a result.

"The teacher has the greatest role in moulding the future of a country. Of all professions, his is the noblest, the most difficult and the most important. He should be an example to his pupils. If a teacher has a vice, thousands are polluted. If he is dedicated and pure, thousands of children will be improved and the nation will gain from educated men and women of character. The field of education has long been afflicted by confusion and contradictory ideals. Many have spent deep thought on the problem, but they have not been able to arrive at a solution that could help to make the life of the educated person both useful and full. Meanwhile, the system is fast sliding into the depths of degradation. Freedom has led to licentiousness; reverence has receded from all relationships; institutions dedicated to the worship of the Goddess of Learning have changed into temples for the worship of the Goddess of Wealth.

"Appreciation and encouragement are offered not for virtue and good character, but for money and its accumulation. In the conduct of individuals and in human relationships, no trace of morality, charity, justice or rectitude are visible. The situation is fraught with enormous danger for the future of humanity. Life today is riddled with fear, despair and doubt. Man rolls uneasily on a bed infested with fleas, finding no rest or peace.

"A school should not be considered just a commonplace arrangement designed for teaching and learning. It is the place where the consciousness is aroused and illumined, purified and strengthened, the place where the seeds of discipline, duty and devotion are planted and fostered to fruition. It is said that schools have developed science and technology to supreme heights. But, though man has explored millions of miles of space, he has not mastered the skill of exploring even half an inch of his own inner space! He is acquainted with the ups and downs on the surface of the moon, but he makes no attempt to know the joys and sorrows of his next-door neighbour.

"The first task of the teacher is the cultivation of virtue in the hearts of his pupils. This is far more vital than the promotion of learning. Teachers have to be examples who can inspire their pupils. They must practise what they preach. As the teacher, so the pupils. We hear much of intellectuals today. It is only through the intellectuals that the world has degenerated in so many directions today. From the non-intellectuals, the world has to learn many lessons in conduct and behaviour. The intellectuals pay no attention to common truths, since they are too low; they do not grasp the higher truths since their intellect is capable only of confusing them by doubts. While defining human values, you may enumerate sixty different points. But all the sixty are included in these six: compassion, fear of evil, forbearance, serenity, patience and non-attachment.

"Another characteristic of the educated, the intelligentsia, is their pride. They move around wearing the crown of conceit. Pride is the wall that hides the truth from untruth. This obstacle has to be removed so that unity might be realised and Divinity manifested. Parents entrust their dearly beloved children to the teachers in the schools, believing that they are capable and willing to guide them and to instill in them skills and habits that can later help them to stand up against the hardships and temptations of the world. Teachers are, therefore, burdened with a great responsibility. When a child needs help it rushes to the mother; when the mother needs help to equip the child with knowledge and strength of character, she rushes to the teacher. Therefore, the teacher has to be more than a mother to the children. His anxiety about the child's physical, mental and moral health, and his vigilant attention and care, have to be more constant and knowledgeable than that of the mother.

"Teachers must speak to one another in loving terms only. They should not indulge in mutual recrimination. For the tender minds of children will be tarnished by the slightest tinge of hatred that pollutes the atmosphere of love. Teachers have to discriminate and develop firm faith in the *Atma*. As the seed, so the crop. Unless they are able to implant this seed of knowledge, value orientation cannot happen. Teachers and students must develop constructive companionship. The teacher must share the sorrows and joys of the pupils as keenly as if they were his own.

"Students have to cultivate gratitude, compassion and tolerance. Students now believe that the study of books is all that is needed. But what is the result to be gained? The test for scholarship is: are soft and sweet words uttered? Are good works planned and executed? Are scholars involving themselves in good works for their society? Are they avoiding acts that injure others? Are they grateful to those who promote their happiness? These are the tests, not how many books they have read or how many degrees they have collected. Consider the learned scholars of today. They are bondslaves to greed, suspicion, envy and factionalism. They have no steadiness of conviction. So they cannot sleep, they do not relish food, and each one suspects the other. The reason for this sad condition is that they have no spiritual outlook or experience.

"Educated people today are all afflicted with selfishness. Why? They have been rendered so helpless by this disease that they do not pay attention to the misery of even their parents. This is no sign of education. Education must broaden the heart, it must expand one's love. Fortitude and equanimity belong to the reality in man. One must express this truth in every act, and with gratitude, too, for all kindnesses shown. People forget those who helped them advance in life, they repay kindness with injury. The very teachers who contributed to the progress of students in their studies, are hit on the head by their students. Teachers may have faults, but the student has no authority to look for faults, expose them and retaliate.

"Students! Uproot from your minds the idea that you are undergoing education for the sake of money. Do not be enslaved by money. Educate yourselves into a worthy character, earning virtues. Learn to give in plenty, not receive in plenty. Develop renunciation, not acquisitiveness. Be eager to participate enthusiastically in those activities that help others, even more than in activities that help yourselves. And pay attention to activities that could be pleasing to God. God is in everyone. So, when God is pleased, everyone is pleased. Your first duty is to give happiness and satisfaction to your parents. You should not be preoccupied with your own personal comforts and pleasure.

"Teachers are not the only moulders of the country's future. They should not be blamed exclusively for the kind of students we now are worried about. It has been said that the peace and prosperity of a country rests on the teachers and guardians of the law. I must add a third and crucial group, parents. They must bear the main burden of blame for ruining the character of their children, by being overindulgent and giving them too much freedom. They do not provide them with examples of honesty, sense-control and discipline. Some people talk of an educational theory advocating full freedom to the child, allowing it to grow just as it likes. The parents are advised not to curb or control it. This is a sure way of making the child wild, a burden to itself and a nuisance to society. Knowledge can be given by the teacher; however, the discipline, the rigorous control of the senses and behaviour must be administered by the parents. Then the children become sacred souls, holy, sanctified individuals. Even while their minds are tender and their hearts unsoiled, children must be trained to purify and sweeten their thoughts, words and deeds.

"The homes in which the children grow, as indeed all homes, have to be clean and with vibrations free of hatred, envy, greed, spite or hypocrisy. The food that the child eats must be pure. From the age of two to five, the child looks up to its mother, and so the mother's behaviour has to be very proper. Women these days rush for jobs even more than men. But of what avail is the money they earn, when they are not able to tend to their children, a mother's sacred and first duty? In former times, the tradition and custom in our homes was that, when women were pregnant, they would read or listen to sacred stories to fill their minds and hearts with pure and holy thoughts and feelings, thereby creating in the foetus 'the purest vibrations'.

"The ideal of Sai Spiritual Education (*Bal Vikas*) is to raise a generation of boys and girls who have a clean and clear consciousness. Teachers of Sai Spiritual Education should cultivate love for their students. They should treat them as their own children. But they should be careful not to be too lenient. Discipline should be enforced with love and understanding. The children should be taught to cultivate respect and veneration for all the religions. Love of one's own religion should expand into love for all other faiths. Religious animosity should never be allowed to sprout in children's minds. We should teach them the basic unity and the common goal of all the religions, though the practices may seem different. Children should be taught the essential teaching not only of their own scriptures, but of the scriptures of other faiths, too." (2)

"All faiths have emphasized one common factor, that there is only one God, and Truth is His form. There are no differences between Hindus, Muslims and Christians on this basic concept. All religions, all scriptures, all spiritual teachings point only to one truth, the unity of Divinity. Instead of realising this, men are lost along wrong paths.

"Jesus sacrificed His life for the regeneration and welfare of mankind. Today there are some who exaggerate the so-called differences between different faiths, and for their own selfish purposes, exploit these differences and thereby bring a bad name to the great founders of these religions, who were spiritual giants. No prophet or messiah asked his followers to hate other religions or the followers of other faiths. Every religion has declared that God is One and that the Divine dwells in every being. Jesus also proclaimed the truth that the One Spirit resides in all beings. When Jesus was addressing the Jews, an ethereal voice declared: 'All lives are one, my dear Son. Be alike to everyone.'

"When Jesus was being crucified, the same ethereal voice declared that the human body is only a vesture for the spirit. The body is subject to constant change. But the indwelling spirit is immortal. This was the truth proclaimed in *Vedanta* when it said: 'The body is a temple in which the eternal spirit resides as the indweller.' The inner meaning of this is that wherever you may go, the eternal spirit remains with you. You must regard the body as the temple of the spirit; bear in mind that Divinity is ever within you. Only when you realise this truth can you begin to experience the Divine.

"Whether in Hinduism or Buddhism, Jainism or Sikhism, Christianity or Islam, Divinity is One and One only. Those who profess great love for their particular religion are indulging in make-believe. Hindus regard Hinduism as the greatest religion. Wherein lies its greatness? If you declare that the God of all religions is one, why claim superiority for Hinduism and decry other religions? Does that bespeak your love for Hinduism? This applies also to those professing Christianity. They say: 'We are Christians. We believe in the unique Divinity of Jesus. There is no other Divine saviour.' One may claim that Jesus is Divine. But does that entitle one to deride other religions?

"No religion should allow the decrying of other faiths. It is not a religion at all that cavils at other religions; it is a form of arrogance. The great saints who worshipped Christ or Rama or Krishna or Allah were inspired by their profound teachings. But how many of the followers of these faiths live up to these teachings today? If the teachings of the founder of a religion are not followed, can it be called a religion? Those who, in the name of religion, further their selfish interests, are bringing discredit to the founder of the religion.

"The first thing to be learnt is that there is only one God. Men may be different in form and name and colour, and their country and historical circumstances may vary. But God has no such differences. Hence, you should not cavil at any religion, or attack or deride it. You may profess whatever faith you like. But, you should not disparage another's beliefs. It is a travesty of devotion. Sri Krishna says in the *Gita* that the mark of a true devotee is absence of ill-will towards anyone (*adveshta sarvabhutanam*). We must respect the Divine that is in every creature." (3)

"God is neither distant nor distinct from you. You are God. You are *Sat-chit-ananda*. You are being (*asthi*), awareness (*bhati*), loving kindness (*priyam*). You are all. When will you cognise this truth? When you shake off the delusions which hide the truth? If your yearning to experience *Brahmananda*, the *Sat-chit-ananda* is sincere and pure, from this day, keep ever in your memory what I am about to tell you:

1. 'I am God, I am not different from God.' Be conscious of this always. Keep it ever in mind. 'I am God I am God, I am not different from God.' Be reminding yourself of this. Pray that you may not fail in this spiritual exercise.

2. 'I am the Invisible Supreme Absolute.' (*Akhanda Para Brahman*). This is the second truth to be established in the consciousness by unremitting repetition and prayer.

3. 'I am *Sat-chit-ananda*' (being-awareness-bliss).

4. 'Grief and anxiety can never affect me.' Develop this faith and convince yourselves of this truth by repeated assurance and prayer.

5. 'I am ever content; fear can never enter me.' Feel thus forever. Pray that this conviction grows stronger and stronger. Exhort yourself, 'O Self!' Utter *Aum tat sat,* the threefold symbol of Brahman. As the physical body is maintained healthy and strong by the five vital airs *(prana),* these five prayers will endow you with the awareness of Brahman which is the same as the status of Brahman Itself. (4)

References :
1. Sathya Sai Baba, *Sanathana Sarathi,* December 1992. pp. 290
2. *Sathya Sai Education in Human Values,* taken from Discourses given by Sathya Sai Baba, Compiled by Lorraine Burrows, 1988, pp. 1 - 2, 9 - 15, 19, 39 - 40, 54 - 63, 67, 71 – 75, 80, 89 – 90, 99, 115 - 121
3. Sathya Sai Baba, *Sanathana Sarathi,* January, 1986, pp. 2 -3
4. Sathya Sai Baba, *Sanathana Sarathi,* January 1984, pp. 7 - 8

APPENDIX

Some people relentlessly seek spiritual knowledge at the expense of secular learning. This is not desirable. They miss both and wander aimlessly between the two; such a predicament, too, is undesirable. Secular learning should not be neglected.

(Sathya Sai Baba, *Sathya Sai Vahini*, pp. 170)

We live in times which, for many people, the gap between man and nature is becoming wider and wider. The environment, outer and inner, is becoming extremely polluted. This is so for the air, the water, the soil, the trees, the rivers, the seas, as also for our blood, our digestive and nervous systems and, thereby, for our mind.

An ever-increasing number of people fall ill. Diseases break out at an increasingly younger age. In the industrialized countries nearly half the population dies of cardiovascular diseases and twenty five percent of cancer. The number of people with cardiovascular diseases, cancer, and other serious diseases is increasing. They are mainly toxic diseases caused by a wrong way of living and eating. Seen from the theory of the five elements of space (ether), air, fire, water and earth, further causes of disease are to a very huge extent noise, too little exercise, polluted air, too little sunlight, electro-magnetic pollution, polluted water and a wrong way of living. The toxic diseases are also called civilization diseases.

Most people nearly always eat industrialized food, heated and reheated food, bread; they use all kinds of stimulants, like alcohol, soft drinks, chocolate, coffee, tea, refined sugar, tobacco, *rajasic* and *tamasic* condiments and salt, besides other faulty food, such as meat, fish, animal fats, and eggs. Most articles of food come from crossed or genetically manipulated, so-called 'improved' strains of plants and animals. Nowadays, there are several kinds of genetic manipulation. The oldest method is genetic manipulation without expedients. In the last ten to fifteen years methods of genetic manipulation have been developed with expedients such as chemicals and irradiation. The latest development is DNA - manipulation.

Grains, pulses, potatoes, fruits, etc. contain natural poisons for protection against worms, moulds, bacteria, etc. Scientists have discovered that genetically manipulated natural products contain much greater quantities of these natural poisons than those which have not been genetically manipulated. Some scientists say that these natural poisons are much more harmful for man than preservatives, artificial flavours and colours, residues of fertilizers, insecticides, etc. When that is true, all foodstuffs coming from genetically manipulated plants, grains (especially wheat), potatoes, etc. are *tamasic*. Even fruits like apples, oranges and bananas which are manipulated very badly may be *tamasic*. Nearly all the consumed food is *rajasic* and *tamasic*. In digesting these foods so many toxic substances are released that the body cannot eliminate them. The blood is polluted, putrefaction symptoms appear in the bowels, the tissues acidify and the nervous system degenerates. The body, literally, becomes poisoned and acidified. The immune system of the body thereby becomes undermined, giving all sorts of diseases their chance.

Lysosomes (organelles) filled with indigestible substances (residual bodies) accumulate in the body cells, especially in the cells, of the nervous system, the heart muscles, the liver and the skin, and cause premature aging. Eighty percent of the volume of the braincells of old people contain residual bodies filled with old-age pigment (lipofuscin, ceroid and amyloid); this may cause senility with the concomitant symptoms: loss of memory, depression, irritability, anxiety, tiredness and loss of appetite. The great majority of the diseases mentioned can be prevented and even cured by directing the mind Godward and by eating *satvic* food, which is living food. Living food is Divine; cattle and plants must be tended with love and wisdom. The cattle must be fed with good food and be allowed to die a natural death.

According to Sathya Sai Baba, fresh, raw, uncooked, unheated, unirradiated fruits, nuts, coconuts, vegetables, roots, tubers, and soaked or just germinating pulses, eaten in moderation and grown without the aid of artificial fertilizers and other chemical substances, are the best *satvic* food. The vegetables, if necessary, may be cooked for a short duration provided they are consumed immediately. Small quantities of uncooked biological germ-free milk, from cattle tended with love and wisdom, and milk-products prepared from this milk, such as buttermilk, yogurt, curds and butter are also *satvic* food; buttermilk is better than milk.

Further, small quantities of starch-containing foodstuffs, such as *ragi* and rice, for example, in the form of liquid gruel, or rice soaked in curds may be taken. The rice also may be cooked for a short duration. Here too it is important that the warm rice be consumed immediately. What is more, a meal can only be called *satvic* if one eats it sparingly and in the right attitude of mind. Sathya Sai Baba attaches much value to pure water energized by the sunlight with the life-force (*prana*). During an interview Sathya Sai Baba said: "Eat the best food you can find." As a matter of fact, finding real *satvic* food is very difficult nowadays.

To make the importance of *satvic* eating habits clearer and in order to help to change over to *satvic* food, we will speak about *ayurveda* and survey a number of important sciences of nutrition of western naturopathy. There are a lot of similarities between *ayurveda* and the western natural healing arts. Further *ayurveda*, is universal and more all-embracing than western naturopathy; *ayurveda* also includes the study and the working of the *Atma*, the *gunas* and the *pranas*. Western medical science and even several branches of western naturopathy have only a materialistic view. *Ayurveda* and the teachings of the Essenes delve much deeper. The *gunas* not only govern the material world but also the mental and the spiritual.

A. AYURVEDA

1. History

The golden age of Indian culture was between 2700 B.C. to 600 A.D. The millennium from the time of Atreya (700 B.C.) up to 700 A.D. (i.e. almost till the beginning of the Mohammedan invasion of India), was the heyday of *ayurveda*, the golden era in the medical history of India, comparable to that of Hippocrates and Galen in the West. This was followed suddenly by dark centuries of stagnation, neglect and decay. Much of the old literature of the various branches of medicine has been lost or destroyed by foreign invasions and domination of India.

The *Rig Veda* and the *Atharva Veda* are variously claimed as the source, or the original tree of which *ayurveda* is a branch. Thus it is sometimes called an *upa-veda* (subject) of the *Atharva Veda* by most and of the *Rig Veda* by some. To Bharadwaja goes the credit of first propogating *ayurveda* in the world. Later on, Charaka emphasized the point that the science of life *(ayurveda)* is beginningless and has existed for all time.

It is remarkable that the birth of the Buddha coincided with the height of intellectual development of India. The age between 600 B.C. and 200 A.D. was the time when scientific medicine evolved and took definite shape. It was the Buddha who extended the benefits of scientific medicine to humanity at large, motivated by the spirit of compassion. The same spirit of compassion was later on expressed by Christ.

Bharadwaja acquired through *ayurveda* unmeasured life endowed with happiness. *Atreya* and other great sages learnt *ayurveda* from Bharadwaja, Agnivesha from *Atreya*, Charaka from Agnivesha, Dridhabala from Charaka. Dridhabala edited the 'Charaka Samhita'. According to the Sushruta and Kashyapa *Samhitas*, which are more or less contemporaneous with the 'Charaka Samhita', the original teachers of these treatises, namely

Dhanavantari and Kashyapa, claim to have received the science from Indra, and were therefore on par with Bharadwaja. The Bharadwaja (or Atreya) school is primarily one of medicine, the Sushruta of surgery, and the Kashyapa school of pediatrics and obstetrics.

2. The Rishis

From the very beginning of the *Vedic* period there appears on the field a class of *Rishis* (sages, seers) who not only composed hymns and performed sacrifices, but also fought wars and ploughed fields. They devoted their lives to disinterested inquiry into thinking, imagination, reasoning and generalisation. These *Rishis* lived apart from the world in quiet forest retreats.

The forest dwellings *(ashramas)* gradually grew to be the centres of highest learning. The priestly, or preceptor class *(Brahmanas)*, became the dispensers of religion, law and medicine. They believed that all the ills of humanity are rooted in ignorance and all progress and happiness in unclouded knowledge. The *Rishis* evolved a system of education which had for its aim the inducing or drawing out of the latent capacities of a man, the individual or the whole, integral man in potential. This education aimed at securing for its votary his well-being both here and hereafter as is claimed for the science of *ayurveda* by its author: "It is the science of life which teaches mankind what constitutes their good in both the worlds." The *Rishis* built up an elaborate educational organization which succeeded in making the highest fruits of education available to the humblest member of society.

The faculty that enabled the rich as well as the poor to launch themselves on an educational career, was the absence of the compulsion to pay any fee at all, at the start. At the end of his education, the disciple could, of his own volition, make a suitable payment to his preceptor. In this society, where the love of knowledge and service to fellowman was held high, everyone was educated.

Each *Rishi* family was an autonomous university. The unitary *Rishi-kulas*, or educational settlements, developed into a form more complex, first as *ashrama-kulas* in the forest, and later on as *Guru-kulas*. Some of the more renowned *Rishis* had ten thousand pupils studying under their direction. Admission to these universities was by no means easy.

The first three classes of men were compelled to undergo a long period of rigorous studentship; the compulsion was not governmental but a far stronger one, the compulsion of religio-social convention. A member of the serving class (*shudra*) could be, and frequently was, as highly educated as any of the upper classes.

Taxila, situated in the north-west, was undoubtedly the most important seat of learning in ancient India. Its history goes back into hoary antiquity. It was founded by Bharata. This famous university attracted students not only from far off places in India, but also from foreign countries, such as Babylonia, Egypt, Phoenicia, Syria, Arabia, China and Greece. The catholicity of the curriculum amazes the student of history.

The Alexandrian school, established in the 4th century B.C., was probably the result of inspiration derived from Taxila during Alexander's invasion of India. In spite of the hazards of travel in those days, parents sent their sons to Taxila at the tender age of sixteen. The course lasted five to seven years.

3. Ayurveda, the Science of Life

In ancient India an elementary knowledge of medicine was considered necessary for all students. They were taught elementary rules of the preservation of health and how to live a full span of life in perfect health by taking care of one's diet, personal hygiene, actions and character. This shows the importance attached to medical science as the basic knowledge for every individual.

Ayurveda is primarily the science of positive health and it is only secondarily a science for the curing of diseases. Hygiene plays a very important role in Indian medicine. This code of health lays down in full detail the regimen of daily life in general, with its modifications and variations during different seasons. The most important point emphasized is that these rules are to be applied according to the individual constitution of the person. It comprises instructions on diet and activity, work, rest and sleep, sense-purity, sex-hygiene and behaviour in general.

Its definition of man is complete. Man is an aggregate of body, mind and spirit. *Ayurveda* inculcates the discipline of the senses and the regulation of the moral life so as to accord with the happiness and good, not merely of the individual, but of society as a whole. It is therefore social and universal in its conception and application. It is an entire way of life that *ayurveda* expounds - embodying philosophy, eugenics, ethics and healing. The human body is no doubt a machine, but the metaphor should be applied in a limited sense only. Even as a machine it is self-stoking, self-adjusting, self-repairing, self-preserving, self-asserting and a self-multiplying machine. It has intelligence and feelings, individuality and purposiveness.

According to *ayurveda*, moral excellence is the very basis of true education. Therefore, the vast majority of required qualifications of a student of *ayurveda* concerned the ethical side of the student's personality. In addition, much importance was attached to physical and intellectual items. The student lived in the closest association with the teacher. The teacher should have unbounded affection for his disciples, and had to devote a personal and individual care and thought to every pupil, and be his source of inspiration and guidance.

In his daily conduct the student was required to observe strict rules. During student life, special emphasis was laid on celibacy, abstinence from meat-foods and intoxicating drinks. The student was allowed to eat only pure articles of food. He had to be righteous, self-controlled and free from greed, anger, passion, envy and ridicule. Because of the oral education his memory was developed to a degree almost incredible in our times. The student, who lived a life of celibacy and discipline in his preceptor's home, was not allowed to drink wine, just like a hermit striving for liberation. Men who, out of an innate purity and strength of mind lived a life of discipline eschewing wine and meat and resorting to a wholesome diet and clean habits, were regarded as immune from disease, whether endogenous or exogenous, especially from mental disease. Of course, *ayurveda* could not prescribe this way of living to everyone. In general, *ayurveda* advocated moderation and limitation. *Ayurveda* did not dictate total abstention from food meat and wine, except for those on the spiritual path.

4. The Triumvirate of Vata Pitta, and Kapha

The central theory of *ayurveda* is the theory of the triumvirate of *vata*, *pitta* and *kapha*. The five elements of ether, air, fire, water and earth are transformed into three by combining ether and air into *vata*, turning fire into *pitta* and combining water and earth into *kapha*. *Vata*, *pitta* and *kapha* are the names of the three organizations of the body. These three organizations must be appreciated in their united and integrated whole as mutually checking and balancing forces in the body. *Kapha* and *pitta* are relatively static, and need, at every point of their existence and functioning, the co-ordinated impulse and motivations of *vata*.

The body, like all living organisms, needs a minimum tripartite *(doshas)* organization for its life processes:

1. The *kapha* organization of fluid balance in the body (water balance system). The matrix of the material pattern that life requires for its existence and expression, is provided by water, the daily purifier and refresher, and the elixir of life. The counterpart in the body of the water in nature is the body-fluid, the colloid fluid *(sleshma)*, known as protoplasm. This integrative organization regulates constantly the physical and chemical structure of the body-fluid, as well as its circulation. It maintains the proper balance

between fluids in the various parts of the body. The colloid fluid holds the joints together, performs all cohesive, nutritive, developing and stabilizing functions.

2. The *pitta* organization of thermal balance. Specific heat is necessary to digest and assimilate material from the environmental world and also to maintain the optimal temperature of the body. The internal thermal balance is sustained by the anabolic and catabolic processes constantly taking place in the body.

3. The *vata* or *vital* (life-sustaining) organization. It initiates all activities and maintains the specificity of all vital processes. The *vata* is the very self of the five forms of *vata* in the body, viz. *prana, udana, samana, vyana* and *apana*. No part or cell of the body can function without the motivation of *vata*. Its function is to cause all movement, including that of conveying sense impressions and thought and emotional impulses. Thus all neuro-muscular activity and all sense-functions belong to *vata*. All life functions, including the daily metabolic processes of maintaining the proportion and tone of body-elements, belong to *vata*. *Vata* is indeed the very life principle.

From the moment of conception some men are equibalanced in *vata, pitta* and *kapha,* and some have a predominance of *vata*, some of *pitta* and some of *kapha*. Of them, only the first enjoy perfect health, while the rest are ever liable to disease. Charaka propounds that there are three main classes of persons. Those are the three main constitutional groups in each of whom one of the triumvirate of biological organizations is predominantly active or pronounced. Generally speaking there are seven constitutional types: 1. *Vata*, 2. *Pitta*, 3. *Kapha*, 4. *Vata-Pitta*, 5. *Pitta-Kapha*, 6. *Vata-Kapha* and 7. *Vata-Pitta-Kapha*. Charaka says that when the triumvirate is in its normal condition man enjoys perfect health; and when it is in an abnormal or pathological state man suffers from disease.

The triumvirate organization, body tissues and the excretory and secretory matter become vitiated in the disease condition. Once *vata, pitta* and *kapha* are vitiated, they spread their vitiating effects to all the body parts and channels, for they pervade the whole body. *Vata, pitta* and *kapha* are then called the three *doshas*, derived through vitiation or pollution, becoming impure, bad or corrupted. Sushruta says, "*Vata, pitta* and *kapha* are the cause of all disease. Just as the entire universe cannot transcend the triad of natural forces of *satva, rajas* and *tamas*, similarly the totality of disease cannot transcend, but falls within the triad of *vata, pitta* and *kapha*."

There are *vata* diseases, *pitta* diseases and *kapha* diseases. *Vata* diseases arise in the large intestine, *pitta* diseases in the small intestine and *kapha* diseases in the stomach. The diseases can manifest themselves in other places. *Vata* disorders are gasification, constipation, diarrhoea, dizziness, rheumatism, nervousness, neuralgia, depression, headache,etc. *Pitta* diseases are gastric ulcer, high blood-pressure, gall-bladder complaints, liver-complaints, etc. *Kapha* diseases are asthma, bronchitis, lung-congestion, inflammation of the sinus cavities, etc. Suppressed fears cause *vata* disorders, rage or hatred gives *pitta* disorders, and jealousy, greed and attachment develop *kapha* disorders.

The experienced *ayurvedic* doctor has at his disposal several methods to determine the constitution and the disturbances of the three *doshas* of the patient. After that he can balance the three *doshas* by several modes of treatment, among other things by a proper diet. To compose such a diet is rather complicated: each food has a specific influence. Every constitution needs its own food. To increase or to decrease *vata, pitta and kapha*, special foods can be used. Ayurveda also gives rules for correct food combinations. First of all, the three *doshas* have to do with the body. The three *gunas* have, in the first place, to do with the mind, but also with the body. Fortunately for us, the system of *satvic, rajasic* and *tamasic* food is less complicated; in addition, it is essential for people on the spiritual path. Healthy spiritual people do not need to pay attention to the three *doshas*; they can concentrate on the three *gunas*.

To end this very short summary of *ayurveda* here are a few simple remarks. Safflower oil is excessively irritant and provokes all body-humours. Grapes are the best of fruits. Milk, especially cow's milk, is said to be foremost among the vitalizers and rejuvenators. Buttermilk is considered to be the best in assimilation disorders, owing to its digestively stimulant, astringent and light qualities. It is beneficial to *vata* and *kapha* and does not provoke *pitta*. Another vitalizer is the well known *ginseng* (from Korea).

Eat in proper proportions. The food eaten in the right measure does not disturb the balance of *vata*, *pitta* and *kapha*, but exclusively promotes life, is easily passed down to the rectum, does not disturb the gastric fire and is easily assimilated. Eat after the digestion of the previous meal. The food that is eaten while the previous meal is lying undigested in the stomach, getting mixed with the semi-digested chyme of the previous meal, immediately provokes all the humours. Do not eat hurriedly or too leisurely. Do not talk or laugh while eating. Sri Swami Shivananda says that onions and garlic are *rajasic* foods. Sai Usha says that cumin and cardamom are *satvic* whereas cloves and cinnamon are *rajasic* and onion and garlic *tamasic* foods.

The great sages made use of the *rasayanas*, or vitalizers such as the *Brahma rasayana*, to obtain great longevity, heightened memory and intelligence, freedom from disease, youth, excellence of complexion and voice, optimum strength of body and senses, etc. They were able thereby to develop an intense devotion to God. These vitalizers, or life-extension preparations, work best for people with a high consciousness, but not for worldly-minded people.

It is remarkable that recently in the West, a new science, viz. the life-extension science, has come into being. Well-known names in this field are Professor Linus Pauling, Professor D. Harman and Professor Dr. J. Bjorksten. Unfortunately the ideas and modes of treatment of the western life-extension science are sometimes not in accordance with the Divine laws (abuse of animals).

B. THE WESTERN NATUROPATHY

1. The Bio-Electronigram of Professor L. C. Vincent

The human body can be looked upon as a 'field'. According to Professor L.C. Vincent, a person does not fall ill when his field remains in good condition. In certain circumstances this field may become a fertile soil for diseases. He distinguishes four 'fields', illustrated in a diagram. Along the x-axis the acidity (pH) is plotted, along the y-axis the redoxpotential (rH2) and along the z-axis, vertically upon the paper, the electronical resistance (R). The quality of water and other liquids can be fixed by means of these three physical quantities. The acidity reveals something about the quantity of free hydrogen ions (H^+) in a liquid, the redoxpotential (rH2) indicates the number of available electrons for the reduction-oxidation reactions, and the electronical resistance (R) mentions the quantity of minerals in the liquid.

A liquid is neutral when pH = 7. We talk about acid liquid when the pH is less than 7, and about alkaline liquid when the pH-factor is more than 7. A liquid is electrically neutral when rH2 = 28. There is a shortness of electrons when the rH2-factor is higher than 28 and there is a remainder of electrons when the rH2-factor is less than 28. The pH-factor of the blood of man is expressed by his vitality. When this pH-factor rises, his vitality goes down. The rH2-value is, above all, important for the absorption of oxygen, while we breathe. When the redoxpotential is higher than 24, suffocation of the cell-breathing sets in.

The health of the human 'field' can be measured by the values of the pH, rH2 and R-factors of the three tissue-fluids: blood, saliva and urine. The triangle drawn in the diagram holds good for a human being with optimum health. The 'egg' is the life-limit of the blood. Beyond that limit death is instantaneous. Each 'field' from the diagram forms a culture for certain diseases.

FIELD 2		35	shortage of electrons	FIELD 3
acid			bad absorption of O_2	basic
oxidised			chlorinated tap water	Oxidised
youth			800-2000 Ω cm	adulthood
moulds				viruses
				indust. food
		30	cooked	anticoncept
			potatoes	pill
				cancer line
				irreversible
electric	pasteurized	28	sterilized	
neutral	milk		milk	
	≈ ≈		pre- cancerose	
	uncooked		line	
	milk			
	vegetables	25	heart and	
fruit			vascular diseases line	
vegetables		opt		
		□ health ○		
5.5	6	6.5 7.07	7.5 8 8.5 pH 9
		22 raw		
		potatoes		
		20 vegetables		
		rH2		
		life		
		limit		
		of		
		15 the		
		blood		
mineral water 400Ωcm				
Spa 1700Ωcm		polluted water		
Konigstein 7000 Ωcm		(bacteria)		
Volvic 7000Ωcm				
FIELD 1		10 many electrons	FIELD 4
acid reduced		good absorption	basic
procreaton vitamins		of O_2	reduced dead
uncooked food			bacteria

BIO-ELECTRONIGRAM of Professor L. C. Vincent

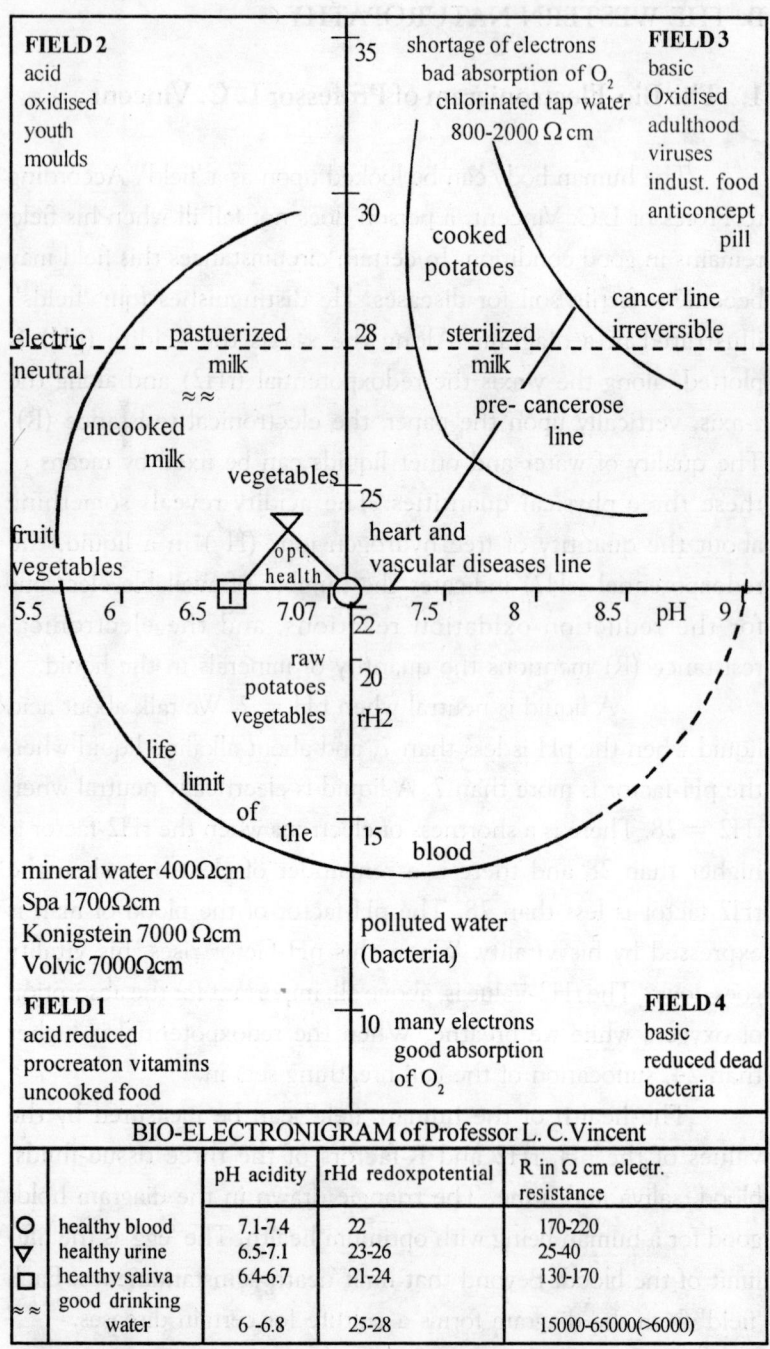

		pH acidity	rHd redoxpotential	R in Ω cm electr. resistance
O	healthy blood	7.1-7.4	22	170-220
▽	healthy urine	6.5-7.1	23-26	25-40
□	healthy saliva	6.4-6.7	21-24	130-170
≈ ≈	good drinking water	6 -6.8	25-28	15000-65000(>6000)

Compile from several sources e.g. "Orthomoleculair," August 1986, pp. 30

Field 1: for diabetes, high blood pressure, cramps, etc.
Field 2: for childhood diseases, infantile paralyses, tuberculosis, etc.
Field 3: for (present urban) civilization diseases, cancer, cardiac and vascular diseases, AIDS, multiple sclerosis, neurosis, irritation, stress, depression and ageing.
Field 4: for pneumonia, dysentery, typhoid fever, cholera pestilence, syphilis, etc.

By using industrial nutrition, heated food, meat, fish, etc., in short, *rajasic* and *tamasic* food, the physical tissues acidify. In consequence of this, the urine becomes more acid (lower pH) and the blood compensatorily more alkaline (higher pH). Saliva becomes more alkaline as well. The rH2-values increase in many cases. In this way the triangle is stretched out to top right and the 'field' of the person becomes susceptible to various civilization diseases. At the right side of the line of cardiac and vascular diseases, there is a great chance of catching these diseases. When somebody is suffering from a heart-disease, the pH-value of his blood will be found at the right side of the relevant line. Nowadays, eighty-five per cent of all diseases are civilization diseases.

Uncooked food, especially fruit and vegetables, restores the triangle of the optimum health. The measurings and the theory of Professor L. C. Vincent of France form a scientific proof of the curative effect of uncooked food and the degenerating effects of industrial food, heated food, stimulants, meat, fish, etc.

As shown in the diagram, chlorinated tap water stretches the triangle out to field - 3. Water, polluted with bacteria, stretches the triangle out to field - 4. Good drinking-water complies with the conditions that are mentioned in the index. Pure water is of vital importance to man. Therefore they advise one not to drink chlorinated tap water. It contains too many minerals, poisons and viruses. Drinking-water, which is purified by way of the method of reverse osmosis', or water such as Spa water from Belgium, Konigstein water from Germany or Volvic water from France, can be recommended. (Dr. H. M. Shelton and others prefer distilled water). Put the purified water in sunlight, it is then loaded with *prana*.

Man functions best in a slightly negatively charged environment (surplus of electrons). This we find in the woods, by the sea, or in the neighbourhood of a waterfall. Motorcars, concrete, electric apparatuses, synthetic materials and the like produce a positively charged environment. This kind of electrical pollution (shortage of electrons) can be reduced by some simple measures like the use of natural materials for clothes (cotton, wool and silk), wearing non-isolating shoes, by now and then going out into the country when the dew is still on the grass, and avoiding as much as possible, all electrical apparatuses (television, neonlamps, etc.).

Use only silk from 'wild' silkworms, such as *Antheraea mylitta* from India, *Antheraea yamamai* from Japan and *Antheraea pernyi* from China, because these silkworms are not killed by heated air; mostly, the silk moths may fly out. Do not use silk from 'cultivated' silkworms, such as the *Bombyx mori*. They are killed in their cocoon by heated air.

Besides, there are many ionizing apparatuses (air ionisers) which negatively charge a part of the oxygen-molecules in the air. We must also pay attention to the electro-magnetic pollution in our life-environment. In California a foundation has developed the life field polarizer. It is a complex antenna system in the form of a simple cone. The inventors say that the life field polarizer harmonizes the electromagnetic environment and clears interfering vibrations from the electrical fields of biological systems. It protects all forms of life against the harmful electromagnetic radiation produced by TV sets, radio, TV and radar stations, overhead power lines, tools and appliances powered by alternating current motors, spark plugs in cars, etc.

Do not use aluminium pots and pans; aluminium compounds are toxic. Finally, a healthy set of teeth is extremely important for optimum health. More and more naturopaths and dentists point out the disease-producing properties of amalgam fillings and recommend composite fillings. Consult an acupuncturist and a dentist who is an expert on composite fillings.

2. Uncooked Food

In natural food diet, and the nutritional therapy of western naturopathy, plain, raw, biological food is central. Uncooked food has been eaten all over the world since times immemorial. That is why certain primitive races still enjoy excellent health. Man is by nature vegetarian. Richard Leakey, a prominent palaeo-anthropologist, came to the conclusion that prehistoric man was a fruit eater. The digestive tract of modern man still most resembles that of fruit-eating animals.

Almost without exception, poets, philosophers and historians of antiquity picture the diet of primitive man as being very simple and consisting largely of fruits and nuts. Porphyro, a Platonic philosopher of the Third Century, after carefully investigating the subject of diet, tells us that "the ancient Greeks lived entirely on the fruits of the earth." The myth of Prometheus, who first stole fire from heaven, points back to a time when man did not cook his food, when he was not a sickly, suffering creature as we see him today, but a long-lived, healthy, happy being.

The temperature of our body is 37ºC. At that temperature foodstuffs are not damaged while being digested. Above 40ºC, injury sets in. The boiling temperature of water is about 100ºC. The frying temperature of butter, oil and fat is above 200ºC. At these temperatures, several nutritious substances are partially or totally lost. Moreover, their molecular structure and spatial form can also be transformed.

It is common knowledge that the most important food components are proteins, carbohydrates, oils and fats, vitamins, enzymes, minerals, trace elements, fibres, flavourings, water and oxygen. Proteins, composed of amino-acids which are the most important components of the body, are denatured at raised temperature, that is to say, deprived of their vitality; moreover, they are partially or totally destroyed.

Protein molecules in plants, animals and the cells of the human body are really living molecules. Each protein molecule in the human body has its own characteristic duration of life; they live from a few hours up to some days. After that they are destroyed, digested and replaced by new protein molecules. This activity of the human body is truly bewildering and has been observed and understood with the aid of the electron microscope and the most advanced biochemical methods. This rejuvenating activity forms the basis of the possibility of so-called 'eternal youth'. Eating pure *satvic* food is a precondition. The properties of the protein molecules, depend among other things, on their shapes. These shapes are changing continuously. What is more, every human body is unique and this uniqueness expresses itself in the fact that every human body has specific protein molecules, just as specific as finger-prints. God's creation is wonderful! Through heating the protein molecules become stiff and lifeless.

Carbohydrates undergo several transformations as do the facts composed of glycerol and fatty acids, and they, too, are denatured. Fats that are heated over 180°C are considered to be a causative agent of cancer.

Vitamins are sensitive to heat, and in cooking them, an important part of them is lost; some vitamins are totally destroyed. Enzymes are organic catalysts necessary to the digestive process; they are also destroyed by cooking and frying. Minerals and trace element compounds also cannot stand the cooking and frying temperatures; they are partly converted into inorganic substances which no longer have any nutritional value. In Germany, proteins, unsaturated fatty acids, vitamins, enzymes, fibres and natural flavourings are called life-substances. All these life-substances are destroyed or made useless to the body because when food is cooked about eighty five percent of the extant nutritious substances are destroyed or made useless to the body. People who solely eat heated food have a chronic shortage of vitamins, minerals, etc.

The food value of uncooked food is considerably higher than that of cooked or otherwise heated food. Unfortunately, a greater portion of the population feed themselves on heated and especially cooked food. How, then, can many people remain fairly healthy? Cooked food is not totally useless food, although it is dead and poor food. People eat large amounts of food so that, all the same, they may dispose of sufficient nutritious substances. They are more liable to diseases than eaters of uncooked food. Here follows an illustrative story from Dr. Ann Wigmore. In her book *Be Your Own Doctor* she says: "The most moving experience I can remember was to see how cancer-cells from the human body could excellently prosper on cooked food, but that they could not survive on the same food, but now uncooked." Someone who only eats uncooked food will generally have at his disposal exceptionally good health and will be capable of great physical and mental efforts.

Man has probably eaten uncooked and plain food for millions of years. With civilized man, uncooked food has practically completely disappeared from his daily diet. This has induced degeneration, weakening of the nervous system and an undermining of the resistance power against disease. Man is not free from the consequences of the choice of life. These consequences are decided by the laws of nature, by the Divine laws.

Unfortunately, modern man is stuck in wrong eating habits. Yet, it is best only to eat food which can be digested and assimilated easily and well, and from which useless substances can easily be eliminated. Food must supply the nutrients and energies necessary for growth, maintenance, recovery and the efficient functioning of all cells, organs and tissues of the body. When food is not well digested, toxins which may cause diseases develop. Therefore, the food must be simple, natural and not degenerated.

Spoiled, refined, machined, bleached, demineralized, preserved, potted, tinned, smoked, chemically treated, improved, cooly warehoused and other kinds of treated food, should be avoided, because it is food that has been made unsuitable for consumption and has no more nutritional value; it is dead food.

Nature offers us food in a faultless form. Every treatment and heating destroys the natural structure and diminishes the nutritional value. Only uncooked food can optimally be digested by a well-functioning digestive tract. Uncooked food is living food. Living food contains vital strength. It contains germinal force, as in nuts, seeds, tubers and roots. Fruits contain seeds and are living food. Germinating grains, pulses and seeds are living food, as well. Leafy and stalky vegetables should be used soon after harvested. Food is ranged under uncooked food when during the preparation temperatures over 40°C have been avoided. Yogurt, buttermilk, curds and cheese made from uncooked milk at 18°C can thus be considered uncooked food.

A living body is held together by living food which contains much water. This water is necessary for the transporting of the various foodstuffs to body cells and for the expulsion of poisonous waste products. Fresh fruit and vegetables contain all the necessary materials for the body and much water. All fruits consist of eighty to ninety percent purifying, life-giving water. Water from fresh fruit and vegetables contains several enzymes, vitamins and other nutritious substances necessary to the life processes.

Uncooked food provides for an efficient digestion and a good acid /alkali balance. Uncooked food contains a minimum of bodily inimical, toxic substances and exerts a cleansing effect on the bowels. Uncooked food leads to the restoration of the bacterial balance in the mouth, throat, stomach and intestines. Uncooked food promotes the transport of oxygen to the cells and purifies the blood through which the skin and liver are cleansed. The skin reflects the body's condition. Uncooked food strengthens the nervous system and restores the sleep rhythm and mental balance.

Uncooked food is the best medicine. In short, uncooked food has great advantages.

3. Uncooked Food and Vital Strength

Fruits, nuts, pulses, grains, seeds and vegetables only maintain their vital energy for a certain period of time. Fruit and vegetables rot very quickly. Nuts, pulses, grains and seeds are, in the long run, affected and finally destroyed in a natural way by all sorts of micro-organisms, such as bacteria, ferments and moulds. These micro-organisms may produce very toxic substances, which even may be fatal. That is why one must see to it that this living food is kept under the best possible conditions. Do not keep the seeds in a place that is either too damp or too hot. Otherwise the seeds will begin to sprout, as do potatoes. To make just germinating cereals, pulses and seeds for consumption, it is very important to do it in very hygienic conditions. Hygiene is very important. For hygienic reasons it is sometimes necessary to cook the food.

To counteract the decomposition process of foodstuffs, people have developed all sorts of auxiliaries and techniques. For example, grain is refined and anti-oxidants and other additives are added to other foodstuffs. Owing to this, the food loses its original nutritional value. It is best to let the food keep its natural structure and to preserve it under the most preferred circumstances. When apples and other fruit are peeled, they soon turn brown through oxidation. Leafy and stalky vegetables quickly lose their juice after being harvested. Stored peeled nuts lose a part of their *satvic* qualities. The fresher the fruits, vegetables and nuts, the more they are living food. In most cases uncooked food is much more hygienic than cooked food, regardless of all stories about bacteria and insects. Cooked food disturbs the bacteria balance in the mouth, throat, stomach and intestines. By this the enamel of our teeth is affected. Cooked food decays fairly quickly. Bread, for instance, gets mouldy very soon.

4. Uncooked Food and Healing Power

Uncooked food has great healing power. We can illustrate this with some examples. In Europe and America, nearly half the population dies of heart and vascular diseases even though the heart is a very strong organ. People having a heart attack, or other vascular disease, have a too great cholesterol percentage in their blood. This is caused by an over-production of cholesterol produced by the body itself and by sluggish elimination, rather than by eating food which is rich in cholesterol. Heart and vascular diseases are caused by mental tension, lack of exercise, polluted air, poor quality drinking-water and, especially, by a disturbed metabolism and degeneration of the nervous system caused by the wrong food, such as meat, fish, animal fats, too much cheese, all industrial sugars including refined cane-sugar, table luxuries like alcohol, soft drinks, chocolate, coffee, tea, tobacco and salt. The blood contains too much cholesterol, too much protein and too much uric acid. Animal fats contain too much saturated fatty acids. Together with cholesterol, inorganic salts, polysaccharides and proteins, these saturated fatty acids give cause for arteriosclerosis (hardening of the arteries).

The change-over from animal fats to vegetable oils that have a higher percentage of P.U.F.A. (Plurally Unsaturated Fatty Acids) has a favourable effect, but is insufficient to prevent heart and vascular diseases. Plurally Unsaturated Fatty Acids are substances which are necessary for the synthesis of prostaglandins. The latter are hormone substances which protect man from heart and vascular diseases. Consumption of too many plurally unsaturated fatty acids is also harmful for health. That is one of the reasons why *ayurveda* advises against the use of safflower oil. Olive oil is an excellent oil, for it contains relatively few though sufficient polyunsaturated fatty acids.

Heart and vascular diseases can be prevented and cured by sufficient rest, sleep and exercise, and by consuming food which is rich in vitamins, enzymes, minerals, trace elements and fibres. Fruits and vegetables play a very important role in this. Generally, a heart attack manifests itself after a period of forty years, so a cure will take time!

Cancer is a much dreaded disease which affects people of all ages these days. Just as with heart and vascular diseases, cancer can be prevented and in many cases even be cured by consuming the proper food. There are different well-known diets, like the Moerman diet, the Nolfi diet, the Gerson diet, the Wigmore diet, the Jan Dries diet, etc. It is striking that many cancer diets are rich in vitamins and minerals, whereas the use of starch is limited. In the Jan Dries cancer diet the following foods are forbidden: cooked and fried food, deep-frozen food, preserved food, all cereals and cereal products, like bread, pastry, macaroni, spaghetti, etc., meat, fish and shell-fish (cooked, fried or raw), table luxuries like alcohol, soft drinks, chocolate, sugar, coffee, tea, tobacco and salt. There is no true explanation for this complex disease. Often cancer is considered to be a metabolic disease. Jan Dries considers that cancer has something to do with a disturbance of the energy-picture. According to him, cancer is often accompanied by a metabolic disturbance, but this disturbance is not the cause of cancer.

Man not only functions on the basis of foodstuffs like proteins, carbohydrates, oils and fats, vitamins, enzymes, minerals, trace elements, fibres, natural flavourings, water and oxygen, but also on certain energies. An item of food does not just have a chemical structure, it also has an energetic aspect. The idea of vital strength is probably becoming clearer to us.

Plants are able to take in sunlight and store it. In the Max Planck Institute in Heidelberg, in 1984, it was scientifically demonstrated that plants take in light energy in the form of biophotons and store it in their DNA-molecules. Light can be imagined as a flow of particles of light (photons), or as electromagnetic waves with a certain wavelength, frequency, amplitude and energy (intensity). The greater the wavelength the smaller the frequency, the greater the amplitude the greater the energy. The organs of our body and the various foodstuffs produce specific waves. Each organ transmits waves with a certain wavelength and a variable amplitude and intensity (bio-energetic value). Through sickness the character of waves changes and the amplitude and bio-energetic value decrease.

Now it is possible to cure a certain organ or clinical picture by using foodstuffs which transmit waves having the same wavelength as the organ concerned, but the bio-energetic value of which is high, so high that this energy can be transferred to the sick organ. By this the organ in question will be cured and the clinical picture will disappear. So it is said that some foodstuffs have a high intensity on the wavelength of the stomach, and other foodstuffs on the wavelength of the kidneys, etc. Grapes, for example, have a high bio-energetic value for everything that concerns the blood, but a low intensity on the intestines. That is why grapes are never advised for intestinal complaints.

The highest bio-energetic value can be found in fruit, especially in tropical and subtropical fruit, with the exception of bananas and oranges, because these fruits have been too greatly refined through genetic manipulation. Cultivated fruit has a much lower bio-energetic value than wild fruits. The root-plants have a relatively low value. Nuts and seeds have a fairly high bio-energetic value. Herbal tea has a high bio-energetic value, spring-water has a low one. When we reduce a food by grinding, grating or cutting it into pieces, the bio-energetic value decreases fairly slowly during the first half. But thereafter the bio-energy quickly disappears because the natural structure is lost. By cooking or frying the bio-energy disappears and the food becomes dead food.

Within the framework of these bio-energetic considerations, a distinction is made between diseases with a left polarity and diseases with a right polarity. Cancer is a disease with a left polarity, whereas diabetes is a disease with a right polarity. Because fruit has a high bio-energetic value with a left polarity, a fruit-diet is extremely well suited to the healing of cancer, but not for a diabetic patient. In the cancer diet of Jan Dries there are fruits like apricots, avocados, pineapples, bilberries, cactus fruits, raspberries, Galea melons, yellow Spanish melons, honeydew melons, kaki, cherries, kiwis, mangoes and papayas on top of the list, as also almonds, chervil, mushrooms without stems, pollen, Maya honey and honey comb.

The bio-energetic value of a food can be measured by a Lecher measuring instrument. This discovery is particularly valuable in food therapy but also in the dietetics. What man needs is a living, natural food, having a good bio-energetic value. Only *satvic* food fully meets this criterion.

The third example is rheumatism. Rheumatism is a collective noun for a large number of diseases which are concerned with the organs of locomotion. It impairs especially the joints. It is no longer possible to count the number of people who have a serious or less serious form of rheumatism. Almost everyone sometimes has some particular rheumatism or other. Most rheumatic patients get continual treatment and think that their disease is incurable. In the usual medical science, i.e., allopathic therapeutics, rheumatic complaints are treated with a great variety of medicines. These medicaments are, when used for a long time, detrimental to the digestive tract. Thousands of people have freed themselves from rheumatic complaints by using solely natural means. A good food therapy which gives enough attention to the acid-alkali balance mostly gives the best results.

The Swedish biochemist Professor Dr. R. Berg is the founder of the theory concerning the acid-alkali balance. Foodstuffs contain metals like calcium, magnesium, potassium, sodium and iron, and non-metals like chlorine, phosphorus and sulphur. His calculations started from these eight elements. With chemical processes, as also through digestion and the other life-processes, non-metals can form acids, whereas metals form alkalis. When we determine the percentages of these non-metals and metals of the various foodstuffs, and reduce these percentages into acid and alkali percentages, we find that one article of food has an acid surplus and another foodstuff a alkali surplus. In this way, Dr. R. Berg formed a table of foodstuffs with an acid surplus (acid-forming food) and foodstuffs with a alkali surplus (alkali-forming food).

Acid - Forming Foods	Alkali - Forming Foods
- concentrated foods	- bulky food
- little water	- much water
- rich in energy	- poor in energy
- rich in non-metals	- rich in metals
- meat, fish and shellfish	- pumpkin and black radish
- oils and fats	- gherkin and avocado
- eggs and margarine	- potatoes
- butter, curds and cheese	- vegetables
- brown shoot grain rice and white rice	- fresh fruited
	- dried fruit
- cereals and seeds	- dates and figs
- nuts	- coconuts
- pulses	- Soya beans
- bread and dough products	- milk
- beer, wine, tobacco	- cream
- coffee, tea, cocoa	- buttermilk
- antibiotics	- yogurt

Free acids, like apple, citric and lactic acids, have no influence on the acid-alkali balance. All acid fruits have an alkali surplus. Man is unable to digest large quantities of proteins. They form acids, which irritate the gall bladder and the liver and create disturbances in the stomach and intestines. The toxic acids accumulate among others in the weak connective tissue round the joints, where they may cause rheumatic processes. The acid value (pH) of urine is a measure for the acidity of the body tissues. The pH of urine should lie between 6.5 and 7.1. The pH of blood should lie between 7.1 and 7.4. We fall ill when these limits are surpassed. We die when these limits are too greatly surpassed. When the body acidifies, because the digestive system and the excretory organs are unable to eliminate the redundant toxic acids, the urine becomes too acid and the blood becomes too alkaline. The blood becomes too alkaline because it tries to counteract, to compensate the acidifying of the tissues. For good health our body needs food having a alkaline surplus.

It is advisable to choose a food packet of which 80% has a alkaline surplus and 20% an acid surplus. In this case we are using balanced food. Then we can speak of an acid-alkaline balance. Not all naturopaths subscribe to this theory. Yet this nutritional rule could be important for each person who wants to remain well and for each rheumatic who wishes to be cured. As with heart and cancer patients, meat, fish, shell-fish and various stimulants are forbidden foodstuffs for a rheumatic, whereas fruit and vegetables play the leading part in his cure. The three examples (heart and vascular diseases, cancer, and rheumatism) illustrate the particularly great healing force of uncooked food.

5. The Digestive System

The digestive system of man consists of the following parts:

The mouth, or the natural kitchen, the pharynx and the tongue, the cutting teeth (incisors), the eye teeth (canine teeth) and the grinding teeth (molars) for cutting up finely and grinding the food, and the salivary glands. The tongue contains the sense of taste. The four main tastes are sour, sweet, salty and bitter. Taste is, for the greater part, affected by the olfactory sense in the nose. We discriminate between three large salivary glands: the parotid gland, the under-the-tongue salivary gland and the lower jaw salivary gland, and many small salivary glands in the tongue, the cheeks and the palate. Every twenty-four hours about one and a half litres of saliva are secreted.

The esophagus, or gullet, for the passage of food from the mouth to the stomach.

The stomach, with its most important functions, such as the digestion, movement, storing and absorption of foodstuffs: In the stomach wall there are about five million glands which excrete gastric juices. To provide a certain acidity, hydrochloric acid is produced. Every twenty-four hours three litres of gastric juice are secreted.

The stomach is a J-shaped bag built of three muscular layers with an entrance (cardia) and an exit (pylorus). The stomach works best when all muscles of locomotion are at rest. That is why it is good to rest for a while after eating. The stomach is constantly in motion. By means of strong contractions the contents of the stomach are literally shaken back and forth. The most important activities take place in the lowest part of the stomach (antrum).

The stomach is a strong organ, just like the heart, but we should not overburden it. Do not eat more than 500 millilitres of food in one meal. To ensure a good healthy stomach we should prevent nervous tension, eat the right food and engage in proper eating habits, such as chewing well, eating slowly and moderately without drinking during meals. An inflammation of the stomach (gastritis) is caused by nervous tension, wrong food, and the use of chemical medicaments such as aspirin, antibiotics and antirheumatics. According to Sathya Sai Baba, the stomach is in a key position and all diseases find their origin in the stomach.

The small intestine is four to five metres long, while the total length of the digestive system, from mouth to anus, is six to eight metres. The small intestine consists of the duodenum (the part leading out of the stomach), the jejunum or middle portion, and the ileum (the lowest part opening into the large intestine). The secretions of the liver (with the gall bladder) and the pancreas (large gland behind the stomach) empty themselves into the duodenum. The duodenum is the central place of digestion. Man can live without a stomach, but not without bile or pancreas juice.

Every twenty-four hours, one and a half litres of pancreas juice is excreted. The most important function of the gall is the emulsifying of the fats; it also has an anti-bacterial effect.

The surface of the small intestine is covered with innumerable projections for enlarging the surface (4500 square meters) where the digested foodstuffs are absorbed into the venous blood and carried to the liver. The most important function of the small intestine is digestion, movement and absorption of food. All these functions of the body are surprisingly attuned to the nature and the quantity of the ingested food. Here, the senses also have an important role. The whole forms an unbreakable unity. In the small intestine the digestion is almost entirely completed.

The work of the cells of the intestinal wall is very intensive; they die off after two days and are replaced by new cells. This means a few billion cells a day.

The large intestine, is composed of the blind gut (caecum) with the vermiform appendix, the ascending (colon ascendes), the horizontal (colon transversum) and the descending large intestine (colon descendes). From the small intestine, small quantities of intestinal contents are transported via the valve of Bauhin to the blind gut.

According to Doctor Keith, in the blind gut a fermentation activating bacteria-flora is produced which ensures a faultless functioning of the large intestine. According to classical medical science, the large intestine is not so important; the large intestine absorbs water from the contents of the intestine and can produce several vitamins and break down cellulose.

In naturopathy, the large intestine is given a much greater importance. Dr. Keith says that the large intestine is one of the biggest workshops of our body.

According to Jan Dries, due to the use of animal food, like meat, fish, shell fish and also cheese, the functioning of the blind gut is eliminated and putrefactive bacteria develop. The result is a shortage of vitamins and minerals, and the intestine becomes less active and may become constipated. Instead of fermentation bacteria, rotting bacteria appear and, with this, the large intestine becomes a filthy sewer. Healthy intestinal flora are supremely important. A clean, well-working large intestine is, according to various naturopaths, the basis for good health. A great many diseases disappear when the large intestine is reconditioned. The building-up of healthy intestinal flora can only be done with the help of the right food. The intestinal flora are destroyed by antibiotics.

According to naturopathy, the large intestine has a number of important functions. In this purpose are included the extraction of water from the contents of the intestines, the intake of minerals, glycocholic acids, vitamins and foodstuffs, the forming of several B-complex vitamins, of which vitamin B-12 is the best known, the forming of vitamine K, biotin, folic acid and niacin, and the storing and transport of the contents of the intestines. Water passes through the kidneys via blood. Detrimental substances, like urea and creatinin and all sorts of salts, are drained away with the urine via the urinary bladder. With certain disturbances, like diarrhoea, water is not extracted from the contents of the intestines and thereby the body can lose much fluid. Owing to this, one can have a serious shortage of minerals.

The rectum. This is a passage for the roughage (faeces).
The lower opening of the rectum (anus).

The shorter the transit time, or stay, in the digestive tract the better. The normal transit time is twelve hours. The transit time may even be shorter, especially if the food is rich in fibres. Many people have a much too long transit time, sometimes from two to three days. Healthy people, with well-functioning intestines, have three motions a day. Then the faeces is odourless, pulpy, homogeneous and light in colour, and has the form of a long sausage which is covered in a layer of slime. The faeces shows us the quality of the digestion. The transit time can be measured in a simple way, for example by drinking a big glass of red beetroot juice and seeing how long it takes before the faeces become red in colour.

According to the dietetics of the naturopathy, there are a great number of foodstuffs that an intestinal patient should not eat. He has to stick to a number of nutritive rules, like thorough chewing, eating slowly and moderately, food that is neither too hot nor too cold, no drinking whilst eating, sticking to the acid-alkaline balance, sticking to the food combinations of Dr. H. M. Shelton (improved by Jan Dries), and following a specific intestinal diet for each intestinal complaint. It is also necessary to prevent as much nervous tension as possible. With the necessary patience, for the intestines recover quite slowly, the intestines can be totally healed.

These regimens are not only very instructive for intestinal patients but, as a matter of fact, for everyone, because the intestines of practically all people do not function well under the influence of current eating-habits.

Unsuitable for human bowels are alcohol, soft-drinks, chocolate, refined sugar, coffee, tea, tobacco, salt, vinegar and other strong acids and condiments, like pepper and nutmeg. Also meat, fish, shellfish, eggs and cheese are not fit to be eaten, especially not for sick intestines. Meat cannot be completely digested, it is rich in rotting bacteria, contains no fibre, passes awkwardly through the intestines, acidifies the body and causes rotting in the intestines. Meat is not necessary as a supplier of protein. The same is true of fish, shellfish, eggs and cheese. Hard-boiled eggs are especially taboo. It is better for intestinal patients not to drink any milk. Milk is not ideal for the nose and throat mucous membranes or for the intestines. Milk has also to be drunk separately. It is difficult to combine milk with other food. A limited use of yogurt and buttermilk is allowed; these are easier to be digested and combined.

In all cereals, except corn, rice and some varieties of millet, we find gluten, which seriously can affect the intestines. White bread can easily cause constipation, whereas wholemeal bread contains bran. Bran contains a number of substances which irritate the intestines. The intestinal wall can also be disturbed by leaven bread. All sorts of bread are dead food. During its preparation it is heated and then cooled down again. That is why it is *tamasic* food. Sathya Sai Baba says that starch is *tamasic*. He says that only small amounts of certain freshly ground cereals such as *ragi* and rice soaked in water (gruel), or rice soaked in curds, are *satvic* food. In the intestinal diet of Jan Dries, all cereals and cereal-products are omitted.

When the intestines have recovered, a limited amount of grain and rice may be eaten again. Pulses also do not belong to the intestinal diet. Pulses are difficult to digest and can lead to all sorts of digestive problems, like intestinal gas, rotting dyspepsia, constipation, etc. Doctors often prescribe cooked food for intestinal patients. We may say that cooked food spares the intestines, but it does not cure them. Cooked food is strange to the body. It is dead food.

Cooked cabbages, cooked pulses and cooked onions are very bad for the intestines. Garlic, and even grapes, do not belong to an intestinal diet. Unfortunately, raw leafy vegetables, like endive, cabbage, lettuce, lamb's lettuce and witloof chicory, are also not good for intestinal patients. Raw leafy vegetables are very difficult to digest and may cause all sorts of intestinal problems. That is why it is necessary, with a diet for the intestines, to be very careful with raw vegetables. We have to give preference to root and tuberous plants. All vegetables should be very well sliced and, preferably, eaten together with mashed potatoes. Fermented vegetables, like sauerkraut, digest fairly well. It is better not to combine sauerkraut with potatoes.

It is not good to switch over to uncooked food too casually because weakened and sick intestines cannot digest raw vegetables. Yet, in the healing of sick intestines, switching over to the right food comes first of all. No single treatment, not even a treatment by a natural healing practitioner, is significant so long as a good intestinal diet is not followed. An intestinal patient should learn again how to eat. Because fruit is the best digestible food, giving the least problems and containing all the needed ingredients, it is good to begin with fruit juices. The Jan Dries intestinal diets begin with fruit juices, after which, step by step, one switches over to fruit paps, fruit salads, vegetable juices, fermented vegetables, like sauerkraut, cooked vegetables, raw vegetables and, finally, to a variety of raw food.

With fruit as a binding agent, yogurt or unsweetened cream may be used. With vegetables, oil sauces and herbal oil sauces may be used. The best ones are cold pressed vegetable oils, like olive oil, coconut oil, sesam seed oil, and sunflower oil. Vegetables can also be combined with butter, ghee (clarified butter), nuts or seeds, especially linseed. Potatoes can be combined with a little butter or ghee. There are many possibilities. As vegetable juices, carrot juice and potato juice are especially recommended.

It is recommended that only those fruit and vegetables that have not been cultivated with any fertilizers or other chemicals are to be eaten. All fertilizers are suspect. Some are very bad, some destroy the value of foods, some make them injurious. Of the different kinds of fruit juices for an intestinal diet, the preferred ones are kaki, pineapple, shaddock (pomelo), apricot, bilberry, kiwi, cherry, ripe medlar, red and black currant and plum. They have a good effect on the stomach, the small intestine, the large intestine and, for the most part, also on the liver. For solving intestinal problems there are a number of simple aids and appliances, like bilberry juice, pineapple juice, honey dissolved in camomile tea, and clay.

The intestinal diet is highly purifying, and through it a number of unpleasant reactions may occur, especially in the beginning. Some of them may be headache, depression, irritability, dizziness, tiredness, temporary emaciation, fears, eruption of the skin, stomach aches, intestinal pains, diarrhoea, etc. The total detoxification of the body can take months, even years. Still, good results can be achieved in a short time. Immunotherapy begins with a clean intestine. In the immune system of man, the Peyer's patches around the small intestine play an important role.

6. The Digestion

The digestion of starch begins in the mouth. In the weakly acid saliva is ptyalin (salivary amylase), which converts starch into maltose, and the enzyme maltase which converts maltose into glucose. Ptyalin works best at pH 5.5 - 7. The enzyme maltase is also found in the pancreatic juice and in the intestinal juice. In the mouth starchy food has to be mixed very well with the saliva to take in the enzymes. Ptyalin is broken up by acids (pH < 5.5) and strong alkalines. Acid food can destroy the ptyalin in the mouth.

In the stomach the process of digesting starch is temporarily stopped and the gastric acid stabilizes the already freed sugars so that they may not ferment. The starch is stabilized by the gastric acid as well. If one eats too much, the stomach becomes overfull. All the food will not come into contact with the stomach wall and the gastric acid. In that case, fermentation of starch and sugars can take place in the middle of the upper part of the stomach. A food volume of 250 millilitres is ideal, 500 millilitres is admissible. The capacity of the stomach is 1500 millilitres: this quantity is inadmissible. The starch which is not digested in the mouth, and most other compound sugars, are broken up in the small intestine under the influence of various enzymes into simple sugars.

The digestion of protein starts in the stomach. The stomach wall contains gland-cells which produce hydrochloric acid and about eight different enzymes called pepsins. These enzymes can only work in an acid environment. It is hydrochloric acid which sees to this. The pepsins are functioning optimally at pH 2–4. Much undigested starch slows down the digestion of protein. In the stomach the proteins are under the influence of the pepsins, broken down into polypeptides, which, in turn, are broken down by the enzymes trypsin and chymotrypsin from pancreatic juices in the small intestine, into dipeptides. Finally the dipeptides are broken down into amino-acids by the enzyme dipeptidase. The amino-acids are transported through the intestinal wall to the blood.

The enzyme lipase causes the transposition of the fats in the fatty acids and glycerol. This enzyme occurs in the pancreatic fluid. In the small intestine the enzyme lipase is aided by gall secretions, which emulsify the fat.

The pancreas also produces, apart from the pancreatic fluid with its various enzymes for the digestion of proteins, carbohydrates and fats, two more hormones, insulin and glucogen, which get into the bloodstream and play an important role in sugar metabolism.

All the venous blood, which comes from the intestines, loaded with all kinds of foodstuffs, first goes to the liver. The rectum vein is the only one, which does not go directly to the liver. Medicines that are taken via the mouth can, to a greater or lesser extent, be made inactive by the liver. But through the rectum vein this is not the case, as with medicaments, which are administered in the form of a suppository.

The liver is the largest gland (1.5 kilograms). It contains nearly one fifth of the total bloodmass. It has a number of important functions, and these may be mentioned:

1. The liver continually produces gall. This gall can go directly or via the gall bladder to the small intestine. Gall helps to break down fats by making an emulsion of them. This is a colloidal solution.

2. Via the portal vein the liver receives blood from the intestines. This blood is loaded with elementary foodstuffs, such as amino acids, simple sugars, fatty acids, glycerol, vitamins and minerals. The amino acids, the simple sugars, the fatty acids and the glycerol are, if necessary, sent on via the blood or, if possible, changed into glycogen or other products. Glycogen can, if necessary, be changed into glucose. Glucose is an important energy supplier (fuel). Energy is essential for a healthy life. The liver stores glucose in the form of glycogen. The hormone glucogen from the pancreas, and the hormone adrenalin from the adrenal glands, stimulate the release of glucose. The hormone insulin from the pancreas slows down the release of glucose. The greater part of

the fatty acids and the glycerol does not go to the liver, but via the so-called chyle vessels, straight to the fat deposits in the body. A normal liver contains little fat. Fats can provide energy as well, but they have to undergo a longer and less efficient digestive process than carbohydrates. The fats are only put into action as fuel when the carbohydrate reserves are exhausted.

The liver itself also produces proteins from amino acids (among others, for the coagulation of the blood).

3. The liver takes part in the amino acid bank. In the blood and in the lymphatic vessels there is constantly present a circulating stock of amino acids. This stock is called the amino acid bank. When the quantity of amino acids is too large, then the liver absorbs amino acids; or the liver stores these amino acids. When the quantity of amino acids in this system has become too small, the liver puts the absorbed amino acid into circulation again. Most of the body cells, indeed, also have the capacity of storing amino-acids and putting them into circulation again. There are eight amino acids, which the body cannot make, but certainly needs, and therefore, has to take them from the food. All fruits, nuts and vegetables contain most of these eight amino acids, whereas some fruits, nuts and vegetables contain all the eight amino acids. Because of the amino acid bank it is not necessary to eat protein food which contains all eight essential amino-acids at each meal, nor even each day.

4. The liver is the storehouse of all kinds of vitamins and for the many trace elements (oligo-elements), such as iron, copper, lithium, manganese and zinc. These trace elements are only found in small quantities in our body. However, just like vitamins, they are absolutely necessary.

5. The liver is a source of heat. Especially in rest the liver is the most important source of heat for the maintenance of body temperature.

6. The task of the liver is to make poisonous particles harmless and in so doing to protect the body from poisons. After that, waste products are removed from the body via the kidneys together with

the urine. With the ingestion of pure food, the liver has already enough work to do. But if we consume impure food, the liver gets overburdened and is, finally, damaged. When this happens you can take it for granted that the whole body has become polluted. With liver complaints, the following stuffs are banned: industrial food, heated fats, roasted nuts and peanuts, sweet biscuits, cake, white bread, meat, fish, eggs and stimulants like alcohol, chocolate, coffee (coffee-substitutes as well), tea, refined sugar, tobacco and salt (sea-salt as well). Alcohol, chocolate, coffee, tea and salt are exceedingly bad for the kidneys. According to Jan Dries, the best medicine for liver patients appears to be fruit, especially kaki, kiwi, pineapple, apricot, bilberry and honeydew melon. Also, potatoes and vegetables, such as carrots, beetroots, radish, black radish, pumpkin and leeks play an important role in a liver diet. Of all bodily processes the digestion needs the most energy.

To regain health and energy, the liver, gall-bladder and kidneys must be cleansed and kept free-flowing. The steady and consistent use of moderate quantities of the following juices (they are best taken either first thing in the morning or thirty minutes before eating) can be recommended :

1. Wheat grass juice which contains much chlorophyll.
2. Beet juice (high in vitamins A, C, B2, B6 and folic acid, and minerals such as iron, calcium, phosphorus and potassium) has a stimulating and fortifying effect on the liver, gall-bladder and kidneys. Sip small quantities or add to other juices. Try juicing the beet greens also. Wheat grass and beet juice are the most powerful cleansers on this list.
3. Carrot juice, high in pro-vitamin A, has a beneficial effect on the liver and stimulates the flow of bile.
4. Lemon juice contains citric acid and other acids that have an antiseptic action. Lemon juice is mildly diuretic.
5. Green drinks, rich in vitamins, minerals, and chlorophyll, are made from sprouts, greens, vegetables and, if desired, a little sauerkraut.

6. Apple juice is high in malic acid, pectin and enzymes that act as a bile solvent and liver stimulant.
7. Watermelon juice is an effective diuretic that can be used every morning for breakfast. Juice the rind, seed and all.

Sea vegetables provide vital minerals necessary for the detoxification and stimulation of kidney functions. Either whole sea vegetables or powdered forms may be used. Sea vegetables are one of the richest food sources of minerals and trace elements. Up to two tablespoons of kelp, dulse, arame etc. can be used each day. They can be added to salads, dressings, etc. Other rich food sources of minerals and trace elements are nuts and dried fruit.

7. The Natural Physical Cycles

In the book *Fit for Life* by Harvey and Marilyn Diamond, of the Natural Hygiene Movement in the United States, it is said that in each day of one's food intake and digestion there are three natural physical cycles distinguishable:

Cycle I : 12 noon to 8 p.m. : Food intake(eating and digestion)
Cycle II : 8 p.m. to 4 a.m. : Assimilation(absorption and use)
Cycle III: 4 a.m. to 12 noon: elimination (of bodily waste and food remnants)

A well-combined meal will stay in the stomach for about three hours. A faulty combined meal may stay in the stomach as much as twelve hours. That is why it is recommended to eat good living food (many vital substances) and to bear in mind the various alimentary rules, such as the acid-alkali balance and the principle of the proper food combinations. Moreover, eat in the evening as early as possible; the food pulp should have left the stomach before you go to bed. The best times to eat are from 12 noon to 2 p.m., and from 5 p.m. to 7 p.m. It is good to keep five hours between meals. It is very beneficial to cut out the traditional breakfast and solely to eat fruit and drink fruit juice before twelve o'clock noon.

Whole fruits are better than their juices. Probably noon is the best time for a starchy meal, whereas, in the evening, it would be best to take a protein meal. Eat moderately, not too hot and not too cold, eat slowly and chew well.

Do not drink during meals. Many people eat and drink at the same time. This is a bad habit. Liquid thins the saliva in the mouth. The best way is to drink water ten to fifteen minutes before a meal. The best eating order during meals is to eat first the most juicy food, then the less juicy food and finally the driest and most concentrated food. Nothing is better for the elimination cycle than regularly eating a sufficient quantity of food with a high percentage of water. Drink good water. Sathya Sai Baba also stresses the importance of drinking pure water. "Drink much water," He says, "…long time before or after a meal, not during a meal. Pure water contains *prana* and this is necessary for life." *Prana* comes from sunlight.

Besides the prevention of the intake of toxins and their formation during the digestion, the elimination of the various toxins is exceedingly important. These toxins are secreted in the stool, via the liver, and via the kidneys with the urine, via the skin with the respiration. The elimination of toxins needs much energy. Therefore it is wise to fast now and then.

When you follow up the alimentary rules and you have a full night's rest, which as often as possible has to begin plenty of time before midnight, the body is able to finish the assimilation cycle at 4 a.m.

8. The Correct Fruit-Consumption

Someone who is still relatively healthy and has always eaten cooked food will be able to switch over to raw fruit without too many problems.

The switchover to uncooked vegetables is much more difficult for most people. Yet it goes without saying that, besides fruit, we do eat vegetables. Eating only fruit is not practical. Indeed, nuts and seeds are also fruits. Healthy people need not feed themselves on fruit alone. It is good to strive each day to eat half a kilogram of fruit. Do not eat more than 500 grams of fruit in one meal. It is possible to live on one and a half kilograms fruit per day. Over-eating of fruit is not good; it overburdens the kidneys and the bladder. Eat fruit always slowly and chew well; pieces that are too large will ferment in the intestines. In food therapy, fantastic results are attained with fruit diets.

Fruit contains everything that the body needs; it has an ideal food structure for the human body. Fruit has the highest percentage of water of all food. The solid substance contains, on an average, 90% glucose and fructose, 4% to 5% easily digestible proteins, 3% to 4% minerals, 1% fatty acids and less than 1% vitamins. The vital strength which is inherent in fruit is unexcelled. Fruit belongs to the most delicate and best of all foodstuffs; they have delicious tastes, exceptional delicious scents and it is a treat to look at their colours. Just like leafy vegetables and nuts, fruit forms a diet of full value. Fruit purifies and does not constipate. Fruit protects the heart by preventing the blood from becoming too thick and the arteries from becoming clogged.

Energy is essential for a healthy life. Digesting fruit requires less energy than any other food; the relative fuel value of fruit is high. Together with this, fruit plays an important role in the detoxification of the body and in getting rid of excessive bodily weight provided it is eaten in the right way. By just reducing one's caloric units one will not be able to reduce excessive bodily weight if the consumed calories come from denatured, poorly combined, toxic and constipating food.

How should fruit be eaten in a proper way? Harvey Diamond says: "In the very first place: fresh!" And that also applies to fruit juices. Baked apples, all canned fruit, cooked applesauce and fruit tarts are all injurious to health. Dr. M. O. Bruker says that whole fruits are much better than fruit juice because important vital substances are left behind the fruit pulp.

Fruit undergoes little or no digestion in the mouth or in the stomach. It just stays for twenty to thirty minutes in the stomach. An exception to this is bananas, dates and dried fruit, which stay in the stomach for fifty to sixty minutes.

When you wake up in the morning you are refreshed and at the highest energy level of the day. This energy should not be used for a solid breakfast. Most traditional breakfasts are poor food combinations, forcing the digestive system to work for hours, wasting much energy. Even when the breakfast is properly composed, it remains in the stomach for three hours or longer. The energy can only be built up when food is absorbed from the small intestine. In contrast to the traditional breakfast, fruit just remains in the stomach for a short time. Its digestion requires little energy and with the digestion, energy is soon released.

One of the greatest problems of the digestive tract is the elimination of the toxins which develop during the demolition of old cells and of the toxins which develop and are released during the digestive process of eaten food. Instead of giving special attention to fresh living food, we buy processed food and bake, fry, grill, cook, roast, steam or stew nearly everything we eat. Moreover, we use poor food combinations. Owing to this, many toxic by-products develop during digestion. The elimination of these toxins takes place mainly in the morning hours. Fruit has a great detoxifying effect because of the high percentage of water and the abundance of enzymes, vitamins and minerals in it. Because of this, it is a very suitable food to eat at that time. It is, therefore, most advisable to consume only fruit and fruit-juice before noon. Forget the traditional breakfast and take a fruit breakfast in the morning.

Do not add any sugar to the fruit. The acids and sugars of the fruit do not combine well with starch and proteins. Therefore do not eat fruit with or immediately after eating anything else. If you do, the fruit will be held up in the stomach by the other food; as a result the fruit may start fermenting and producing all kinds of toxins. In consequence of this, the other food goes bad as well, especially in the intestines. The proteins that are present start rotting, while the carbohydrates start fermenting.

Hence, the golden rule: "Take fruit and fruit juice only on an empty stomach." When you have eaten anything else you will have to wait a few hours before being able to take any fruit or fruit juice. The waiting period after uncooked vegetables is two hours, that after a well combined meal without meat is three hours, and that after all wrongly combined meals is eight hours. Best of all is not to eat any fruit at all between meals and no fruit juice either. It disables the digestive system. After having eaten fruit you will have to wait about half an hour before being able to eat anything else. After having eaten bananas, dates and dried fruit, you will have to wait a whole hour before you eat anything else. Switching over to uncooked food should be done step by step. Applying the correct fruit consumption by dropping the traditional breakfast is probably the best first step.

9. The Swith-Over to Raw Food

As a result of having eaten inferior food for years on end, our digestive tracts usually get degenerated, and often not able to digest uncooked food with any benefit. Because our body, through overburdening of the digestive tract, was unable to eliminate all the toxic substances, which have accumulated in the muscles, the fatty tissues, the arteries, and the brain cells, etc. for years. That is why we often have an ungainly body-weight and may have fallen ill. A toxic, acidified body is recognisable by a poor skin, a swollen body, excessive weight, baldness, nervous outbursts, and dark shadows around the eyes, and premature wrinkles on the face.

Depending on the extent of the degeneration and the quantity of toxins stored up in the body, the changeover to uncooked food, especially in the beginning, will entail more or less discomfort. What are the possible discomforts? When, for example, you start eating fruit according to the rules of the correct fruit consumption, the purifying ability will disturb the accumulated toxic refuse in the walls of the stomach and the intestines and may cause eructations and a puffy feeling. You may get headaches or other pains, you may feel, all of a sudden, tired and frightened, turn giddy, get a thin motion or excessive mucous secretion from the nasal cavity (this is not a cold!), be subjected to cutaneous eruptions, get irritable or depressive and even fall ill. These discomforts may last a few days or a few months.

It is possible to eliminate all accumulated toxins from the body. The correct fruit consumption plays an important role here. Eventually the body-weight will return to normal and the body will be more energetic and healthier than ever before. The total detoxification of the body will require much effort and can take months or even years.

The various different digestive upsets which range from eructations and wind, to far more serious chronic pains and inflammation of the digestive tract, create a serious problem. The correct consumption of fruit and the correct combination of food are the most important means to prevent these disturbances and diseases. Especially sick people are advised to consult a naturopath (physician) who has a profound knowledge of food therapy when they want to switch over to raw food. Just using food as medicine can heal many diseases, but each disease requires careful handling, while, in addition, all kinds of complications may arise. And healthy people, too, should orientate themselves very well and get instructed in a right way.

The mix of foods should contain all necessary nutrients. For example, we run the risk of getting a shortage of vitamin B12 when we switch over to an exclusively vegetable diet, because vitamin B12 is especially found in animal foodstuffs. Meat, fish and eggs and dairy products contain vitamin B12. If we use some dairy products we will not need meat, fish or eggs. A deficiency of vitamin B12 slows down the formation of normal red blood cells, which carry oxygen to the cells and tissues.

The switchover from cooked to raw food cannot in many cases be done overnight; we need time for that. For a number of people it can be a long time, because their intestines are degenerated or sick to such an extent that they work inefficiently. Step by step more heated foods should be replaced by living food. Wrong eating habits should be replaced by good eating habits.

Most people hardly chew their food and swallow it at the same time as chewing and, often, they consume much larger portions than they actually need. Raw food should be eaten slowly and masticated very well; otherwise the stomach and the intestines will not be able to digest it properly.

The digestive difficulties, which may be experienced at the switchover to uncooked food, are caused by the old fixed and wrong eating habits and by the degenerated condition of the digestive tract. Due to wrong foods eaten over the years, the action of the stomach has become too sluggish to be able to digest raw food properly. So the food remains in the stomach for too long. The poorly digested contents of the stomach then pass into the intestines, where they cannot be digested either. Stomach and intestinal cramps may arise and the stomach and the intestines may fill with gases. The gases cause flatulence and swollen intestines. They may be very toxic. A part of the gases will be found again in the blood and is exhaled via the lungs (evil-smelling breath). Because of the poor digestion only few nutritious substances are got from the food. Because of this we are inclined to eat larger quantities again, and, with this, a vicious circle is begun.

Through such beginnings we may think that raw food is difficult to digest, and in the end, we might even reject raw food. That would be a big mistake, a mistake which many doctors commit as well. To make the switch-over to raw food successfully we should improve our eating habits radically and give our digestive tract time to recover. The regeneration of our digestive tract can only take place with the help of raw food. Fruit is the easiest food to digest. That is why the very first step for switching over to living food is the application of the correct fruit consumption.

10. The Second Step Towards Raw Food

If processed and wrongly combined food is digested, then, under the influence of fermentative and putrefactive bacteria in the gastric-intestinal canal, various toxins like alcohol, indole, skatole, phenol, cresol, uric acid, neurine, cadaverine, agmatine, tyramine, putrescine, histamine, mercaptans, ammonia and hydrogen sulphide will develop there. The carbohydrates may begin to ferment, while the proteins may start rotting. Carbohydrate fermentation can result in chronic autointoxication, which resembles in every way the symptoms of chronic alcoholism. The alcohol produces chronic irritations in the system and results in the formation of scar tissue. The decomposition of the food by the putrefactive bacteria is stimulated by everything that slackens the digestive processes. Therefore, it is advisable to stop little by little the use of processed food, that is, no refined, bleached, preserved, potted, tinned, smoked, chemically treated or bottled foodstuffs.

Also, the use of alcohol, vinegar, soft drinks, coffee, tea and chocolate should be cut out or cut down as much as possible. The same applies to the use of sugar, kitchen salt and wrong condiments. Alcohol causes great strain on the liver and kidneys. Alcohol impedes the calcium absorption, necessary for the bones, by decreasing the capability of the liver to activate vitamin D. Alcohol destroys a number of B-complex vitamins. Vinegar is very sour and disturbs the environment in the mouth and the stomach. Soft drinks are pointless: they contain all sorts of toxins, like much refined sugar, phosphoric acid and caffeine.

Refined sugar is dead food and extremely injurious to one's health. Coffee and tea contain caffeine, chocolate contains theobromine. Caffeine is connected with many diseases, such as diabetes, birth defects, gastric ulcers, kidney disease and hypertension. Caffeine causes the excretion of twice as much calcium from the body as normal. According to Dr.Bruce Ames of the Univerity of California, Berkeley, theobromine strengthens certain cancer-producing substances in the cells of the human body. It also causes atrophy of the testicles. There are many types of herbal teas. They taste good, and most of them are by nature caffeine-free. Salt is bad for the kidneys and is one of the main causes of hypertension. Condiments are seldom good. Asafoetida, black pepper, cayenne, cinnamon, cloves, mustard, nutmeg and tamarind should be replaced by *satvic* spices and herbs (see part C).

Dr. H. M. Shelton says: "The effect of condiments is the opposite of what it is popularly supposed to be. They depress and hinder rather than aid the digestion. Their continued use results in the hardening of the mucous lining of the alimentary canal. This hardening renders the delicate membranes less sensitive to their irritating qualities, but cripples the efficiency of the membranes. Cayenne or red pepper is about the most fiery of all condiments. If this is taken by the non-user its burning may be felt in the stomach. It may even result in diarrhoea. Repeated irritation from condiments produces irreparable injury to the stomach, liver, intestines, kidneys, blood vessels, heart and other vital organs." +

Our real vitamin and mineral needs are very often exaggerated. Fresh vegetables and fruit contain an abundant supply of all the vitamins we need. For the body, the so-called law of minimums is what counts. The overspill is removed and treated as toxic waste. Owing to this, the liver and the kidneys are additionally burdened and valuable energy is used up. Many health and food experts have expressed their serious concern about the threat to our health through swallowing a multitude of vitamin and mineral pills.

+ Dr. H. M. Shelton, *The Science and Fine Art of Food & Nutrition*, pp. 196 - 97

Smoking needs a chapter for itself. Heaven knows how many diseases are caused by smoking. What is known of its effects is a blood-curdling story: cancer, birth defects, inflammation, hypertension, pathological acceleration of the heart-beat and, from that, resulting heart injury, narrowing and slackening of the blood vessels, increased excretion of gastric acid and destruction of the vital cells from the lips to the lungs. Cigarette smoke contains more than 3000 chemical substances. In 1960 they discovered that tobacco smoke contains the radioactive element polonium. Each cell, each organ, in short, the whole body, cannot function optimally because of the use of tobacco. There is no healthier goal than trying to stop smoking.

Finally, we have eggs, fish and meat. Eggs contain much sulphur, which is a heavy burden on the liver and the kidneys. Egg yolk is rich in cholesterol. The human body cannot use this. Fried eggs are difficult to digest. Fish is comparable to meat. Fish from polluted seas or lakes is worse than meat. The subject of meat can fill a whole book. Man is by nature not a meat-eater; our digestive tract is not able to digest meat well. Meat-eating animals (carnivora) have special teeth and short intestines to be able to digest food that putrefies very quickly. No matter how carefully handled, meat very readily undergoes putrefaction and it is impossible to get it so fresh that some degree of putrefaction has not already set in. There is seldom a fattened animal killed that is free of disease.

During the digestion of meat, large quantities of uric acid are released in the body. Uric acid is a dangerous toxin. Unlike meat-eating animals, man does not have the enzyme uricase to break down the uric acid. By heating meat, many proteins are lost, and many toxins are formed with their consequences. Moreover, the meat of today contains several toxic, chemical substances added by man. The only effect that meat has on our health is that it diminishes it. Among other things, owing to the fat content, meat causes all forms of cancer, hypertension and heart-attacks. It is not necessary for man to eat meat. We only need a little protein: probably just 25 to 50 grams per day. Proteins consist of aminoacids. There are eight amino acids which the body itself cannot produce, but which are certainly necessary, and therefore, it has to absorb them from food. Cow's milk, many fruits, nuts and vegetables and soybeans contain all the eight amino acids. Try, step by step, to use less meat, and finally, drop it completely. Meat production is a great economic loss. A tract of well-cultivated land will sustain at least twenty times more people by its crops than by the meat of cattle nourished by the same area.

11. The Principle of Correct Food Combinations

The right food combination plays a prominent part in having an optimum digestion. *Ayurveda* is the very first source of the teachings regarding the rules for correct food combinations. In the United States, this principle has been brought to the fore by Dr. H. M. Shelton (1888 -1987) who studied at an *Ayurvedic* university in India. Recently Jan Dries, a well-known nutritionist of Belgium, has completely revised and improved Shelton's food combination doctrine according to the latest insights of digestion physiology. This chapter is a brief summary of Jan Dries book about food combining which I can recommend.[+] Good food combinations lead to a maximum amount of energy, form minimal amounts of toxins, stimulate the detoxification of the body, and prevent all kinds of digestive upsets and diseases. The proper fruit consumption is the very first and important rule about food combination.

All articles of food contain proteins, carbohydrates and fats. The carbohydrates, or saccharides, can be subdivided into starch and the sugars, such as the disaccharides beet-and cane-sugar, and the simple sugars, such as glucose (grape-sugar) and fructose (fruit-sugar). During digestion, proteins are converted into amino

---

+ Jan Dries, the new book of food combining (see references 11).

acids, starch and sugars into simple sugars, and fats into fatty acids and glycerol. In addition to proteins, starch, sugars and fats, there is the group of free acids, such as citric acid. The other nutritious substances, such as water and rough fibrins, aid the digestion but have no influence on food combinations.

All foodstuffs contain proteins, starch, sugars, fats and free acids in a specific ratio. Mostly, one of these five nutritious substances dominates. Such a nutritious substance is called a 'dominant'. In a foodstuff rich in protein, protein is the dominant. So there is food rich in protein, food rich in starch, etc. If various articles of food are combined, several dominants can be present; these dominants can counteract each other and cause serious digestive problems resulting in fermentation of the carbohydrates and putrefaction of the proteins and thence sleep disturbances, flatulence, acid eructations, distension of the stomach and intestines, food allergy, corpulence, constipation, fermenting diarrhoea, putrefaction diarrhoea and other ailments.

Eating one article of food (monodiet) in big quantities does not change the mutual ratios of the five nutritious substances. It is possible to combine several articles of food if the mutual ratios of the five nutritious substances in those foodstuffs suit each other. The ratios are decisive; we call them 'the keys of the food combinations'. A well-composed meal has one dominant. In rice starch dominates, in bananas sugars, and in lemons free acids, etc. Our digestive system is not capable of digesting well a meal with several dominants.

Pulses have two dominants: starch and proteins. Their starch-protein ratios are unfavourable. That is the reason why pulses are difficult to digest. With grains, the starch-protein ratios are somewhat more favourable, but at the same time, mostly unfavourable. The starch-protein ratio of rice is the most favourable. That is why rice is the most easily digestible kind of grain. There are ten food combinations of paramount importance, six bad combinations and four good combinations. Protein-fat combinations

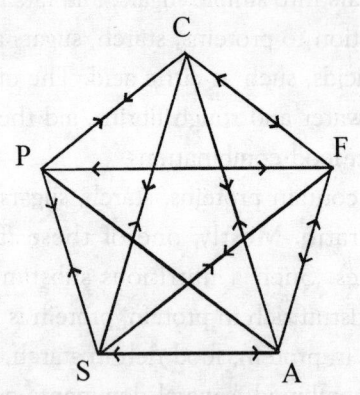

Food Combinations Pentagon (Jan Dries)

P : protein
C : starch <----------> good
S : sugar
A : acid (free) ------><------- bad
F : fat

are natural combinations. The most important food combinations can be united in a pentagon.

* Starch-protein combinations. Dr. H.M. Shelton said that all starch-protein combinations are more or less bad food combinations. In reality the starch-protein combination is not what is decisive, it is the starch-protein ratio. Some natural starch-protein combinations can be digested quite easily. In a wonderful way the stomach is able to attune to the acidity, the composition, the total amount and the speed of secretion of its gastric juices to the kind and the quality of food ingested.

The digestion of starch begins in the mouth under the influence of ptyalin, is interrupted in the stomach and continued in the duodenum. Fermentation can only occur in the middle of the upper part of the stomach (see chart stomach) because the sugars cannot be stabilized by gastric acid there if the stomach is

Filling Stomach
(According to Jan Dries)

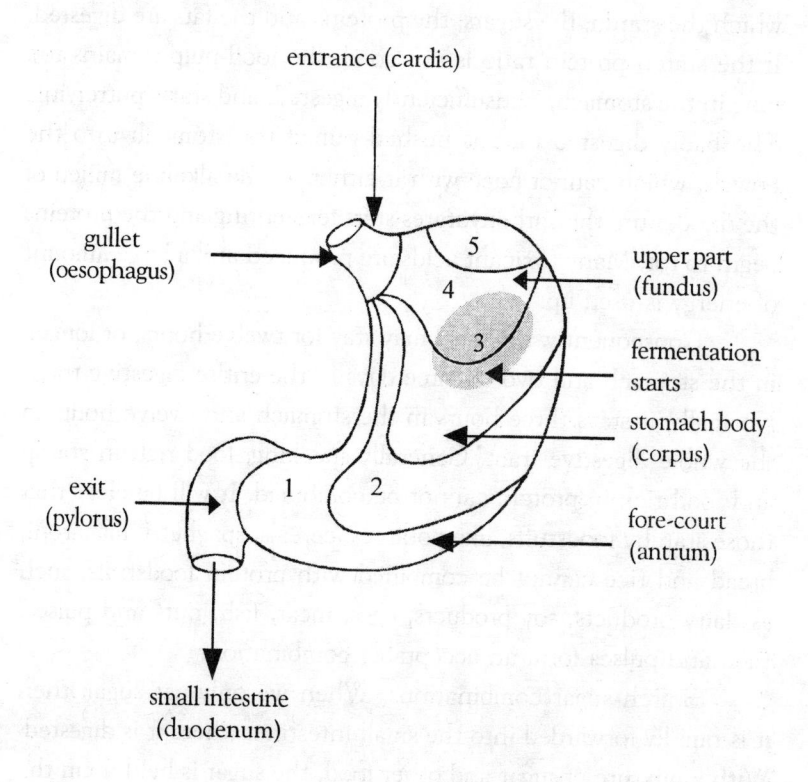

Diagram labels:
- entrance (cardia)
- gullet (oesophagus)
- upper part (fundus)
- fermentation starts
- stomach body (corpus)
- fore-court (antrum)
- exit (pylorus)
- small intestine (duodenum)

"The stomach is the key point." (Sathya Sai Baba)

Overfull stomach with:

1. first course
2. soup
3. main course
4. dessert
5. air

too full. Normally, the sugars cannot ferment in the stomach because they are stabilized by gastric acid. The digestion of protein starts in the stomach under the influence of pepsins. The contents of the stomach are little by little transported to the duodenum in which the starch, the sugars, the proteins and the fats are digested. If the starch protein ratio is not good, the food-pulp remains too long in the stomach, is insufficiently digested, and starts putrefying. The badly digested food is pushed out of the stomach into the bowels, which cannot cope with it either. In the alkaline milieu of the duodenum the carbohydrates start fermenting and the proteins begin to rot. Many toxicant acids are produced and a large amount of energy is used up.

Consequently, the meal may stay for twelve hours, or longer, in the stomach and two to three days in the entire digestive tract. Normally, it stays three hours in the stomach and twelve hours in the whole digestive tract. Generally speaking, food rich in starch and food rich in protein cannot be combined. It will be clear that those starchy foodstuffs, like potatoes, cereals, spaghetti, macaroni, bread and rice cannot be combined with protein foodstuffs, such as dairy products, soy products, eggs, meat, fish, nuts and pulses. Rice and pulses form an acceptable combination.

* Starch-sugar combinations. When we only eat sugar, then it is rapidly forwarded into the small intestine, where it is digested. With a mixture of sugar and other food, the sugar is held up in the stomach till the other food has been digested. The sugars may start fermenting in the middle of the upper part of the stomach because it is not stabilised by gastric acid there. So, starchy and sacchariferous food cannot be combined. Thus corn products cannot be combined with beet sugar, cane sugar, jams, syrups, honey, dates, raisins, figs and other fruit. But two different kinds of starchy foods, like potatoes and cereals, can certainly be combined.

* Starch-fat combinations. Starchy foods can well be combined with oils and fats, like potatoes or cereals, with creamy butter or vegetable oils.

*   Starch-acid combinations. Acid food destroys the enzyme ptyalin, which is necessary for digesting starch, in the saliva. So, do not combine potatoes or corn products with vinegar, sour gherkins, fruit, tomatoes, sauerkraut, etc. Spaghetti or macaroni combined with tomatoes and cheese or meat are bad combinations. Leavened bread is a starch-acid combination and because of that difficult to digest. Leavened bread with honey gives a starch-acid-sugar combination and this is worse still. Be careful with sauces made of oil, yoghurt, vinegar or lemon juice. The acidity (pH) of oil is about 4.5, but with lemon juice its acidity is lowered. Industrialized sauces have an acidity of 2.9 - 3.6. Never use them. With potatoes or rice all these sauces give bad combinations Also be careful with home-made sauces. Most industrialised drinks have a low acidity (pH) too. Cola is very sour.

*   Starch-vegetable combinations. Fresh, uncooked vegetables contain an abudance of vital substances and much water. Fresh vegetables and fresh fruit are much better than all kinds of cooked preparations. Vegetables have no specific digestive juices; they are digested in a basic milieu as well as in an acid milieu. Vegetables form good combinations with starchy foodstuffs. It is recommended that starchy meal, is to be combined with a substinal vegetable salad.

*   Protein-protein combinations. The digestive tract cannot comply with the digestive demands of more than one protein foodstuff. Meat cannot be combined with nuts, eggs, milk, etc. It is possible to combine various kinds of nuts in the same meal. Several kinds of cheese can also be combined in the same meal.

*   Protein-sugar combinations. All sugars have a checking effect on the secretion of gastric juices and, by that, they impede the digestion of proteins. And what is more, the sugars remain in the stomach till the proteins have been digested. That is much too long. The sugars may start fermenting in the stomach. So, protein foods and sugar cannot be combined.

Protein-fat combinations. Oils and fats have a restricting effect on the secretion of gastric juices. They reduce the amount of pepsins and hydrochloric acid in the gastric juice. Therefore it is better not to combine protein and fatty food. The digestion of foodstuffs which contain protein as well as fats, like cheese, milk and nuts needs more than the digestion of protein food with only very little fat. An abundance of fresh uncooked leafy vegetables neutralizes the restrictive action of the fats.

* Protein-acid combinations. With the combination of protein food and, for instance, sour fruit, the acid upsets the digestion in the stomach, either by making the pepsins inactive or by preventing the secretion of hydrochloric acid. Owing to this, protein in the stomach cannot be well digested and results in rotting in the stomach and the intestines. Therefore, never combine protein food with acid food, like meat with sour fruits.

* Protein-vegetable combinations. All vegetables, especially leafy vegetables, can very well be combined with protein foodstuffs. Vegetables containing little starch, like red beet roots, cauliflower, pumpkin, turnips, scorzonera and carrots may give problems. Beans, peas and lentils are starch-protein combinations. It would be best if you ate them without any combination or in combination with leafy vegetables.

* Fat-sugar combinations. These combinations are bad food combinations. Natural food, rich in sugar, such as fruit and honey, contain little or no fat. Fat and sugar do not belong together. Sugars enveloped with fat cannot come into contact with gastric acid and becuase of that they are not stablilized and start fermenting. So do not eat nuts with raisins (matrimony), nut-paste with honey, olives with bananas, sweetened cream, ice, marchpane, nougat, etc., Acidic and semi-acidic fruit can be combined with a little unsweetened whipped cream.

* Fat-acid combinations. Fat is a concentrated food and because of that difficult to digest. Becuase sugar in the body can be converted into fat there will never be a shortage of fat. The addition of acid, such as citric acid (lemon juice), makes fat more easily digestible. Acidic oil-sauces from good combinations with

vegetables but not with items of food rich in starch or protein. Acid curbs the movements of the stomach, therefore do not use too much acid.

* Sugar-acid combinations. All fruits are by nature sugar-acid combinations. Acidic, semi-acidic and sweet fruit form good combinations. If certain fruit combinations are not eaily digested it is an individual problem and not a general combination problem. Yogurt with honey or sweet fruit is a good combination.

* Fruit-vegetable combinations. Fruit is rich in sugar and acid and poor in protein. Vegetables are poor in sugar and acid and relatively richer in protein. Fruit and vegetables form difficult combinations. It is best not to combine fruit with vegetables. The acidity (pH) of vegetables is 5.2 - 6.6, so they are a good combination with starch or protein. Fruit is much more acidic. Even sweet bananas have an acidity of 3.8. So fruit forms bad combinations with starch or protein. Vegetables are difficult to digest. With an oilsauce they stay longer in the stomach whereby they can be better digested. Raw vegetables without oil are difficult to digest. Waterfruits are considered vegetables. They form a seperate group. It is best to eat melons on their own. Cucumber, tomato, gherkin, paprika, aubergine, courgette and pumpkin can be combined with other vegetables.

Dr. H. M. Shelton has summarized in some schedules all the rules concerning the correct food combinations. Jan Dries improved the theory of the correct food combinations and made a new and up-to-date schedule which is totally in harmony with modern digestion physiology (see food combinations charts 1 & 2 Jan Dries)[+].

Jan Dries distinguishes between good, bad and difficult combinations. To judge a food-mix it is necessary to consider both the food combinations and the quantities. If the starch-protein ratio is 5 to 1 it is a good combination, but if the ratio is 1 to 1 it is

---

+ Jan Dries, The New Book of Food Combining (see Reference 11)

	FOOD COMBINATIONS CHART 1 JAN DRIES + good combinations 0 difficult combinations - bad combinations	Mushrooms	Milk	Vegetables, sprouts	lactic acid vegetables	yogurt-buttermilk	tomatoes/ midly sour	vinegar-mustard/sour	fruit-berries	fruit rich in sugar	sugar-honey
					ACIDS					SUGAR	
PROTEIN	meat- fish- fowl	+	-	+	-	-	+	-	-	-	-
PROTEIN	cheese-curds	+	-	+	-	0	+	-	+	-	-
PROTEIN	nuts-seeds-stones	-	-	+	+	0	+	-	+	-	-
FAT	oil-fat-egg yolk	+	0	+	+	+	+	+	+	0	-
FAT	butter-(whipped) cream	+	0	+	+	+	+	+	+	0	-
FAT	avocado-olive	+	-	+	+	+	+	+	+	-	-
STARCH	cereals-bread-paste	+	-	+	-	-	-	-	-	-	-
STARCH	potatoes	+	-	+	-	-	-	-	-	-	-
STARCH	starchy vegetables	+	-	+	+	+	0	0	0	0	0
SUGAR	sugar-honey	-	-	-	+	+	+	+	+	0	■
SUGAR	fruit rich in sugar	-	-	-	+	+	-	0	+	■	0
ACIDS	fruit-berries	-	0	0	0	+	0	+	■	+	+
ACIDS	vinegar-mustard/sour	+	0	+	0	-	+	■	+	0	+
ACIDS	tomatoes/mildy sour	+	-	+	+	+	■	+	0	-	+
ACIDS	yogurt-buttermilk	-	+	+	+	■	+	-	+	+	+
	lactic acid vegetables	+	0	+	■	+	+	0	0	+	+
	vegetables - sprouts	+	0	■	+	+	+	+	0	-	-
	milk	-	■	0	0	+	0	0	0	-	-
	mushrooms	■	-	+	+	-	+	+	-	-	-

For most people all pulses are difficult to digest and combine badly. Only people with a strong, healthy digestive system can digest pulses well, and may combine peanuts, legumes, beans and peas as starch.

		STARCH			FAT			PROTEIN		
FOOD COMBINATIONS CHART 2 JAN DRIES + good combinations 0 difficult combinations − bad combinations		starchy vegetables	potatoes	cereaks-bread-paste	avocado-olive	butter-(whipped)cream	oil-fat-egg yolk	nuts- seeds- stones	cheese-curds	meat - fish - fowl
PROTEIN	meat - fish - fowl	0	−	−	−	−	−	−	−	■
	cheese - curds	0	−	−	−	−	−	−	■	−
	nuts- seeds- stones	0	−	−	−	−	−	■	−	−
FAT	oil - fat - egg yolk	+	+	+	−	−	■	−	−	−
	butter - (whipped) cream	+	+	+	−	■	−	−	−	−
	avocado - olive	+	+	+	■	−	−	−	−	−
STARCH	cereals - bread - paste	+	+	■	+	+	+	−	−	−
	potatoes	+	■	+	+	+	+	−	−	−
	starchy vegetables	■	+	−	+	+	+	0	0	0
SUGAR	sugar - honey	0	−	−	−	−	−	−	−	−
	fruit rich in sugar	0	−	−	−	0	0	−	−	−
ACIDS	fruit-berries	0	−	−	+	+	+	+	+	−
	vinegar-mustard/sour	0	−	−	+	+	+	−	−	−
	tomatoes/mildly sour	0	−	−	+	+	+	+	+	+
	yogurt-buttermilk	+	−	−	+	+	+	0	0	−
	lactic acid vegetables	+	−	−	+	+	+	+	−	−
	vegetables - sprouts	+	+	+	+	+	+	+	+	+
	milk	−	−	−	−	0	0	−	−	−
	mushrooms	+	+	+	+	+	+	−	+	+

Combine germinating cereals, pulses and seeds as mildly starchy food or starchy vegetables. Combine sprouts as vegetables. Melons should not be combined with any food, nor with other fruits as well.

a bad combination. In those cases where the food contains only small quantities of starch and protein then the 1 to 1 combination is all right. If a meal consists of several courses the meal must be considered as a whole. The choice of the main course mostly determines the whole meal. A preceding light soup does not influence the main course. Never eat fruit after the main course. Eventually, fruit may be eaten as a first course. A good first course is a small dish with raw vegetables. Be careful that in all your meals not more than one nutrition substance dominates.

12. The Fourth Step to Living Food

For several reasons, most people cannot totally switch over to living food from one day to the next. As has already been said, the best first step is probably practising correct fruit consumption, while the traditional breakfast is cut out. At the same time, or as a second step, all stimulants and processed foodstuffs ought to be cut out. As a third step we have mentioned the application of the principle of correct food combinations.

The fourth and last step is undoubtedly the most difficult step. Bread and other corn products are dead food. In bread, pastry and biscuits, animal fats, refined sugar and fruit may have been worked in. Anyhow, do not use wheat flour and bread, pastry, etc. made from white flour. It would be best to bake bread yourself from fresh wholemeal ground by yourself. It is good to reduce the consumption of this popular food, but it is better still to cut it out completely.

While bread is still consumed, use three to four tablespoons of uncooked grains of corn per day in order to eliminate a shortage of B-complex vitamins and other vital substances. The best way to do this is in the form of sprouting grains of corn, like germinating wheat or rye. It is also possible to prepare a thick porridge of freshly ground corn and pure water no warmer than 40ºC. The grains of corn can also be soaked in water and flocked in a flocker of your own. Do not use industrial flocks. That is dead food. And, especially, do not forget to eat uncooked vegetables with the bread. Bread may be buttered. Potatoes should not be fried. Never fry with vegetable oils that are rich in poly-unsaturated fatty acids (use coconut oil, olive oil, butter or ghee for frying). It would be best to eat the potatoes uncooked or mushy or very quickly steamed; you may, if necessary, mash them together with butter and hot water.

It is becoming an ever greater problem to find foodstuffs of good quality. It is difficult to be sure of the quality unless you grow your vegetables and fruit yourself or buy them from a trusted address. The vegetables and fruits bought in ordinary shops and supermarkets are mainly heavily chemically polluted, and often, radiated as well. Products grown by using chemical manure and products which have been radiated, are of very poor quality. Therefore it is necessary to use biologically grown products which have not been radiated. Alas, these products are often very expensive.

Fortunately, we still have a group of foods of which the value is increasingly discerned and which are not very expensive. It is the germinating cereals, pulses and other seeds. These sprouting natural nutritious sources might be the least polluted foodstuffs we can find at the moment. And it is living food. Germinating cereals, pulses and seeds are much easier to digest than the non-sprouted ones. During the germinating process, there arises an enormous activity: starch is converted into sugar, the proteins are converted into amino-acids, the enzymes are activated and large quantities of vitamins are formed. Sprouting cereals, pulses and other seeds contain all the required nutritious substances. Sathya Sai Baba only mentions just-germinating pulses. There are good manuals about sprouting available.

Finally, the diet will consist entirely of living, biological nourishment, of fruits, nuts, coconuts, vegetables, roots, tubers, soaked or just-germinating pulses, a little uncooked milk, buttermilk, yogurt or coagulated milk (curds), a bit of creamery butter and a few potatoes, cereals and rice prepared in a special way. Drink pure water and herbal teas, like camomile tea, lime blossom tea or one of the many other available herbal teas. There are many medicinal herbal teas.

13. Classification of Food According to Jan Dries

Food items can be subdivided into five groups: food rich in protein, food rich in starch, etc.

Food rich in protein. If food contains more than 10% protein it is called food rich in protein. We distinguish between animal proteins present in meat, fish and shell-fish, milk proteins in milk, buttermilk, yogurt, cheese, curds and eggs, and vegetable proteins in ground-nuts, nuts, cereals, pulses and seeds.

Food rich in starch. Starchy foodstuffs are cereals (wheat, rye, oats, barley, maize), rice, buckwheat, bread, biscuits, pastry, spaghetti, macaroni, potatoes, chestnuts, ginger, horse-radish, peas, chick-peas, soya beans and lentils. Mildly starchy foodstuffs are garlic, pumpkin, black radish, radish, kohlrabi (turnip-cabbage), chicory, asparagus, endive, paprika and parsley.

Food rich in sugar. All kinds of milk contain milk sugar (lactose). Industrial sugar is found in syrups, chocolate, jams, sweets, soft drinks, etc. The following fruits contain more than 10% sugars: dried fruit, bananas, bilberries, rose-hip, grapes, kaki, mirabelles, greengages, figs, mangoes, cherries, nectarines, honey-melons, plums and pomegranates.

Food rich in fat. We distinguish between animal fats present in meat and fish, milk fats in milk and milk-products, and vegetable fats in margarine, safflower oil, soya bean oil, palm-kernel oil, sunflower seed oil,, cotton seed oil, olive oil, maize oil, linseed oil, sesame seed oil, nut oil, ground-nut oil, coconut oil, mayonnaise, avocados, etc.

Food rich in acid. There are acidic expedients like vinegar and leaven, sour soft drinks, wines, beer, etc., lactic acidic vegetables and mildly acidic, semi-acidic and acidic fruit. Mildly acidic fruit (pH 3.6 to 3.9) are papaya, mango, kaki, pear, cherry, apple, banana, pomegranate, plum, strawberry, grape, peach, orange and pineapple. Semi-acidic fruit (pH 3 to 3.5) are elderberry, apricot, raspberry, (red) bilberry, kiwi, semi-acidic orange, semi-acidic grape, blackberry, grapefruit and morello. Acidic fruit (pH 2 to 2.9) are acidic cherry, rose-hip, barberry, lemon and cranberry. Fruit contains oxidases which catalyse the biological oxidation by activating oxygen. Fruit stimulates the absorption of oxygen during breathing. Fresh fruit and fresh vegetables are purifying food. They are extremely important for the detoxification and purification of the body, for the removal of waste products and toxins produced during the dissolution of old cells as also during the digestive process.

14. Proteins, the Most Important Nutritious Substances

Proteins are probably the most important nutritious substances. Proteins are indispensable 'building stones' for plants, animals and men. Proteins are divided into animal, milk, vegetable and bacterial proteins.

Animal proteins are found in meat, fish and shell-fish. Milk proteins in milk, buttermilk, cheese, cottage cheese, yogurt and eggs.

Vegetable proteins are found in ground-nuts, avocados, olives, cereals, nuts, pulses, rice and seeds, and in small quantities also in fruit and vegetables. Half the dry substance of the cells in the body consists of proteins; the antibodies, the enzymes and several hormones are proteins. Proteins are able to combine with carbohydrates and form glycoproteins; together with fats they give lipoproteins; with phosphoric acid they give phosphoproteins and with certain metals they give metalloproteins. Proteins are for the greater part built up out of amino-acids. During digestion, the proteins from the foodstuffs are broken down into amino acids;

then the body synthesizes new proteins from these amino acids. Of the twenty-four amino acids, eight are called essential, because the human body is unable to produce them. These essential amino acids are isoleucin, leucin, methionine, lysine, phenylalanine, threonine, valine and tryptophan (tryptophan is a natural narcotic present in bananas and milk). The amino acid histidine is essential for babies, but arginine remains in doubt.

While proteins may also contain substances other than amino acids, the three dimensional structure, and thus the biological properties of proteins, are determined largely by the kinds of amino acids present, the order in which they are linked together in a polypeptide chain, and thereby the spatial relationship of one amino acid to another.

An actual picture of very small objects can be obtained with the electron microscope. Magnifications as high as 100,000 diameters can be obtained with this instrument. This permits the visualization of proteins of high molecular weight, such as virus particles, enzyme complexes and oligomeric proteins. Proteins have all kinds of forms. Some proteins are spherical, other proteins have distorted forms: bent, twisted together or showing knotty swellings. Again other proteins end in thin threads often spirally rolled up. All these forms are continuously changing - they are expanding, palpitating, lengthening, contracting or unrolling themselves, sometimes all of a sudden. The spatial forms are very important. The biological activities of proteins, such as enzymes, depend on the native structure and form. Proteins are really living structures. The disruption of a native structure is termed denaturation. The biological activity of most proteins is destroyed by exposure to strong acids or alkalis, heat, detergents, heavy metals, etc.

Very important proteins are the enzymes. Enzymes are protein catalysts for chemical reactions in biological systems. Essentially, all biochemical reactions are enzyme-catalysed. For almost every organic compound in nature, and for many inorganic compounds, there is an enzyme in some organism capable of reacting with it and catalysing a chemical change. Many enzymes catalyse reactions of their substrates only in the presence of a co-enzyme. Vitamins B form part of the structure of many co-enzymes.

Over 25% of all enzymes contain tightly bound metal ions or require them for activity. There are functional and non-functional plasma enzymes. Certain enzymes and pro-enzymes are present at all times in the circulation of normal individuals. Non-functional plasma enzymes perform no known physiological function in blood. Their presence in plasma at levels elevated above normal suggests an increased rate of tissue destruction. Measurement of these non-functional plasma enzyme levels can thus provide the physician with valuable diagnostic and prognostical clinical evidence. There is an optimal temperature and also an optimal acidity (pH) at which enzyme-catalysed reactions are most rapid. All of the water-soluble vitamins serve as co-enzymes or co-factors in enzymatic reactions. Enzymes are extremely important. Athough once thought to be a vitamin in the true sense, vitamin D is a hormone intimately involved in the regulation of calcium and phosphate metabolism. Enzymes and hormones really are mediators between the gross and subtle worlds.

Modern biochemistry teaches that the digestive processes are very complicated, and that every nutritious substance has to cover a long distance. If food is heated, all kinds of toxic substances are formed, and over and above that, denatured, slightly misshapen molecules. Guy Claude Burger of France has launched the theory that the enzymes of our body are only adjusted to undamaged living molecules, and that they are not capable of easily digesting heated food. The damaged, slightly deformed molecules are dangerous; they are used as building-stones of the tissues or simply stored because they cannot be converted further. In addition to toxic substances, these slightly deformed molecules are the real pathogens. We can speak of molecular pathology.

Guy Claude Burger says that one of the tasks of the immune system is to eliminate these dangerous, slightly misshapen molecules in cooperation with useful viruses and bacteria. What is more, the immune system has to supervise these viruses and bacteria and to destroy the superfluous ones. That is why diseases can be cleaning processes. They become destructive in case the body cannot control these processes. He arrived at the conclusion that eating raw, natural food is absolutely necessary for physical and mental health.

The essential amino acids are found in mother's milk, cow's milk and in most fruits, nuts and vegetables. Meat, fish, cereals and pulses do not contain every essential amino acid. Almonds, peanuts and soya beans contain them all; they are the only vegetable sources of complete protein. The almond is the king of the nuts. Almonds contain 21% protein, 17% carbohydrates and 55% fat (much oleic acid), the vitamins A, B1 and B2, and the minerals potassium, phosphorus, calcium, magnesium, sulphur, chlorine, sodium and iron. Though not alkaline, like the soya bean, the peanut is valuable as a source of complete protein (27%). The soya bean is the most valuable of the legumes. Besides 30-35% protein, it contains 15% fat and 20% carbohydrates. Though rich in phosphorus, it is alkaline in reaction, being well supplied with potassium, calcium, magnesium and sodium.

A shortage of proteins leads to under-nourishment and loss of strength. A surplus of proteins causes all sorts of diseases, like heart and vascular diseases, cancer, rheumatic complaints, kidney diseases, food allergies, etc. Most people in Europe and America eat far too much protein, as many as 100 - 300 grams of protein per day. Man needs a minimum of 15 grams of protein per day. A good norm is probably 25 - 50 grams per day. Young people and people engaged in heavy work require more. The need for protein depends on several factors. With a vegetable diet, the need is smaller than with an animal diet.

Raw food, living, natural and unheated food, contains highly valuable proteins, and leads to a lesser requirement. The daily requirement of protein is lower when the food is rich in magnesium and when we keep to the rules of food concerning the acid-alkaline balance and the food combinations. The better the digestive tract functions, the lower the need for daily protein.

The higher the percentage of protein in a foodstuff, the more difficult it will be to digest. Meat, fish, cheese and pulses are, in fact, difficult to digest. That also counts for cocoa, peanuts and peanut butter, often loved by children. Foods rich in protein pollute and acidify the body; it is not easily digested and causes putrefaction in the bowels. Foodstuffs which are poor in proteins are much healthier than foodstuffs rich in proteins. When food poor in proteins is regularly used and the rules of food are adhered to, the need for proteins will steadily decrease. Dependent on the kinds of fruit, one kilogram contains about three to fifteen grams of protein; with vegetables, one kilogram contains five to sixty grams of protein. To provide for the daily requirement of proteins, carbohydrates and fats, it will be sufficient to eat one kilogram of fruit per day, half a kilogram of vegetables (including potatoes) with an oil sauce, a little yogurt or whipped cream, and a few nuts.

Up to noon it is best to eat only fruit or nothing at all. Then two meals may be taken. The best times are from 12 noon till 2 p.m. and from 5 p.m. till 7 p.m. We may take two vegetable meals, or one vegetable meal and one fruit meal. The vegetable meals may either be combined with starchy food, like potatoes and rice, or with protein food, like nuts, yogurt, curds and eventually, cheese. With fruit, yogurt or unsweetened whipped cream may be used as a binding agent. Vegetable oil sauces or herbal oil sauces may be used as binding agent. Butter may also be used as a binding agent with potatoes.

15. Milk and Milk-Products

According to Sathya Sai Baba, a little pure milk, buttermilk, yogurt or curds are good *satvic* food. In addition to purity, He emphasizes a small quantity. Moreover, He prefers soured milk-products. Use, therefore, only raw, fresh, biological milk free of germs and the milk-products prepared from that at a low temperature (lower than 40° C), all produced in very hygienic circumstances. The cattle must be tended with love and wisdom, be fed with good food, and be allowed to die a natural death.

For a baby, mother's milk is the best nourishment. After breast milk they often switch over to cow's milk. In Europe, America and Australia much milk and many milk-products are consumed by adults. In western naturopathy, there are proponents and opponents of the use of milk and milk-products, whereas some people claim that moderate use of these products is good. All agree that milk, in any case, must be raw, pure, biological, and therefore, not denatured (heated) and not polluted with all kinds of chemicals. In contrast to other people, Europeans go on producing enzyme lactase for the digestion of milk-sugar (lactose) after infancy. People who cannot produce lactase become ill after drinking milk. This is called lactose intolerance. This is especially found in Asia. These people may certainly use milk-products soured by lacti-acid-bacilli, such as yogurt. The lactic-acid-bacilli convert milk-sugar (lactose) into lactic acid. Lactic acid prevents cancer and lactic-acid-bacilli have a favourable influence on intestinal flora. That is why yogurt is used with the reconstruction of disturbed intestinal flora.

Milk is a complete food. One litre of milk gives about thirty-three grams of protein. Protein from milk has a fairly favourable amino-acid composition. Milk contains lecithin and choline which prevent the fattening of the liver, enrich everything with oxygen and also stimulate the activity of the detoxification of the liver. Milk has a draining effect, contains much water and can be considered as a forcing body-building food. Milk should always be drunk slowly and may not be mixed with other foodstuffs. In the stomach it forms a coagulant, which deposits itself upon other food particles by which these particles are inaccessible for the gastric juice.

Milk contains casein which can cause various problems. With some people milk causes mucus secretion in the throat, nasal mucus membranes and in the intestines. Slimy substances are a protection of the respiratory system and are required for progressing of the digestion, but they must be drained off in good time. Too thick slimy layers cause difficulties. An allergy to cow's milk is another much occurring disease.

Pasteurized, sterilized and UHT-milk, and their by-products, are connected to a large number of diseases, like respiratory problems, allergy, headache, cancer, inflammation of the ear (otitis), arthritis (synovitis), osteoporosis (decreasing of the percentage of lime in the bones), etc. Dr. H. M. Shelton says: "The process of pasteurization is intended to destroy bacteria which are supposed to cause disease. It does destroy some of the germs in milk including the lactic-acid-bacilli, which are the natural protectors of the milk. Many bacteria or their spores are not killed, especially the harmful, even by boiling. The bacteria that survive even ideal pasteurization multiply rapidly thereafter. By pasteurization there is a great reduction of the bone-nourishing salts of the milk, its vitamins are destroyed, its digestibility is impaired, its proteins are rendered less valuable and its value as a food is greatly reduced."[+]

Milk cannot be combined with most foodstuffs (see charts) or with cereals. That is a pity, for corn proteins are poor in essential amino-acid lysine, which is richly found in milk proteins. In this respect milk and cereals complement each other. Buttermilk and yogurt combine well with vegetables, with almost all fruits, and with oils and fats. Therefore we prefer soured milk-products like buttermilk, yogurt and curds. Curd is a soft cheese which develops by souring milk. The percentage of protein varies between 10% and 14%. Curds may be used with herbs or vegetable juices and for all kinds of sauces. Low fat curd, or cottage cheese, is a wonderful product with a high nutritional value. It is lightly digestible and has a favourable influence on the liver and on the whole metabolism.

[+] Dr. H. M. Shelton, *The Science and Fine Art of Food and Nutrition* PP. 508 - 51

Cheese is, in contrast to curds, a very much more concentrated food. Many sorts of cheese contain as much as 25% protein. That is why the digestion of cheese is particularly difficult. It rots very soon in the intestines. Cheese is not fit to be eaten. Never eat fat and old cheese. Never eat cheese with bread. Creamery butter is an excellent adipose (fatty) foodstuff. Together with herbs we can prepare various kinds of herb-butter. Ghee is clarified butter.

He who stops using milk and milk-products should take care about not to become short of vitamin B12 and lose intestinal strength, for the lactic-acid-bacilli fall off then. Goat's milk has certain medicinal qualities.

16. Nuts and Seeds

There are two sorts of fruit, soft and hard. Hard fruits are nuts, pulses, cereals and hard seeds. So nuts are fruit. In addition to fresh, soft fruits and uncooked vegetables, raw, unheated, non-radiated, not genetically manipulated, biological nuts are important *satvic* food. It is possible to live exclusively on nuts, fruit and vegetables. What nuts have to offer is unbelievable. In natural food they take a central place. In combination with vegetables they form a food of full value. In general, because of ignorance, they are eaten very rarely.

Our digestive tract is attuned to the digestion of fruit and nuts. Fresh nuts contain water and are light to digest. Unfortunately, most nuts are peeled, dried and heated. Owing to this they are difficult to digest. They are dead food. Therefore we should always try to get raw unhusked nuts. This is often not simple, for in many cases it is difficult to discover if the nuts have been heated or not, even in health-shops. Dried nuts are best soaked some hours in good water. Nuts can also be ground, after which water can be added. Raw nuts do not contain injurious bacteria and they can be kept for a long time.

Nuts, and seeds as well, because they are similar to nuts, are concentrated foodstuffs rich in proteins, fats, vitamins and minerals and mostly poor in carbohydrates. Moreover, they have got a high combustion value. Nuts are forcing food. Due to their richness in vitamins and minerals they have a healing effect. Nuts contain much phosphorus, potassium and sulphur and they are very rich in vitamins B1 and B2. Therefore they have a good effect on the nervous system. Nuts contain much calcium, phosphorus and magnesium, necessary to the development and the maintenance of the skeleton. They contain many minerals, iron, zinc, copper, manganese, chromium, selenium, etc. The minerals in nuts and seeds are combined with other substances and belong to a living whole. The human body needs these active minerals for its enzyme-catalysed metabolic processes. Mineral supplements, like calcium tablets, are dead substances and are ingested by the body with difficulty. As a source for minerals, nuts (like dried fruit and sea vegetables) are much better.

Nuts are rich in chlorine, phosphorus and sulphur. Therefore, when one eats nuts one should expect a good acid-alkali balance. That means that with a fruit and vegetable diet, a small amount of nuts may be eaten without any danger. One should also pay attention to the food combinations. Nuts and seeds combine well with leafy and stalky vegetables, as with sour and half-sour fruit, but combine with difficulty with yogurt and buttermilk and badly with most other foods.

Many people like nut and sesame seed paste as a bread spread. These, however, are bad food combinations. When one kilogram of base-forming food, like fruit, vegetables, potatoes and yogurt, is eaten per day, then one may eat between fifty to hundred grams of nuts and seeds per day. Especially in winter, it is advisable to eat at least thirty grams of raw biologically grown nuts each day.

The most commonly used nuts are hazel nuts from Europe, walnuts of Asian origin (adapted to Europe) and almonds from the area round the Mediterranean. Furthermore, we know the Brazil nut, the pecan, the cashew nut, the pistachio nut, not to forget the coconut! The cashew nut is distinguished by its high carbohydrate content (25%). Almonds have uncommonly good qualities and are used in the biological fight against cancer. Fresh coconut-milk is very healthy and the pulp of the coconut is rich in selenium which makes it suitable to fight against heart and vascular diseases and for the building up of the immune system. Once again, it must be emphasized that the nuts obtainable in ordinary shops are mostly those that have been heated at high temperatures. Sometimes they have also been chemically treated. Only biologically grown, unheated, unirradiated, raw nuts are *satvic* food. Stored peeled nuts are less *satvic*. Peel them just before eating.

Several seeds have characteristics in common with nuts. When ground, they are easy to digest. The most commonly used seeds are linseed, mustard seed and sesame seed. Sesame seed is very rich in calcium. Unground sesame seed is indigestible, so it should be ground. Further, we have sunflower kernels rich in oil of a high quality, and pumpkin kernels which have a favourable effect on the prostate gland.

Groundnuts (peanuts) are not nuts but pulses. They are nearly always heated. They are difficult to digest and not often used in natural food. Peanuts are more digestible when lightly roasted than raw. Taken in moderation, the peanut is a most useful addition to the diet. Other edible fruits are sweet chestnuts with 35% carbohydrates, dried dates with 75% carbohydrates, and olives which form the raw material of olive oil.

17. Germinating Cereals, Pulses and Seeds

Many naturopaths agree that fruit is the ideal nourishment; they mean fresh, biological, not genetically manipulated, fruit that has been grown without chemical fertilizers and insecticides. Unfortunately, this kind of fruit is difficult to find nowadays, and when found, is very expensive. Germinating, biologically grown cereals, pulses and seeds and also grasses like wheat-grass, fresh and cheap foodstuffs, containing many vitamins, minerals, enzymes and chlorophyll also called sprouting vegetables are good. For very little money one can have a big sprout-salad. Germinating is a natural way of preparation, much better than cooking. The vital strength remains intact. Cereals, pulses and seeds are easy to preserve.

Pulses are difficult to digest; they are only suited to a healthy digestive tract. They often cause wind and problems in the stomach and intestines. It is said that raw pulses contain several natural poisons such as the harmful phytates. Phytates are nature's insecticide, provided by her to protect seeds against micro-organisms in the soil during the delicate germination process. Yet, Sathya Sai Baba and many others speak well of germinating pulses. According to Sai Usha, green pulses are *satvic* food, but red pulses are not.

It is an established fact that germinating pulses are much more easily digestible than only soaked or cooked pulses. During germination, the seeds, whole grains and legumes absorb water, the proteins are converted into amino- acids, the starch is converted into sugars, the phytates are neutralized by certain phytate-splitting enzymes, the saturated fatty acids are converted into unsaturated fatty acids, the percentage of vitamins often increases considerably, and there is a remarkable increase of enzymes, etc. Germination is a kind of pre-digestion.

When germinating cereals, pulses and seeds are exposed to sun light, chlorophyll is formed. Of the vegetables, parsley, celery, broccoli, chives and spinach are richest in chlorophyll. Chlorophyll and haemoglobin in the blood have a similar structure. Therefore, it is not so surprising that chlorophyll is a medicine. Germinating cereals, pulses and seeds have regenerating and rejuvenating qualities, and are used during the healing of several diseases. Raw, uncooked, germinating cereals, pulses and seeds, grasses and baby greens, together with fruits, nuts and vegetables form the base-food of the famous Ann Wigmore Foundation in Boston and Puerto Rico.

In Rancho La Puerto (known both in Mexico and the United States) of Dr. E. B. Szekely, the same food is used; goat's milk is also used there. The daily bread of the Essenes was prepared by drying in the sunlight the flat loaves made from germinating cereals. So this bread was not baked, but dried. The Essenes ate exclusively living, uncooked food. Starting from the doctrine of the Essenes, Dr. E. B. Szekely has developed a new classification of foodstuffs. He distinguishes them as:

* Biogenic, or vivifying food, such as nuts, whole cereals, pulses, seeds, germinating cereals, pulses and seeds, and baby greens; arsenal of rejuvenation
* Bioactive or life-keeping food, such as fresh raw fruits and vegetables (soil-to-stomach principle); nutrition for health
* Biostatic, or ageing food, such as cooked and stored food; cause of biostasis (antithesis of the life-generating capacity of biogenic foods)
* Biocidic, or life-destroying food, such as all processed, chemicalized foods and all flesh foods; cause of disease and death.[+]

Biologically grown lucerne (alfalfa), fenugreek, sesame seed, buckwheat, wheat, aduki beans, mung beans, lentils, soy beans, green peas and chick-peas can easily be germinated without the use of soil in a (glass) pot. Germination in a glass pot is the simplest method. First remove, before germinating, all damaged seeds, because they will rot.

The biogenic method of sprouting of pulses, cereals and seeds consists of five steps:

1. *De-chemicalizing.* The initial soaking in plenty of tepid water to get rid of the protective inherent chemicals of the pulses, cereals and seeds, as well as the possibly added synthetic chemicals. The

---

+ Dr. E.B. Szekely, *The Chemistry of Youth*, pp. 22-25

water after soaking should be thrown away as it may contain toxic substances. Soya beans need double de-chemicalizing, with additional changes of water.

2. *Potentializing*. A second soaking in good water, just enough to cover the food and to be absorbed. Potentializing mobilizes the dormant, potential life forces around a nascent, small, central germ by generating plant enzymes and plant hormones, splitting harmful phytates and getting rid of them. The remaining water must be eliminated. Soak the smallest seeds for about three hours, the others about twelve hours (hulled buckwheat 15 minutes).

3. *Germinating*. Cover the pot with a small gauze cloth and put it upside down in the (half)dark in a tilted tray. Carefully wash the germinating cereals, pulses or seeds gently and regularly twice a day. Throw the water away. By keeping them moist, but not soaked, we stimulate a biogenic outburst of spectacular increase and multiplication of vitamins in the cereals, pulses or seeds as the little central germ starts to grow.

4. *Sprouting*. Further increases of plant enzymes and hormones in the damp darkness creates a complete plant embryo. After three to five days the sprouting cereals, pulses or seeds are ready.

5. *Chlorophyllizing* (optional). Rice germinates slowly. For nuts, such as almonds, de-chemicalizing and potentializing is enough (they will double in size); for whole grain to make bread, these two processes are sufficient. For germinating cereals, pulses and seeds the first four processes are enough, with an additional half-day in indirect light, to add some chlorophyll.

Exposing the developed plant embryos to light (not direct sunlight) until they reach a minimum of five and maximum of ten cm in height, becoming a tender, dark green baby plant (total development in normal temperature, about a week). Baby greens of wheat, rye, barley, buckwheat and sunflower-kernels need a thin, few-cm thick soil to be kept moist for the duration of growth. The baby greens can be harvested twice with a pair of scissors for immediate consumption, to avoid oxidation, wilting, and staleness.

Always germinate (sprout) in favourable circumstances: 20 to 25°C, not directly exposed to light, but with sufficient water, sufficient air, etc. Always take cereals, pulses and seeds of the best quality, and always of biological quality. Seeds of a bad quality and old seeds rot very soon. Rotting also sets in with too much moisture and unclean water.

18. Grasses, Grass Juices, and Fermented Seeds

After using germinating cereals, pulses and seeds, and baby greens, we may use grasses as well. Wheat grass is a panacea (magic grass). It contains much chlorophyll and its detoxification effect is great. It is used for both acute and chronic diseases. Wheat grass can be grown inside the house on a layer of soil. After one or two weeks it can be harvested. The same holds good for rye grass, barley grass, etc. Wheat grass can be chewed, it can be used as a vegetable, or made into juice with the help of a special little mill. Fresh juice made of wheat-grass should always be drunk on an empty stomach. It has a very detoxifying effect and can provoke violent reactions. For some people it produces nausea due to its smell. Those who cannot bear wheat grass juice may take an enema of it; in this way the juice is directly brought into the large intestine. An enema of wheat grass juice should always be preceded by an enema of pure water of body temperature.

In the Ural Mountains, the Himalayas and in the Andes there are people who live very long. The most lasting impression Dr. E. B. Szekely had of the Hunzas of Central Asia, when he visited them in the twenties, was not so much their unusual longevity (100-120 years), but the seemingly total absence of the loss of vitality, so characteristic of the process of ageing. They seemed to have discovered the secret of preventing old age. In addition to fruit and germinating cereals, pulses and seeds, they eat pre-digested food by lactic acid fermentation like yogurt, sour beetroots, sauerkraut and fermented leafy vegetables. The natural lactic acid and the enzymes which are formed during the fermentation process have a beneficial influence on the digestion and a healing influence. The lactic acid destroys the injurious intestinal bacteria. Fermented food cleans the intestines and favours its own production of vitamins in the intestines. The growth of bacteria and fermenting agents depends very much on the temperature.

A temperature which is too high or too low may help to develop undesirable micro-flora. In general the temperature should be kept between 20-25°C. For making ferments and yogurt and cheese prepared from seeds, the following varieties of seeds may be used: rough sesame seed, a mixture of rough sesame seed and sunflower seed, almonds, cashew nuts, soaked soya beans, germinating soya beans and peanuts.

When we let wheat ferment for two to three days we get 'rejuvelac', a wholesome and delicious fermented drink containing many B-complex vitamins and great enzyme activity. We also may use rye, barley, sweet brown rice or rough buckwheat. Rejuvelac can be prepared with the whole grain, with freshly ground flour or with pulverized germinating grains. Of course, the best way is to start from whole grains or whole germinated grains, because then the vital strength remains at maximum. With the help of the rejuvelac we can make yogurt or cheese from seeds.

Fasting is the best method to purify the body. A period of fasting gives the body rest and gives nature the chance to recover and cure the body. When fasting exclusively with water it is possible that, all at once, too many toxins are liberated. That may result in serious consequences. Especially for sick people, fasting is ideal for a few days, for example seven days with the juice of wheat grass (if necessary, alternated with water melon juice). The body gets all the necessary food elements in a form which is concentrated and easy to digest, without being exposed to the dangers connected to total abstinence from food. The toxic acids are neutralized.

For healthy people fasting with water is best. See further the books of Dr. Ann Wigmore and V. Kulvinakas. In the book *The*

Essenes Way of Biogenic Living by Dr. E. B. Szekely it is written : "You will not be freed from the power of evil and from all diseases that originate from evil without fasting. Fast and pray ardently and seek the power of the living God for your recovery. Renew yourself and fast. Fast in solitude and do not tell anybody. God will see and reward you."

19. The Corbohydrates

Carbohydrates or sugars are substances which are composed of the elements carbon (C), hydrogen (H) and oxygen (O). There are several types of sugars. We distinguish between simple sugars (monosaccharides), disaccharides composed of two molecules of the same or different monosaccharide(s), oligosaccharides composed of three to six monosaccharide units, and polysaccharides composed of more than six monosaccharide molecules.

In nature the most important simple sugars are glucose (grape-sugar) and fructose (fruit-sugar). They are especially found in fruits and as building materials of the double and complex sugars. Glucose is the principal sugar in blood, serving the tissues as a major metabolic fuel. Saccharose or sucrose (beet and cane sugar), maltose (malt sugar) and lactose (milk sugar) are the best known dissaccharides. Saccharose consists of glucose and fructose, maltose consists of glucose, and lactose consists of glucose and galactose. Lactose is found in milk products and can be converted by the enzyme lactose which, for instance, occurs in yogurt.

Starch, cellulose and glycogen are well known polysaccharides. All three of them consist of glucose. The two most important components of starch are amylose and amylopectin. Glycogen is an animal form of starch. Foodstuffs which are rich in starch are potatoes, groundnuts, beans, peas, cereals (wheat, rye, oats, barley and maize), lentils, coconuts and rice. Cellulose occurs in fruit, vegetables and whole grains and assures a good stool.

The body can absorb only simple sugars. The double sugars and the complex sugars have to be broken down into simple sugars during digestion. For these breaking-down processes, especially for starch, large quantities of vitamins and minerals are needed. In both refined beet sugar and refined cane sugar these vitamins and minerals are absent. In starchy foodstuffs, like bread and pastry, only very few of the necessary vitamins and minerals are found, so that all starch cannot be converted. Alcohol, refined beet and cane sugar and starchy foodstuffs, like bread and cakes, are real robbers of vitamins and minerals. For this and other reasons, all alcoholic drinks, all refined sugars, including those that are coloured brown, and all articles of food made from wheat flour, like white bread, pastry, biscuits, spaghetti, macaroni and *chapatis* are therefore injurious to health. Avoid these products.

According to Jan Dries, insanity, diabetes and cancer are the three oldest diseases of civilized society which are closely related to the over-consumption of grain products. This reminds us of the words of Sathya Sai Baba. He says that heated food which is thereafter completely chilled is *tamasic*, and that starch has a *tamasic* effect on the body. So, baked bread, and, wholemeal bread as well, is *tamasic* food.

Yet, Dr. M. O. Bruker of the "Gesellschaft fur Gesundheitsberatung' (Society for Health Instruction) in Germany still gives a modest place to wholemeal bread on our daily menu. It is true, he advises one to eat many uncooked vegetables and three or four tablespoons full of raw grains of corn, whether or not germinating. Ready-made and paper-wrapped wholemeal bread is unhygienic and has no vital energy.

Probably, it is best to bake your bread yourself at a temperature as low as possible from fresh wholemeal grains ground by yourself, or better still, just like the Essenes, by moulding flat loaves from flattened germinating cereals, then let them dry in the sun. We can also dry this kind of bread on a radiator, in an oven at a temperature as low as possible or better still in a food-dehydrator at less than 50ºC. Above all, eat grains in the form of liquid gruel, only soaked or just germinating grains. Always de-chemicalize the grains before using. Not all kinds of grain are *satvic*. Probably some kinds of rice such as red rice, *maha* sali rice and *basmati* rice, *ragi*, millet, blue maize from the Hopi Indians in North America, *quinoa* from South America, spelt wheat and *kamut* wheat from Egypt are the best grains.

The digestion of grains and grain products especially needs vitamins B1 and B2, niacin, pantothenic acid and biotin. The required vitamins and minerals have to be provided for the most part by articles of food, like fruit, vegetables, nuts and germinating grains, pulses and seeds. When we eat much bread and other such things, we lay the basis for all sorts of diseases. The digestion is disturbed etc.

The starch from grain products is difficult to digest. On the other hand the starch from potatoes is easy and quick to digest. Moreover, potatoes contain much water, several enzymes and many vitamins and minerals. Potatoes can even be eaten raw. If we eat sufficient fruit, vegetables, potatoes and germinated cereals, pulses and seeds, we have, in fact, no need of grain-products like bread, spaghetti, macaroni, *chapatis* and pancakes to fulfil our need of carbohydrates. Added to this, our body is able to convert proteins and fats into glucose and to store it in the form of glycogen in the liver. When it is needed, this glycogen is converted into glucose. Glucose is necessary as an energy-supplier (fuel). Energy is essential for a healthy life. We probably need about two hundred grams of carbohydrates per day. This produces 800 kcal.

Twenty five to fifty grams of protein per day equal 100 to 200 kcal. forty to eighty grams of fats per day equal 400 to 700 kcal. Together, this amounts to 1300 to 1700 kcal per day. Sathya Sai Baba says that an adult needs about 1500 kcal per day and young people 2000 kcal per day. Nowadays, most people eat far too much, sometimes up to 5000 kcal per day. According to Dutch food-tables, adults need between 2200 to 2500 kcal per day, young people between 2400 to 3000 kcal per day and people older than sixty-five about 1800 kcal per day.

Cereals have a number of disadvantages:

* All cereals, except maize, rice and some types of millet, contain gluten. Gluten can seriously affect the small intestine. Gluten aggravates schizophrenia. Cereals have an acid surplus.

* In bran is found phytin acid. This acid combines with zinc, iron, calcium and magnesium, making these metals unabsorbable by the body. A one-sided grain diet causes a shortage of these metals. A lack of zinc causes difficulties of growth, and a lack of calcium and magnesium causes the decalcifying of bones. But germinating of the whole grains neutralizes the phytin acid.

* In bran is found lectin. This substance can cause inflammation of the mucous membranes of the intestines. Bran contains fibres. Fibre induces a good bowel motion. Even so, this is not equivalent to the negative influence of lectin. There exists a special diet-bran without lectin.

* Especially in bran is found phytohemagglutinin. This substance causes a clotting of the red blood corpuscles.

* Cereals contain anti-trypsin and anti-chymotrypsin. These substances inhibit the activities of the corresponding enzymes trypsin and chymotrypsin.

* Wholemeal flour oxidizes fairly quickly. If flour is not kept cool and dry, it goes bad very quickly. All kinds of moulds and bacteria develop and small insects like corn weevils, meal moths and meal mites multiply rapidly. In order to eliminate the injurious substances from the whole grain, they are refined. Refined grain-product, however, consists exclusively of starch, which is injurious to health. Besides, refined grain-product does not give one the feeling that one has satisfied one's appetite, and this results in one eating far too much. White bread can be compared to refined sugar. Do not eat white bread. The preparation of bread demands high baking temperatures. Owing to this, many valuable nutritious substances, like proteins, vitamins and minerals, are destroyed for the greater part.

"Bread is dead, wholemeal bread as well," says Jan Dries. Bread is really *tamasic* food. Bread is absolutely not necessary. In natural nourishment bread is used very sparingly. It would be best not to eat baked bread at all. Bread can be combined with butter and vegetables, but absolutely not with milk, curds, cheese, meat, fish, eggs, sesame paste, nut pastes, peanut butter, chocolate, honey, jam, sugar or fruits.

* A very much disputed article of food is wholegrain rice or brown rice. The pellicle is very rich in fibres and in vitamins B1 and B2, but it also contains much phosphorus and sulphur; that is why wholegrain rice has a very high acid-surplus on the list of Dr. R. Berg. That is probably the reason why all over the world people eat hulled or white rice. Wholegrain rice may only be eaten very moderately and certainly not every day, otherwise we run the risk of getting rheumatic ailments. Rice may be used instead of potatoes for a change, especially in combination with vegetables. Rice may also be combined with sprouting pulses. Probably rice is the best of the cereals.

Raw honey is a good source of energy, some vitamins, minerals, and enzymes. Dark honeys contain more minerals than lighter varieties. Limit quantity to one or two tablespoons per day or less. Honey consists nearly completely of sugar.

20. Oils and Fats

We distinguish between simple lipids, such as fats, oil and waxes, compound lipids, such as phospholipids, glycolipids, sulfolipids, aminolipids and lipoproteins, and derived lipids, such as fatty acids, glycerol, cholesterol, etc. The lipids hardly dissolve in water or not at all; their transport through the blood takes place in the form of lipoproteins; these are combinations with proteins and other compounds. All animal foodstuffs contain cholesterol.

Oils and fats are composed of glycerol and fatty acids. The dietary fats contain about twenty fatty acids. We distinguish between saturated fatty acids, like stearic acid and palmitic acid, mono-unsaturated fatty acids, like oleic acid, and polyunsaturated fatty acids, like linoleic acid, a-linolenic acid and arachidonic acid. These three last-mentioned acids cannot be made by the body and, therefore, they are called essential fatty acids. All other fatty acids can be made by the body from carbohydrates and proteins. We probably need forty to eighty grams of fat per day.

We can classify oils and fats as follows:

* Animal fats. These fats almost exclusively contain saturated fatty acids.

* Milk fats, like butter and cream. Milk fats contain both saturated fatty acids and unsaturated fatty acids. Butter contains saturated fatty acids (60%), oleic acid (30%), linoleic acid (3,6%) and other fatty acids.

* Mother's milk contains almost exclusively saturated fatty acids and only a few polyunsaturated fatty acids.

* Vegetable oils and fats are, with some exceptions, rich in unsaturated fatty acids. Rich in polyunsaturated fatty acids are safflower oil, sunflower oil, soya bean oil and maize sprout oil. Olive oil is an excellent oil, it contains saturated fatty acids (14%), oleic acid (78%) and relatively few poly-unsaturated fatty acids (8%). Sesame oil has the reputation of being a particularly good oil. Linseed oil has a good effect on the stomach and the intestines. *Ayurveda* advises against the use of safflower oil.

Peroxidation (auto-oxidation) of lipids exposed to oxygen is responsible not only for deterioration of foods (rancidity) but also for damage to tissues, *in vivo* where it may cause cancer. The deleterious effects are initiated by the so-called free-radicals produced during peroxide formation from poly-unsaturated fatty acids. Lipid peroxidation is a chain reaction. That is why consumption of too many polyunsaturated fatty acids is harmful for health. Never fry with vegetable oils that are rich in polyunsaturated fatty acids. Use coconut oil, olive oil, ghee or butter for frying.

Use only vegetable oils of the first cold pressing (maximum 70° C) of biologically grown seeds. The second pressing goes quite as high as 180°C (hot pressing). In any case do not use extracted and refined oils. Avoid just as much margarine, also margarine from the health shop. margarine is *tamasic* food, dead food. it is only a short while ago that the cause of heart and vascular diseases was sought in the consumption of animal'fats, in particular in the consumption of saturated fatty acids. It has been proved that switching over to vegetable oils is insufficient to prevent heart and vascular diseases.

The consumption of meat, fish, refined sugar and grain-products made from white flour is much more harmful than the consumption of fats containing saturated fatty acids. So do not use these foodstuffs. Most animal fats fall automatically into disuse. Butter and cream may, indeed, be used in spite of the fact that they contain saturated fatty acids. As a matter of fact, mother's milk also contains saturated fatty acids. In much processed food, animal fats of a low quality are worked in. That is one of the reasons for avoiding processed foodstuffs. It is good to use cold-pressed oil, but it is still better to eat the oil-containing foodstuffs, like nuts, kernels and seeds. Olives are better than olive oil, etc. Oils and fats perform a number of functions:

* They protect and sustain the organs
* They form emulsions and lubricants
* Fats are a form of reserve-energy (fat depots)
* Fats are necessary for the nervous system
* Lipoproteins are important cellular constituents
* Several vitamins (A, D, E, F, K) dissolve in fats
* Fats provide plasticity to the body, especially to the skin.

21. Vitamins

If we eat sufficient fruit, nuts, vegetables and germinated cereals, pulses and seeds, we need, in fact, not worry about a shortage of vitamins. The same applies to minerals and trace elements. These foodstuffs contain all the well known vitamins and undoubtedly, still many more unknown vitamins and substances necessary for life. We do not know exactly what vitamins do. They are complex organic combinations which are, among other things, likely to work as enzymes (bio-catalysts). Vitamins work together and also with enzymes and hormones. Some vitamins have a protein structure. All of the water-soluble vitamins serve as co-enzymes or co-factors in enzymatic reactions.

Dr. H. M. Shelton says: "There is a great difference between natural vitamins and synthetic vitamins. Some synthetic vitamins are soluble in water, whereas similar natural vitamins do not dissolve in water. Synthetic vitamins may be regarded as drugs. Especially an over-consumption of synthetic vitamins may cause diseases."

The doctors and biochemists of the life-extension science endorse the great importance of good and natural food, but they state that in these days, with present-day environmental pollution, it is still necessary for the sick and the ageing to use extra vitamins, minerals, trace elements and other nutrients in the form of capsules or tablets. They say that certain limited quantities of these nutrients, even if they are synthetic, are not harmful, and that they can have a curative and rejuvenating effect. Probably, it is good to pay attention to the results of this science and to make use of these capsules or tablets with natural or synthetic nutrients when necessary. In any case, care must be taken with these supplemental vitamins, minerals, etc.

By heating food, most vitamins in it are totally or partly destroyed. Some vitamins go to pieces at freezing temperatures, by oxidation, too much sunlight, etc. With regard to vegetables, dark coloured vegetables contain more vitamins and minerals. The outermost leaves of lettuce, cabbage, celery, etc. contain more vitamins and minerals than the innermost leaves. For the formation of vitamins sunlight is exceedingly important. We distinguish two groups:

* Those vitamins soluble in fat, like vitamins A, D, E, F and K.
* Those vitamins soluble in water like vitamins B - complex and C.

We can give but only a very short description of the best-known vitamins:

* Vitamin A (retinal) and pro-vitamin A (b-carotene) occur in alfalfa sprouts and in all orange and yellow fruits and vegetables, especially carrots. It is also found in all the green parts of plants and milk products. This vitamin is particularly necessary for vision, reproduction, mucus secretion, and the maintenance of differentiated epithelia and for the growth processes of children. The loss of night vision is an early sign of vitamin A deficiency. A shortage causes drying up of the skin and mucous membranes, severe growth retardation (including that of the nervous system), glandular degeneration, and sterility. Because vitamin A can be stored in the liver, both acute and chronic toxicity many result from excessive intake.
* Vitamin D and pro-vitamin D are found in mushrooms, butter, cream, green vegetables, almonds, nuts, coconuts and sunflower seeds. In the sunlight, vitamin D is formed in the skin out of pro-vitamin D. Vitamin D is of vital importance to the bones and the teeth; it is essential for the absorption of calcium (Ca) and phosphorus (P). A shortage of vitamin D causes deformation of the bones; rickets is a childhood disorder. Vitamin D deficiency in the adult result in osteomalacia.
* Vitamin E (a-tocopherol). Six different kinds of vitamin E are known. It is found particularly in wheat germ, rice and cotton seeds and in beets, celery, cabbage, lettuce, soya beans, nuts and seeds, germinating cereals (especially wheat), vegetable oils and milk. Vitamin E is required in higher animals for fertility. Although there is no reliable evidence that vitamin E is necessary for human fertility, it is clear that a vitamin E deficient state exists in humans with severely impaired intestinal fat absorption. The signs of vitamin E deficiency in humans are muscular weakness, creatinuria and

fragile red blood corpuscles (erythrocytes). Vitamin E has at least two metabolic roles. It acts as nature's most potent fat-soluble anti-oxidant, and it plays a specific but imperfectly understood role in selenium metabolism. As an anti-oxidant, vitamin E appears to be the first line of defence against peroxidation of cellular and subcellular membrane lipids.

*   Vitamin F. To this vitamin belong the essential fatty acids and lecithins. The essential fatty acids are found in many vegetable oils and in maize, peanut, cotton seed, nuts and soya beans; a-linolenic acid, particularly in linseed oil and arachidonic acid in peanut oil. The essential fatty acids are necessary for the formation of prostaglandin's and leukotrienes. The leukotrienes cause vascular permeability and attraction and activation of leukocytes. A shortage causes inflammation of the skin and impaired transport of lipids.

*   Vitamin K is found in green plants and is required for blood clotting.

*   Vitamin B-complex. We already know of many and various kinds of vitamin B. The vitamins forming the B-complex family are of paramount importance to life. These vitamins are found in all cereals, pulses and seeds, especially in their husks and germs. All young sprouts, especially germinated cereals, pulses and seeds, contain many of them; also in leafy vegetables and dairy products. Because of their water-solubility, these vitamins can be excreted in urine and thus rarely accumulate in toxic concentrations. Deficiency diseases caused by the lack of a simple vitamin are rare; they frequently occur in the setting of a multiple vitamin deficiency state. In general, the lack of water-soluble vitamins affects tissues that are growing or metabolising rapidly in skin, blood, the digestive tract, and the nervous system. Vitamin B complex is essential to respiration, the conversion of carbohydrates and the nervous system.

*   Vitamin B1 (thiamine) is found in rice husk, cereal bran, nuts, leafy vegetables and fruits. It is essential to the metabolising of carbohydrates, the formation of glycogen in the liver, the metabolising of proteins, the synthesising of fats, the liquid balance, and the activity of the endocrine glands and the nervous system. A shortage causes a whole series of ailments, depressions and headaches.

* Vitamin B2 (riboflavin). This vitamin is found in fresh fruits, vegetables, nuts, seeds, germinating cereals, pulses and seeds, milk and yogurt. It is essential to the metabolising of carbohydrates and proteins. Horny, mat and very brittle nails, just like small ulcers in the corner of the mouth, and indicate a shortage of vitamin B2.

* Vitamin B5 (pantothenic acid), is found in fruit, cereals, pulses, potatoes and cauliflower. It occupies a key position in the metabolising of the carbohydrates, proteins and fats.

* Vitamin B6 (pyridoxine) is found in fruit, leafy vegetables, nuts and seeds, pulses, potatoes, cereals and milk. Essential to the metabolising of proteins, the nervous system and the skin. Pellagra is a frequent accompaniment of vitamin B6 deficiency.

* Vitamin B12 (cobalamin). It appears that this vitamin cannot be found in most plants but it is found in fermented leafy vegetables (sauerkraut), bean sprouts, dulse (sea vegetable) and wheat grass. It is plentiful in breast milk and also in cow's milk, meat and fish. A healthy intestine is able to produce this vitamin. Vitamin B 12 is essential to the making of read blood corpuscles. It is also necessary for metabolising of proteins, carbohydrates and fats and for the nervous system.

* Vitamin B15 and vitamin B17. They are important in the struggle against cancer. B15 is found in seeds and several nuts. B17 is found especially in the pips of apples and the stones of apricots, nectarines and plums and also in bitter almonds, cashew nuts, buckwheat, full rice, alfalfa, lentils and several grains.

* Folic acid. This is vitamin B. It is found in broccoli, spinach, endive, Brussels sprouts, beets, potatoes and fruits. Folic acid deficiency is probably the most common vitamin deficiency in the U.S.A.; it causes megaloblastic anemia.

*   Niacin (nicotinic acid, nicotinamide) is vitamin B. This vitamin is found in fruits, nuts, seeds, leafy vegetables, cereals, pulses and milk. A shortage causes inflammation of the skin (dermatitis), diarrhoea, mental disturbances, dementia and pellagra.
*   Biotin is also a vitamin B. This vitamin is found in full grain rice, potatoes, tomatoes, bananas, soya bean, yeast and milk. A large portion of the human biotin requirement is probably supplied from the intestinal bacteria. Biotin is necessary for the metabolism. A shortage causes dermatitis, drying-up of mucous membranes, and in some cases, immune deficiency diseases.
*   Vitamin C. This is the best known vitamin. We find this vitamin in abundance in all fruits and vegetables, grown in most regions. Vitamin C is essential to the building-up and maintenance of all organs and tissues. It promotes resistance against infections; it is the known remedy against scurvy and helps to regulate the respiratory system of the cell, hence its anti-cancer nature. The bioflavonoids are substances which cooperate with vitamin C; together with vitamin C they are called vitamin C-complex.

With the electron microscope scientists have discovered that the living cells in our body are very complicated and contain many different small organs (organelles). There are the ribosomes for the synthesis of proteins, the mitochondria for the production of energy and the lysosomes for the destruction and storage of residual products and toxic substances.

Unfortunately, the lysosomes have the weakest membranes, which can be destroyed by free radicals. Free radicals are atoms or molecules with an uncoupled electron and are formed when oxygen acts on substances such as polyunsaturated fatty acids (membrane lipids). If the membranes of the lysosomes break down, the powerful lysosome enzymes can cause DNA-damage and thereby early ageing and all kinds of illnesses. This process is accelerated by a premature decay of the hormonal system and the immune system (thymus, etc.). The so-called anti-oxidants protect the body against the free radicals. A healthy body produces anti-oxidants (enzymes) such as superoxide dismutase, catalase and glutathione peroxidase, and food can also supply anti-oxidants. Anti-oxidants are the vitamins A, b-carotene, B1, B5, B6, B12, C, E and K, the bioflavonoids, the amino-acid cystein, and the metals selenium and zinc. The production of free radicals is increased by overeating and by metals: lead (in petrol), mercury, nickel, cobalt, platinum, copper, cadmium, polonium, aluminium and local deposits of calcium. Life-extension science pays much attention to the free radicals and the anti-oxidants.

22. Life - Extention Science and Premature Ageing

The *Vedas* say that life span of man should be one hundred sixteen years. According to western life-extension science man can live for at least one hundred twenty years, healthily and happily. Premature ageing, and its culminating phase, senility, and also diseases like cancer, cardiovascular diseases, rheumatism and diseases of the digestive and nervous systems are caused by:

1. Stress and a wrong view of life
2. Smoking, drinking and using drugs (dope)
3. Over-eating
4. Eating meat, animal fat, fish, industrialized food and cooked food
5. Refined sugar, white bread, white macaroni, white spaghetti, white rice and too many grain-products
6. Frying with vegetable oils rich in polyunsaturated fatty acids, such as safflower oil, sunflower oil and maize sprout oil
7. Rancid fat and too much vegetable oil rich in polyunsaturated fatty acids
8. Eating too little fruit, vegetables, and nuts
9. Absorbing too few anti–oxidants (vitamins, enzymes, selenium and zinc)

And the consequence of this is also:
1. Damage of the cellular and subcellular membranes and all other cell parts by free radicals; DNA-damage by free radicals

2. Declining effectiveness of the DNA-repair enzymes
3. Cross-linking of protein molecules to bigger molecules under the influence of free radicals and calcium deposits
4. Accumulation of residual bodies in the body cells, especially in the cells of the nervous system, the heart-muscles, the liver and the skin. Residual bodies are lysosomes filled with indigestible toxic substances
5. Inefficient breathing
6. Insufficient energy production in the mitochondria in the cells
7. Cell calcification, hardening of the arteries and osteoporosis
8. Premature degeneration of the digestive system, the nervous system, the endocrine system and the immune system
9. X-rays and radioactive rays?

The most important function of the immune system is to control cybernetically the growth and repair of all body tissues. The second function is the defence against micro-organisms, such as bacteria, moulds and viruses, and also against poisons and cancer cells. In connection with ageing, the key organs are the hypothalamus, the pituitary, the gonads, the adrenal glands, the thyroid, the liver and the thymus, the central organ of the immune system. Stress leads to shrivelling of the thymus. To prevent and to cure diseases we need a strong and healthy immune system. Positive thoughts, feelings and emotions, the vitamins A, B -carotene, B-complex, C, D and E, a-linolenic acid, linoleic acid, and many minerals and trace elements like magnesium, iron, zinc, selenium, manganese, chromium and iodine, strengthen the immune system.

23. Minerals and Trace Elements

The minerals, which we need in very small quantity, are called trace elements or olig-elements. We use about fifty minerals. Of these minerals we can mention the metals, sodium (Na), potassium (K), calcium (Ca), magnesium (Mg), iron (Fe), and zinc (Zn), and the non-metals, chlorine (Cl), phosphorus (P) and sulphur (S). Trace elements are fluorine (F), iodine (J), selenium (Se), silicon (Si), manganese (Mn), copper (Cu), chromium (Cr), cobalt (Co), nickel (In) and tin (Sn). There are poisonous elements as well, like arsenic (As), cadmium (Cd), mercury (Hg) and lead (Pb). The required quantity of potassium is one to two grams per day; of the other required minerals, less than one gram per day, and of the trace elements, we need only very small quantities. If we eat sufficiently uncooked food we get enough minerals and trace elements.

Louis Kervran and Professor Baranga (Paris) have discovered that the human body has the capacity to transmute biologically one element into another, for instance, potassium into calcium.

Living plants consist of 70% to 90% water; the rest is dry substance. The dry substance consists of 90% organic compounds and only 10% of minerals. Yet these minerals play an important part in the whole system. Plants are the only living organisms able to well and easily absorb inactive minerals from the realm of inorganic compounds and fit them into a living, organic whole. For animals and men, it is very difficult to absorb minerals from mineral water and mineral tablets. Animals and men should eat plants in order to provide for their need of minerals. In man, shortage of minerals is mainly caused by:

* A badly functioning digestive tract through which minerals are not absorbed
* A shortage of vitamins, enzymes and co-enzymes
* The use of kitchen salt, which disturbs the sodium-potassium balance and, as a consequence, the water balance, which forms the basis of mineral balance. It is good to know that man eliminates about two and a half liters of water from his body per day, one and a half liters via urine, half a liter via the skin, half a litre via the lungs, and 150 grams in the faeces
* The use of processed food, refined sugar, white flour and alcohol
* The presence of phytin acid in food (cereals)

*   The use of certain medicines

Only when eating a sufficient diet and having a well-functioning digestive tract, can a sufficient absorption of minerals and trace elements be guaranteed. Man absorbs active minerals, that is to say, minerals of a living unit. Use mineral tablets with trace elements only in case of need. Too large quantities of these tablets can become disease producers.

The very common current methods of medical science are to fight against symptoms, which may cause difficulties. People with the shortage of a certain mineral are apt to use foodstuffs rich in that mineral. There is also a reciprocal connection between the minerals, the vitamins, and the enzymes. For example, when we use much sesame seed in cases of calcium shortage we disturb the calcareous regulation. Sesame seed does indeed contain much calcium, but it does not contain phosphorus, which is necessary. It can be used with nuts which contain calcium, magnesium and phosphorous, the three building blocks for our bones. Here follows a short description of a number of minerals:

*   *Calcium* (Ca). More and more people have problems with their backs, rheumatism, etc. at an ever younger age. The skeleton of modern man shows symptoms of decline already at the age of twenty-five. This is caused by the consumption of heated food, meat, fish, alcohol, refined sugar, chocolate and too many grain products. Bone is constantly being remodelled, as much as 700 mg of calcium may enter and leave the bones each day. The immediate source of new bone calcium is that which is present in body fluids and cells; this amount is small (<10 g) but critically important to the regulation of a large number of vital cellular activities: nerve and muscle function, hormonal activity and others.

Absorption is inhibited by compounds that form insoluble calcium salts (oxalates, phytates, phosphates) and by undigested fat through the formation of insoluble calcium soaps. Most of ingested calcium is not absorbed. Calcium deficiency causes tetanus and related muscle and neurologic disorders. Excessive intake may contribute to cancer. Sesame seed and sweet fruits are the best calcium suppliers besides potatoes, nuts, sea vegetables and milk-products. Spinach, beet tops, and rhubarb should be used rarely, if at all, because of their high content of oxalic acid, a calcium antagonist.

* *Magnesium* (Mg). This mineral plays a part in various metabolic processes, and especially in the nervous system. Five mg magnesium is necessary for the digestion of one-gram protein. There are as many as two hundred and fifty enzymes which become active only when magnesium is present. Malabsorption in chronic diarrhoea from any cause, protein malnutrition and alcoholism can result in magnesium deficiency. A shortage of magnesium causes depression, nervousness, heart and vascular diseases, stomach and intestinal ailments and muscle troubles. The best sources for magnesium are nuts, vegetables and fresh and dried fruits.

* *Phosphorus* (P) is essential. In practically all-metabolic processes it performs a function; it is a building block of the skeleton and is necessary for the blood, the liver, the nervous system and the brain. Nuts are good suppliers of phosphorus, but so are many vegetables, sea vegetables, sprouts, fruits and milk-products.

* *Sodium* (Na). Without sodium life is impossible. It plays a special part in the total metabolism, in the forming of blood and the forming of acid in the stomach. Sodium is the major metal of the extracellular fluid. The need for sodium is supplied by raw foodstuffs. Kitchen salt, sea salt as well, is a dangerous flavouring. It has a great effect on the water balance. Consequently, the secretion of water passes too slowly, and undigested food deposits and other by-products may accumulate in the tissues. Hypertension, and finally, a heart attack, are often the result of using too much salt.

* *Potassium* (K). What calcium is for the skeleton potassium is for the muscles. Potassium is the principal metal of the intracellular fluid. It plays a great part in the blood, in the water balance, the metabolism and for the nervous system. A shortage manifests itself by a fall-out of hair, bad teeth, brittle fingernails, stress, fatigue depression, muscular weakness, poor appetite, several metabolic problems and heart and vascular diseases. Stress stimulates the secretion of potassium by the kidneys which creates a vicious circle. When potassium intake falls below the minimal requirement extracellular alkalosis and intercellular acidosis occurs. Potassium is the friend of the heart and sodium is the enemy. Potassium is rejuvenator.

    A large number of old people suffer from a troubled potassium balance. With heart and vascular diseases, the sodium-potassium relation is most essential. Fruits contain much more potassium than sodium. Processed food, processed meat, fish, cheese and bread always contain much more sodium than potassium. Sodium keeps the water within the body and causes constipation. Diuretics and laxatives worsen the condition, for they also expel the potassium out of the body. Probably, the element potassium is involved in every disease. Man needs a large supply of potassium and relatively little sodium. Fresh and dried fruit, nuts and vegetables cope with this criterion. Potassium is, among other things, found in potatoes, apples, grapes, carrot, pulses and milk.

*   *Iron* (Fe) is found in haemoglobin and is for the absorption of oxygen. It prevents anaemia. Vitamin C promotes the absorption of iron. Parsley, lamb's lettuce, black salsify and spinach are the richest sources of iron. Asparagus, artichokes and kale are high in iron content. It is also found in bean sprouts, lentil sprouts, cereals, pulses, fruits, nuts, seeds and sea vegetables.

*   *Zinc* (Zn) is also very important. It is found in nuts, seeds, whole grains, legumes, figs, dates, avocados and potatoes. There are two dozen known zinc metallo-enzymes; therefore a deficiency of zinc is accompanied by multi-system dysfunction. Significant quantities of zinc can be lost in sweat, particularly in the tropics. Zinc deficiency can occur in diseases characterised by dermatological, gastrointestinal and neuropsychiatric signs; it can also cause growth retardation.

*   *Selenium* (Se) is an integral component of the enzyme glutathione peroxidase, an anti-oxidant that provides a second line of defence against peroxidation of cellular and subcellular membrane lipids. Vitamin E forms the first line. Selenium spares vitamin E. Selenium intake is highly dependent upon the soil in which the foodstuffs are grown. Selenium deficiency causes a dilatation of the heart and the resulting congestive heart failure. Selenium is required for normal pancreatic function. The coconut is rich in selenium.

* *Manganese* (Mn) is present in several manganese metalloenzymes. It is required for superoxide dismutase activity (antioxidant) and the metabolism. It is widely distributed in nuts, cereals and vegetables.

* *Chromium* (Cr) plays a functional role in glucose metabolism and plasma lipoprotein metabolism. Most cereals contain chromium.

* *Iodine* (I) is necessary for the thyroid hormones (thyroxine), which are important for general metabolism, development, and tissue differentiation. Iodine deficiency causes goitre, retardation of the life-processes and diminution of the oxygen absorption. Sources for iodine are sea vegetables (dulse and kelp), wheatgrass, spinach, potatoes, milk, vegetables, broccoli, carrots, fruit and sunflower seeds.

* *Sulphur* (S) is present in amino-acids. There is little knowledge about the need for sulphur. Onions, garlic and garden-cress contain some toxic sulphur compounds.

24. Rough Fibrins

Fibrins consist of fibres of plants (cell walls). These substances are found in all fruit, leafy, stalky, root and tuberous plants (vegetables), nuts, cereals, pulses, kernels and seeds. The animal foodstuffs do not contain fibrins and processed food only contains few or no fibrins. Fibrins are made up of cellulose, lignin, pentose, pectin and gummy substances. Undigested, they pass through the stomach and the small intestine.

Human food should be rich in fibrins. We need forty to sixty grams of fibrins per day. Fruit and vegetables are the best sources of fibrins. An evenly balanced diet consists of 80% fruit and vegetables. Any one who has a feeling of being in need of extra fibrins should take dried fruit as the best nourishment. This contains plenty of fibrins. Dried fruit should always be soaked in pure water for six to twelve hours. Diet-bran can also be used; this is bran which does not contain flour remains nor a number of other harmful substances. It is good to soak this bran first. Fibrins have a number of good qualities:

* They absorb water. They improve the action of the large intestine. The contents of the intestine become voluminous. The stool passes more easily. In the case of a shortage of fibrins, stool elimination is difficult, the faeces become hard. Owing to this, we strain, and become vulnerable to heart attacks or cerebral haemorrhages.
* They shorten the transit time. Bad food together with few fibrins cause a transit time of two to three days, sometimes even a few weeks.
* Fibrins absorb toxins, especially in the rectum.
* In the small and large intestine they act upon cholesterol and glycocholic acids.
* Fibrins have a great effect upon the feeling of being satisfied. Consequently, the appetite is slowed down. And then it is easy to eat moderately. By cooking, the fibrins are smashed and their activity has come to nothing. A shortage causes various diseases.

25. Fruit and Nuts, A Nourishment of Full Value

Fruit and nuts belong to the best *satvic* food, provided they are eaten in moderation. Fruit purifies the body, restores the water balance and stimulates the absorption of oxygen. Fruit has a alkahine-surplus and is rich in vitamins, minerals, trace elements, fibrins, enzymes, monosaccharides, fruit acids (citric acid, etc.) and pure water. Per hectare the fruit culture yields by far the most; banana culture as much as a hundredfold wheat culture. Besides, nuts are rich in protein and fats.

It is said that our ancestors were fruit eaters and that modern man still has the digestive tract of a fruit eater. The Greeks and Romans ate much fruit. The Romans even planted fruit trees on top of their houses. We can distinguish between plain fruit and fruit rich in fat, such as avocados, olives, nuts and seeds. Ripe fruit is the best digestible food. When we eat only fruit and nuts we need at least one and a half kilograms per day.

Freshly gathered and biological, that is to say, grown without artificial manure, insecticides, growing-substances and other chemicals, not genetically manipulated fruit, is the best fruit there is. Fruit from its own region is important. Unfortunately, many sorts of fruit in Europe, are very much 'improved'. Owing to this they have a very low bio-energetic value and an even lower food value. Subtropical and tropical fruit have great value. Bananas should be eaten when they are ripe. Yellow bananas are not yet ripe, wich should have brown spots. Avoid, as much as possible, fruit that has not been grown biologically.

Of course, we can also choose a fruit and vegetable diet, a fruit and nut, plus vegetable diet, a fruit-grain-dairy food diet, or a fruit and vegetable plus grain diet.

When people abruptly switch over to a fruit diet or a fruit and nut diet, the toxins heaped up during many years are then liberated all at once, too rapidly, causing poisoning. Headache, nausea, wind, cold shivers, fever etc., can appear. Suppressed diseases can break out again. That is why, preferably, we should switch over gradually. As a support, we can also drink purifying herbal teas, like stinging nettle tea, birchleaf tea, elder blossom tea or lime tree blossom tea. And also take sufficient bodily exercise, fresh air with regular bathing.

26. One Two or Three Meals Per Day

Sathya Sai Baba often repeats the pronouncement that a *yogi* takes one meal a day, whereas a *bhogi*, or a person who enjoys life, takes two meals per day and a *rogi*, or a sick man, takes three meals per day.

In the book *The Gospel of Peace of the Essenes*, Dr. E. B. Szekely quotes Jesus: "Trouble not the work of the angels in your body by eating often. For I tell you truly, he who eats more than twice in the day does in himself the work of evil. And the angels of God leave his body, and soon evil will take possession of it. Eat only when the sun is highest in the heaven, and again when it is set. And you will never see disease, for such finds favour in the eyes of the Lord. And forget not that every seventh day is holy and consecrated to God. On six days feed your body with the gifts of the Earthly Mother, but on the seventh day sanctify your body for your Heavenly Father. And on the seventh day eat not any earthly food, but live only upon the words of God."

Both the Greeks and the Romans, at the height of their power, only ate one meal per day. The Romans took this meal in the cool of the evening. Ever since Moses' time down to the beginning of our era, the Jews ate as a rule only one meal per day; besides, they sometimes took a lunch of fruit. During a period of more than one thousand years, it was the law of civilized peoples all round the Mediterranean to have one meal per day. The decline of the Roman Empire coincided with giving up this rule. Several naturopaths propagate two meals per day, one meal about noon and the second meal towards the evening.

27. Fasting

Sathya Sai Baba states that it is good to fast one day in the week, and then to exclusively drink pure water. Fasting is abstaining from food of one's own free will, except water. When only fruit juices or vegetable juices are taken we speak of purification cures. Fasting is an absolutely natural method and an old religious custom in all cultures. It is probably the oldest method of curing diseases; it was a method employed over ten thousand years ago. A sick or wounded animal withdraws and fasts till it has regained its health. Healthy people can fast in order to purify body and mind, and sick people just to heal. For sick people especially it is best to have themselves attended to by an experienced fasting therapeutist. Healthy people can do without the help of a therapeutist if they have informed themselves about the fasting procedure they are to pursue and the possible complications.

A fasting cure for sick people usually lasts from twenty-one days to six weeks. Healthy people are advised to fast for no longer than one or two weeks. Pregnant women are dissuaded from fasting, as are those with a number of diseases, like heart and vascular diseases, lung diseases and diabetes, or those with mental instability. There is probably no method which is more suitable for purifying the body. All accumulated refuse-substances and toxins and sick cells are removed. The blood pressure is normalized, the nervous system is stabilized and resistance against infections is much increased.

Just as a fruit diet liberates too many toxins causing rebirth of suppressed diseases (as for instance with antibiotics) by fasting sensory and mental faculties are improved. The control of the sense organs and the mind is increased. Fasting is the best and fastest method for breaking through drug addition.

A fasting cure should be preceded by at least two fruit days, by eating apples and oranges, pineapple, kiwi and honeydew melon so that during fasting the glycogen stock in the liver, the fat deposits and the protein reserves are used up. Especially in the beginning there is an excessive formation of urine; the loss of weight is mostly 300 to 600 grams per day. During a fasting cure one can use a water enema at body temperature. Dr. H. M. Shelton is a believer in this. Others are opposed to water enemas.

The Essenes thought it necessary to purify the intestines while fasting. During fasting one should rest sufficiently. Not too much walking, but regular air and sun-baths and water-baths of about 37ºC (body temperature). The water bath temperature should not be higher when fasting; a higher temperature can strain the heart. The end of a fasting period is announced by a pure tongue, a fresh breath, a shining skin, clean intestinal rinse, etc.

The most delicate moment of a fasting period is the so-called breaking of the fast. The first day after fasting, one may slowly eat an apple in the afternoon. A different method on the first day is to take a little bit of orange juice every hour. The second day two fruit meals can be taken, etc. Purifying cures (one to two weeks) can be performed with fruit and vegetable juices and herbal teas (camomile, stinging nettle, etc.), five times 200 cc of juice per day. We know the grape cure for the kidneys and the nervous system, the black current cure for kidney and metabolic troubles, the bilberry cure for diarrhoea or other intestinal problems, the cherry cure for heart and vascular diseases, the carrot juice cure and the orange juice cure for intestinal ailments, and the pineapple cure for stomach and intestinal complaints.

28. A Few Instructions and Recipes

In most of the following recipes, especially in the sauces, the soups and the vegetable dishes, you can use in moderation (not more than half a teaspoon) *satvic* spices and herbs such as coriander, cumin, ginger and turmeric (do not heat them, use them raw). Never use *rajasic* and *tamasic* spices and herbs such as *asafoetida*, black pepper, cayenne, cinnamon, cloves, mustard, nutmeg and tamarind (use them only for medicinal purposes, see part C of this appendix).

In the morning hours, it is best to have nothing at all or only fruits and fruit juices. Fresh fruit is better than dried fruit. Never use sulphurated dried fruit; and before eating them, let dried fruits like dried apricots, prunes and raisins always soak well for about six to twelve hours in pure water. Soaked raisins are good sweeteners. Soaked figs are very tasty as well. Also, when eating fruit, the food combinations should be kept in mind. Never eat too much fruit at the same time. As a rule, do not combine more than three kinds of fruit. The best way is always to eat one kind of fruit at a time, then wait half an hour or longer before taking the next kind of fruit.

Fruit whipped cream

For fruit meals at midday and/or in the evening, most kinds of fruit can well be combined with unsweetened whipped cream, about forty grams of whipped cream per person. Fruit rich in sugar forms difficult combinations with whipped cream. Melons cannot be combined. Apart from a little bit of protein and milk sugar (lactose), whipped cream contains 36% fat.

Fruit yogurt

All kinds of fruit, except melons, combine well with yogurt. In saying this, we especially think of yogurt which is prepared from uncooked biological milk at a low temperature. A deep plate with about 250 grams of yogurt and small pieces of fruit forms a good meal. You can, if necessary, add some whipped cream, and at the same time, some honey and some vegetable oil may be added.

Fruit curds

Curds and cheese combine well with sour and half-sour fruit, but they form a bad combination with sweet fruits, melons, honey and whipped cream. Curd or soft cheese is easy to digest and contains ten to fourteen per cent protein. It is made by letting the milk go sour and by separating the curds from the liquid (whey). We prefer home-made, skimmed milk curds. It is easy to prepare it yourself. You can add a little vegetable oil to a fruit curds dish. It is possible to use cheese instead of curds, but only with skimmed milk young cheese or ripe cheese, not with fat or old cheese by any means.

Fruit nuts

Nuts can be combined well with sour or half-sour fruits, but not with sweet fruits, melon, honey and whipped cream.

Volume for one person: 40 grams of almonds, 10 grams of walnuts, 4 big sweet tangerines. Soak the almonds for about eight hours and the walnuts for about three hours in pure water. Do not forget to refresh the water for de-chemicalizing. Then remove the brown skin from the almonds. Before removing the skin it is useful to put the almonds first in warm water (40C) for about ten minutes. Get the pips out of the tangerines and mix two tangerines together with the almonds in a kitchen-blender. Then put the pulp on a plate and mix it with the two other tangerines which, in the meantime, you have cut into pieces. Garnish the plate with walnuts.or : from the preceding example replace the tangerines by a half or a third part of a pineapple or cut half a melon and a mango into pieces. Cover this with four tablespoons of a freshly ground coconut. Grind with the help of a kitchen-blender.

Raw soups

Easy to digest, raw soup is a delightful addition to any meal. All kinds of raw soups can be prepared, like cauliflower soup, vegetable soup, tomato soup, carrot soup, etc. They are easy to make. Besides water the following ingredients can be used: fresh potato juice (juicer) in order to thicken the soup, vegetables, some herbs, a little bit of vegetable oil, butter or ghee, and if required a little bit of kelp powder, tamari or seasalt. Cut up the vegetables and the herbs as finely as possible. Use, if possible, fresh herbs, otherwise dried herbs will do. Suitable to eat are: parsley, celery, dill, thyme, borage, lavender, rosemary, mint, sage, savory and lavas (Lavisticum officinale). Fresh herbs are much better than dried herbs. During winter you may use warmed but not boiled water. Alternatively, you may pour the soup into a heat-resistant glass container and place it in hot water until it is warmed. Preserve the enzymes and vitamins in the soup by preventing direct contact with the heat source. If you use avocados, take only ripe ones. First, warm the water, then dissolve a little bit of kelp powder, tamari or seasalt in it and add the herbs. If using fresh potato juice, the temperature must be rather high and the juice must be added rapidly (before it turns brown). Stir and finally add the vegetables. The soup should be eaten at body temperature.

An example: Tomato soup

Ingredients for two persons: One to two cups of water, four to eight tomatoes, one teaspoon of jaggery or unrefined cane sugar, some herbs like basil, celery, parsley, lavas (*Lavisticum officinale*), thyme, sage, rosemary and cumin, a small dollop of olive oil and a little bit of kelp powder, tamari or seasalt. Remove the skins from the tomatoes by plunging them into hot water for some seconds (as short as possible). Mix all ingredients in a kitchen-blender and put the mixture into warm water. Keep the soup warm (body temperature). Garnish the soup with chopped parsley and celery and a small dollop of creamery butter or ghee.

A second example: Potato soup

Ingredients for two persons: Four cups of warm water, four to eight potatoes, ten to fifty grams of creamery butter or olive oil, a little bit of kelp powder, tamari or seasalt, some herbs, and if required, one teaspoon of cumin ground by yourself. Steam the potatoes in their jackets for five minutes; after that remove the jackets. Mix all ingredients in a kitchen-blender. If using fresh potato juice, the juice must be added rapidly to the mixture of the other ingredients. If required, add some raw vegetables; the vegetables should be cut up as finely as possible. You can use endive, spinach, cauliflower, cucumber, paprika, etc.

Vegetable dishes

Here we have innumerable possibilities. Of course, we prefer uncooked (biologically grown) vegetables, but half-steamed and half-cooked vegetables can be used as well, especially during the switch-over period from cooked food to uncooked food. Especially in the beginning it is necessary to be very careful with uncooked vegetables. They are rather difficult to digest and they can cause various intestinal troubles. Therefore, it is necessary to chop all raw vegetables very well and preferably eat them together with the potato pulp or mashed potatoes and, later on, possibly, with grated raw potatoes. They can also be eaten with half-cooked rice, and later on, with raw rice, which should be soaked for 24 - 48 hours or, for instance, with millet (soaked for 24 hours). After soaking for 24 - 48 hours, five minutes of cooking is sufficient to get half-cooked rice. Do not forget to refresh the water for de-chemicalization. Use only the best kinds of rice or millet available.

Leafy and stalky vegetables form good combinations with starchy vegetables, potatoes, cereals, bread, rice, olives and avocado, nuts and seeds, germinating cereals, pulses and seeds, whipped cream, yogurt, buttermilk, curds, butter, ghee and cold-pressed vegetable oils like olive oil, sesame oil and sunflower oil.

Starchy vegetables are fairly difficult to combine with protein foods, sugar, tomatoes and fruit; they only combine well with leafy and stalky vegetables, mushrooms, lactic acid vegetables, yogurt, buttermilk, potatoes, cereals, bread, macaroni, spaghetti, *chapati*, oils and fats.

Combine leafy and stalky vegetables either with starchy foods or protein foods, for these two kinds of foods are bad to combine with each other. So for instance, combine them either with potatoes or with yogurt, but not with both. What has been said in the fruit recipes about whipped cream, yogurt, curds, cheese and nuts can also be applied to vegetable meals at noon and in the evening.

The available varieties of potato are mostly grown using a variety of chemical aids, like fertilizers, insecticides and pesticides. Hence, always use biologically grown potatoes. Per person we can use 200 to 300 grams potatoes per meal. Besides uncooked biological milk, free of pathogenic germs, germinating wheat or rye and nuts, the uncooked biologically grown potato plays an important part in the food-therapy of the well known Danish natural physician, Dr. K.Nolfi. The uncooked potato is a remedy, especially for heart diseases, stomach complaints, kidney diseases, rheumatic ailments and cancer. Besides much water the potato contains starch (10% to 22%) which is very easy to digest, 1% to 2% protein, 1% to 2% fibrins and various enzymes. In addition to this, the uncooked potato is rich in vitamins B-complex, A, K, F and C (22 milligrams per 100 grams), further calcium, phosphorus and magnesium (important for the skeleton and the teeth) and aluminium, arsenic, bismuth, gold, cobalt, nickel, iron, silver and zinc. In a ripened potato is found only a little solanine which, in small quantities, has a curative power; in large quantities it is poisonous. Eat potatoes regularly.

In cooking much of the nutritional value is lost, many vitamins are destroyed, and minerals become organically disconnected. In fact, it will be clear that uncooked potatoes are better than cooked potatoes. At least, we can have a few raw potato pieces with our vegetable meals. The potato pulp is nearest to uncooked potatoes. To make it, first peel and slice the potatoes very thinly, then grind them in a kitchen-blender. Put the ground potatoes immediately into boiling water while stirring and put out the heat as soon as possible. Never cook them.

For preparing mashed potatoes it is best to steam the potatoes in their jackets for five minutes. Before steaming them, cut the potatoes into pieces and, after steaming, remove their jackets. Do not prepare the puree with milk but with boiling hot water and creamery butter. Steamed potatoes can also be eaten without making them into a puree. Never cook potatoes with household salt, but use herbs like ground dill leaves, or if required a little bit of kelp powder or seasalt. Never eat fried potatoes. Oils and fats which are heated over 180°C are thought to cause cancer. With potatoes and vegetables you can eat butter or ghee (clarified butter).

Oil sauces and herbal oil sauces

With vegetables as a binding agent, you can use oil sauces or herbal oil sauces. It is possible to sprinkle the vegetables with a little cold-pressed oil, like olive, sesame or sunflower oil. The term 'cold-pressed' is misleading, for the kernels and seeds are mostly steamed and pressed with the help of filter-presses at a temperature of 60 to 90°C. Hot-pressed oil is pressed at still greater temperatures (180°C). In fact, cold-pressed oil is no longer raw food. That is why Dr. K. Nolfi and Dr. Ann Wigmore do not use 'cold-pressed' oil in their food therapies. The normal requirement of fat is probably 40-80 grams per day.

An example: simple salad dressing

Ingredients for two persons: two tablespoons of vegetable oil, a teaspoon of savory, a teaspoon of thyme, a teaspoon of sage, a teaspoon of rosemary, two teaspoons of unrefined cane sugar (dried cane juice), a teaspoon of lemon juice and a cup of grated cucumber. Grind all the ingredients and mix them in a kitchen-blender.

A second example: paprika sauce

Ingredients for two persons: one large red paprika, two to four tablespoons of sesame oil, two teaspoons of lavas (*Lavisticum Officinale*), two teaspoons of savory, a teaspoon of thyme, a teaspoon of sage, a teaspoon of rosemary, a little bit of ground cumin seed, two teaspoons of unrefined cane sugar, a teaspoon lemon juice and, if required, some seasalt. Peel the paprika and remove the pips from the paprika. Grind all ingredients and mix them in a kitchen-blender. In order to thicken the sauce, a large potato cut into pieces can be steamed for five minutes and after having removed the peels, together with a dollop of butter and hot water, mashed in a blender; then mix this puree with the sauce.

Cumin potato sauce

Ingredients for two persons: two large potatoes, some butter, two teaspoons of ground cumin seeds, half a teaspoon of savory, half a teaspoon of rosemary, a teaspoon of lavas (*Lavisticum officinale*), a teaspoon of unrefined cane sugar and, if required, a little bit of seasalt. Cut up the potatoes into pieces and steam them for five minutes. Then remove the peels. Now mash the potatoes in a blender together with a dollop of butter and some boiling hot water. Mix the puree with the chopped herbs and the ground cumin seed.

Home-made sauerkraut (without salt)

Ingredients: Two large heads of cabbage, a small handful a caraway seeds, a few stalks of whole dill and or two teaspoons of dill seeds, finely ground, one teaspoon of celery seeds, finely ground, and one or two slices of whole-wheat bread of the most wholesome variety. Wrap one or two slices of whole-wheat bread in cheesecloth and place this at the bottom of a crock or pot made of glass, stoneware or stainless steel, but not of alminium or other metal. Shred over the slice(s) of bread the two heads of cabbage and sprinkle at intervals the other ingredients. Fill the container to cover the cabbage with pure, fresh, tepid water. Put a plate over the cabbage and a stone on the plate to weigh it down. Cover the container with a cloth and put in a warm place. If a little mould forms in a few days, it may be lifted off very carefully. In 1–2 weeks the sauerkraut will be ready. The juice may be drained off. Refrigerate the sauerkraut immediately in cheesecloth-covered glass containers. It must be eaten within two weeks.

It is recommended to eat 100 gram of sauerkraut daily. Home-made sauerkraut is very wholesome. Due to its lactic fermentation and cellulose content sauerkraut stimulates the growth of friendly, useful intestinal bacteria. Vege-kraut is sauerkraut with other vegetables added, preferably red cabbage, carrots, cauliflower, celery, and beets.

Growing and juicing wheatgrass

Use plastic trays or boxes and spread an even layer of a mixture of compost and good topsoil 3 cm deep at the bottom. For a 25 x 35 cm tray you need one small cup of dry grains of wheat. Before planting, the soak the grains of wheat for twelve hours and let them germinate for 12 - 24 hours. Spread the germinated grains on top of the soil. Water the tray, cover it with another tray or some dark material and set aside for 2 - 3 days. After that put it in indirect light. Keep it moist. Harvest wheat grass with a sharp knife or a pair of scissors when it reaches 18 - 25 cm in height, cutting as close to the roots as possible. If you have harvested the wheatgrass once or twice you can recycle the mat of roots and soil into compost.

The wheat grass should be juiced immediately after cutting. There are special wheatgrass juicers. Do not drink too much, especially in the beginning. You can start with 25 - 50 grams a time. In the healing regimen, the 25 - 50 grams can be taken three to four times a day, always on an empty or nearly empty stomach.

The most sane and direct approach we have towards finding the fountain of youth, to life extension and rejuvenation is through proper nutrition, utilizing potent foods like wheatgrass and germinating cereals, pulses and seeds and moderate exercise. Wheatgrass is a super nutritive.

Wheat grass juice contains:
- Seventeen amino-acids with all eight essential amino acids
- Hundreds of enzymes. They are life energy itself. Enzymes are especially vital to the blood cleansing. The most important enzymes in wheatgrass are: Cytochrome oxidase (anti-oxidant), lipase, protease, amylase, cattalos, peroxidase, transhydrogenase and superoxide dismutase (anti-oxidant, anti-enzyme)
- A lot of chlorophyll (concentrated sunpower)
- Oxygen
- The natural anti-oxidants vitamin C, E and pro-vitamin A
- Many B vitamins (including B17), vitamin F and K
- Bioflavonoids, compounds related to vitamins (vitamin C-complex)
- Sodium (Na), potassium (K), calcium (Ca), magnesium (Mg), iron (Fe) and many trace elements
- P4D1 stimulates the natural repair of DNA

Wheat grass juice protects us against environmental hazards, such as air pollution. Wheatgrass can prevent both free radicals and lipofuscin pigments (in brain cells) from accumulating and doing their damage (ageing, dementia). Wheatgrass may be used as a rejuvenator. Read Dr. Ann Wigmore's book, "The Wheatgrass Book."

Essene bread

Ingredients: One to two cups wheat, barley or rye or any combination of the three. Half a teaspoon ground caraway seeds or two teaspoons kelp. Soak the grain twelve hours; germinate for 24 - 48 hours until sprout is the length of the grain. Grind the germinated grains and add caraway seeds or kelp. Spread batter

1/2 cm thick on an oiled tray (olive oil). The batter may be thicker. Dry in the sun, a food-dehydrator or an oven at less than 50C. You can make many Essene bread variations, with other cereals and with finely chopped vegetables, herbs, germinated lentils, etc.

Raw rice porridge

Soak 100 grams *basmati* rice for forty eight hours. Refresh the water after twenty four hours. Grind the rice with some fresh warm tepid water in a blender and add a little honey or unrefined cane sugar. It is also possible to add some butter or ghee. This recipe is only for people with a healthy digestive system!

Ice-cream

Run frozen fruit through high-speed juicer and serve immediately. You can use frozen bananas, mangoes, peaches, strawberries, etc.

Some remarks:-

- Avocados, bananas, figs, grapes and mangoes contain a lot of enzymes. All melons are excellent foods and valuable for their vitamins, minerals, sugars and pure water.
- Dried fruit, such as dried apricots, prunes and raisins, contain a lot of minerals (also iron and zinc). Dried prunes are very rich in iron and silicon.
- Cruciferous vegetables, such as broccoli, cabbage, cauliflower, brussels sprouts and turnips, contain protecting substances against cancer (Wiener & Gooses, 1983).
- Parsley, stinging nettle, dandelion and garlic (against infections) are important herbs.
- The almond is the king of nuts.
- Black sesame seeds are best.
- Sunflower seeds are rich in enzymes and contain all the essential amino-acids (25% of its full weight), all the essential polyunsaturated fatty acids, all the known minerals, many trace elements and all the vitamins except vitamin C. Sunflower greens (10 cm cultivated in earth) and buckwheat lettuce is the most nutritious greens available. Cultivate them in an indoor garden.

Flaxseed has the highest vitamin E content of any known seed, excels in complete bulk fibre, is mucilaginous for easy digestion, is high in complete protein and is rich in minerals. Flaxseeds are good for the colon; they strengthen lung tissue and promote the healing of the lung membranes. They are excellent for chronic, degenerative lung disorders. They have similar properties to sesame seeds, particularly for strengthening the bones.

- Jaggery powder and primeval sweetener made from unrefined cane sugar (such as Panellist from South America) are good sweeteners.
- Kelp and dulse are miracle foods containing all of the trace elements and other elements we know of. They are rich in iodine (I). Use kelp powder instead of salt in foods.
- Miso and tamari are made mainly from fermented soya, kozi and unrefined sea salt. In her book, *The Wheatgrass Book* Ann Wigmore says: "While studies have indicated that inorganic minerals can be taken into the body and will serve a specified function, you need to take about ten to twenty times more of them to get the same effect as from organic mineral salts. To meet your bodies mineral needs I recommend you get salts from wheat grass and other live foods. When using inorganic minerals, you run a greater risk of upsetting the delicate balance of mineral salts and reaping chaos internally."
- Spirulina is a natural combination of essential vitamins and minerals.
- Brewers yeast tablets contain vitamin B1 (thiamine), vitamin B2 (riboflavin) and vitamin B3 (niacin).
- Green (or white) clay is a powerful detoxifying substance with a number of healing effects. It absorbs a lot of substances that are harmful to the body and prevents bacteria and parasites from reproducing themselves. All you have to do is to take in clay daily for the length of the normal life cycle of the bacterium or parasite (usually for a few weeks). The body can also assimilate some minerals out of the clay. Clay applied as a

cataplasm attaches itself to the skin and sucks out any substances that are alien or harmful to the body. All forms of diarrhoea are stopped in a few hours by the intake of a few Spoonfuls of green or white clay. Use white clay for babies and infants. Clay can be used in the fight against cancer and other serious diseases (HugoHymens, Belgium).

- Antibiotics kill the intestinal bacteria that ensure a good digestion and remove all the vitamins of the vitamin B complex from your liver, causing depressions, nervousness, etc. Several people taking many antibiotics end their days in mental hospitals. Forty tablets of brewers yeast and half a litre of yoghurt (made from raw milk) daily, together with clay (daily seven times two full teaspoons of clay), vitamin C and static food are sufficient to cure a completely depleted liver in three weeks. In consequence of this, depressions and anxiety can miraculously disappear. Constipation must be avoided at all costs when taking a lot of clay (Hugo Hymens, Belgium).
- *Chapatis* better than rolls, common bread, macaroni and spaghetti. They are only heated a short time and can be made just before meal-time and eaten while warm.
- Everyone is unique. The needs of our bodies are different and changeable, so everybody has to find out which foods are the best for him or her, when and where.
- Hygiene is very important. For hygienic reasons it is sometimes necessary to cook the food.

29. Living Food and Motherhood

Should a pregnant woman eat natural, living food? Yes, of course! Pregnancy is a special experience and is a great responsibility. In pregnancy special consciousness of the needs of the mother and child is required. The mother should have optimum health. This can be guaranteed through good food, sufficient rest, bodily exercise, fresh air and sunlight, and a healthy, good attitude to life.

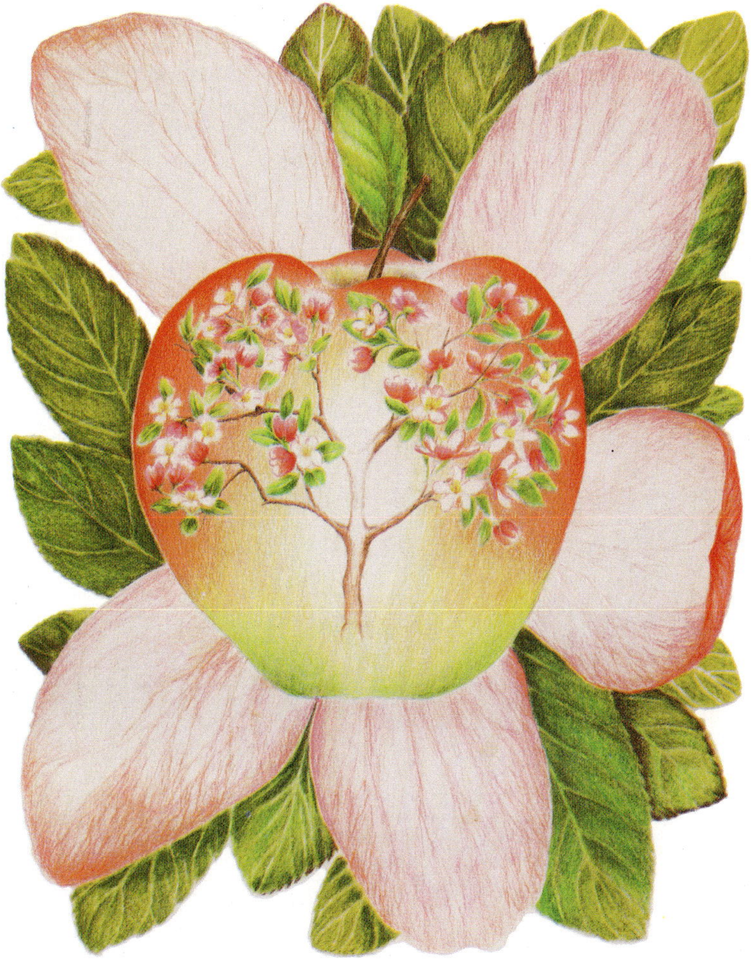

In ample time beforehand, six or more months before the start of the pregnancy, a woman's health should be brought to its optimum level. However, it is never too late. Also, during pregnancy, eating habits can be improved carefully step by step. Special attention must be given to the inclination of eating too much. Eating too much and wrong food combinations cause a shortage of calcium, too. Useful calcium is found in sufficient quantities in germinating sesame seeds, nuts, sweet fruit, potatoes, cabbage, lettuce, sea vegetables and figs.

That the natural and ideal food of a baby is its own mother's milk is so obvious it hardly needs stressing. Human milk is peculiarly and specifically adapted to the needs of the human infant. Especially the first time, mother's milk contains large quantities of antibodies against various diseases. One of the most important factors in assuring an adequate milk supply, is the mother's diet. Mother's milk is readily affected by tobacco, alcohol, coffee, tea, chocolate, narcotics and nearly all drugs. That is why they should be avoided. If mothers are healthy, without stress and worries, if they feed themselves properly and give adequate attention to essential details, the milk glands of nearly all of them can be brought to the required degree of activity.

The advice is to give exclusively mother's milk during the first year. After that, supplemental food, such as fresh fruit juices or cow's milk or goat's milk may be started. Breast-fed babies have a better start in life. Give your baby mother's milk as long as possible. Dr. H. M. Shelton says: "I hold that the natural nursing period of the human infant ranges from three to five years, depending on whether it is born in the tropics or in the far north. Even after the child is eating other foods, it should still be receiving its milk supply from its mother's breasts."

The best substitute for mother's milk, and the best supplementary food is fresh fruit juice. Grape juice and orange juice are specially recommended. Give milk and juice at different times. Fruit juice can be given very well between breast-feedings.

Other substitutes for mother's milk are cow's milk and goat's milk; they can also be used as supplementary food, if required, alternated with fresh fruit juices. Never give artificial baby foods; they are dead foods. No other except milk and fruit juices should be given to the child for the first eighteen months of its life. At about eighteen months of age soft fruits may, however, be added to the diet. Beginning with the second year, fruits, nuts and vegetables may be added to the child's diet. Vegetables may be given raw or half-cooked, preferably raw.

No starchy foods or cereals should be given under two years. Dr. Tilden says: "It is a mistake to feed starchy food too soon, before the end of the second year. Children under two or three years of age have trouble in converting starch into sugar. They should get their sugar from fruits! Many of the troubles from which children suffer are due to the practice of feeding them starchy food." Meat should never be fed to a child under six years of age and, better, never at all. For the physical and mental health of the children, it is very important to give them the correct food.

30. Bodily Exercise, Fresh Air, Bathing and Sunlight

For a good functioning of all the bodily-cycles, the heart and blood circulation, it is all-important to combine good eating habits with necessary bodily exercise. Of all possible bodily exercises, walking, especially walking fast, bicycling, and swimming are excellent activities. Harvey and Marilyn Diamond recommend jumping elastically on a mini-trampoline. The ideal time for these exercises is early in the morning. The minimum necessary is a quick walk of twenty minutes. A walk in the woods, along the seaside or a cycling-tour performs wonders for our health.

It is of paramount importance to sleep with an open window at night. During this time the body removes a lot of water and toxins through breathing and the skin; when the body gets fresh air it can function effectively. Taking a bath or a shower once or twice a day is very good. We can look upon the sun as the source of life. The rays of light, the heat-rays and other rays of the sun are indispensable to plants, animals and men. All foods that grow above ground in the sun are superior to food that grows underground, a fact known to the ancients. Try, when the sun is shining, to stay in the open air for half an hour.

C. AYURVEDA AND THE WESTERN NATUROPATHY

1. A Comparison

In opposition to western naturopathy, *ayurveda* does not accept health-care without spirituality. *Ayurveda* and western naturopathy agree that the best health-care is self-care. *Ayurveda* emphasizes that correct diet is the essence of self-care, and that wrong diet is the main physical causative factor of disease. It states that things we do for ourselves, such as giving up wrong foods, and overcoming negative emotions like anger, fear and worry, will do more for our health in the long run than taking many medicines and consulting various doctors. Spiritual discipline, rest and silence, diet, herbs and simple exercises (*yogasanas*) are the most important medicines of *ayurveda*. Sathya Sai Baba has said, "In the past, illness was cured by simple remedies provided by nature, rest, regulation of diet and spiritual discipline."

Western naturopathy says that most diseases are caused by the accumulations of toxins and the deficiency of our nutritional requirements, such as enzymes, vitamins and minerals. *Ayurveda* is not as concerned with enzymes, vitamins, minerals and other nutritious substances, as with the energetics of food. According to *ayurveda*, foods can be classified according to different degrees of increase or reduction of the three biological humours and the three qualities, *satva*, *rajas* and *tamas*, in man. *Ayurvedic* regimes keep us in harmony with the cosmic life forces and qualities, with the universe and with God.

According to *ayurveda*, though mental and physical diseases are of many kinds, and pathogens are of many varieties, all are products of disharmonies of the three biological humours *vata, pitta and kapha*. The classification of diseases and the identification of pathogens are considered to be of secondary importance. *Ayurveda* does not treat symptoms, but deals with the underlying causes. In balancing the humours, it deals with the the root of the disease process is cut off.

Generally, all the mental and physical diseases an individual is prone to can be treated through methods of balancing the three humours. One method of balancing the three humours is to move from their *tamasic* and *rajasic* sides to their *satvic* side. This should be done with a *satvic* diet, originally devised for the purification of the mind, and the practice of *yoga*. A *satvic* diet is very important in the treatment of mental disorders, but also in the treatment of most modern so-called physical diseases. These physical diseases are mostly very strongly related to psychological factors. A *satvic* diet aids in the tonification and rebuilding of higher quality tissue in the body. Eating *satvic* food is tantamount to purification of the mind and healing of the body by balancing the humours, removing the toxins supplying nutritional requirements, and strengthening the immune system.

Most diseases arise from poor or wrong functioning of the digestive system. A *satvic* diet is important, but also the right functioning of the digestive fire *(agni)*. *Ayurveda* emphasizes the importance of *agni*. *Agni* not only absorbs nutrients, but also destroys any pathogens. Undigested food becomes like a pathogen in the body, breeding toxins and upsetting the immune system. The digestive fire should also be fed and cared for to give it the power to adequately digest the food. Hence, in *ayurveda*, regulating *agni* is considered a root treatment for most diseases. *Ayurveda* says that spices and herbs are usually the best thing for increasing *agni*. Spices and herbs are also best for destroying accumulations of toxins *(ama)*. *Ama* blocks the functioning of *agni* and the assimilation of nutrients. In western naturopathy little attention is being paid to the use of spices and herbs.

Ayurveda and western naturopathy agree that the modern lifestyle is deleterious to health. Modern life is excessively *rajasic*. We are always preoccupied with one thing or another and entertaining ourselves with reading, television, all kinds of sports and travelling. We do not have time for heart-to-heart communication and for silence, peace and prayer. When we grow old we become more and more *tamasic*. The number of demented people is increasing and is becoming a great problem in modern society.

The food we eat is predominantly *rajasic* and *tamasic*. Generally speaking, *rajasic* food aggravates *vata and pitta*, *tamasic* food increases *kapha* and *ama* (toxins). The mass media as a whole has an influence that strongly aggravates *vata*. Watching television, reading newspapers and magazines, talking and doing business during meals are very bad habits. Meals should not be taken when excessively nervous, thoughtful or worried. Mind-altering drugs, stimulants, weight reduction pills and most medicinal drugs, such as pain-relieving drugs are strongly disruptive.

The great majority of our activities increase *vata*. Sitting in front of a computer all day and playing computer games aggravates *vata*. Rock music disturbs the nervous system and aggravates *vata*. A number of New Age practices such as channelling, wrong meditational practices and excessive imagination can increase *vata*. Frequent travelling, particularly by airplanes, fast forms of sports and excessive running aggravates *vata*.

2. The Living Foods Lifestyle of Dr. Ann Wigmore

Dr. Ann Wigmore teaches in her institutes in America her 'living foods lifestyle.'[+] According to her, enzymes are probably the most important nutritious substances. Hundreds of enzymes are already known. The functions of enzymes are infinite: digesting

---

+ Dr. Ann Wigmore, Rebuild your Health with High Energy Enzyme Nourishment (See Reference 48)

food, fighting infection, rebuilding the body, etc. The human body can manufacture all kinds of enzymes when it is healthy; in living food there are many enzymes.

Dr. Ann Wigmore claims that all kinds of 'incurable' diseases such as AIDS, cancer, heart diseases, diabetes, arthritis, allergies and all forms of depression can be healed with her living foods lifestyle method. She says, "Because of the unprecedented severe digestive and assimilation problems that now exist, the average person cannot digest raw food. Foods such as hard root vegetables, tough fibrous vegetables and ungerminated grains, nuts and seeds are indigestible. Therefore the living foods lifestyle incorporates these foods through special preparations such as germinating, fermentation and blending with rejuvelac for easy digestion. Food should never be cooked or fried. You may have noticed that I no longer advocate juicing, except for wheatgrass and watermelon juice. Juices can be too cleansing for most people's bodies which have become extremely toxic from environmental and dietary abuse. Blend instead. The whole food contains fibres and nutritious factors found in the pulp which is discarded when juicing."

Dr. Ann Wigmore advocates the use of the blender as a means to help the body assimilate nourishment and the use of rejuvelac made from germinated wheat. She states that the most important key in getting back to health is to use blended foods in small amounts frequently throughout the day; eating nutritionally balanced food in a blended form is a big help to the digestive system and also to the immune system. Blending is more efficient than simple chewing and mixing in the stomach. Blended foods can restore health much more quickly than eating the foods as salads. Her key foods are wheat grass juice, rejuvelac and 'energy soup'. Energy soup is a complete meal containing every nutrient in a balanced form that the body needs.

Rejuvelac

Rejuvelac is a very nutritious fermented beverage and one of the best aids for digestion. It contains many enzymes, vitamins

B, C and E, and healthy bacteria which enables the colon to function properly. The high vitamin E content in rejuvelac acts as an anti-oxidant. To make rejuvelac, cover two-day-old germinated wheat seeds with twice their volume of water. After standing for two days at room temperature, pour off the formed rejuvelac into another jar. The germinated wheat seeds can be recovered with water, and allowed to stand one additional day for another batch, and this can be repeated once more. Good rejuvelac is a cloudy, and very faintly yellow liquid. It has a tart lemon-like flavour, tinged with a doughy yeasty flavour. The very best rejuvelac is slightly carbonated. Make everyday fresh rejuvelac. Rejuvelac has remarkable capacities; it can even help to correct candida problems. It is important to rinse the wheat seeds twice a day while they are germinating to ensure that mould does not grow.

Some people are allergic to foods and fear that certain foods such as wheat will cause bad reactions. In thirty-five years, Dr. Ann Wigmore has never known one person to have an allergic reaction to wheat (or other foods) when it is uncooked, germinated and given in an easy-to-digest form. As a matter of fact, allergies are extremely misunderstood. Most people see allergies as simply an intolerance to substances like dust, pollen or certain foods. People do not realise that allergies are severe digestive disorders resulting from a lack of enzymes and a faulty state of the digestive fire (*ayurveda*). It is believed that over ninety per cent of the population in the West suffers from 'allergies'.

Energy soup

One of the most important aspects about energy soup (blended soup) is that it is easy to digest, which is so vital for those suffering from allergies, or, shall we say, digestive difficulties. In the living foods lifestyle programme, blended soups and drinks are the main source of nutrition at every meal of the day. It is possible to eat nothing else. However, especially when starting the transition to the living foods lifestyle, salads, sauerkraut, soaked almonds, etc. can provide variety, as an occasional supplement to the blended foods. Making blended soups and drinks is a matter of individual creativity. Every soup or drink can have a different combination of ingredients. The only difference between soup and a drink is its thickness. It is important to blend the ingredients in the right order; otherwise it is possible that some foods will not be well blended. First of all, put in all the ingredients that are tough and are the hardest to break down together with rejuvelac or other liquid. Be aware of your food combining, avoid all wrong food combinations! The energy soup of Dr. Ann Wigmore has the following basic ingredients:

- a little seaweed such as dulse or kelp (for minerals and trace elements),
- rejuvelac (it prevents energy soup from oxidizing),
- alfalfa and germinated mung beans, lentils and green peas (all together one handfull per meal),
- A variety of greens and vegetables (in moderation). Buckwheat and sunflower baby greens are best. Also watercress, celery, parsley, endive, spinach, kale, etc.,
- One or two peeled apples or some watermelon (including rind), or some Papaya. Apples mix well with vegetables in a blended recipe. You can also use sweet potatoes.

Occasionally you can use in the energy soup:
- potatoes and carrots,
- sweeteners such as a little raw honey, jaggery, soaked raisins, soaked prunes, dates, etc.
- thickeners such as avocado and soaked almonds (never eat avocado and nuts or other seeds in the same meal).
- other vegetables ingredients (no-milk-products) such as germinated grains and sesame seed.

Consume blended soups and drinks immediately. They will not keep for more than a few hours, even when refrigerated. Dr. Ann Wigmore never uses milk and milk products and other non-vegetrian food stuffs.

- For breakfast Dr. Ann Wigmore suggests to take some simple combinations of fruit or watermelon juice or germinated buckwheat cereal. Energy soup is the main dish for lunch and dinner. She does not pay much attention to spices and herbs. She advises against strong spices and herbs and recommends mild flavours. To my mind her living foods lifestyle could be improved considerably by correctly applying *ayurvedic* spices and herbs.

3. Ayurvedic Spices and Herbs

It is said: "Where the herbs are gathered together like kings in an assembly, there the doctor is called a sage who destroys evil, and averts disease." Spices and herbs are like subtle foods. In small dose they are like strong food supplements. *Ayurveda* teaches that almost everyone should take spices and herbs on a regular basis; they are part of our necessary foodstuffs.

Herbal therapy requires the support of proper food to be effective. Diet can enhance, neutralize or counter the effect of spices and herbs. It may take a month or more of a natural remedy, particularly in treating a long-standing complaint, to have a noticeable effect. It may take several months to notice major changes.

Ayurveda offers the largest variety of herbal preparations of any herbal tradition. Not only must we have the right diagnosis and right prescription to adequately treat a disease, the herbs must also have the right potency. Many old or commercially-prepared herbs may lack this. In some respects it is misleading to speak of the general properties of an herb. These vary according to the way in which the herb is grown, prepared and combined. Miraculous powers can be found in very ordinary herbs when they are specially grown and prepared. Fresh herbs have a special power. Home-grown herbs, cultivated with love and wisdom, possess much more healing power. Wild herbs are best. The right combination of herbs allows the individual herbs to function synergistically. Many *mantras* can be used for potentiating herbs. The *mantra Om* is generally used. Mediums such as ghee or honey can help to direct the effects of herbs.

According to *ayurveda*, the digestive fire (*agni*) is central to health. When the digestive fire is normal, there is good digestion, circulation and complexion, adequate energy and a strong immune system. When the digestive fire is abnormal, there is poor digestion, poor circulation and bad complexion, offensive body odour, flatulence, constipation, low energy and poor resistance to disease.

The digestive fire has four states: high, low, variable and balanced. The digestive fire (*agni*) is usually high in *pitta* types with excessive appetite. *Pitta* usually have types with a strong circulation, but the stool, will tend to be loose with some diarrhoea. Their resistance to disease is generally good, but when they occur, diseases are apt to be sudden and severe. *Agni* is usually low in *kapha* types, with poor appetite and a tendency to gain weight. There will be excess mucus, bloating and congestion; diseases are not often severe. *Agni* is usually variable in *vata* types, with periods of strong appetite, alternating with loss of appetite. Gas distention and constipation are usually signs of variable *agni*. Circulation is also variable, as is resistance to diseases.

Ayurveda says that spices are usually the best thing for increasing the digestive fire, for destroying accumulations of toxins from indigestion, and for inhibiting the formation of *ama*. Hence, the right intake of spices can be a major aid in the treatment of most diseases. *Ama* is opposite in properties to the digestive fire, and serves to block its functioning. *Ama* not only tends to cause disease, it also blocks the assimilation of nutrients. For detoxification the deep-rooted toxins should be burnt up, particularly with the very hot spices, such as cayenne, black pepper, long pepper, ginger, asafoetida, and mustard. Most of these spices are *rajasic*, only ginger is *satvic*. Here we need a very good *ayurvedic* doctor or a lot of wisdom, otherwise the treatment may do more harm than good. The *satvic* spices cardamom, coriander, cumin, fennel and turmeric are also helpful for detoxification. Sometimes chillies together with ghee, are used.

When the digestive fire is high, spices should generally be avoided. When the digestive fire is low, all kinds of spices can be taken, but preferably *satvic* spices. When the digestive fire is variable, some spices such as cumin and ginger can be taken. When the digestive fire is normal, mild *satvic* spices – cardamom, coriander, fennel, turmeric - can be taken to maintain balance. Always use spices in moderation and knowledgeably.

Sometimes it may be necessary to use *rajasic* and *tamasic* spices, herbs or foods and even allopathic medicines to cure the body, but we must realize that at the same time the mind becomes more *rajasic* and *tamasic*. After the required changes have been brought about, we should purify the mind by eating *satvic* food and through other spiritual methods.

Ghee (clarified butter) is good for restoring vitality, nourishing the nerves and improving *ojas* the essential energy of the body. Ghee is prepared by heating one kilogram of raw, unsalted butter on a medium fire for about half an hour (yield of ghee: 800 g). The butter will melt and start to boil. As it boils, foam will rise to the surface. Do not remove this foam for it contains medicinal properties. Turn the fire to low. When a drop or two of water placed in the ghee produces a cracking sound, the ghee is ready. The finished ghee should be golden-coloured and clear. Let it cool slightly and then pour it through a strainer into a container. Ghee may be stored without refrigeration.

Ghee is regarded as much easier to digest than butter and less mucus-forming. Ghee is *satvic*, promotes intelligence and perception. According to *ayurveda*, the best oils are ghee and sesame oil. Unrefined sesame oil, coconut oil and olive oil are *satvic*. *Ojas* literally means vigour. It is not a physical substance. We could say it is something like the essential energy of the immune system. *Ojas* is replenished by special foods like milk and ghee, and by special tonic herbs like *ashwagandha*, *shatavari* and *guduchi*.

Cardamom, coriander, cumin, fennel, ginger and turmeric are *satvic*. Most other spices such as asafoetida, black pepper, cayenne, cinnamon, cloves and mustard are *rajasic*. Tamarind is *rajasic* and *tamasic*. Sathya Sai Baba has literally said, "Indians use a lot of tamarind which is detrimental to health." Nutmeg and valerian are *tamasic*.

Satvic herbs are: holy basil (*tulsi*), *bhringaraj*, calamus, camomile, celery, gotu kola *guggul*, *jatamansi*, lotus, mint, rose, saffron, sandalwood and *shankhapushpi*.

Satvic rejuvenative herbs are: aloe gel, *amalaki*, *ashwagandha*, astragalus, comfrey root, ginseng, *guduchi*, *haritaki* and *shatavari*.

Satvic herbal jellies (*rasayanas*, *rejuvenators*) are *Brahma rasayan chyavan prash*, *ashwagandha* compound, *shatavari* compound, *shilajit* and *triphala*.

Chillies, garlic, onions and radishes are *rajasic* and *tamasic*. During an interview, Sathya Sai Baba said that garlic is better than eggs the latter being *rajasic*. All cabbage family plants and most beans are *rajasic*. Mushrooms are said to be *tamasic*.

Satvic spices can help balance the effect of too much fruit and dairy products. According to the sages of ancient India, milk is an ideal food for children when taken properly and balanced with the right spices. In addition, milk (raw, fresh, biological and free of germs), especially cow's milk, is considered to be the best rejuvenator and vitalizer. Unfortunately most milk is pasteurized and therefore *tamasic*. Dairy products are *ama*-increasing and mucus-forming, particularly when pasteurized. When you have no other choice you can add mucus-decreasing spices such as cardamom and ginger to make the milk more digestible. Warm milk is a good mild sedative promoting sleep. Yogurt is best taken mixed with fresh cucumber and spices such as cumin and coriander. Cheese is the most mucus-forming of all dairy products; here, cumin can be helpful.

Children may use *satvic* spices and herbs; the dosage is less with the child's age. For old people, *satvic* spices and herbs, especially *rasayanas*, are good. Balding and greying of the hair are part of the aging process. Its treatment involves *satvic* food and herbs, especially milk, almonds, sesame seeds and herbs such as *amalaki, ashwaganda, bhringaraj* and gotu kola. For retaining the memory and revitalizing the brains cells *Brahma rasayan and* gotu kola are excellent.

4. Some Special Satvic Spices and Herbs

Spices and herbs should be cultivated without fertilizers and other chemicals and should not be irradiated, otherwise they will not be *satvic*. They are used in dishes and in *ayurvedic* medicines. The other ingredients for *ayurvedic* medicines such as ghee, raw sugar or honey should also be *satvic*.

Turmeric (rhizome). It is said that turmeric bestows the energy of the Divine Mother and purifies the *chakras* and the channels of the subtle body. It is good for the practice of *hatha yoga*. In India, turmeric is called the kitchen queen. It can be used in most sauces, soups and vegetable dishes. Do not heat the turmeric but use it raw. Half a teaspoon is not too much. It has many curative qualities. It is antiseptic and an excellent natural antibiotic. Turmeric purifies the blood and promotes the right metabolism in the body. It helps the pancreas and the spleen, and helps improve the intestinal flora. Be careful in case of pregnancy, acute jaundice and hepatitis.

Coriander (seed, plant). This spice can also be used in many dishes, half a teaspoon is not too much. Do not heat the coriander. It increases digestion and absorption and is good for diarrhoea and dysentery. Coriander, cumin and fennel seeds have similar properties and are often used together for digestive disorders. Coriander helps the kidneys. Cumin is good for the stomach.

Fennel (seed). Raw, unheated fennel seeds can be taken after meals. Fennel seeds are one of the best spices for digestion, increasing the digestive fire without aggravating *pitta*, stopping cramping and reducing flatulence. They are good for digestive weaknesses in children or in the elderly. They are calming to the nerves and they promote mental alertness. They can also help promote menstruation, and milk flow for nursing mothers. Fennel is a good general spice for all constitutions.

Ginger (rhizome). This spice can also be used in many dishes. It is perhaps the best and most *satvic* of the spices; it is called the 'universal medicine'. Ginger can be used in digestive, respiratory and arthritic diseases. It relieves gas and cramps in the intestines. It is a tonic to the heart. Fresh ginger is especially good for deranged *vata*. Dry ginger promotes discharge of phlegm and mucus from the lungs and throat better than fresh ginger does. Be careful in case of inflammatory skin diseases and high fever.

Cardamom (seed). Cardamom powder can be used in several dishes. Do not heat it, but use it raw. Cardamom is one of the best and safest digestive stimulants. It helps the spleen and removes excess *kapha* from the lungs and stomach. It is good for opening and soothing the flow of the *pranas* in the body and clarifies the mind. It gives joy.

Basil (herb). Holy basil *(tulsi)* is one of the most sacred plants in India; it is devoted to Vishnu. It is said that holy basil augments faith and compassion, love and devotion. It clears the *aura* and makes the immune system stronger. Basil removes excess *kapha* from the lungs and excess *vata* from the colon. It increases memory. Basil can be taken as a tea with honey for promoting clarity of mind. Do not boil the tea; add the basil to boiling hot water and infuse it for fifteen or twenty minutes. The fresh herb can be used in many dishes; do not heat it but use it raw.

Camomile (herb, flower). Camomile tea is very popular; a little ginger improves this tea. Used in moderation it is good for all constitutions. It helps relieve digestive headaches, it sedates nerve pain and it strengthens the eyes. Camomile is very balancing to the emotions.

Mint (herb). There are three main mints, peppermint, spearmint and horsemint. They have a mild soothing action on the digestive and nervous system. They help relax the body and clear the senses and the mind. Peppermint is the best mint to improve digestion.

Peppermint tea and spearmint tea are good for all constitutions. Be careful in case of neurasthenia.

Aloe (gel). Aloe is a rejuvenator. It bestows joy. It brings about the renewal of the female nature. Aloe gel is a wonderful tonic for the liver, the spleen, the blood and the female reproductive system. It tonifies all digestive enzymes of the body. Take two teaspoons three times a day, together with a pinch of turmeric, as a general tonic. It can be taken mixed with water or apple juice. Aloe powder is a powerful laxative; use it only in small amounts. Be careful in case of pregnancy.

Triphala (*rasayana*). *Triphala* a combination of the three fruits, *amalaki*, *bibhitaki* and *haritaki*, is one of the best medicines emerging from India. It is the safest and most strengthening of the purgative herbs. *Triphala* cleanses the bowels of all toxins and improves the digestive fire. It has a strengthening effect on the deeper tissues.

Triphala is a balanced *rasayana*. *Amalaki* is a rejuvenator for *pitta* and the basis for *chyavan prash*, that is the main all-round tonic and rejuvenator in *ayurvedic* medicine. *Bibhitaki* is a rejuvenator for *kapha*, *haritaki* for *vata*. *Haritaki* feeds the brain and the nerves, promotes intelligence, vision and voice, and aids longevity.

Gotu kola (rejuvenative herb). Gotu kola is perhaps the most spiritual and *satvic* of all herbs. It is used by *yogis* to improve meditation. It helps balance the left and right hemispheres of the brain. *Gotu kola* is the main revitalizing herb for the nerves and braincells. It increases intelligence, memory and longevity; it decreases senility and aging.

Gotu kola fortifies the immune system and strengthens the adrenals. It is a powerful blood purifier. It is called *brahmi* as it aids knowledge of *Brahman*, the Supreme Reality. Gotu kola is good for all constitutions, and it is the basis for *Brahma rasayana*. Be careful because large doses may cause headaches or temporary loss of consciousness.

Ashwagandha (root). *Ashwagandha* is the best rejuvenative herb, particularly for the muscles, marrow and semen and for *vata* constitution. It is used in all conditions of weakness and tissue deficiency in children, the elderly, those debilitated by chronic diseases, those suffering from lack of sleep or nervous exhaustion. *Ashwagandha* inhibits ageing and is one of the best herbs for the mind. It regenerates the hormonal system. *Ashwagandha* has similar properties as *ginseng*, yet it is far less expensive.

Shatavari is the main *ayurvedic* rejuvenator for the female as is *ashwagandha* for the male; *shatavari* is a *rasayana* for *pitta* constitution. *Ashwagandha* is good for weak pregnant women.

5. Purification and Cure

In summary, we can say that the causes of disease may be: 1.Dearth of spirituality, 2. *karmic* causes, 3. negative emotions, feelings and thoughts, 4. disequilibrium of the three *gunas*, 5. imbalance of the three biological humours, 6. accumulations of toxins (toxemia), 7. deficiencies of enzymes, vitamins, minerals, etc., 8. bacteria and viruses. In *ayurveda* it is said that most diseases arise from poor or wrong functioning of the digestive system. *Kapha* diseases arise in the stomach, *pitta* diseases in the small intestine and *vata* diseases (all nervous disorders) in the colon. That is why the cleansing of the gastric-intestinal canal is very important.

A *satvic* diet can cleanse the gastric-intestinal canal but usually slowly. In many cases it will be necessary to make use of stronger purification methods simultaneously. Several western naturopaths think that all problems with the digestive system result in serious problems with the colon and that all diseases originate in the colon. They say that most colons really do resemble a sewage system loaded with impacted, putrefying decay, toxic gas, toxic material, noxious bacteria and parasites.

Dr. Ann Wigmore believes that less than five per cent of the American population has healthy colons and that over ninety per cent has parasites. When the colon does not eliminate regularly and efficiently - there should be an elimination for every meal that is eaten - impacted material begins to harden on the walls of the colon. Autopsies have confirmed that a colon can carry from a few pounds to thirty-five pounds of hardened material. In that case the colon cannot absorb nutrients properly and various highly toxic substances are absorbed into the bloodstream.

Even diarrhoea can be a sign of constipation due to the fact that hardened material is preventing the proper working of the colon. Dr. Ann Wigmore advocates the use of enemas, wheatgrass juice implants and colonics for loosening hardened material and for detoxifying and bringing the colon back to health. A colonic is a continuous enema given by a professional therapist. Everyone can use enemas and wheatgrass juice implants. Wheatgrass juice implants should be taken only after the colon has been cleaned with a water enema. Use an enema bag that can hold up to two quarts of water. Take two to three of these size bags of water at one enema session. Some people have found it beneficial to lie on their left side when the water is first entering the descending colon and after that to lie on their right side when the water is entering the ascending colon. You can take an enema once a day for a long period. In fact, it is extremely important to cleanse the colon when you change to a healthy lifestyle with *satvic* food. It is also important to help the colon back to its natural position through exercises. Rebounding on a mini- trampoline can be particularly effective for helping shape the abdomen muscles. Bicycling and walking are also excellent for the colon. One of the most beneficial things for your colon is squatting. Squatting is our natural position for elimination.

In *ayurveda* there are many different methods given to cleanse the body and the mind.[+] Keep in mind that body and mind have a strong interaction. All *ayurvedic* methods can be defined under two groups, reduction or elimination therapies and tonification or supplementation therapies. Reduction methods decrease excesses

---

+ Dr. David Frawley, *Ayurvedic Healing, A Comprehensive Guide* (See Reference 16)

in the body and are indicated for accumulations of toxins, aggravated humours and overweight; they are especially suitable in the acute stage of disease. Reduction methods are also employed to eliminate deep-seated toxins, as part of a disease prevention, internal cleansing programme. In *ayurveda* reduction therapy has three parts:

1. Palliation or preliminary, mild detoxification therapy. Palliation therapy consists of an anti-toxin diet (*satvic* diet), spices and herbs for stimulating the digestive fire and for burning up toxins, fasting, exercises, sunbathing and exposure to wind. Palliation methods are for reducing *ama* (deep-seated toxins) and calming the humours by separating them from *ama*.

2. Oleation and sweating therapies to help bring the aggravated humours into the digestive tract for elimination. If they are not eliminated after these therapies, they will be reabsorbed and go back into the tissues. Oleation therapy is mainly concerned with the application of oil, not with body massage. After adequate preliminary detoxification for some weeks, a period of daily oil application and sweating therapy should be done for at least one week for health maintenance and a longer period for treatment of severe diseases. Large amounts of warm sesame oil are applied all over the body. At the same time oils are taken internally (mostly ghee). Many of the same effects of short-period intense oil massage can be gained by mild daily application of oils over a long period of time. Sweating is usually done in a sweat box; saunas, warm baths or showers can also be used. Oils can also be applied to special parts of the body such as the forehead, the top of the head and the feet, followed by a warm shower; this can be done to treat insomnia. Giving a warm sesame oil massage to a child is very good. It calms its nervous system and increases the child's feeling of being nurtured and cared for.

3. Purification or detoxification therapy (*pancha karma*) for removing excess humours from the body. It cannot be done without the proper preparation. Purification therapy is indicated when the

aggravated humours are in the gastro-intestinal canal. If the aggravated humours are lodged in the tissues or mixed with toxins, they cannot be directly eliminated; in that case palliation methods and oleation and sweating therapies must first be applied. Purification therapy is said to consist of five parts: cleansing enemas, purgation, therapeutic vomiting, nasal application of herbs and blood-letting. Cleansing enemas are used to dispel high *vata* from its site in the colon. Purgation is used to eliminate high *pitta* from the small intestine. Most of *pancha karma* is a clinical practice but several of its methods can be used as part of self-care.

Ayurveda brings clarity into detoxification programmes. Many of the *ayurvedic* methods are also used in western naturopathy, but not so systematically. It will depend on your state of health which path you have to follow so as to be able to switch over to *satvic* food in the best possible way, and to give nature all scope to heal you completely.

If you are relatively healthy, it will probably be sufficient to use an *anti-ama* (*satvic* diet), spices and herbs, cleansing enemas with pure water, wheatgrass juice or decoctions with herbs and oils, one or two cleansing colonics and some purgatives such as *triphala* or gel. Wheatgrass juice implants - keep them in your colon as long as possible - are also very beneficial; they cleanse and nourish various parts of the digestive system. Except for the colonics, it can all be done by yourself and is excellent self-care.

Colonics can be helpful but they are not advisable for the weak, emaciated, tired or those suffering from nervous system disorders. A colonic should be followed up by spices and herbs to promote digestion, as it strongly reduces the digestive fire. Purgative herbs have the same effects as colonics.

Tonification therapies nourish deficiencies in the body and are indicated for tissue weakness and underweight; they are specially indicated in chronic disease, in convalescence, malnutrition and in states of nervous exhaustion or after reduction therapies have been used. The usual rule is first to reduce and then to tonify. The main tonification method is dietary: rich, nutritive, *satvic* food, along with spices and herbs, external and internal oleation therapy, tonifying enemas (oils and herbs), mild massage, rest and relaxation.

Rejuvenation or *rasayana* therapy is a special form of tonification therapy. Rejuvenation therapy properly follows deep cleansing and the elimination of the excess humours from the body. The *rasayanas* are *satvic* herbs. Spiritual therapy, the four medicines of Sathya Sai Baba, includes the use of *rasayanas*. It is said that the *rasayanas* harmonize the functions of the body by modulating the neuro-endocrine-immune system. Treatment with the four medicines of Sathya Sai Baba (SSSB) is the most effective integrated treatment for all mental and physical diseases, also for those diseases in which the immune system and emotional problems are involved. In *ayurveda*, surgery is well known, but it is only applied when it is thought absolutely necessary.

In the West, life-extension scientists endorse the great importance of good and natural food (*satvic* food), but they state that in these days, with present-day environmental pollution, it is necessary for the sick and the old to use extra vitamins, minerals and trace elements (tablets). As already said, green (or white) clay is a powerful detoxifying substance. Hugo Symens (Belgium) combined all this knowledge to develop his miracle treatment. He claims that all kinds of incurable diseases such as cancer, heart and vascular diseases, arthritis, allergies and all forms of depression can be healed with his 'miracle treatment'. In most cases an amelioration of some sort becomes evident almost instantaneously after starting the treatment. Even patients with terminal cancers are cured in a period which seldom exceeds three months. Hugo Symens makes use of *sativc* food, a lot of clay, a lot of vitamin C (powder) and tablets of brewers yeast, kelp, spirulina, vitamins and minerals. He emphasizes the importance of raw, fresh, biological milk free of germs and the milk-products yogurt and buttermilk prepared from that milk at a low temperature (lower than 37°C), all produced in very hygienic circumstances.

6. Correct Breathing, A Straight Back and Correct Singing

All western and eastern musical systems state that correct breathing forms the basis for the training of a good musician. The Indian music of the *Vedic* era, which is called *Ghandarva Ana* or heavenly music, attaches great value to breathing. Correct breathing is of paramount importance for physical and mental health. The respiration does not only see to the supply of oxygen and the discharge of carbon dioxide and waste products, but also to the supply of *prana* (universal energy). Sources of *prana* are sun rays, water, air and food. *Prana* is taken up via the skin (sunbath), the tongue (therefore prolonged chewing), the nostrils and the lungs.

The only correct way of breathing is the natural respiration or complete *yoga* respiration with abdominal muscle control; this respiration should travel via the nose and consists of three steps:

1. The controlled abdominal respiration (with back respiration) with the help of the diaphragm. The diaphragm works like a piston and forms a kind of second heart.
2. The chest or flank-respiration in the middle area (above the diaphragm) by expanding the ribs and swelling up the lungs.
3. The high respiration or collar bone respiration by lifting up the collar without hunching up one's shoulders.

To start with, these three respirations' can be practised separately and afterwards as a whole.

Practise of the natural basis respiration: By preference practise lying on the floor. First of all, relax the body, especially the face, the jaws and the throat completely. After that raise the knees or lay a little cushion under the knees. Place the left hand on the belly between the pubis and the navel and the right hand between the navel and the breastbone. Start breathing in slowly and deeply

NATURAL WAY OF BREATHING
WITH ABDOMINAL MUSCLE CONTROL

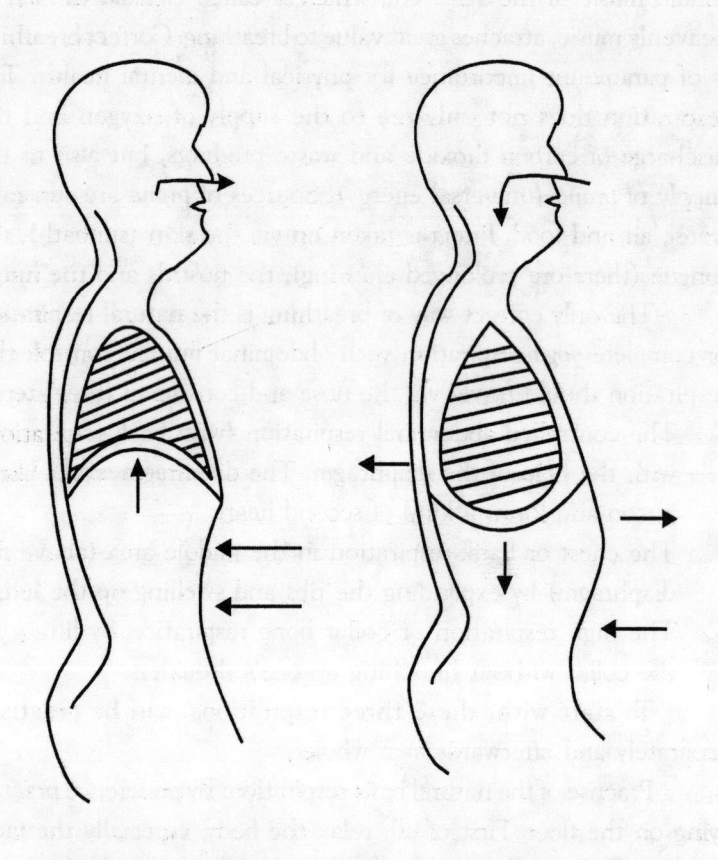

BREATHING OUT **BREATHING IN**

with the belly. Only the area between the navel and the breastbone may expand; the area between the navel and the pubis must be kept flat by controlling the abdominal muscle. If required, help with the left hand. Secondly, expand the ribs and finally have the collarbones lifted up. Hold the breath for two seconds, then breath out; first out of the belly and finally out of the lungs. Thus from bottom to top. Empty the lung completely. As a general rule the breathing out should last twice as long as the breathing in.

It is also possible to practise this breathing standing or sitting. If standing, the knees must be kept a little bent. The spine must always be as straight as an arrow, also in the sitting posture. Sit always on the two seat bones and keep the shoulders loose, the face relaxed and the breastbone a little forward. Never pull up the shoulders when breathing in. There are several exercises to straighten the back. The so-called sun salutation (*Surya namaskara*), a system of several exercises, can be specially recommended. It is very important to do all these exercises under good guidance.

The natural basis respiration and a straight back are of paramount importance for correct recitation and singing. The practice of music in totally surrendered mode is called *nadopasana*, the veneration of sound (*nada*), in order to purify body and mind and merge the soul into God. The *Upanishads* declare that the human body is a reflection of the cosmos and is nothing other than *Nada Brahma* (*Brahma* as sound).

Vemu Mukunda says: "The human voice comprises three octaves. Our emotions influence our breathing pattern; besides, they move the focus of the body consciousness to a specific part of the body, for example, fear is located just above the navel. This causes a change in the frequency of the voice (voice height). All human emotions can be located as positions of consciousness between the navel and *agna chakra* and this comprises an octave.

"In the system of *Ghandarva Ana* the octave is subdivided into twenty two frequencies or *shrutis* (consequently three octaves,

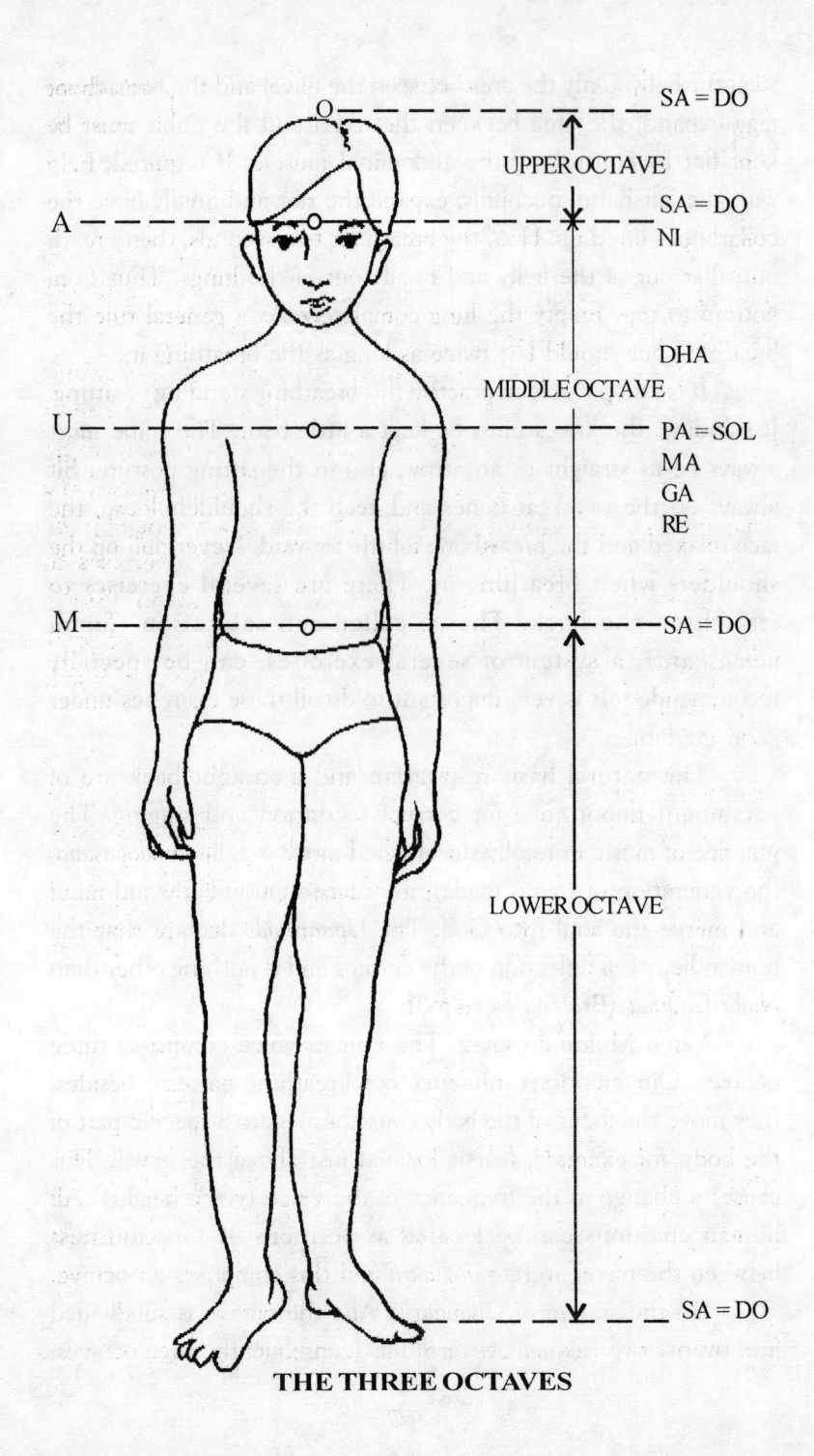

```
                    O  — — — — — —  SA = DO
                                      ↕ UPPER OCTAVE
A  — — — — — — — — — — — — — — — —  SA = DO
                                       NI

                                       DHA
                                       MIDDLE OCTAVE
U  — — — — — — — — — — — — — — — —  PA = SOL
                                       MA
                                       GA
                                       RE
M  — — — — — — — — — — — — — — — —  SA = DO


                                       LOWER OCTAVE



                   — — — — — — — —  SA = DO
```

THE THREE OCTAVES

sixty six *shrutis*). The twenty two *shrutis* result in twelve notes (*swaras*). Seven *swaras* form the *raga* scale with the notes Sa, Re,Ga, Ma, Pa, Dha and Ni. The tonic Sa corresponds to the western keynote Do, and the note Pa with Sol. Everyone has a specific tonic or basic tone (Sa/Do). The cosmic basic tone is G. That is the reason why in groups it is best to recite or sing from the basic tone G. D and C are also possible because these notes harmonise best with G.

"The *mantra* 'Aum' is the source of all creation and envelopes all disciplines and expressions of music. Mostly this *mantra* is recited or sung in an incorrect way. At least a complete octave must be used. When the *mantra* 'Aum' is sung correctly – from the personal or cosmic basic tone – from lower to upper tonic on the continuing spectrum of sound, consciousness moves through twenty two emotional energy points (shrutis) from one emotion to another. Hereby the concerned energies are activated and can be transformed into spiritual energies. The different *prana* streams are stimulated and body and mind are purified. This forms the basis of a music therapy for curing psychological and psychosomatic ailments. Body and mind can be protected against outer negative influences through meditation and the recitation and singing of *mantras*. It is very important to do this in the correct way.

"If the A of the *mantra* 'Aum' is sung correctly, with the consciousness at the navel, mind becomes quiet and peaceful; U sung with the consciousness at the *anahata chakra*, in the area of the heart, brings brightness and joy to the mind; and M sung with the consciousness at *agna chakra* gives spiritual bliss to the mind." In the singing of *bhajans* melody and rhythm are equally important. Everyone not only has a specific basic tone, but also a specific basic rhythm corresponding to the heart-beat.

7. My Personal Experiences and Vision

According to Sathya Sai Baba, fresh, raw, uncooked, unheated, unirradiated fruits, nuts, coconuts, vegetables, roots, tubers and soaked or germinating pulses, all grown without the aid of artificial fertilizers or other chemicals, a little uncooked biological germ-free milk from cattle tended with love and wisdom, and milk-products from this milk, such as buttermilk, yogurt, curds and butter, a little rice soaked in curds or water and *ragi* gruel are the best *satvic* food. If necessary, the vegetables may be very briefly cooked (half-cooked) and the rice up to a third (*Prema Vahini*, p.67), provided they are consumed immediately, otherwise they become *tamasic* food. Everything should be eaten in moderation; overeating makes food *rajasic* and *tamasic*.

In the beginning, I could hardly believe that I should eat only raw food, raw rice, and raw, germinated pulses, but now I do! For some years I had to fight with my desires, to overcome several resistances, to gain experience with many recipes and to study modern biochemistry and the most important schools of naturopathy. And now I am convinced that only pure, fresh, natural, raw, unheated food is really healthy, *satvic* food. Genetic manipulation, irradiation and cultivation with artificial fertilizers and other chemicals are unnatural. Only an ecological health garden and cattle tended with love and wisdom can provide real *satvic* food. Mankind should start realizing that living *satvic* food is Divine. If *satvic* food is heated it loses its Divine qualities, it becomes *rajasic* food and, in the end, *tamasic* food.

Because of the purifying, detoxifying working of *satvic* food, I experienced a number of unpleasant reactions such as diarrhoea and suddenly appearance infectious diseases; at the lowest point of my body weight I was only fifty kilograms (my height is 1.72 m). But I also experienced many positive results: several physical degeneration phenomena disappeared, a better sense-control and mind-control, an improved memory and power of concentration, more equanimity and joy, a deeper feeling for nature and more love and understanding of the Divine laws.

Finding real *satvic* food is a great problem. We have to use our sense organs and all our mental faculties to discover whether certain food is *satvic* or not. For some time I have known intuitively if food is predominantly *satvic, rajasic or tamasic*. My digestive system has also become very sensitive; for instance when I eat some *tamasic* fruits I get diarrhoea at once.

To my mind much native fruit in Holland is predominantly *tamasic*. Even subtropical and tropical fruit can be predominantly *tamasic*, especially oranges, lemons and bananas. Many nuts (mostly heated), vegetables, roots, tubers, cereals, pulses, seeds and milk-products are also predominantly *tamasic*. For this there can be several causes, such as cultivation with artificial fertilizers and other chemicals such as pesticides, herbicides and fungicides, treatment with chemicals for storage and transport, irradiation, radiation fallout, genetic manipulation, too early harvesting and the selling of stale and old items of food.

Sathya Sai Baba has said: "Eat the best food you can find." This is a very important statement. It is difficult to find *satvic* food, but at the same time, it is possible. We have to exert ourselves. In Holland it is possible to buy *satvic* coconuts and subtropical and tropical fruits on the market with the exception of bananas. All the bananas I bought were *tamasic*. Only in health shops is it possible to buy *satvic* native fruits, dried fruit, nuts (in the husk and unheated), vegetables, roots, tubers, *basmati* rice and pulses. Of course, most of these articles of food are not totally *satvic* but only predominantly *satvic*.

Even in health shops you must be careful. It cannot be helped that even in health shops certain articles of food can be predominantly *rajasic or tamasic*. I have to cycle four hours (up and down) to find *satvic* milk products. Therefore I decided to use very few milk products. It is a very good idea to keep a goat for milk (not for meat!), and to have your own ecological health garden and indoor garden; at least you can plant some fruit trees in your garden.

Many people have asked me why Sathya Sai Baba does not give only raw food in the canteen of His *ashram* in Puttaparthi. Of course, I do not know. I think it must be because a lot of people would fall ill for they cannot digest raw food. Over and above this, nobody knows what He does with this food on a subtle level. During an interview, He has said that it is very important not to go outside the *ashram*, because within a very short time, we lose all energy He has given to us. Therefore we should not go outside the *ashram* to have meals.

8. Satvic Food and Family Life

Sathya Sai Baba often says, "One who eats three meals a day is a sick person *(rogi)*, one who eats twice a day is an enjoyer *(bhogi)*, one who eats just once a day is a *yogi*." If you want to become a *yogi*, it is clear what to do. However, most of us are still *bhogis* or more or less *rogis*. Therefore, we are used to eating twice or thrice a day.

Satvic food is of paramount importance for our spiritual life and health. Eating stavic food is tantamount to purification of the mind and healing of the body and balancing the humours, removing the toxins *(ama)*, supplying required nutritious substances, and strenghtening the immune system. For a devotee of God it becomes necessary to switch over to *satvic* food. When we are ill we shall have to detoxify our body and mind thoroughly and switch over to *satvic* food step by step, using the blender. When we are relatively healthy, we may have to do the same thing, but the purification is easier; in any case, it will be necessary to use enemas to cleanse our colon and occasionally the blender to help our digestive system.

Many people believe that it is not possible to live on *satvic* food in a family. That is totally untrue. Everyone can cut out the usual breakfast and instead eat some fruit or some gruel made of pure water, fresh ground grain such as wheat or *ragi*, and some raw honey or jaggery. Do not forget to dechemicalize the grains. For breakfast, you can also take simple combinations of fruit blended with rejuvelac or simply watemelon juice; juice the entire watermelon including the rind and seeds. Sesame milk made by blending soaked sesame seeds with rejuvelac and some soaked raisins is also adequate. With a little rejuvelac you get cream or paste.

Everyone can prepare meals according to the recipes listed in chapter twenty-eight. To most of these recipes, especially the sauces, soups and vegetable dishes, you can add *satvic* spices and herbs in moderation (half a teaspoon), such as cardamom, coriander, cumin, fennel, ginger and turmeric (do not heat them, use them raw). With these spices you feed the digestive fire *(agni)*. In *ayurveda* it is said that turmeric destroys the process of aging and fills the body with youthful vitality. Whether it be North India or South India, all Indian cuisine has turmeric as an indispensable item. Besides making the vegetables and other foods aromatic and aesthetically more tempting, it is the anti-septic effect of turmeric that preserves the food from a variety of small insects that can pollute it.

Do not use *rajasic* spices, such as asafoetida, black pepper, cayenne, cinnamon, cloves and mustard and *tamasic* spices such as nutmeg and valerian. Tamarind is both *rajasic* and *tamasic*. The pungent vegetables chillies, garlic, onions and radishes are also *rajasic* and *tamasic*; avoid them as much as possible.

For family life you can prepare all kinds of tasty vegetable dishes consisting of half-steamed / half-cooked potatoes, potato pulp or half-cooked rice and half-steamed / half-cooked or raw vegetables with oil sauces, herbal oil sauces or curries. You can make a good curry from tomatoes, ghee, turmeric and coriander. Use just germinating cereals, pulses and seeds and baby greens such as sunflower and buckwheat greens (Chapter 17). Try to make rejuvelac, energy soup, sauerkraut and vege-kraut (without salt). There are many possibilities; use your own creativity. The following guidelines are important:
1. Never forget to pray and to offer the food to God before eating it.
2. Eat in silence, with *satvic* feelings and thoughts, in good company, in a clean room, slowly and at regular intervals, and chew the food well.

3. Always eat in moderation, never overeat.
4. Eat the best food you can find and afford.
5. Heat your food as little as possible. Never reheat it. Eat preferably uncooked food.
6. Use the blender if necessary; avoid pure juices but blend instead.
7. Do not forget the rules for correct food combinations.
8. Use moderate amounts of *satvic* spices and herbs to feed the digestive fire.
9. The mix of food should contain all necessary nutrients.
10. Fast one day a week.
11. Drink pure water, herbal teas, blended fruits, rejuvelac or almond milk (blend soaked almonds with rejuvelac).
12. Eat cereals in the form of liquid gruel, only soaked or just germinating.
13. Fruit and several milk-products are *satvic* provided they are eaten in moderation and cultivated/made in the correct way.
14. The switch-over to *satvic* food should be done step by step, carefully and with the necessary knowledge or guidance. Do not forget that everyone is unique and that the needs of our bodies are different and changeable.

Avoid as much as possible the following foodstuffs:
1. Food cultivated with fertilisers and other chemicals.
2. Food treated with chemicals for storage and transport purposes.
3. Processed industrialised food.
4. Old, stale and reheated food. Never put heated food into the refrigerator and reheat it after some time for a meal.
5. Heated food that has totally cooled down (bread, etc.).
6. Fried, grilled and roasted food.
7. Alcoholic drinks and soft drinks such as cola.
8. Tobacco and drugs.
9. Animal fats, margarine, meat, fish, shell-fish and eggs.
10. Refined sugar, sweets and commercial ice.
11. Chocolate, coffee (also substitutes) and tea.
12. White flour and products made of white flour such as bread,

biscuits, pastries, pancakes, macaroni, spaghetti and teapots. If possible, also avoid whole-meal bread.
13. Pasteurised, sterilised and UHT-milk and their by-products.
14. Salt, vinegar, industrialised sauces and *rajas* and *tamasic* spices and herbs.

"The proper care of children is the foundation of a culture," "Prevention is better than cure" and "Health is wealth" are golden sayings. Therefore, parents should teach their children, and teachers should instruct their pupils, how to prevent and cure diseases, how to maintain physical, mental and spiritual health. That is the reason why parents should teach their children to eat only *satvic* food. Drinking pure water is very important. At the 'Fluorosis' conference in Puttaparthi (29 - 30 January 1994) Sathya Sai Baba said, "In India only about twenty-five per cent of the population are employed in some work or other; nearly half of the remaining seventy-five percent are not able to do any work due to physical disability. We have to start investigations in the primary schools where children are susceptible to attacks by diseases such as fluorosis. Fluorosis affects the movement of the joints and weakens the bones; it is caused by contamination in food, water and air. Many diseases are caused by drinking polluted water. If there is one milligram of fluoride in a litre of water it is all right. If there is four or five milligrams of fluoride in a litre, it is positively injurious to health. Meat, fish, black and red salt, black coffee and tea cause the spread of fluorosis and aggravate it. To prevent fluorosis you can take curds, lime, orange, tomatoes, potatoes and other vegetables which contain vitamin C. You should also eat more carrot to build bones."

In the industrialized countries nearly half the population dies of cardio-vascular diseases. At the second International Symposium on Cardiovascular Diseases in Puttaparthi (21st - 23rd January, 1994) Sathya Sai Baba said: "Food plays a major role in the upkeep of health. Care should be taken to see that the food consumed does not have much fat content, for the fats consumed in large quantity are detrimental not only to one's physical health but also to mental health, whereby man loses human values. Meat and alcohol take a heavy toll of man's health, causing many diseases in him."

Birds and beasts do not suffer from cardiac and digestive ailments, as does man. Human beings indulge in taking all sorts of fried and cooked items of food, being slaves to the tongue. Modern man has come out with many artificial foodstuffs and a variety of alcoholic drinks, which gravely endanger his health. When man observes moderation in diet he can be saved from diseases. We should avoid viewing TV, video, etc. while eating food, as they cause mental disturbances. Man should make an earnest endeavour to lead a serene and pure life.

"Hurry, worry and curry (fatty foods) are the root cause of cardiac ailments." The presence of large quantities of fat is the cause of cardiovascular diseases. Fatty foodstuffs cause increase in weight resulting in susceptibility to cardiac diseases. The presence of toxins inflicts equal damage.

It is wrong to conclude that surgery is the only way of curing heart disease. Some of the diseases can be cured even by medicine. In my opinion it is the primary responsibility of every individual to prevent himself, from becoming a victim of heart diseases by regulating his food and other habits. Prevention is better than cure. There can be no room for cardiac ailments if your food habits are properly controlled and regulated. If the vegetarian food consumed is balanced and wholesome, it should contain liberal doses of vitamin C and vitamin E which are available in vegetables like carrot, for the presence of these vitamins prevents heart ailments in a large measure.

"Good people eat moderately, people who practise spiritual austerity fill only half their stomach; the noble ones eat only for living, the fools live only to eat."

During an interview on the thirty-first of December, 1993, Sathya Sai Baba emphasized the importance of the principle of control in food habits, work, sleep, and in everything. He said that everything in life is limited, so we should not exceed limits. Among other things He mentioned fruit and milk. Fruit and milk are *satvic* foodstuffs, but only when eaten in moderation; in large quantities they are *rajasic* and *tamasic*. So, it depends also on the quantity whether a food is beneficial or harmful.

9. Epilogue

The switch-over from current eating habits, with its food patterns, to *satvic* eating habits and *satvic* food, is drastic. Much discipline and perseverance is needed and also much knowledge and time, but the results can be staggering. The goal of this appendix is to teach the necessary knowledge of natural healing arts in order to make the switch-over to *satvic* food as effective as possible.

Sick people especially are advised to be guided by an experienced naturopath (doctor) while switching over to *satvic* food. This naturopath should know the ins and outs of food therapy. Everybody should orient himself as well as he can. Current eating habits make man sick and weak. They shorten man's life and make advances on the spiritual path practically impossible. With *satvic* food, man can resist all diseases with fair success and attain longer life. With *satvic* food, man has at his disposal more energy and becomes capable of greater physical and mental efforts.

Sathya Sai Baba says: "It is necessary to cleanse the mirror of the mind of the impurities covering it. This cleansing is done by regulating one's food and other living habits, including recreation. This cannot be done in a day or a month. This requires persistent and prolonged practice."

References :

1. The *Charaka Samhita*, Expounded by the worshipful Atreya Punarvasu, compiled by the great sage Agnivesa and redacted by Charaka & Drdhabala, six volumes, Shree Gulabkunverba Ayurvedic Society, Jamnagar, 1949, India.

2. Doug Cutrell, *The Living Foods Manual,* as developed by Ann Wigmore, Ann Wigmore Foundation, 196 Commonwealth Avenue, Boston, MA 02116, U S A.
3. Prof. Dr. J. G. Defares, 120 *jaar jong, De praktische wetenschap van een gezond langer leven,* Strengholt's Boeken, Naarden, 1987, Holland.
4. Prof. Dr. J. G. Defares, *Langer vitaal blijven,* Strengholt's Boeken, Naarden, 1982, Holland.
5. H. & M. Diamond, *Fit for Life,* Warner Books, New York, 1985, U. S. A
6. Harvey & Marilyn Diamond, *Living Health,* Warner Books, New York, 1987, U. S. A
7. Jan Dries, *Natural Food for Daily Use*, Arinus, Weg naar As 267, 3600, Genk, Belgium.
8. Jan Dries, *Kennismaking met de vegetarische voeding*, Arinus, Genk, (tel. 011 – 355246) 1986, Belgie.
9. Jan Dries, *Kanker genezen volgens de Dr. Nolfi-therapie,* Arinus, Genk, 1986, Belgie.
10. Jan Dries, *Het Dries-dieet ter vorrkoming van en ondersteuning bij kanker,* Arinus, Genk, Belgie.
11. Jan Dries, *The New Book of Food Combining, A Completely New Approach to Healthy Eating,* Element Books Ltd, The Old School House, The Courtyard, Bell Street, Shaftesbury Dorset, SP7 8BP, England.
12. Jan Dries, *Tijdschrift Naturleven,* Genk, Belgie.
13. Christian de Duve, *A Guided Tour of the Living Cell,* W. H. Freeman and Company New York 1984, U. S. A.
14. Prof. Dr. I. Elmadfa, Prof. Dr. E. Muskat, Prof. Dr. H. D. Cremer, D. Fritzsche and W. Aign, *Die grofle GU Nahrwert Tabelle, Grafe and Unzer Verlag GmbH,* Munchen Deutschland.
15. H. Elmau, *Bioeletronik nach Vincent and Saurer-Basen-Haushalt in Theorie and Praxis,* Haug Verlag, 1985, Deutschland
16. Dr. David Frawley O. M. D., *Ayurvedic Healing, A Comprehensive Guide,* Motilal Banarsidass Publishers Delhi, 1922, India.
17. Dr. David Frawely and Dr. Vasant Lad, *The Yoga of Herbs, An Ayurvedic Guide to Herbal Medicine,* Motilal Banarsidass Publishers, Delhi, 1994, India.

18. T.C. Fry, *Dynamische Gesundheit*, Walthausen Verlag, Ritterhude, 1990, Deutschland; American edition: *Program for Dynamic Health*.
19. Claude Gelineau, *Kiemen in onze veoding*, De Driehoek, Amsterdam, 1983, Holland.
20. Dr. B. S. Goel, *Third Eye and Kundalini, An Experiential Account of Journey from Dust to Divinity,* Third Eye Foundation of India, Shri Siddheshwar Ashram Bhagaan – 131033, Harayana, 1992, India.
21. L. Kevran en O. Ohsawa, *Biologische transmutatie,* Oost West Centrum, Amsterdam, Holland.
22. V. Kulvinskas, *Leben and uberleben,* F. Hirthammer Verlag, Munchen, 5. Auflage, 1988, Deutschland; American edition: *Survival into the 21st Century* - Planetary Healers Manual.
23. D. W. Martin, Jr. P. A. Mayes, V. W. Rodwell & D. K. Granner, *Harpers Review of Biochemistry,* Lange Medical Publications, Los Altos, California 94023, Twentieth Edition, 1985, U. S. A.
24. H.C. Moolenburgh, arts, *Beschavingsziekten en gezondheid,* Uitg. Ankh-Hermes bv, Deventer, 1987, Holland.
25. Vemu Mukunda, *De involved van muziek bij psychische en psychosomatische problemen,* Tijdschrift Prana 53, Holland.
26. Vemu Mukunda, *Aspecten van pranayama en Ghandharva Gana,* Tijdschrift Prana 64, Holland.
27. R.A. Nieuwenhuis *Vrije radicalen, schales tussen voeding en ziekte,* Orthos Media Den Haag, 1992, Holland.
28. Jamila Peiter, *Die Heilkraft der Vital-Erndhrung,* Access Verlag, Konigstein-Falkenstein, 1989, Deutschland.
29. Dr. A. J. Salome, Dr. A, Huson, Prof. P. J. Brouwer, *Functionele anatomie,* 7e druk, 1987, Uitg. Spruyt, Van Mantgem & De Does bv Leiden, Holland.
30. Dr. A. J. Salome, and Gita Sellman, *The Complete Sprouting Book,* Thorsons Publishers Ltd, 1986, Great-Britain.
31. H. M. Shelton, *The Science and Fine Art of Food and Nutrition, The Hygienic System,* Volume, II, Natural Hygiene Press, 6th revised edition, 1984, P. O. Box 1083- Oldsmar, Florida, 335577 (The Health Library Life Science Institute, 1108 Regal Row, P.O. Box 609, Manchaca, TX 78652 – 0609)

32. Dr. H. M. Shelton, *The Science and Fine Art of Fasting;* Natural Hygiene Press, 5th revised edition 1978, Chicago, U S A.
33. Dr. H. M. Shelton, *Orthobionomics, The Hygienic System,* Volume I, Health Research, California, 1972, U S A.
34. Dr. H. M. Shelton, *An Introduction to Natural Hygiene,* Health Research California, 1963, U S A.
35. Sri. Swami Sivananda, *Health and Happiness,* The Divine Life Society, 1984, India.
36. Hugo Symens J. C. *The Miracle,* Belgium.
37. Dr. E. B. Szekely, *The Essene Way – Biogenic Living,* I. B. S. International Box 205, Matsqui B. C., Canada VOX 1 SO.
38. Dr. E. B. Szekely, *The Chemistry of Youth,* I. B. S. Internacional, Box 205, Matsqui B. C. Canada VOX 1 SO.
39. Dr. E. B. Szekely, *The Ecological Health Garden,* I. B. S. International Box 205, Matsqui B. C., Canada VOX 1 SO.
40. Dr. E. B. Szekely, *De leer der Essenen, Het vredesevangelie van Jesus Christus,* Servire bv. Katwijk aan Zee, 1983, Holland.
41. Dr. J. H. Tilden, *Mit Toxamie fangen alle Krankheiten an,* Waldthausen Verlag Ritterhude, 1990, Deutschland Amercian edition; Toxemia, *The Basic Cause of Disease.*
42. Vasant Lad, *Ayurveda, the Science of Self-Healing,* Lotus Light Press, Wilmot, 1984, U. S .A.
43. H. Wandmaker, *Willst Du Gesund Sein? Vergiss den Kochtopf,* Walthausen Verlag Ritterhude, 1990, Deutschland.
44. Dr. M. Weimer, *Weerstand tegen ziekten,* Uitgeverij Kosmos, Utrecht / Antwerpen, 1987, Holland / Belgie.
45. Dr. Ann Wigmore, *Wees uw eigem dokter,* Elman Delft, Holland; American edition: *Be Your Own Doctor.*
46. Dr. Ann Wigmore, *The Hippocrates Diet and Health Program,* Avery Publishing Group Inc., Wayne, New Jersey, U S A.
47. Dr. Ann Wigmore, *The Wheatgrass Book,* Avery Publishing Group Inc., Wayne, New Jersey, 1985, U. S. A.

48. Dr. Ann Wigmore, *Rebuild Your Health with High Energy Enzyme Nourishment, Living Foods Lifestyle,* Quality Printero, Aguadilla, Puerto Rico, 1991.
49. Dr. Ann Wigmore, *The Sprouting Book,* Avery Publishing Group Inc., Wayne, New Jersey, 1986, U. S. A.
50. Dr. Ann Wigmore, *Recipes for Total Health and Youth,* Ann Wigmore Press, 196 Commonwealth Ave., Boston, MA 02116, 1990, U S A.

Note: 11, 16, 38 and 48 can be specially recommended.

"The desire to know God, to love God and be loved by God is not a desire that binds. When awareness of God dawns in all its splendour, every worldly sensual desire is reduced to ashes in the flames of that awareness."

OUR PUBLICATIONS

01. 70 QS & AS. ON PRACTICAL
    SPIRITUALITY AND SATHYA SAI BABA - O. P. Vidyakar — Rs. 90
02. A COMPENDIUM OF THE TEACHINGS
    OF SATHYA SAI BABA(4th Ed.) - Charlene Leslie-Chadan — Rs. 600
03. "ALEX" THE DOLPHIN - Lightstrom — Rs. 90
04. A JOURNEY TO LOVE (4th Ed.) - David Bailey — Rs. 180
05. A JOURNEY TO LOVE BOOK II
    Love & Marriage - David Bailey — Rs. 200
06. A JOURNEY TO LOVE (Spanish) - David Bailey — Rs. 375
07. A JOURNEY TO LOVE (Telugu) - David Bailey — Rs. 60
08. ANOTHER JOURNEY TO LOVE - Faye Bailey — Rs. 200
09. ASHES, ASHES WE ALL FALL DOWN - Gloria St. John — Rs. 80
10. A STORY OF INDIA AND PATAL
    BHUVANESWAR - Jennifer Warren — Rs. 60
11. AT THE FEET OF SAI - R. Lowenberg — Rs. 120
12. BAPU TO BABA - V. K. Narasimhan — Rs. 120
13. BUDO-KA - True Spiritual Warriors - Deena Naidu — Rs. 200
14. CRICKET FOR LOVE - Sai Towers — Rs. 250
15. CUTTING THE TIES THAT BIND - Phyllis Krystal — Rs. 110
16. CUTTING THE TIES THAT BIND
    Symbol Cards - Phyllis Krystal — Rs. 120
17. CUTTING THE TIES THAT BIND - Posters - Phyllis Krystal — Rs. 600
18. CUTTING MORE TIES THAT BIND - Phyllis Krystal — Rs. 120
19. CUTTING THE TIES THAT BIND - Work Book - Phyllis Krystal — Rs. 140
20. DA PUTTAPARTHIA PATAL
    BHUVANESHWAR (Italian) - Sandra Percy — Rs. 150
21. DEATHING (Indian Edition) - Anya Foos-Graber — Rs. 195
22. DISCOVERING MARTIAL ARTS - Deena Naidu — Rs. 265
23. EDUCATION IN HUMAN VALUES (3 Vols.) - June Auton — Rs. 750
24. FACE TO FACE WITH GOD - V. I. K. Sarin — Rs. 150
25. GLIMPSES OF THE DIVINE - Birgitte Rodriguez — Rs. 150
26. GLORY OF SAI PADHUKAS - Sai Towers — Rs. 100
27. GOD AND HIS GOSPEL - Dr. M. N. Rao — Rs. 120
28. GOD LIVES IN INDIA - R. K. Karanjia — Rs. 75
29. GOD DESCENDS ON EARTH - Sanjay Kant — Rs. 75
30. GOOD CHANCES (2nd Reprint) - Howard Levin — Rs. 120
31. HEART TO HEART (2st Reprint) - Howard Levin — Rs. 120
32. HOLY MISSION DIVINE VISION - Sai Usha — Rs. 80
33. IN QUEST OF GOD - P. P. Arya — Rs. 120
34. JOURNEY OF GRACE - Cynthia Harris — Rs. 140
35. KNOW THYSELF (2nd Revised Ed.) - Gerard T. Satvic — Rs. 200
36. LET ME SOW LOVE - Doris May Gibson — Rs. 120
37. LETTERS FROM A GRANDFATHER - S. K. Bose — Rs. 180

38. MESSAGES (Japanese)	- Dr. M. N. Rao	Rs. 150
39. MESSAGES FROM MY DEAREST FRIEND SAI BABA	- Elvie Bailey	Rs. 130
40. MIRACLES ARE MY VISITING CARDS	- Erlendur Haraldsson	Rs. 180
41. MOHANA BALA SAI (Children's Book)	- Sai Mira	Rs. 120
42. MUKTI THE LION FINDS HIMSELF	- Regina Suritsch	Rs. 85
43. ONENESS OF DIVINITY	- Ratan Lal	Rs. 100
44. PATH OF THE PILGRIM	- Richard Selby	Rs. 120
45. PRASANTHI GUIDE (Revised Ed.)	- R. Padmanaban	Rs. 100
46. SAI BABA AND NARA NARAYANA GUFA ASHRAM Part III	- Swami Maheswaranand	Rs. 30
47. SAI BABA GITA	- Al Drucker	Rs. 200
48. SAI BABA & SAI YOGA	- Indra Devi	Rs. 110
49. SAI BABA'S SONG BIRD	- Lightstorm	Rs. 80
50. SAI BABA: THE ETERNAL COMPANION	- B. P. Misra	Rs. 100
51. SAI HUMOUR	- Peggy Mason, et. all.	Rs. 70
52. SAI NAAMAAVALI	- Jagat Narain Tripathi	Rs. 90
53. SATHYA SAI'S AMRITA VARSHINI	- Sudha Aditya	Rs. 75
54. SATHYA SAI'S ANUGRAHA VARSHINI	- Sudha Aditya	Rs. 90
55. SAI SANDESH	- Sai Usha	Rs. 50
56. SAI'S STORY	- Shaila Hattiangadi	Rs. 75
57. SATVIC FOOD & HEALTH (2nd Revised Ed.)	- Gerard T. Satvic	Rs. 45
58. SATVIC STORIES	- Benjamin Kurzweil	Rs. 40
59. SELF REALISATION	- Al Drucker	Rs. 50
60. SPIRITUAL IMPRESSIONS A Bi-monthly Magazine	- Sai Towers	Rs. 100
61. SPRINKLES OF GOLDEN DUST	- Jeannette Caruth	Rs. 65
62. SRI SATHYA SAI BABA AND WONDERS OF HIS LOVE	- John Elliott	Rs. 90
63. SRI SATHYA SAI CHALEESA	- B. P. Mishra	Rs. 25
64. SRI SATHYA SAI BABA PRAYER BOOK	- Sai Towers	Rs. 10
65. SRI SATHYA SAI BABA YOUNG ADULTS PROGRAMME	- L. A. Ramdath	Rs. 80
66. STUDY CIRCLES FOR DIVINITY	- Ross Woodward & Ron Farmer	Rs. 390
67. TEN STEPS TO KESAVA	- Lightstorm	Rs. 150
68. THE ARMOUR OF SRI SATHYA SAI	- O. P. Vidyakar	Rs. 10
69. THE DIVINE LEELAS OF BHAGAVAN SRI SATHYA SAI BABA	- Nagamani Purnaiya	Rs. 100
70. THE GRACE OF SAI	- R. Lowenberg	Rs. 120
71. THE HEART OF SAI	- R. Lowenberg	Rs. 130
72. THE OMNIPRESENCE OF SAI	- R. Lowenberg	Rs. 120
73. THE PROPHECY	- Barbara Gardner	Rs. 120
74. THE THOUSAND SONGS OF LORD VISHNU	- Jeannette Caruth	Rs. 150
75. THY WILL BE DONE	- C. D. Mirchandani	Rs. 90
76. TOWARDS A BETTER LIFE - Word Images from Sai Teachings (10 cards)		Rs. 50

77. WAITING FOR BABA	- V. Ramnath	Rs. 95
78. WHO IS BABA?	- Margaret Tottle-Smith	Rs. 60
79. YOU ARE GOD	- M. N. Rao	Rs. 150
80. YOUR LIFE IS YOUR MESSAGE	- Charlene Leslie Chaden	Rs. 225

FORTHCOMING PUBLICATIONS ...

01. A COMPENDIUM OF SAI BHAJANS — R. Padmanaban
02. DIRECTORY OF MASTERS, SAINTS AND ASHRAMS IN INDIA — R. Padmanaban
03. FOUNTAIN OF LOVE
    An Overview of Sathya Sai Water Supply Project — R. Padmanaban
04. I AM I — Ratan lal
05. IN SEARCH OF A MIRACLE — Dr. Teri O' Brien
06. KRISHNAMURTHI AND THE FOURTH WAY — Evan Gram
07. LOVE IS MY FORM VOL. I The Advent
    Pictorial Biography of Sri Sathya Sai Baba — R. Padmanaban
08. ONE SOUL'S JOURNEY — Leni Matlin
09. TRYST WITH DIVINITY — Swapna Raghu
10. VOICE OF THE AVATAR - Compilation of Yearwise Volumes of Discourses of Bhagawan Sri Sathya Sai Baba

OUR DISTRIBUTORS

Australia
Mr. James Somers
13 Hunter Street, Parramatta
NSW 2150
Phone : (02) 9687 2441
Fax : (02) 9687 2449

Canada
Sri Sathya Sai Books & Information Centre
290 Merton Street, Toranto
Ontario M 4S 1 A9
Phone : (416) 481 7242
Fax : (416) 498 0270 / 345 9212
E-mail : saibooks@idirect.ca

England
Sai Books UK Limited
21, Greystone Gardens
Harrow
Middlex, HA3 0EF
Phone : (181) 907 1267
Fax : (181) 909 3954
E-mail : saibooks@btinternet.com

India
Sai Towers Brindavan
23/1142, Vijayalakshmi Colony
Kadugodi, Bangalore 560 067
Phone : (080) 8451648
Fax: : (080) 8451649

Sai Towers
3/604 Main Road
Prasanthi Nilayam 515 134
Phone : (8555) 87270 / 87327
Fax : (8555) 87302
E-mail : saitower@vsnl.com
Web : www.saitowers.com

D. K. Publishers and Distributors P. Ltd.
1/4224, Ansari Road
Darya Ganj
New Delhi 110 002
Phone : (011) 327 8368 / 326 1465
Fax : (011) 326 4368
E-mail : dkpd@del3.vsnl.net.in

Europe (excluding England)
Sathya Sai Book Shop
Laurenzenvorstadt 87
CH 5000 AARAU
Switzerland
Tel / Fax: (62) 822 3722
E-mail : 113042.2123@compuserve.com

Malaysia
Sathya Sai Baba Centre of Bangsar
24, Jalan Abdullah
off Jalan Bangsar
59000 Kuala Lumpur
Phone : (3) 254 5224 / 241 3646

New Zealand
Sathya Sai Publications
P.O. Box 56-347
Dominion Road
Auckland 1003
Phone : (9) 638 8210
Fax : (9) 638 8159
E-mail : ravi@titan.co.nz

Singapore
P. Ramanathan
Block 1M
Pine Grove No. 01- 43
Singapore 591201
Phone : 466 5983

West Indies
Ace Printery Fed Traders Ltd.
34-36, Pasea Main Road
Tunapuna, Trinidad & Tobago
Phone/Fax :
 (868) 663 (2273) 663 2152, 3223
E-mail : ramdhan@carib-link.ne

U.S.A.
Jai Sai Ram
PO Box 900
Trinidad, CO 81082 U.S.A.
Phone : (719) 846 0846
Fax : (719) 846 0847
E-Mail : jaisairm @ ria.net
 or
 jaisairm @ rmi.net